Social Change
in the Southwest,
1350–1880

STUDIES IN HISTORICAL SOCIAL CHANGE

Scott G. McNall and Jill S. Quadagno, editors

Social Change in the Southwest, 1350–1880

THOMAS D. HALL

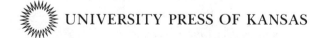 UNIVERSITY PRESS OF KANSAS

Published by the University Press of Kansas (Lawrence, Kansas 66049), which was organized by the Kansas Board of Regents and is operated and funded by Emporia State University, Fort Hays State University, Kansas State University, Pittsburg State University, the University of Kansas, and Wichita State University

Portions of this book appeared in slightly different form as "Incorporation in the World-System: Toward a Critique," *American Sociological Review* 51:3 (June 1986): 390–402, and "The Transformation of the Mexican Northwest into the American Southwest: Three Paths of Internal Development," in *Rethinking the Nineteenth Century: Contradictions and Movements*, Francisco O. Ramirez, ed. (Contributions in Economics and Economic History, No. 76, Greenwood Press, Inc., Westport, Connecticut, 1988), pp. 21–42 (copyright © 1988 by Francisco O. Ramirez). Reprinted with permission.

Library of Congress Cataloging-in-Publication Data

Hall, Thomas D., 1946–
    Social change in the Southwest, 1350–1880 / Thomas D. Hall.
        p. cm. — (Studies in historical social change)
    Bibliography: p.
    Includes index.
    ISBN 0–7006–0497–9 (pbk.)
    1. Southwest, New—Social conditions. 2. Southwest, New—Economic conditions. 3. Indians of North America—Southwest, New—Cultural assimilation. 4. Southwest, New—Ethnic relations—History.
    5. Social change. I. Title. II. Series.
    HN79.A165H35 1988   88-14250
    306'.0979—dc19
Printed in the United States of America

10 9 8 7 6 5 4 3

To Bryan, Jean and Robert
who patiently endured my captivation by *los indios bárbaros*

For my book:

- Yaqui didn't become okay dependent on nearby non-Indian communities for food (livestock), like Apaches did   (p. 130)

- See pp. 28-29 for discussion of bands, tribes, tribe-formation, and terminology.

- p. 208 - CW command withdrawal of US troops - replaced by Vols who were determined to exterminate Indians

- p. 217 - AZ Indians as obstacles to mining [I need a
  234   more sophisticated explanation of assault on Yaquis] - Indian-hating
  had a motivation - elements of obstacle

p. 226 - even tho fine book ignores Yaquis!

Contents

List of Figures, Tables and Maps

FIGURES

TABLES

Preface

How does one come to write a book such as this? The answers are many. The first, riveted firmly in my mind, is found atop Black Mesa in northern Arizona on the Navajo reservation in summer of 1972. I had recently completed a master's degree in anthropology and had been hired to teach at Navajo Community College on the Navajo Nation. Navajo Community College was then a novel experiment in Native American self-determination, in which Navajos ran their own college, oriented toward Navajo needs. I was on Black Mesa with Al Henderson, a young Navajo economist, friend, colleague and co-teacher. We had brought two vans of students to see the Peabody Coal strip-mining operation first hand, and were watching a dragline take house-sized bites of coal from the earth and load them into gargantuan trucks that carried the coal to slurry lines for transportation to electricity generating stations across the desert.

I was trying, even then, to make sense of a variety of "anomalies": How was it that "traditional" Navajos could be displaced from their land by fellow tribesmen to make way for strip mining coal intended to generate electricity that would be used, among other things, to air-condition the sidewalks of the Las Vegas strip? How was it that Navajo and Hopi coal was sold to finance cultural and educational centers to preserve native "traditions"? Why was Navajo Community College dedicated to preserving such "Navajo traditions" as silversmithing, rug weaving, sheepherding, and religious traditions—many of which had come from outsiders, and yet were clearly vital elements of contemporary Navajo culture? I was also wondering how an Anglo anthropologist could teach Navajo students about culture and ethnocentrism. Finally, there was the irony of an Anglo anthropologist and a Navajo economist discussing,

xiii

dissecting, arguing about Adam Smith and Karl Marx and the processes of modernization and self-determination, only to find that the insights of either slipped away like cedar smoke from a campfire every time understanding seemed to be within our grasp.

Then, not even a year later I found myself back in Los Angeles suddenly paying double prices to fuel my little VW bug to visit friends in the Navajo Nation, and worrying about something bug drivers seldom fretted over—getting a speeding ticket for exceeding suddenly lower speed limits. On that trip I wondered how OPEC, half a world away, shaped events even on the remote Navajo reservation, changing the price of oil, and therefore of coal, and therefore Navajo tribal politics, and even the funding situation at Navajo Community College.

I found myself contemplating how all these things, and many more, were intertwined: centuries-old patterns of continuance and change, contemporary global interconnections, Navajo tribal politics and the peculiar version of academic politics practiced at Navajo Community College in those days. My drive to understand these things led through the Sociology Department of California State University at Los Angeles to a Ph.D. at the University of Washington in Seattle. I owe Dan Chirot a profound debt for allowing me the freedom to think widely about social change while insisting that history be taken seriously in its own right and not be used as ammunition for theoretical fantasies. The ideas first developed there evolved through a long path into this work.

This book, then, has a complex agenda. If there is one overriding thesis it is that social change is complex in several ways. First, social change is multi-leveled. Global, regional and local changes all shape and influence each other. Thus the following analysis proceeds whenever possible from local to regional to global sources of change, using the inadequacies of explanation of change at one level to demonstrate the need for additional explanation at a broader level. Consequently, the analysis does not always proceed in strict chronological order. Second, the processes of social change have themselves been changing, often in ways that are not altogether clear. Third, many of the groups that we so often take as traditional are themselves the products of complex processes of social change. Fourth, the "victims" of social change in conventional liberal analyses played significant, and frequently vital roles in the very processes that affected them. This is not to say that they are either responsible for the results or that the results are as they would have wished, but to underscore their active role in their own histories. Finally, I take both social theory and social history seriously, and treat each as independently significant. To proceed from history ("the facts") to theory, or from theory to interpretation of history, is to do violence to the truth. It is the interaction of the two that is central; each informs and counterbalances the other. If this work must be put in only one category of endeavor, it is clearly a work of historical sociology, despite the fact that its substantive subject and chronological settings are unusual in sociology.

A second reason for writing this book is found in a bit of southwestern folklore that I learned from a Navajo friend who was pulling me into an Anasazi ruin we were exploring. Never mind that "Navajos do not enter ruins," and that while holding my hand he was probably pulling my leg, as was his wont. Anyway, according to this legend, Anasazi ruins contain, in addition to pot sherds and ancient corn kernels, peculiar microbes that can infect visitors with a strange disease that causes the victim to languish whenever he or she remains away from the Southwest for too long. The disease is certainly terminal, if not fatal, for no one has ever recovered, having once contracted it. The only relief available is found in periodic visits to the Southwest. In a pinch, reading or writing about the Southwest provides temporary relief. So in some ways the research and writing of this book have constituted a form of preventive medicine. I am indebted to many friends in the Southwest for stronger cures in the form of friendly accommodations over the intervening years: Jim Martin and Leigh Hoover, Jim and Marcy Matlock, Owen Seumptewa, Al Henderson, Ken, Alice, Joey, and Tanda Nuendorf.

I have benefitted from the help and advice of many scholars: Terry Kandal, Fred Shanley, Daniel Chirot, Pierre van den Berghe, Michael Hechter, Hubert M. Blalock, Jr., David Hodge and Tom Barth all had important, if sometimes conflicting, effects on my education. Since my arrival at the University of Oklahoma, many colleagues have been of considerable help: Joseph Whitecotton, Richard Pailes, Tim Baugh, Fred Shelley, Gary Sandefur, Nancy Langton, Paul Minnis and Patricia Gilmore have all read and critiqued parts of this manuscript. Many of them also lent their time and insights to my attempts in several papers to address knotty theoretical problems raised by events and processes in Southwestern history. Besides several maps and tables that I have "stolen" from him, I owe Richard Nostrand for an especially timely "cure" by shanghaiing me to El Cerrito with his geography seminar during the fall of 1983. Other scholars have also given their time and advice: William Griffen, David Wilcox, Randall McGuire, and Clark Knowlton. The Research Council of the University of Oklahoma Graduate School provided funds to gather the materials to construct the maps used in this work. The maps were drawn by Mary Goodman, with advice from James Goodman and Richard Nostrand. The College of Arts and Sciences provided a summer research grant that enabled me to concentrate on some of the more intractable theoretical issues I encountered in constructing this work. I also owe a special debt to the various research assistants who have helped me over the years: Vicki Page, Shahin Gerami, Gary McClelland, Travis Patton and John Packham. All of them carried out tedious tasks cheerfully and willingly.

Scott McNall has been a valuable editor and friend, who gives timely advice and criticism in a way that always inspires me to dig in and go to work. I owe debts of an entirely different kind to Professors William Ray and Luther White of the Oklahoma University Mathematics Department for sharing computer terminals that allowed me access to word-processing facilities, thus easing the many revisions of this manuscript. Their generosity far exceeds the expectations of normal collegiality. John Bryan and Tanya Stewart helped solve many word-processing problems, and showed me innumerable shortcuts. Finally, I owe my family, Jean Poland, Bryan Hall and Robert Poland, for support and forbearance while I was captivated by Southwestern nomads. Jean did me the singular honor of marrying me, and the book, and has subsequently improved both substantially.

As is always the case, the many colleagues and friends mentioned above do not include all who helped produce this work and improve its contents. Nor are they to be blamed for the author's recalcitrance in rejecting some advice. They do, however, deserve a share of the credit for any contributions this book makes to the understanding of social change.

CHAPTER I

Introduction

Generalization is beyond question what we seek from the empirical and concrete. But it is generalization *from* the empirical, the concrete, and the historical; not generalization achieved through their dismissal; not generalization drawn from metaphor and analogy. Whatever the demands of a social theory, the first demands to be served are those of the social reality we find alone in the historical record. All else is surely secondary (Robert Nisbet, 1969, pp. 303–304).

In the course of European expansion, groups that were more or less autonomous—bands, tribes, chiefdoms—were engulfed by expanding states, and thus transformed into ethnic groups. The consequences of incorporation for these new ethnic groups were far from uniform. Some groups were destroyed, some were assimilated, some survived, barely or prosperously. What accounts for these varied results? What are the causes of these changes? What is the relative importance of the social organization of the engulfed group or groups? What is the significance of various constellations of engulfing and engulfed societies? Are there any general patterns in the process of incorporation? Why and how do "societies" become ethnic groups? Although events of this nature have been common throughout the world over the last half millennium, this work explores these questions by examining the history of several groups in what is now the American Southwest, but for most of the time was known to Europeans as the northwest frontier of New Spain.

THE "DIALECTIC" OF HISTORY AND SOCIOLOGY

A sociologist working with historical materials is obviously limited to available data. Beyond that, though, there is the perpetual tension be-

1

tween seeking general patterns and seeking a unique constellation of past events. Well-executed historical sociology and history do both (Abrams, 1982, pp. x–xiii). Yet how are the disciplines different? Abrams suggests that they differ in the types of questions asked and the strategies employed to pursue them. He classifies these in two broad categories: (1) questions of how and why an event occurred, and (2) questions about conditions when an event happened (Abrams, 1982, p. 301). In more familiar terms, this is a distinction between explanatory and narrative accounts of events. His point is that both sets of strategies use both theory and evidence to achieve different goals. These goals are not so much conflicting as complementary. Thus, it is important to sketch the goals of this work.

This study seeks generality, but a generality that is grounded in and emerges from "the facts" (Stinchcombe, 1978; Tilly, 1981, 1984; Hopkins, 1979; Ragin and Zaret, 1983; Abrams, 1982). Tilly is " . . . a bit more enthusiastic about general theories than Stinchcombe" (1981, p. 7). He argues that historical sociologists:

> . . . are not learning to do archival research; nor are they taking their questions from the prevailing historical agenda, or suppressing their inclinations to explicit modeling, careful measurement, and deliberate comparison. They are, on the other hand, edging toward the adoption of genuinely historical arguments—arguments in which where, and especially, when something happens seriously affects its character and outcome (Tilly, 1981, pp. 43–44).

Hopkins stresses that the complementarity of "statistical" and "narrative" approaches are " . . . not two versions but two halves of a full account" (1979, p. 42). The statistical side stresses "the plausibility of the general propositions" with "an incidental interest, if any, in one case" (Hopkins, 1979, p. 44). The narrative side stresses "the plausibility of the complex interpretive account offered of *those* changes in *that* place through *that* time period" (Hopkins, 1979, p. 44, emphasis in original). According to Hopkins the narrative approach is the more general form of inquiry and explanation in the study of social change. Ragin and Zaret (1983) echo this argument. This study favors the narrative approach, using "history to develop theory" (Stinchcombe, 1978, p. 1).

An immediate consequence of this approach is that a number of comparisons—internal and external, explicit and implicit—are required. To some extent questions about why in one instance a given event has different effects on similar groups and in another instance produces similar effects on dissimilar groups may be addressed through judicious internal comparisons. But given that the "where" and especially the "when" of an event are crucial, these anomalies may only be explained by external comparisons. External comparisons are sometimes necessary to establish just what is unique to the where and when of an event, and to untangle the constellation of factors that make such an event special. The goal here is to find answers to these questions for the Southwest, and to sketch the potential limits of their generality.

THE ISSUES

The facts never speak for themselves. They must always have an interpreter. The questions that guide one in developing theory, however, do not come from a vacuum, but from preceding theoretical discussions. These are sketched briefly here.

European expansion began over half a millennium ago. Midway through this expansion the industrial revolution began. Since then debate has continued over the necessity of imperialism for European development. On the one hand, some claim that without the resources taken from the rest of the globe Europe could not have developed and the industrial revolution would never have occurred. Others claim that European conquest and colonization of the globe were side effects of its own internal development, and are indicators of the vigor of capitalist societies. Today the debate is not couched in such broad terms. Rather, the debate centers around the role of European expansion and seizure of wealth in its own development and the development, or its absence, in the rest of the world. The questions addressed by this work derive from this debate. The goal is to study the connections between social changes in one region and their global context, highlighting the interactive and exogenous sources of change.

Such a study of social change may be approached from three different directions. First are questions about how European states affected the course of social change in various nonstate societies. Second is the inverse, and too often neglected, question of how the structure and organization of nonstate societies shaped the changes that were the product of interaction with European states. Third, and theoretically the most interesting, is the question of how the course of change is affected and shaped by the interaction, or particular combination, of state intervention and nonstate social organizations. Modern European states, of course, are not the only states to have profound effects on nonstate societies, nor does Europe hold a monopoly on imperialism. The Chinese, Roman, Greek, Persian and other early empires also had significant impacts on nonstate societies.

Since their first appearance some 5,000 years ago (Wright, 1977; Service, 1975; Lenski, 1966; Lenski and Lenski, 1982) states have been major agents of change among nonstate societies. But the very dominance of Europe may in part be due to earlier state-induced social change among the nonstate societies of early Europe (McNeill, 1963, 1980; P. Anderson, 1974a, 1974b). Thus, increased understanding of these processes holds the possibility of better understanding of the history of European world dominance.

The study of social change has been marked by its own peculiar dialectic that involves a process of making various simplifying assumptions, testing theory against the facts, and being forced to treat some assumptions as problematic. Thus, unilinear models of social evolution have given way to multilinear models; uniformitarian assumptions have given way to the distinction between general and specific evolution; and pristine accounts of change are giving way to reactive accounts. This study seeks to further these trends, contribute to a more refined theory, and force some re-examination of the facts. Rather than assuming that a form of social organization is traditional, social organization is treated as problematic. Rather than assuming that the groups discussed here are traditional raiders, the origins of raiding are investigated.

One consequence of European dominance is that much of the ethnographic evidence upon which various theories of change are based is itself both a product of agents of those states, and more importantly, was gathered from already vastly changed societies (see Wolf, 1982, Ch. 1). For instance, the various ethnic resurgences around the world (Yancey et al., 1976; A. D. Smith, 1981; Horowitz, 1975; Hechter and Levi, 1979; Olzak, 1983a, 1983b, 1983c; Nagel and Olzak, 1982) find some of their roots in the transformations produced by European expansion. Previously autonomous groups were transformed into ethnic groups by conquest; others, by more-or-less voluntary migration, became ethnic minorities. These phenomena are not limited to the past, or to the third world, but continue today. Such ethnic changes have deep historical roots. Less obviously, the types of transformations that produced ethnic groups may have changed over time.

WHY THE AMERICAN SOUTHWEST?

The Southwest is an appropriate locus for this study for several reasons. First, the relatively slow speed and moderate intensity of social change facilitates consideration of subtleties and nuances obliterated elsewhere. The efforts to colonize the northern frontiers were less intense than those in central Mexico or central Peru. Indigenous groups were gradually pushed into volatile alliances with Spanish settlers rather than overwhelmed by them. Indeed, the very mildness of frontier changes requires examination and explanation. Second, a wide variety of indigenous groups allows examination of similar effects on diverse groups, and conversely, diverse effects on similar groups. Yet this diversity makes generalization difficult. To the degree that events are peculiar to the Southwest, the generality of the analysis is limited. Finally, an abundance of historical scholarship makes it possible to study the processes of incorporation through close analysis of events. However, that analysis is complicated because the authors of assorted documents, the compilers of those documents, and the interpreters of those documents were seldom interested in the issues raised here.

The existence, role, and changes of the frontier must be explained by events outside the frontier, either regionally within New Spain, or globally in the various rivalries among European powers vying for control of parts of the New World. Changes in the state had effects on frontier administration and life, and consequently on the processes of social change among indigenous groups adjoining the frontier. The most dramatic of these wider issues is the conquest of the region by the American state.

The American conquest brought several major changes in quick succession. The central area of New Mexico (approximately the region of the State of New Mexico) declined in significance, while the tenuous colonies of Texas and California became major centers of development. Once the American Civil War was settled, a presumed solution to the so-called Indian problem was achieved through the establishment of Indian reservations. But probably the most significant change was the shift from a frontier of an underdeveloped state to a frontier of a rapidly developing state. Once the conquest was complete, the dynamics of change were so drastically different that subsequent changes warrant a separate study.

AUDIENCES

The following account will have different sources of interest for different audiences. Within sociology, the analysis of imperialism in an early frontier area will be a central issue, since this aspect of European expansion has been seldom studied by sociologists. There is much to be learned about social change by the study of frontiers, since some processes of change cannot be studied in Europe, but only outside of it. Second, the relatively low intensity of these state–nonstate confrontations facilitates the study of processes that were too rapid and too poorly recorded elsewhere to allow careful analysis.

This work also contributes to the trend in anthropology toward a self-reflective ethnography and ethnology, which recognizes that the study of social change is based on evidence that is itself rooted in changing circumstances. Rather than trying to hold change constant and discover pristine forms, the goal is to use change to understand change. As with with older ethnohistory, the history of the western United States, and the Southwest in particular, has suffered from a parochial focus (Steffen, 1979). This study uses theoretical analysis to place local and regional events in a wider context and to raise new questions about past events. Thus, it offers a theoretically grounded rationale for the study of regional history.

Historically, this study emphasizes the dynamism of the Southwest and thereby undermines tradition as an explanation of events. This is not to say that there is no such thing as tradition, but to emphasize that a tradition is an adaptation by a group of people to a specific set of circumstances. As long as those circumstances continue, the tradition will continue. When circumstances alter, pressures for change are created. Whether tradition is used to explain the barbarity of nomadic groups in the seventeenth and eighteenth centuries, the feudalism of nineteenth-century New Mexico, or the warrior tradition among Native Americans, it masks dynamic changes and denies the role of history in shaping the present.

Clearly, this is a work of historical sociology, with the accent on sociology. Its aims are explicitly guided by theoretical concerns, and its goal is to construct an improved theoretical account of frontier social change as a part of general processes of incorporation of new areas into an expanding European world-system. Consequently, the analysis is not a thorough narrative, nor does it adhere to a strict, chronological ordering of events. Such accounts are found in the many histories of the region cited throughout this work. While deviations from chronological sequence are minimized, the focus on theoretical issues and, especially, the imprecisions of geographical and chronological boundaries make some deviations necessary. Temporal processes overlap; as one process begins to decay, another begins to emerge. The two are distinct when viewed from their respective peaks, but from the zone of overlap, events appear chaotic. Thus, the American conquest of New Mexico did not occur in a few months, but rather took over half a century—from the opening of the Santa Fe Trail until the coming of the railroads and the firm implantation of a territorial government. Some might argue that it is still not complete.

Finally, it is useful to give an overview of what is to follow. Chapter II addresses the theoretical issues raised here. Because of the conceptual ambiguity in the terms used in ethnographic, ethnohistorical, and historical accounts, this theoretical overview should clarify the terms used throughout this book. Thus, the major social groups indigenous to the Southwest, and the region itself, are not describes in detail until Chapter III. Chapter III also sketches the indigenous situation in the centuries immediately preceding Spanish contact. Chapter IV describes how Spanish policies that engendered a state of endemic warfare in Mexico were recreated in New Mexico. Chapter V recounts the first two waves of colonization (before and after the Pueblo Revolt). The stress is on patterns of interaction, the formation of a particular type of frontier, and the state of endemic warfare.

Chapter VI describes the temporary peace that was established on the frontier in the late eighteenth and early nineteenth centuries. Some attention is paid to the variety of strategies employed by colonial officials, and how these were systematically undercut by various local trading, raiding, and ecological conditions. Chapter VII discusses the same time period, but with an emphasis on regional and global inter-relations. The implementation of the Bourbon reforms is reviewed and linked to Mexico's break with Spain and American penetration of northern Mexico. Two major consequences of Mexican independence for the Southwest were the growth of the Santa Fe Trail trade, and the breakdown of the frontier peace.

Chapter VIII reviews the explanations for the American annexation of northern Mexico. The American, Mexican, and Southwestern sources of the conflict are reviewed separately, then merged into a fuller account. Chapter IX traces the consolidation of the conquest. Finally, Chapter X summarizes the "Conclusions, Questions, Speculations" sections of chapters IV through IX, weaving their separate conclusions together into a general account of frontier social change.

CHAPTER II

Social Change and the Southwest: Theoretical and Geographical Background[1]

> I believe that all human societies of which we have record are "secondary," indeed often tertiary, quaternary, or centenary. Cultural change or cultural evolution does not operate on isolated societies but always on interconnected systems in which societies are variously linked within wider "social fields" (Eric R. Wolf, 1982, p. 76).

However one views the connection between European expansion and the industrial revolution, there can be no doubt that the two processes are related. Likewise, there can be no doubt that with the industrial revolution a radically new form of social organization had appeared. Global expansion had brought European observers in contact with a large variety of societies. In the context of the rapid and unprecedented changes of the late eighteenth and early nineteenth centuries, all these newly encountered societies were clearly on the other side of the great watershed through which western European societies were passing. They resembled little in modern Europe, but had some affinity to those portions of Europe that had yet to experience the new changes. This basic similarity lies at the root of all the classical dichotomies between "traditional" and "modern" societies: gemeinschaft and gesellschaft, mechanical and organic solidarity, folk and urban culture. But the traditional–modern dichotomy masks more than it reveals. There are important differences among the types of societies at both poles of the dichotomy. That there are wide variances among state societies has long been recognized by sociologists (e.g., Bendix, 1967; Lieberson, 1961). The study of distinctions among nonstate societies has been a major raison d'etre of social anthropology. Reflection on these differences has given rise to a variety of theories of social and cultural evolution.

THEORIES OF SOCIAL EVOLUTION

In the nineteenth century, unilinear models of social change predominated. These theories all shared underlying assumptions about "progress" (Nisbet, 1969). Each society was expected to follow a fixed trajectory of change that inevitably culminated in a European-style modern society. The change from one stage to another was largely endogenous. Only societies that were somehow "deficient" did not progress through all the stages. The major difference among societies was the timing of the changes, a function of their internal structure. With the acceptance of these assumptions all that was necessary to reconstruct human sociocultural evolution was a synchronic sampling of existing societies that were arrested at the various stages of development.[2]

Both nineteenth- and twentieth-century writers have recognized the diversity among nonstate societies in terms of social organization, complexity, size, and degree of political integration. Such societies vary from small groups of 20 or so foragers, through large chiefdoms, to quasi-states with formal governments. It is widely recognized that many of these societies found in the modern world are the products of interaction of traditional and modern societies, and not static or atavistic remnants of earlier social forms. Twentieth-century evolutionists have devised a number of useful schemes to classify this array of social forms. Godelier (1975, 1977) has revised various Marxist schemes based on the concept of the mode of production. Sahlins (1972) and Dalton (1968, 1969) have devised schemes based on systems of distribution and exchange; Service (1971, 1975), on political integration; Lenski (1966; Lenski and Lenski, 1982), on productive technology; Fried (1967), on stratification and political organization. The particular scheme they use is less important than the underlying diversity they all seek to organize.

These evolutionary schemes are examples of the sequences of stages in general evolution, as distinguished from those of specific evolution, the adaptive changes of a particular society to its environment (Sahlins, 1960, p. 43). This distinction is important because it allows the specification of criteria for change without requiring that all social forms pass through all stages in sequence, thus breaking away from unilinear models. What is problematic is how specific evolution contributes, or fails to contribute, to general evolution. The distinction requires two levels of discussion: (1) general patterns of change in the forms of social organization; and (2) historically specific social systems. While stagnation, regression, or leapfrogging are not problematic at the general level, they remain theoretically intriguing at the specific level.

Steward's (1955, 1977) concept of "multilinear evolution" is useful in dealing with the complexities of specific evolution. A number of factors can produce similar changes in social organization. Hence, similarity of social organization is not necessarily an indicator of similar histories or evolutionary trajectories. Rather, social organization is an adaptation to a constellation of ecological and social conditions. Similar constellations produce similar adaptations, but similar constellations can be constructed in a variety of ways. For instance, increased demographic concentration usually gives rise to increased sociocultural integration (among nonstate societies at least). Increased demographic concentration can arise from several sources—ecological changes, technological changes, external pressures such as war, or any combination of these.[3]

Among many factors affecting evolutionary processes is the wider social setting of a society. It is useful to distinguish between two broad categories of change engendered in different settings. Pristine social change refers to changes in social organization that occur either in isolation or in the context of societies at the same level of sociocultural development. That is, the social environment is homogeneous with respect to general evolutionary types of societies. Reactive, or secondary, social change refers to changes caused in a society by interaction with one or more societies that are "more advanced" in the general evolutionary sense. The distinction is not one of contact versus isolation, but between homogeneous versus heterogeneous social settings. As Wolf (1982, p. 76; 1984) has so forcefully stated, reactive rather than pristine social change has been more common, especially during the last half millennium.

The distinction between pristine and reactive social change has been drawn several times. Fried (1967, 1975) has argued that "tribes" are nearly always products of reactive change. Tribes are formed by the amalgamation of related band societies under the impact of invading states. Thus a tribe cannot be a stage in a sequence of pristine forms leading to the state, since it is only produced by interactions between bands and states. Steward (1955, Ch.9; 1977, Chs.5, 17) has made a similar argument for the formation of large bands. Wolf (1982, Ch.6) has documented the reverse process, the fragmentation of bands into family units under the pressure of the fur trade. B. Price (1978) has extended the distinction to the formation of states. States may appear pristinely (Wright, 1977), or may be reactively produced from bands, tribes, or chiefdoms via interaction with already existing states.

Since more advanced forms of society capture larger amounts of energy from their environment, have higher levels of social integration, and have higher levels of general adaptability (Sahlins, 1960, p. 38), they may be expected to be the initiators and the more independent actors in reactive social change. Still, the mechanism by which more advanced societies affect less advanced societies must be specified. When the effect is in the advanced direction, how is this distinguished from diffusion? If the effect is in the less advanced direction, how is it distinguished from decay? If the effect is static, how is it distinguished from isolation?

From their first appearance, states have absorbed smaller, less complex social groups. The results of incorporation have been highly variable: some groups have been eliminated, either by annihilation or assimilation; others have become ethnic minorities; others have become colonies; still others have been able to regain some autonomy in a variety of plural societies. State incorporation of nonstate societies (and occasionally other states) has been a major form of reactive social change.

THEORIES ABOUT INCORPORATION

Modernization theory, dependency theory, and world-system theory all discuss incorporation in one way or another, although few of them do so explicitly. These theories focus on two types of states: mercantile states and industrial capitalist states. Hence, they are concerned with a relatively narrow range of incorporation—the impact of modern (post–fifteenth century) states on other societies. They do not address earlier forms of incorporation, such as the effects of the Chinese, Roman, Greek or Persian empires on surrounding societies.

According to modernization theory, nation-building involves a process of integration of formerly diverse social groups into one political–economic order with a shared sense of identity. The modern nation-state, according to this theory, was to become the organizing unit of the modern world as various non–nation-states became nation-states, either through conquest and absorption, through colonization, or through diffusion. This prediction has failed at two levels. First, while the nation-state form has spread, it has not become universal, nor have all the new nation-states come to resemble the modern nation-states of western Europe. Second, even modern nation-states have not succeeded in molding uniform national identities. The nationhood of nation-states is more frequently a political aspiration than a social reality. Instead there has been a constant re-emergence of separate local identities (Yancey et al.,

1976; A. D. Smith, 1981; Horowitz, 1975; W. Connor, 1972, 1977; Hechter and Levi, 1979; Foster, 1980; Olzak, 1983b, 1983c). Theoretical discussions of these discrepancies focus on modern states (Nagel and Olzak, 1982; Nielsen, 1985; Olzak, 1983b).

Most theories of uneven development grow out of dependency theory (Portes, 1976; Chirot and Hall, 1982). These theories explain uneven development as the result of expansion of the developed states into undeveloped regions. As developed states expand, they utilize resources taken from undeveloped regions to fuel their own further development. At first this is done through direct seizure of territory and resources. Later the same ends are achieved through capitalist trade (Amin, 1976). The extraction of resources from these regions not only blocks development, but also causes changes that retard development. Underdevelopment is not simply the lack of development, but is a direct consequence of unfavorable economic relations—hence the phrase, "the development of underdevelopment" (Frank, 1969b). Thus, the existence of feudal-like forms in parts of Latin America is not due to the persistence of archaic forms of sociopolitical organization preserved from the time of Spanish colonization, but is a consequence of their position in international trade (Frank, 1969a; Genovese, 1969; Stavenhagen, 1975).

World-system theory elaborates the analysis of dependency.[4] Wallerstein (1974a, 1974b, 1979) distinguishes three types of world-systems: (1) mini-systems, which are small, isolated groups of peoples living in relative isolation; (2) world-empires, in which single polities dominate economic exchange networks; and (3) world-economies, in which several polities coexist within a single economic exchange network. There are few mini-systems left in the modern world. World-economies either fall apart or become world-empires when one agrarian state eventually incorporates the entire exchange network under its political control (Wallerstein, 1979). Braudel (1984, pp. 21–85) argues that this distinction is overdrawn. During the "long sixteenth century" (1450–1650) a world-economy based on commodity production for market exchange developed in Europe. The drive for capital accumulation pushed this world-economy to constant, but uneven, expansion. This "modern world-system" has persisted until it is truly a *world*-system. Thus, the modern world-system has been very successful in absorbing other social units into itself. Conversion to a world-empire has been and continues to be blocked by the dynamics of competition among core powers for hegemony (Chase-Dunn, 1978; Bousquet, 1980). The emergence of the modern world-economy constitutes the single transition from feudalism to capitalism (Wallerstein, 1979, Ch.8). This world-economy set in motion the social forces that generated the industrial revolution, led to the

European colonization of the world, and produced the current world order.

Competition among producers for profits generated by production of goods for exchange eventually causes production to exceed market demand. This crisis of overproduction leads in turn to competition for new markets, new sources of raw materials, and new sources of labor—all of which may be obtained by incorporating formerly external areas into the world-economy. These processes generate a cyclical pattern of growth. A systemic crisis of overproduction leads to expansionary competition, then to relative stabilization under a hegemonic state, and on to a new crisis of overproduction.[5]

Wallerstein holds that the growth of the capitalist economy has been accompanied by the development of a world-economy, a network of economic exchange that transcends national borders. A major contribution made by world-system theory is the recasting of the unit of analysis from the nation-state, which is the implicit unit of analysis in most discussions of incorporation, to the world-system (Bach, 1980; Bergesen, 1980, Chs. 1, 10). Thus, interaction among nation-states and between states and nonstates becomes an explicitly theoretical issue. The emergence of a capitalist world-system constitutes a new level of social organization in an evolutionary sense. This new form began to emerge in the long sixteenth century in western Europe and gradually grew to encompass the entire world. This system constituted one mode of production, a unitary system of producing the material goods necessary to keep the system functioning. The defining characteristic of this mode of production is commodity production, production of goods for sale on the market. As the system expanded, world-wide production and trade processes differentiated the world-economy into central, thriving, modern, diversified industrial states (the core); marginal, retarded, mono-cultural, agricultural, or extractive states (the periphery); and states characterized as intermediate between the other two (the semi-periphery). The class structures of these three types of states are systematically different.

Core states have "typically modern" class structures. The persistence or emergence of ethnic groups within core states is interpreted as a strategy for improvement of class position for specific groups. Ethnic groups occupying superior class positions organize to defend their position; those in inferior positions organize to enhance the possibility of improvement. Ethnicity is used to legitimate their efforts to advance themselves (Wallerstein, 1979, Chs. 10, 11; Arrighi et al., 1983). In cases where such ethnic groups are regionally concentrated, the region bears the same relation to the central state as colonies bear to their mother countries. Residents of these internal colonies (Hechter, 1975) manifest their resistance to their colonial situation in ethnic terms when they are part of a cultural division of labor (Hechter, 1978).

Modes of Production, World-System Theory,
and the Process of Incorporation

Wolf (1982) and Tilly (1981) concentrate on the mode of production as the basic source of the "relations of production," rather than the relations of exchange, which are emphasized by Wallerstein. The under-lying issue in this debate is whether capitalism consists of one mode of production or of several articulated modes of production.[6] If capitalism does indeed constitute a single mode of production, then the persistence and constant re-emergence of forms of social organization that resemble "pre-capitalist" forms is an important problem. However, if capitalism is a system of articulated modes of production, then the articulation of the various modes of production requires explanation. An irony of this debate is that the world-system approach, associated with the single mode of production camp, has an explanation for the articulation of multiple modes of production—the capitalist market.

Wolf argues that " . . . the capitalist mode of production did not come into being until the latter part of the eighteenth century" (Wolf, 1982, p. 298). The transition was the result of continual pressure by merchants to gain control over various aspects of trade. With the rise of the factory system, merchants finally gained control over the means of production, thus ushering in capitalism and becoming the bourgeoisie. Technological changes were the result of intra-bourgeois competition. In contrast, world-system theory concentrates on the accumulation of capital and the transformation of productive processes intended to further that goal. Thus, for both camps, market articulation is a major mechanism of incorporation by which more advanced areas (core states) produce changes in less advanced peripheral areas.

In world-system analysis incorporation is defined as " . . . the integration of its production processes into the interdependent network of production processes that constitute the world market" (Wallerstein and Martin, 1979, p. 193). This is called "effective" or "real" incorporation which is " . . . a situation in which the patterns of production and reproduction typical of external arenas have ceased to be dominant within the region and tend to disintegrate qua systems" (Arrighi, 1979, p. 162). This is distinguished from "nominal" or "formal" incorporation which is " . . . a situation in which political domination by an external power and/or economic relations with the capitalist world-economy have been established but the dominant patterns of production and reproduction within the region are still those typical of external arenas." Furthermore, "even if they are not, should for any reason political domination cease and/or economic relations with the capitalist world-economy be severed, there would be a tendency toward the re-establishment of those patterns" (Arrighi, 1979, pp. 161–162). Sokolovsky adds that "it follows that while power relations are a vital aspect of the system, by itself plunder does not constitute effective incorporation" (1985, p. 49).

Both Arrighi (1979) and Sokolovsky (1985) make it clear that, for world-system theory, incorporation involves only effective incorporation. However, in both "pre-capitalist" (Schneider, 1977) and "ancient" (Ekholm and Friedman, 1982) world-economies, significant social changes occurred without effective incorporation, although effective incorporation also occurred in "ancient" world-economies (Ekholm and Friedman, 1982). By excluding milder forms of incorporation, world-system theory limits the range of social changes examined, masking pertinent variables and processes by inadvertently holding them constant (e.g., strength of an incorporating state, or the types of nonstate societies incorporated).

This inattention arises because

> both Frank and Wallerstein focused their attention on the capitalist world system and the arrangements of its parts. . . . Their choice of focus thus leads them to omit consideration of the range and variety of such populations, of their modes of existence before European expansion and the advent of capitalism, and of the manner in which these modes were penetrated, subordinated, destroyed, or absorbed, first by the growing market and subsequently by industrial capitalism (Wolf, 1982, p. 23).

These same problems run through the analysis of feudalism, the formation of regions of refuge (Aguirre Beltran, 1979) and the North American fur trade—to take them in successively milder forms of incorporation.

Feudalism and Incorporation. According to Wallerstein (1974b) commodity trade between eastern and western Europe produced "development" in western Europe and "underdevelopment" or the "second serfdom" in eastern Europe.[7] This analysis raises the mode of production debate in full detail. The imperialism thesis is at issue in two forms: (1) did the west–east European trade cause (or in refined versions accelerate) the "underdevelopment" of eastern Europe, in particular causing the "second serfdom"; and (2) was this "underdevelopment" vital to the rise of the "modern world-system"? The relevance of this debate to the American Southwest is demonstrated by reviewing the explanations of how incorporation produced feudalization in some peripheral areas of the modern world-economy.

Frank (1969a), Genovese (1969) and Stavenhagen (1975) argue that the feudalism of Latin American societies (in the seventeenth through twentieth centuries) was a direct result of dependent trade relations with Europe—Spain, then Britain, then the United States. Thus feudalism in Latin America is not a recalcitrant, atavistic Spanish tradition, but a constantly regenerated social structure produced by capitalist trade arrangements. Wallerstein (1974b) extends that argument to the origin of feudalism or the "second serfdom" in eastern Europe. Chirot (1975) critiques and extends that analysis.

Chirot distinguishes two types of "servile labor": that which arises in conditions of extensive social and economic isolation; and that which arises as a response to expansion of capitalist markets. The former is the classic feudalism described by Bloch (1961), the latter is not. Both forms appear similar on the surface: agricultural laborers are bound to the land, the results of their labors are taken by the landlord, and the landlord in turn has some obligations to his tenants. This is a clear instance of multilinear evolution—two different paths leading to a similar social form. This is the root of much confusion and controversy surrounding the use of the term feudalism; it can refer to a social form that can be produced in at least two ways, by isolation, or by a particular type of incorporation. According to Chirot (1975) the second type, which he labels servile labor, appears in response to market expansion when there is a potential class of large landlords, a labor shortage, and a labor-intensive technology.

When trade increases—as a result of factors external to the region—the local elite (either an indigenous hereditary elite, or a class of conquerors) attempts to increase production of local goods for the external market. To increase production, the local elite must somehow coerce the local labor force to produce more than its subsistence needs. When land is scarce and labor abundant this is relatively easy: direct producers may be denied access to land necessary for subsistence production unless they also produce a suitable amount of surplus for export. When labor is scarce and/or land is abundant, this strategy will not work as readily, since the producers may simply seize unused land for subsistence production. To control the producers the elite must develop some means of curtailing the freedom of movement of the labor force. The alternative is to employ a production technology that uses less labor. If no such technology is available, the labor force must be constrained. This may be done through formal bondage to the land (serfdom), or through force of arms (slavery), or through economic restraints (debt peonage). Thus, either a labor shortage or an abundance of empty land will produce the same result—a servile labor system.[8] The other side of such labor restriction is the formation of obligations on the part of the elite to care for the producers—hence, the close association of servile labor with patron–client relations.

Clearly this type of feudalism, servile agricultural labor, is a product of incorporation into a wider trade network. Whatever the specific form of servile labor, such systems arise as a response to increased external trade. Indeed, it may be the case that the collection of pristine feudal systems is an empty set. If this analysis is correct, then when its various conditions are met, servile labor systems should appear. The particular form of bondage will vary with the conditions outlined above. This analysis has a double relevance to the Southwest. On the one hand, it offers an explanation for "debt peonage" and "feudalism" references that appear in the literature on New Mexican Hispanic social organization. On the other hand, to the degree that those systems exist and are associated with increased external trade, the Southwest offers an independent test of the theory, shedding some light on the second serfdom and the mode of production controversies.

Peripheries and Regions of Refuge.   Incorporation may also lead to relative stagnation. This issue has been addressed by Aguirre Beltran whose *Regions of Refuge* (1979) presents a theory of a peculiar form of incorporation, enforced stagnation. Not all newly absorbed areas are effectively incorporated. Some regions, called "regions of refuge," are only marginally important to the absorbing state. In marginally incorporated regions, social relations within the region are buffered from the dynamics of the state and suprastate economies, freezing regional development at the time of absorption. Such regions preserve older forms of social relations that are no longer found in the central sectors of the supraregional economy. This leads to the formation of a regional elite whose members act as brokers between the region and supraregional sectors. These areas are also preserves in the sense that they maintain state control of the region in expectation of later development. It is not uncommon for a region of refuge to be a net liability to the absorbing state. Still, the formation and transformation of a region of refuge requires explanation at a supraregional level.

From the vantage of Europe, the important feature of this growing trade network is that other, non-European areas became enmeshed in it. From the vantage of those areas caught in the new trading relations, their primary importance is not the participation in the market, but the consequences for local systems of production, and hence for social organization. Participation in the market generally has two consequences: (1) pressure to intensify existing production processes; and (2) pressure to produce new goods for sale. The North American fur trade illustrates these processes.

The Fur Trade.   The context of the fur trade is significant.[9] "In the European search for wealth, furs were not items of highest priority: gold, silver, sugar, spices, and slaves were all more desirable and profitable" (Wolf, 1982, p. 158). The fur trade supplied luxury goods; it did not make or break empires. Nonetheless, it had profound consequences for the groups that participated. It disrupted existing networks of exchange, created and then destroyed new ones, altered ecological balances, set off large population movements, and even changed the structure of the social organizations of many groups. Among northeastern populations there was a decided shift toward smaller units of organization and productive activities. The older system of extended groups of families broke down, as groups fragmented to improve their relations with traders: " . . . the hunting territory, held and defended exclusively by small family groups against other possible users, was a consequence of the new individualized exchange relationship between trapper and trader" (Wolf, 1982, p. 163; Leacock, 1954). This fragmentation also facilitated missionary efforts to "convert" natives (A. G. Bailey, 1969, cited in Wolf, 1982, p. 163). Obviously the fur trade had a dramatic impact on one set of partners, while having only minimal impact on the other set.

The focus on mode of production facilitates analysis and study of the effects of trade. Yet to label these participants "proletarianized hide collectors," while in some sense "useful," would detract attention from the important and complicated social changes engendered by participation in the trade. Thus, there is far more to incorporation than is suggested by the imperialism thesis.

Toward a Theory of Incorporation

The preceding analysis suggests reformulation of the concept of peripherality as a continuum of degree of incorporation of an underdeveloped region into a core area. But what accounts for variation along this continuum of incorporation? World-system theory suggests that market relations, which presumably benefit the core, may be such a factor. However, because peripheral areas may sometimes use core resources,[10] market relationships cannot be the sole factor. Political interests could also cause a core state to spend resources to maintain a peripheral area, as was the case for New Mexico during the Spanish and Mexican eras (1598–1846), or for France and Louisiana before 1800. This suggests that differences in political power between core and periphery may be another motivation for incorporation.

For capitalist states, the degree of market articulation is one major factor in determining the degree of peripherality of a region. Market articulation refers to the degree of capital and product flow between the expanding state and the absorbed region. Market flow includes amount of goods transferred, the type of goods (e.g., raw products or manufactured goods), relative importance of the transfer to the economy, and degree of centralization of the exchange process. Evaluation of these components is relative to the position of the observer, in the core or in the absorbed region. For instance, furs from North America were in no way vital to European economies, yet their collection and exportation to Europe produced major social and economic changes among indigenous societies.

The degree of incorporation may range from weak through strong. At the lower range of that continuum are areas either outside the world-economy or only slightly connected to it. Toward the middle of the continuum the primary flow of influence remains from the core to the periphery. The core has a strong impact on peripheral areas, but the peripheral areas have weak impacts on the core. At the strong pole of the continuum essential goods are exchanged. These regions experience full scale "development of underdevelopment," and are important to core development. Influence flows in both directions, but net product and capital flows are to the core. Labeling the entire range of relations "peripheral," while recognizing major political and economic differentials, masks these important variations.

Thus it is useful to distinguish among types of peripheries, based on strength of market articulation or degree of incorporation. At the weak pole of the continuum are areas external to the world-economy and areas where contact has barely occurred. These might be called "external arenas" and "contact peripheries," respectively. In the middle range of the continuum are found "marginal peripheries," or "regions of refuge." Finally, at the strong pole of the continuum are found "full-blown," or "dependent," peripheries. These latter are what both dependency and world-system theories typically call to mind, but actually represent only one extreme of a continuum. Where some mechanism other than market articulation is the force behind incorporation, the same types of peripheries may be found. This conceptualization differs somewhat from that of conventional world-system theory;[11] it is summarized in Figure II.1.

	NONE	WEAK	MODERATE	STRONG
STRENGTH OF INCORPORATION		←		→
MARKET ARTICULATION	None	Weak	Moderate	Strong
IMPACT OF CORE ON PERIPHERY	None	Strong	Stronger	Strongest
IMPACT OF PERIPHERY ON CORE	None	Low	Moderate	Significant
TYPE OF PERIPHERY	External arena	Contact periphery	Marginal periphery or region of refuge	Full-blown periphery or dependent periphery
WORLD-SYSTEM TERMINOLOGY		External arena	Incorporation	Peripheralization

Figure II.1. The continuum of incorporation and associated factors

Explaining the consequences for social change of position on this continuum is part and parcel of an empirical examination of the processes of incorporation. This analysis suggests that there are at least two distinct levels of explanation for the impact of state societies on nonstate societies: world-system and local. At the world-system level changes in the world-economy account for changes in a region's incorporation into the world-economy. Explanations for the efforts by core states to bring other regions into closer relations must be sought in the dynamics of the world-system, and the internal dynamics of the core states (Bergesen, 1980, Ch. 10). Changes in incorporation have strong impacts on, and are shaped by, local social organization.

The impact of incorporation also may be expected to differ according to the level of sociocultural complexity of the absorbed society. For instance, there is little possibility of trade with foragers, unless the state creates a demand for goods produced in the state and if the foragers can collect some useful good, for example, furs or slaves (see Wolf, 1982, Chs. 6, 7). When the local population practices some type of agriculture, trade for available surplus is a possibility.

However, shifts in incorporation are not entirely elastic. As a region becomes more tightly incorporated into the world-economy, external pressures impinge more forcefully on local groups. When such pressures are sufficiently strong, and of sufficient duration, the structure of local groups will be changed. Thus a group of autonomous bands may be transformed into a tribe, or independent subsistence producers may be tranformed into peasants. If the transformations are sufficiently drastic, they become increasingly difficult to reverse—even in the event of a core-induced shift to weaker incorporation. Hence, as the incorporation of a region becomes stronger, approaching the full-blown periphery pole of the continuum, loosening of incorporation becomes increasingly difficult. Incorporation operates like a loose ratchet-and-pawl mechanism. Within a narrow range of incorporation change is reversible. The stronger the incorporation the less likely it is that change will be reversible, so change tends to be in one direction (see Wolf, 1982, p. 311). For instance, once the horse had been introduced into southwestern groups in the early seventeenth century, local ecological adaptations were changed so drastically that it was impossible to return to unmounted foraging (see Chapters V and VI). This does not mean that reverses did not occur, but rather that the stronger previous incorporation had been, the larger the obstacles to reversal and the more difficult it would be for the social structure to return to the status quo ante.

Social change is least at low levels of incorporation. As long as such regions remain loosely incorporated into the core economy, relatively small changes in degree of incorporation do not have profound effects on local social organization. For instance, a number of semi-autonomous tribes may be transformed into a mass of peasants who maintain separate identities.

The amalgamation of tribes into a single peasantry is most likely when all groups take the same economic role, such as independent cash-crop production. If, on the other hand, a division of labor due to kin-based access to different local resources emerges among the peasantry, new ethnic identities may form along these natural cleavages. There are two interrelated points here: (1) where there is no division of labor, fragmentation of peasants into tribes is very unlikely due to the uniformity of the mode of subsistence engendered by a prior, relatively strong, level of incorporation; (2) where there is a division of labor, ethnic identities are likely to crystallize along the divisions in the productive system.[12] This re-emergence of ethnicity is not, however, a return to tribal identities, but a newly emerged set of identities. These new identities, surely, will be likely to seize on any distinctions that already exist in the local cultural repertoire. What is problematic is the conditions under which a division of labor emerges.

An explanation for the emergence of a new division of labor must be sought in the analysis of the degree and type of market articulation between a local community and the world-economy. Changes in market articulation alter both the type of products exported to the core and the level of demand for those products. This, in turn, alters the types and distribution of possible subsistence activities, or niches, in the local ecology (Barth, 1969; Orlove, 1980). A new division of labor will emerge in which the divisions will coincide with the various subsistence activities. Ethnic boundaries will form along niche boundaries (Barth, 1969; Hannan, 1979). An explanation of how changing market articulation affects the distribution of niches must be sought in detailed examination of local ecological conditions, local social structures, and the degree of incorporation into the world-economy.

Although market articulation is a key factor affecting incorporation processes, it is not the only factor. The degree of transformation experienced by absorbed societies is also affected by the difference in political power between an encroaching state and the absorbed societies. This factor is probably more important in mercantile states than in industrial capitalist states. In relative terms, the power differential between Spanish invaders of Mexico and Peru and the Aztec and Inca societies was quite low (Lang, 1975; Wolf, 1959, Ch. VIII). In contrast, there was a large differential between English colonizers and the natives of eastern North America, as there was between Portuguese colonizers and the indigenous societies of Brazil (Lang, 1979). The differential between modern India and the large number of tribal societies within its borders is an intermediate case (Schermerhorn, 1978, Ch. 4). In India tribal societies have not posed a serious threat to the Indian state, but have caused considerable administrative and political trouble. The difference between the American state and the various Native American tribes in the twentieth century is an example of a large power differential. The power differential between core states and peripheral areas shapes the incorporation process.

In summary, incorporation must be explained at several levels. First is the contextual, or world-system, level. Changes in this level have their own internal dynamic. While this dynamic is affected by the totality of change in its constituents, no one component, especially a single peripheral area, has major effects on the overall dynamic of the world-system. Second are local or regional dynamics. The degree to which an area, a region, or society is incorporated into the world-system sets the context within which local changes may occur. Third, local social structure shapes the way in which incorporation and changes in incorporation affect local social structures and social processes. Thus social change, at the local level, is a product of both contextual changes and local endogenous conditions. In the language of statistical analysis, it is an interaction effect of local and contextual changes. To emphasize solely endogenous or exogenous factors is to misunderstand fundamentally the dynamics of social change. In terms of the debates reviewed above, both the relations of exchange (Wallerstein, Frank) and the relations of production (Wolf, Tilly) offer useful insights into the processes of social change. The exogenous penetration of the market is crucial to understanding the incorporation process. So, too, is the form of local social organization—mode of production, class structure, kinship system, and style of political leadership. Both camps, however, err in asserting the primacy of one over the other. The interaction of the two is what is crucial.

Finally, intellectual honesty requires that the limits of the above discussion be underscored. While incorporation is a general concept, this analysis emphasizes the last half millennium, the era of mercantile and industrial states. To the degree that capitalism and mercantilism represent something new in social organization—whether only in degree or, as is more commonly held, in kind—the types of incorporation that have occurred in this era might reasonably be expected to be limited. They would also be the most common forms of incorporation and the forms most relevant to the understanding of the present and immediate past. A fuller understanding of the changes in societies and the origins of states will require studies of other, earlier forms of incorporation.

INCORPORATION AND THE SOUTHWEST

With this discussion of the problems and issues of incorporation in mind, it is now possible to explain the value and relevance of studying these processes in the American Southwest. The Southwest has special features at all three levels of analysis: world-system, regional and local. At the world-system level there is the unusual circumstance of two waves of incorporation into the expanding European world-economy: the Spanish and American conquests. This allows comparison of the effects of mercantile incorporation with the effects of capitalist incorporation. The two waves also make it possible to avoid—for this analysis—the debate about whether capitalism originated in the long sixteenth century or only with the industrial revolution. Whatever one's position on that debate, the first conquest was clearly mercantile, the second equally clearly capitalist. The fact that the United States in the mid-nineteenth century was only a nascent industrial power beginning its climb to core status makes the comparison all the more interesting. Even at this early stage it is clear that the capitalist conquest was significantly different. Furthermore, the second conquest allows some assessment of the consequences of the transfer of control of a region from a declining mercantile empire—with a brief Mexican interregnum—to a rising capitalist state. The fact that the region was a frontier for both states is itself another useful feature.

A frontier is where, in social and geographical space, incorporation occurs. Here it is possible to descend from the theoretical clouds to concrete events, and begin to untangle what happens when a state attempts to absorb a nonstate society. The Southwest is unique in that it remained a frontier for so long, for several centuries under three modern states.

The explanation for this marginality is found at a world-system level of analysis, as is the transfer of control from one state to another. However, as a region of refuge, an area occupying the middle ranges of the continuum of incorporation, it experienced a number of significant shifts, back and forth, along that continuum. This back-and-forth slippage makes the region particularly fascinating to study. Throughout the period of study, but in the Spanish era in particular (ca. 1540–1821), political considerations played a major role in the various shifts of context. The area was preemptively colonized to block occupation by various European rivals. The various attempts to expand the initial New Mexican colonies, and to colonize Texas and then California, were motivated as much by considerations of international rivalries as by concerns internal to the empire (Bolton, 1929; Bannon, 1974).

The key to understanding southwestern social change is in understanding the shifting contexts of those relations. In the era of Spanish conquest and control the Southwest passed through several significant changes. The seventeenth century was an era of initial conquest, which drastically altered the nature of local group organization and interrelations. The first two-thirds of the eighteenth century was an era of formation of a region of refuge. The last phase of Spanish control, from the Bourbon reforms until Mexican independence (ca. 1765–1821), was a time of changing relations between a region of refuge and the state. Under the Bourbon reforms the Southwest moved from the marginal toward the dependent pole of the continuum of incorporation. Mexican independence is doubly important because it marks another shift back toward marginality in relation to the Mexican state, and the intensification of American interest in the region. The American conquest (officially 1846–1848) has long been recognized as a benchmark in southwestern history. Not only did the conquest shift the region from one state to another, but the strength of incorporation increased significantly. These changes in incorporation altered relations between and among the various groups living in the region.

While these southwestern features afford special opportunities, they also present special problems. The two successive waves of conquest increased the difficulty of making a full comparison of the consequences of the two types of incorporation. The second conquest affected an already greatly changed situation. The subtleties of these changes in incorporation require a precision of analysis that strains the data available for the task.

ETHNOGRAPHIC TERMINOLOGY AND SOCIAL STRUCTURE

The various evolutionary schemes reflect different theoretical conceptions of social organization, and usually imply different analyses of the processes of social change. They are difficult to separate because they overlap extensively. Furthermore, some terms are tied to specific geographical locations or specific groups. For instance, a band leader in Africa is a "headman," in New Guinea a "big man," and in North America a "chieftain"—yet all three perform similar functions, in similar manners. A big man is the type of leader most common among the various nomadic indigenous groups found in northern New Spain, and describes one whose power comes from persuasion, superior ability in various pursuits including, but not limited to, oration, and who is noted for his generosity (Sahlins, 1963, p. 289).

These conceptual schemes are compared by Moseley and Wallerstein (1978) especially for "pre-capitalist" forms of social organization. These categories label stages of general evolution, and hence become problematic when applied to specific cases. Three sets of terminology warrant further discussion here, those of Lenski, Spicer, and Wolf. All three base their distinctions on somewhat different criteria, but the resultant terminologies are remarkably congruent. Lenski (1966; Lenski and Lenski, 1982) bases his distinctions on technology. He divides societies into four main categories: hunting and gathering, horticultural, agrarian, and industrial. Horticultural and agrarian societies are divided into simple and advanced. Simple horticultural societies are distinguished from hunting and gathering societies by the practice of plant cultivation; advanced horticulturalists add the use of metals. Simple agrarians add the use of the plow; advanced agrarians add the use of iron. The agrarian stage is also marked by the appearance of the state and civilization. Industrial societies use a variety of energy sources.

There is a problem with Lenski's diagnostic traits: in the New World metals were not in extensive use, iron and the plow not at all. By those criteria there were no advanced agrarian societies, and hence no states in the New World. However, most writers classify the Aztec and Inca empires as states or civilizations (e.g., Service, 1975, Chs. 10 and 11). But if the diagnostic elements are taken only as crude indicators, and the entire constellation of common traits is used, there is no problem. What emerges from such treatment, though, is that the entire range from simple horticultural to advanced agrarian societies is a continuum of food-producing groups that do not fall into neat categories.

Spicer (1962, pp. 12–15) divides southwestern groups into four economic types: nonagricultural bands, bands, rancheria people (a term taken over from Spanish descriptions), and village people. Nonagricultural bands are the equivalent of Lenski's hunters and gatherers. Bands are nomadic people who herd, hunt, and practice agriculture upon occasion. Rancheria people are the most varied, ranging from people living in more-or-less permanent homes scattered over a wide area to groups living in moderately compact areas. Village people are distinguished by permanent, compact villages; they frequently made use of irrigation. Bands straddle Lenski's hunting and gathering and simple horticultural types of societies. Rancheria people are primarily simple horticulturalists. Village people range from advanced horticulturalists to simple agrarians. Within the rancheria type there is considerable variety; consequently, most southwestern groups are considered to be rancheria people.

Wolf (1982, Ch. 3) distinguishes three types of societies based on the mode of production: kin-ordered, tributary, and capitalist. He explicitly uses Marx's concept of mode of production as an ideal type with which to compare actual societies. His intent is not to force all societies into a Marxian mold, but rather to draw upon the insights of Marx's analysis of society to present broad classifications helpful in understanding the effects of the expansion of capitalism on other types of society. Wolf says, "The utility of the concept does not lie in *classification* but in its capacity to underline the strategic relationships involved in the deployment of social labor by organized human pluralities" (1982, p. 76, emphasis in original). Thus, his categories are intellectual tools, not empirical realities. If a different problem were being addressed, a different classification might be more useful.

Kin-ordered societies, sometimes called classless or acephalous societies, are those in which all social organization is in the idiom of kinship. The kinship system functions either to organize social relations that facilitate the garnering of resources under conditions of abundance, or to restrict access under conditions of scarcity. In contrast, the tributary mode is marked by central control by an elite. The elite maintains power through the control of some strategic resource such as water, is usually capable of some form of coercion, and controls the local social organization. The direct producers of society's material needs control the means of producing those goods. In the capitalist mode, the means of production are held by a nonproducing class, the bourgeoisie; the non-owners, the proletarians, do the work. Wolf is using standard Marxian analysis. In the kin-ordered mode wealth is accumulated by proliferation of kinship ties. In the tributary mode wealth is accumulated by unequal exchange, one trading partner being able to take advantage of unequal values for some product. In the capitalist mode wealth is accumulated by taking surplus value, that is, by taking some portion of the value generated by the labor of workers.

The kin-ordered mode straddles the hunting and gathering through simple horticultural types of society. The tributary mode ranges from advanced horticulture to advanced agrarian societies. In Spicer's terms, bands and rancheria people are in a kin-ordered mode, whereas village people, and possibly the more compacted rancheria people, are simple tributary types. The Spanish Empire was an advanced tributary system, whereas the American state in the nineteenth century was clearly in the capitalist mode. With Wolf's tributary mode, as with Lenski's horticultural-agrarian continuum and Spicer's rancheria types, a large number of societies are spread along a continuum.

An important feature of these three analyses, as with the term "tribe," is the inherent fuzziness of group boundaries and membership in these forms of society. Bands, tribes, rancherias, and some tributary groups have very fluid memberships, not in the least because their social structures are frequently shaped by the actions of more advanced societies, i.e., they are frequently products of incorporation (see Wolf, 1982, p. 387). This fluidity and permeability of boundaries between both groups and types of societies are why all these classification schemes have a large, central category that represents some sort of continuum with fuzzy boundaries. The lack of clarity is not an analytic failing, but rather an accurate reflection of the outside world.

Here I will use the terms "band," "chiefdom" and "state," and comment on the term "tribe." A band is an acephalous form of organization ranging from a few loosely connected families to hundreds of individuals loosely organized into various kin groups. Chiefdoms are societies with distinct internal ranking, marked both by some internal stratification and by definite political authority structures. A state is marked by strong internal differentiation, definite compact settlements, a clear political structure with institutional means of political regulation (law and government), military defense, and a means of financing these activities—all staffed by full-time specialists. The Spanish, Aztec, and Inca empires are familiar examples of states. These terms differ somewhat from Wolf's modes of production. Bands are part of the kin-ordered mode, typically but not exclusively hunters and gatherers, and definitely lacking central organization and control. Chiefdoms are a vague type, but have some central control, however weak. They fit somewhere in the tributary mode, and are typically horticultural or simple agrarian groups. Tribes straddle the band–chiefdom distinction, and denote groups more complicated than bands, but how much more complicated is problematic. Each of these terms requires more elaborate discussion.

Steward (1977, pp. 118–124) has provided a detailed analysis of bands, in which he distinguishes between "minimum" and "maximum" bands. A minimum band consists of several closely related nuclear families living and working together in an area. This generally means 10–50 individuals, at a population density from one person per 1–40 square miles. The maximum band, in contrast, may consist of up to 500 persons. He says: "The social, cultural, and dialectical [linguistic] frontiers of such bands may be delimited by distances within which people can associate or by such barriers as deserts, lakes, and mountain ranges" (Steward, 1977, p. 123). Any technology or conditions that allow speedier or easier transportation will facilitate interaction over a wider territory. Steward analyzes these factors in some detail for western Shoshonis (1977, Ch. 17), including the Ute bands that enter into this study.

The most general feature of Steward's analysis is the extremely fluid nature of bands. To attempt to bound and define bands, to tie them to a territory, to identify leaders and so on is to misunderstand fundamentally the nature of band organization. The attempt to assign definite membership, boundaries, and leaders to bands has been a consistent error on the part of virtually all state officials in their attempts to establish relations with band societies. As used in this study, the term "band" will refer to any of the types of society ranging from Steward's minimal to maximal bands. His discussion defines the general, and necessarily vague, limits to the term. For these reasons, throughout this study I will refer to various band societies as, for example, "the Ute bands," and avoid the term "the Utes." The latter gives a false sense of a unitary structure, suggesting that a collection of bands is a tribe.

The term "tribe" is highly problematic (Fried, 1967, 1975). It has been used to refer to vague groups fitting anywhere along a range of nonstate societies. Only Service (1971) uses the term with any precision, and his usage marks a range of social organization between large bands and small chiefdoms. But even in Service's more restricted usage, the term conveys a false sense of unitary organization and identity that has led many analysts to refer to such nonexistent entities as the Navajo tribe or the Ute tribe or the Comanche tribe or the Apache tribe. Rather, these were collections of bands that lacked singular, overall organization— until either the Spanish or the American states began to impose one.

Thus, the problem with the term "tribe": it may refer to a form of organization that results from contact with a more complex form of society during which smaller groups are thrown together; or it may refer to a linguistically related, but politically autonomous group of bands. A tribe can arise by an amalgamation of related bands, or by the devolution of an organized chiefdom. Fried (1975) doubts that tribes occur pristinely, and strongly suggests that they are nearly always the result of interaction with a more complex form of society. In short, tribes are reactive forms of social organization frequently produced in the early or mild stages of incorporation.

The term "tribe" will be used sparingly to refer to a group of bands having a collective identity. As noted, such a collective identity is usually the result of interaction with a state society. Many tribes exist mainly in the eyes of the beholder, and not for the members. What are frequently labeled tribes or even nations are in fact collections of bands that share linguistic similarity, and that interact occasionally. Tribes may have some sort of leadership, but such leadership is typically fragile and based on influence more than power. Rather than being discussed in the abstract, tribal groups are best explained and described in context.

The term "chiefdom," in contrast to tribe, refers to a society with a definite structure, and with some systematic form of political organization. A distinguishing feature of a chiefdom is the existence of a definite mechanism for replacing the political leader.[13] Like band and tribe, chiefdom refers to a range of types of society. At one end of the range are tribes with relatively stable social structures; at the other end are incipient states. In the Southwest, Pueblo societies were the only clear chiefdoms, although under severe external pressure Papagos, Mohaves and Comanches approximated chiefdom organization. Pueblo societies, however, are generally located toward the tribal end of the continuum in the ethnographic literature since they have a minimal ruling elite. This may in fact be a mistaken reading of the present into the past. This point will be argued below. The utility of the term "chiefdom" in regard to the Pueblos is to highlight their relatively more structured organization and more stable leadership patterns as compared with other indigenous Southwestern groups.

To summarize, the terms "band" and "chiefdom" represent polar ends of a continuum of nonstate organizations. At the simple pole are groups that are little more than nuclear families in more-or-less regular contact with other such families who share the same language. At the more complex pole are groups that have extensive organization and clear political authority structures, may frequently encompass more than the local living group, and are stratified internally. These terms are conceptual constructs (ideal types) against which empirical cases can be evaluated. Note that Wolf's category, the tributary mode of production, straddles the range from simple chiefdom to agrarian states (e.g., from Pueblo societies to the Spanish Empire), thus obviating discussions of the origins, pristine or reactive, of states. The same can be said of Lenski's range from simple horticultural to advanced agrarian societies. Spicer uses only part of that range, omitting that portion of the continuum between tribes or chiefdoms and states. This may incidentally serve to magnify the apparent gap between village people and the Spanish Empire by giving the impression that there is a void or gulf between the two types, rather than a continuum that happens not to be represented by any empirical examples in the times and places he discusses.

Given the preceding theoretical discussions and terminological analyses, it is now appropriate to turn to the Southwest and its residents. Chapter III describes the region, introduces the various indigenous actors and sketches the condition and trajectories of change immediately before Spanish entry into the region.

NOTES

1. An initial form of this argument appeared in T. Hall (1983). The debate between Wolf and Wallerstein is discussed in T. Hall (1984b). The analysis of incorporation was developed in T. Hall (1986). This chapter integrates these theoretical forays.

2. Appelbaum (1970), Harris (1968), and Lauer (1982) provide some of the more accessible summaries and critiques of these theories. Nisbet's (1969) critique is a classic, as is Lenski's (1976) reply. Bendix (1967) provides a detailed analysis of the traditional–modern dichotomy. Granovetter (1979) discusses the hazards of theoretical discussions of social evolution.

3. Mathematically the number of possibilities is the sum of all the possible nonredundant combinations of factors, taking the factors first one, then two, then three at a time, and so on. With only 3 factors, as is the case here, there are 7 possible constellations. With 5 factors, there are 31 possibilities. With only 10 factors there are 1,023 possible constellations. The point is that a small number of factors can give rise to a very large number of constellations. This is one source of the complementarity between sociological and historical approaches to the study of social change. One approach emphasizes the small number of un-

derlying factors, the other approach stresses the myriad manifestations of various combinations of those factors. Neither approach is complete by itself.

4. The basic statements of world-system theory are found in Wallerstein (1974a, 1974b, 1979, 1980, 1984). These are elaborated in Chirot (1977), Hopkins (1979), Bach (1980), Bergesen (1980), Hopkins and Wallerstein (1982) and Chase-Dunn (1984). Critical assessments are found in Skocpol (1977), Chirot (1980, 1981), Chirot and Hall (1982), Howe and Sica (1980), Aronowitz (1981), Stinchcombe (1982, 1983), J. Hall (1984), and Chirot (1985, 1986). Nash (1981) reviews applications of world-system theory to ethnographic problems. "World-system," "world-economy," and "world-empire" are properly hyphenated in Wallerstein's usage. He intends a unitary concept, not a noun modified by an adjective. A "world-system" or "world-economy" is a new social form, and not simply "system" or "economy" spread over the globe.

5. The notion of cycles in the world-economy is discussed in several places. Mandel (1980) provides a strict Marxist analysis. World-system analyses are found in a two special issues of *Review* (II, no. 4, 1979, and VII, no. 4, 1984), Hopkins and Wallerstein (1980, Pt. I), Bergesen and Schoenberg (1980), and Bergesen (1983).

6. Wolf (1982, Chs. 3,10) provides an especially good summary of this literature. Barraclough (1983) criticizes Wolf's analysis. Major sources on the mode of production debate are Wolpe (1980), J. Taylor (1979), Chilcote (1984) and Chilcote and Johnson (1983).

7. The "second serfdom" refers to a second occurrence of serfdom, this time in eastern Europe, as opposed to the first occurrence in western Europe. It does not refer to a second appearance of serfdom in eastern Europe. The debate centers around issues raised by Perry Anderson (1974a) and Brenner (1976, 1977, 1982), drawing on Blum (1957) and Malowist (1958). Kay (1974), Tilly (1975; 1981, p. 40ff), Chirot (1975), and Hechter and Brustein (1980) contribute to the understanding of the issues. Aston and Philpin (1985) and Denemark and Thomas (1988) provide cogent summaries of this fractious debate.

8. There are two problems with this abbreviated statement: (1) obviously, the connection between various strategies of labor containment and the resultant form of servile labor is much more complicated and contingent than can be elaborated here; and (2) the statement rings of teleological reasoning. The intent is not that elites act in a teleological manner—though, to be sure, they would if they fully understood the situation—but that only those elites who did contain their labor force survived to leave a record of their presence and actions.

9. This brief example is drawn from Wolf (1982, Ch. 6) and some of his sources, especially Leacock (1954) and A. G. Bailey (1969). The fur trade is a clear case of "devolution" due to market participation. Bateman (1986) provides further analysis of the effects of the fur trade on indigenous social organization.

10. Whether a peripheral area is a net asset or liability can be a function of accounting procedures. No doubt the key issue is not net return to the core as a whole, but the class-specific costs and benefits of core-periphery relations. This is an area in need of close empirical investigation, which must, however, remain outside this work.

11. Wallerstein describes the differences between them: "What you [Hall] call 'contact periphery' is exactly what I mean by 'external arena.' The external arena is only of interest if there is some market articulation. The question is what

kind. What you call 'marginal periphery' is what we have been calling 'incorpora-tion' and what you call 'full-blown periphery' we have been calling the process of peripheralization that occurs only after our 'incorporation'" (personal commu-nication, October 15, 1985).

12.   Here I am using the Wallersteinian pole of the mode of production debate to set the context for change, which emphasizes market relations. How-ever, for local analysis, I favor the relations of production (Wolf, 1982; Tilly, 1981) pole of the debate, especially in regard to the formation of ethnic identi-ties. Thus, the two sides are not so much opposed as addressing different issues. I follow Wolf (1982, 1984), Harris (1979) and others in employing material conditions—ecological and technological adaptation—as parameters to which culture (including modes of group identity) must conform. In the long run, cultural and material aspects will be congruent, with material conditions setting the limits within which culture may vary. In the short run, however, both are crucial, and cultural changes may be the prime mover of material changes. Which one will be dominant in any specific setting is as much an empirical as a theoretical issue. Indeed, sorting which processes are long-run and which are short-run remains a challenge.

13.   Sahlins's discussion of the Nuer and the Tiv as segmentary lineages (1961) forms the limiting case. There is no permanent organization, and it is only called into being in the event of either strong external threat or strong internal pressures for expansion. The discussion of the Nuer is of special interest in that the Nuer seemed for a while to have been a reactive state (a state formed from bands or chiefdoms in response to predatory actions of another state). When the original threatening state was displaced by Europeans, the Nuer state collapsed.

CHAPTER III

The Southwest:
The Region, the Peoples
and Prehistory

The Southwest is a distinctive place to the American mind but a somewhat blurred place on American maps, which is to say that everyone knows that there is a Southwest but there is little agreement as to just where it is . . . . The term "Southwest" is of course an ethnocentric one: what is south and west to the Anglo-American was long the north of the Hispanic-American . . . (Donald Meinig, 1971, p. 3).

"Southwestern cultures have the general appearance of attenuated Meso-american cultures . . . ." If Southwestern archaeological research had been initiated in Mexico and moved northward, this would have been apparent much sooner (Richard Woodbury, 1979, p. 26; quotation from Kelley, 1966, p. 95).

Reed (1964, p. 175) facetiously defined the Southwest as reaching from Durango to Durango (Mexico and Colorado) and from Las Vegas to Las Vegas (New Mexico and Nevada). Meinig's point, however, is well-taken: the boundaries of the Southwest vary through time according to one's perspective. Archaeologists and anthropologists have long argued over where the Southwest begins and ends. The United States border has been something of an intellectual barrier for them (Lipe, 1978, p. 328; Hinton, 1983, p. 318; Di Peso, 1979b).

GEOGRAPHY AND PHYSIOGRAPHY[1]

The physical variety of the region usually accepted as the Southwest is tremendous. Of seven major life zones found in North America, six are found in New Mexico alone (Beck, 1962, pp. 9–10). Altitudes in the Southwest range from near sea level to approximately 3,600 meters (12,000 feet). Since temperature varies inversely with elevation, and rainfall increases with elevation, the variety of life zones is readily apparent.[2] According to Lipe (1978, p. 328) the climate, flora and fauna have fluctuated around conditions similar to today since the end of the Pleistocene (8,000–10,000 B.C.). These fluctuations "may have been great enough to affect prehistoric cultures, but they were probably not sufficient to alter the major environmental zones or regions that exist today" (Lipe, 1978, p. 328). However, Woodbury (1979, p. 25) cautions that "recent over-use of some resources has caused conspicuous changes, which must be taken into account in evaluating past landscapes." "Recent" should be read as in the last century or so.

Woodbury, following Lobeck (1948), divides the area into six major physiographic provinces: the southern Rocky Mountains, the Colorado Plateau, the Basin and Range Provinces, the High Plains, and, in Mexico, the Sierra Madre Occidental, and the Sierra Madre Oriental (see Map III.1). The Mogollon Highlands can be seen as a seventh region (see Lipe, 1978, pp. 331–332). The high southern Rocky Mountains extend from Colorado into northern New Mexico. The Rio Grande, the Pecos River and the Colorado River originate in these mountains. Timber and large game are plentiful, but only some of the lower valleys provide arable land. The Colorado Plateau extends over western Colorado, eastern and southern Utah, the northern half of Arizona and northwest New Mexico. Altitudes range from 1,500 to 2,100 meters and rainfall from 25 to 38 centimeters annually. The plateau is interrupted by volcanic intrusions and lava flows, and deeply crosscut by canyons, providing some of the most picturesque territory in all of North America. It is also a highly variable region with significant differences in life zones over short distances. Few streams are permanent; most are intermittent. The vegetation varies from pine forests at the higher elevations, to piñon and juniper, to sagebrush, saltbush, and greasewood. Where soils are deep, shrubs and grasses replace woodlands. At lower elevations cottonwoods and willows are found around seeps and drainages. In the northwest, precipitation comes mainly from the Pacific in the winter and spring in broad, frontal storms. In the southeast, precipitation comes from scattered and localized summer thunderstorms that originate in the Gulf of Mexico. These two sources are approximately balanced in the four-corners region (the area surrounding the point where New Mexico, Arizona, Utah and Colorado meet).

Basin and Range Provinces surround the Southwest on the northwest, west, south and southeast. Western Utah and Nevada are part of the

Map III.1. The Southwest: A context for definition

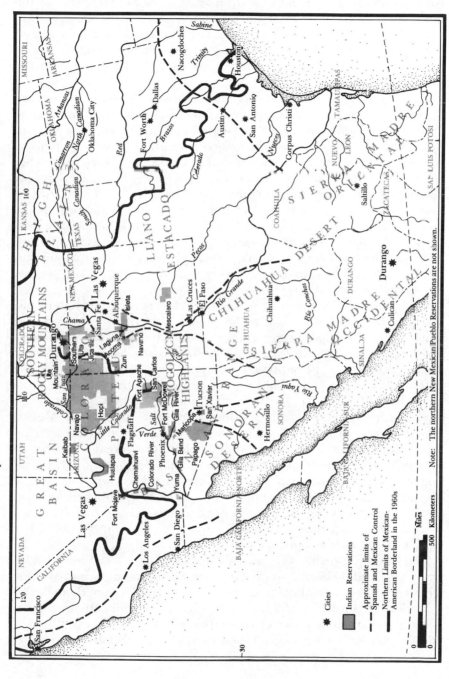

Sources: Meinig (1971:4–5), Woodbury (1979:24), Lipe (1978:332), Nostrand (1970), Dutton (1975).

Note: The northern New Mexican Pueblo Reservations are not shown.

Cities ★

Indian Reservations

Approximate limits of
Spanish and Mexican Control

Northern Limits of Mexican–
American Borderland in the 1960s

Miles
0   500
0   500
Kilometers

Great Basin, an area of interior drainage that is quite dry due to the rainshadow of the California Sierras. The Basin and Range areas are marked by isolated mountain chains, running north–south, scattered throughout basin areas. In the Great Basin region elevations are above 1,350 meters, where the vegetation resembles the lower areas of the Colorado Plateau.

To the west, south and southeast of the Colorado Plateau are the other Basin and Range areas. Elevations rise from near sea level in the vicinity of the lower Colorado River to 1,200 meters in southwestern New Mexico. Rainfall also increases toward the east from less than 12 to more than 25 centimeters. The vegetation here is sparse, consisting of creosote bushes and cacti, with mesquite and acacia near washes. The mountains support oak and juniper woodlands, and pine forests at the higher elevations. The lowlands of southern Arizona and northern Sonora are known as the Sonoran Desert; those of southern New Mexico and northern Chihuahua (between the Sierra Madre Occidental and the Sierra Madre Oriental) are known as the Chihuahuan Desert. Somewhat higher than the Sonoran Desert, the Chihuahuan Desert receives more rain, and has slightly denser and somewhat different vegetative cover.

To the east and northeast of the Colorado Plateau are the High Plains, which, in central New Mexico, include the drainage of the Pecos River. This is a vast grass and shrub area, home of the bison and bison hunters. This area of eastern New Mexico is known as the *Llano Estacado,* the staked plains—a name supposedly derived from the similarity of the bluffs that surround the plains to a huge stockade fence seen at a distance (Lavender, 1980, p. 14; Beck, 1962, pp. 7–8). The Mogollon Highlands are in the center of the Southwest, on the Arizona–New Mexico border. These form the southern edge of the Colorado Plateau. Pine forests are found at higher elevations. As elevation decreases the vegetation shifts to a piñon–juniper woodland, shading into mountain mahogany–oak scrub, and finally to desert steppe in the lower valleys. The southern edge of the escarpment, known as the Mogollon Rim, receives abundant water, since moisture-bearing clouds release their contents upon encountering the highlands. Further from the rim, even at higher elevations, there is less precipitation.

The final two provinces are the two Mexican ranges, the Sierra Madre Occidental and the Sierra Madre Oriental. Both extend far into Mexico. They are rugged mountains, cut by deep canyons. Between them lies an extension of the Basin and Range Province, the Chihuahuan Desert.

If there is any consistency in the southwestern environment, it is variety. This variety is not broad and continuous, but rather narrow and fine-grained, with strong differences occurring over short distances. This makes human adaptations and generalizations about them complicated.

CULTURES, LANGUAGES AND SOCIAL STRUCTURES

The physical diversity of the region is matched by its linguistic and cultural diversity.[3] There is no clear association between the languages spoken in the Southwest and the different cultural groups within the region.

Before reviewing linguistic variations a few cautions are in order. Linguistics, especially historical linguistics, is not an exact science, but is generally more precise than ethnohistory or ethnology. There are a number of techniques for tracing the genetic relations of languages (see Langacker, 1968). Languages are usually divided into "families," "languages," and "dialects." The differences among these levels are not well specified, but the list moves from lesser to greater similarity. Dialects are usually somewhat mutually intelligible. Families, sometimes only discernible to a trained linguist, contain languages that are more similar to each other than to languages not in the family.[4] In the Southwest there are at least six major language families: Uto-Aztecan, Kiowa-Tanoan, Southern Athapaskan, Yuman, Keresan, and Zuni (Hale and Harris, 1979).

Uto-Aztecan (Miller, 1983), one of the largest language families in the New World, is divided into three major groups: Aztecan, Sonoran, and Shoshonean. Nahautl is the most familiar of the Aztecan languages. In the Southwest Pima and Papago are part of the Sonoran group; Shoshoni, Ute, Comanche, and Hopi are part of the Shoshonean group. All of the latter, except Hopi, are part of the Numic subgroup.

Kiowa-Tanoan has three major, mutually unintelligible, branches among the Eastern Pueblos: Tiwa, Tewa and Towa (Hale and Harris, 1979). Only the people of Jemez Pueblo speak Towa, although it is probable that the residents of Pecos Pueblo were also Towa-speakers. Tewa is spoken at San Juan, Santa Clara, San Ildefonso, Nambe, Pojoaque and Tesuque Pueblos. Tiwa is spoken at Picuris, Taos, Sandia and Isleta Pueblos, and was the language of Tigua Pueblo near El Paso, Texas. Kiowa is spoken among the Plains Kiowa. There is considerable controversy about whether the Kiowa are an early Pueblo group that moved to the Plains, or a remnant of a Plains group that adopted Pueblo culture (Snow, 1984). There is also some evidence that Kiowa-Tanoan and Uto-Aztecan were part of the same group about 10,000 years ago (Hale and Harris, 1979).

Athapaskan languages are spoken by groups in the interior of Alaska and northwestern Canada, the northern coast of California, and the Southwest.[5] The far northwest is the homeland of all these groups. The Southwestern groups—known as the "Southern Athapaskans"—separated from their closest linguistic relatives about A.D. 1000. Linguistic differentiation within Southern Athapaskans began about A.D. 1300 when they split into eastern and western groups. The eastern group consists of Kiowa Apache, Jicarilla Apache, and Lipan Apache. The western group consists of Navajo, Chiricahua Apache, Mescalero Apache, and the ethnographic "Western Apache"—San Carlos, White Mountain, Cibecue and northern and southern Tonto. The "Western Apache" dialects are all mutually intelligible. These divisions are a partial reflection of modern reservation organization.

The Yuman family is represented in the Southwest by Yuma (Quechan), Mohave, Walapai, Havasupai, and Yavapai and a few others (Kendall, 1983). Yuman speakers live in southern California, the lower Colorado River area, and Baja California.

Both Keresan and Zuni are linguistic isolates—that is, they cannot be unambiguously related to any other language families. Keresan languages, sometimes considered to be dialects of a single language, are spoken at Zia, Santa Ana, San Felipe, Santo Domingo, Cochiti, Acoma and Laguna Pueblos. Zuni is spoken only at Zuni.

The cultural diversity in the Southwest exceeds its linguistic diversity. Precise descriptions of Southwestern groups are all but impossible since group organization varied considerably during the last five hundred years. The following descriptions are intended to give the reader a general sense of each group.

The major band societies considered here are Apache, Navajo, Comanche and Ute bands. The timing and circumstances of the appearance of Athapaskan-speaking Apache and Navajo in the Southwest have been the subject of controversy, and will be discussed below. Ute and Comanche bands entered the region from the north in the late seventeenth and early eighteenth centuries. Throughout the era under discussion all four groups remained nomadic. All acquired horses and guns from the Spaniards, although Comanches also acquired guns indirectly from the French via other Plains groups. All became formidable raiders until the mid- to late nineteenth century, when the American state forced them onto permanent reservations. Today the Navajo are the most numerous Native American group in the United States.

The main rancheria peoples are the various Yuman groups along the lower Colorado River and the Pima and Papago in southern Arizona. These groups play a less dramatic role in the account that follows, although at times they were crucial to certain events and processes. They have remained sedentary farmers throughout the era under consideration. They were more often the victims than the perpetrators of raids, but occasionally took the offensive against their enemies.

Pueblo societies are the closest to chiefdoms of Southwestern groups. The name Pueblo is taken from the Spanish word for town. The Spaniards granted them the status of *gente de razon* (literally, people of reason)—that is, civilized—because their villages resembled European villages and were organized in accord with Spanish sensibilities of town life (Wolf, 1959, Ch. VIII). The use of the term "Pueblo" (capitalized) to refer to these people has created considerable confusion. "Pueblo" can refer to a single village, a single group that may occupy more than one village, any or all villages inhabited by similar peoples, or a single individual. In the plural the term can refer to more than one of any of these. To help alleviate this confusion I will use the term "Pueblo" (capitalized) as an adjective modifying the appropriate noun, for example, society, village, group or individual. As with labels like "the Navajo," the term "the Pueblos" gives a false sense of unity to a culturally and politically heterogeneous collection.

There have been several important changes among Pueblo societies. Probably the most dramatic event in their history since Spanish contact was the Pueblo Revolt in 1680, when many Pueblo groups united briefly and drove the Spaniards from New Mexico (see Chapter V). The revolt and subsequent reconquest led to many changes among the villages. Laguna, Tigua, the Hopi-Tewa, and Pecos villages all deserve special mention. Laguna Pueblo was founded in the late 1690s by Keresen speakers who had worn out their welcome at Acoma (Ellis, 1979b). The Tigua people were Tiwa speakers who left northern New Mexico with the fleeing Spaniards after the revolt. They now live in the El Paso area and speak Spanish and English (Houser, 1979). Finally, the Hopi-Tewa are a group of Tewa-speakers who were invited by the Hopi villages (ca. 1700) to assist in defense. They have remained at Hano (in Arizona) ever since (Dozier, 1966; Stanislawski, 1979). Pecos, also known as "Cicuye," was abandoned—due to Apache and Comanche raiding—in 1838, when the last Towa-speaking members joined their linguistic relatives at Jemez (Schroeder, 1979d). Today there are 20 Pueblo societies whose members speak languages from four different language families, and use at least six mutually unintelligible languages.

The Pueblo groups all live in compact villages made of adobe. They are all farmers. Those in the east use irrigation systems that involve diverting

water from permanent streams. Those in the west mix occasional irrigation with a variety of dry farming techniques (i.e., they rely on natural
rainfall). They have extensive internal social organization, and have
various kinds of groups, whether organized along clan or moiety lines.
Each group usually has ceremonial functions to perform and has its own
kiva (or *estufa*), a semisubterranean room where religious rituals were
held and religious knowledge was taught. They all have dual leadership
divided between religious and secular leaders. Beyond this it becomes
difficult to generalize because of the variations among Pueblo groups,
and because of historical changes. Nonetheless, the Pueblo groups as a
whole constitute a relatively coherent cultural complex, clearly distinct
from other southwestern cultures (Eggan, 1983; Jorgensen, 1983).

At the time of the Coronado expedition (1540s) there were well over
100 occupied Pueblo villages (Schroeder, 1968; 1979c, p. 254). How
many distinct groups this represents is problematic. Estimates of total
population vary between 130,000 and 248,000 at that time. These may
be high, but given reconstructions of populations after contact (Dobyns,
1966), and a fall-off factor of 20–25, it does agree with population
estimates of about 6,500 in 1706 (Schroeder, 1979c, p. 254). Overall, the
total number of Pueblo residents was large, and marked by considerable
cultural diversity. Furthermore, apparently many of them had relatively
recently occupied their homes; others, however, had been in place for
some time.

Finally, note that the Pueblo societies have long been celebrated in the
anthropological literature for their great cultural stability and conservatism. Spicer says, "Their role in the drama of cultural conflict and
change which began to unfold after the Spanish arrival was one chiefly
of a tenacious and, for the most part, passive resistance" (1962, p. 14).
Dozier, himself a member of the Tewa Santa Clara Pueblo, begins his
ethnohistory of the Pueblos with the claim that "this is an account of a
people who have preserved a distinctive way of life for many years"
(1970a, p. 1). This persistence was not solely due their singular ability to
"compartmentalize" their social life (Dozier, 1964, 1970a, 1970b), but
was also rooted in the marginal interest in their homeland by various
encroaching states that allowed them to compartmentalize and thus preserve their culture.

In a discussion about the use of the ethnographic present to study the
past, Dozier says that "the kinds of social structures found among the
Pueblos today appear to be extremely old. . . . It is not out of order,
therefore, to suggest that probably all of the [social] structures now
found in the Pueblos existed in prehistoric times" (Dozier, 1970b, p.
209). While such staunch preservation and perseverance in the face of

massive assault is the stuff of heroic epics, it is also a phenomenon begging for explanation; if, indeed, it has really occurred.

Having introduced the major indigenous actors and their crosscutting linguistic and cultural diversity, the conditions immediately before Spanish entry into the Southwest will be sketched.

PREHISTORY OF THE SOUTHWEST[6]

Southwestern prehistory is marked by many debates. First, there are the usual archaeological sources of controversy: incomplete evidence, partial excavations, and the problematic reconstruction of human social organization from archaeological artifacts (Schroeder, 1982, 1984). Second, there are changes within archaeology itself. On the one hand, dating techniques have changed over the years from stylistic analyses of pot sherds to far more sophisticated—and reliable—techniques such as trace-element analysis, dendrochronology, paleomagnetization, and palynology (study of pollen) (Longacre, 1970b; Schroeder, 1979a). On the other hand, foci of interest have shifted from a concentration on large ruins to the study of cultural evolution and cultural ecology. Third, there has been a shift of concern from "what happened" to "how, and why, it happened"; a shift from fact to process. Fourth, the international boundary has remained a wide gulf between researchers in northern Mexico and the southwestern United States (Woodbury, 1979, p. 26). Nevertheless, there is some consensus.

Humans appeared in the Southwest sometime between 10,000 and 9000 B.C. Between about 2000 and 500 B.C. life was relatively stable with a mix of hunting and gathering with occasional planting. The first cultivated plants originated in Mesoamerica, where they had been domesticated considerably earlier. Between 500 B.C. and A.D. 500 permanent villages, pottery, and a general dependence on planting became common (Woodbury and Zubrow, 1979). Prehistoric sedentary groups are typically divided into four groups or cultures: Anasazi, Mogollon, Hohokam, and Hakataya.[7] Their definitions are subject to periodic revision, carried out with vigorous debate (Longacre, 1970b; Schroeder, 1979a; Woodbury, 1979, pp. 27–30; Ford, Schroeder, Peckham, 1972).

Ford, Schroeder and Peckham (1972) provide a summary of what is known about the origins of these groups. The Hopi have been at their present location since about A.D. 500–700, and in Oraibi since about 1100 (Eggan, 1979, p. 233). By the early sixteenth century they had contracted to their present location. The Towa were in the Jemez area since about 1250. Sometime after that other Towas settled further east at

Pecos. This latter interpretation is disputed. While there is agreement that Tiwa developed in situ in the Rio Grande Valley since about 950, there is agreement on little else in regard to their internal differences. The Tewa are still more problematic. They apparently split from the Towa ca. A.D. 900. These groups moved to the locations occupied at the time of contact between 1300 and 1500. They moved several times afterward.

The Keres are seen to have originated in the Chaco area. The eastern Keresans moved into their present locations sometime during the early 1300s. The western Keresans moved somewhat earlier. There is disagreement about the origin of the Zuni. Peckham holds that they moved with the Chacoan peoples; Ford and Schroeder accept an in situ development (Ford, Schroeder, Peckham, 1972). In any case they lived in six villages at the time of Spanish contact. The Piros and Tompiros lived in the central and southern Rio Grande Valley. Little is known about these groups of Piro speakers (Vivian, 1964). Both groups disappeared early in the Spanish period.

What little is known about the relations between nomadic and Pueblo groups comes primarily from ethnohistorical materials, particularly early Spanish chronicles (hence, it is properly outside the chronological scope of this chapter). From information collected on the Coronado expeditions (Schroeder, 1983; Schaafsma, 1981, *inter alia*) clearly some of these Plains groups had trading relations with Pueblo villages, and others had attacked them some years previous to Spanish arrival.

Wilcox's (1981a, 1984) model of Pueblo-Athapaskan interaction and trade is most congruent with subsequent patterns revealed in ethnohistorical accounts. He sees the nomads trading with Pueblo villages, and moving into Pueblo hinterland to harvest wild products that were being ignored for lack of people to collect them. Apparently Plains nomads wintered at some of the Pueblo villages. There is evidence for this at Pecos (Schaafsma, 1981; Kessell, 1979). This suggests that the nomadic peoples were either integrated into, or in the process of being integrated into, existing trade networks.

There is some evidence that such relations existed in the late prehistoric period. Baugh (1982a, 1982b, 1984a, 1984b, n.d.) documents trade relations between groups living in what is now western Oklahoma and New Mexico. He posits a "macroeconomy" that was a system in which semi-nomadic groups were middlemen in trade between two sedentary groups. Wilcox suggests that the early Southern Athapaskans may have played a similar role among sedentary groups on the Plains during their southern migration, and that that role was carried over to the Pueblo villages (1981a).[8] Arguments center around the timing and the route of their arrival. It is generally accepted that they left their northern homeland in western Canada and interior Alaska about A.D. 1000, and that the various subdivisions of Southern Athapaskan began to emerge ca. 1300. Wilcox (1981a, 1984) argues that a group of Athapaskan people moved south sometime during the fifteenth century. They contacted sedentary groups on the western perimeter of the Plains from whom they may have learned some agricultural practices. They also may have acted as middlemen in trade among sedentary groups, including some eastern Pueblo villages (especially Pecos). This would have given them access to unoccupied territories under the control of their Puebloan partners. Such a relationship would have been mutually beneficial: the Athapaskans gaining territory, and the Pueblo villages trading for hinterland products such as hides or piñon nuts that they were unable to harvest themselves. Some Athapaskan groups remained on the Plains, others moved into the Southwest proper.

Athapaskan raiding could have caused abandonment of some villages in the thirteenth and fourteenth centuries, and consolidation of settlement in the fourteenth and fifteenth centuries. If they arrived in the late fifteenth century, they could not have caused these changes. The preponderance of evidence supports the latter interpretation.

The Mesoamerican Connection[9]

In broad stroke, a consensus is emerging that the Southwest had important connections with Mesoamerica. Kelley and Kelley (1975), Di Peso (1968, 1974), Reyman (1978) and Lister (1978) present versions of the Mesoamerican connection thesis. Many New Mexican turquoise pieces were traded into the Zacatecas region ca. A.D. 1000. Both turquoise and pottery from New Mexico have been found at the obsidian mining complex in La Joya, Jalisco (Weigand et al., 1977, p. 22; Weigand, 1982a, 1982b, 1982c; Weigand and Spence, 1982). Thus, mining was a "systematically pursued economic activity" in pre-Hispanic New Mexico (Weigand, 1982c, p. 5).

The nature and strength of "the Mesoamerican connection" remains at issue: What is the nature of the connection? What is the relevance to subsequent changes, especially the Spanish invasion? To answer these questions it is useful to take a closer look at the general regional collapse of population in the thirteenth and fourteenth centuries. Local and regional networks account for many trade patterns. The breakdown of these trade patterns may contain the explanation for the collapse of some population centers, and the aggregation of others. The breakdown of a trade network carried with it a simplification of sociopolitical structure. The attempts to incorporate nomadic peoples, especially from the Plains, into new networks sheds light on nomadic–sedentary relations throughout the period.

Upham (1982) analyzes the collapse of a trade network among the prehistoric western Pueblo societies. He shows that 67 different sites were clustered in groups. Since this environment is marked by highly variable weather conditions, trade in subsistence goods could have developed as a means of controlling environmental uncertainty (see also Bronitsky, 1982). Based on demographic reconstructions, Upham argues that thirteenth-century populations were sufficiently large and the environment sufficiently taxed that some system of managing uncertainty was necessary.

Upham argues that local exchange was limited to approximately 50 kilometers due to foot transportation in this terrain. Regional exchange was facilitated by trade in nonlocal and/or symbolic goods that served a banking function. That is, they could be traded for subsistence goods in time of need, but could be stored in the meantime. The exchange of symbolic goods then facilitated the exchange of nonsymbolic goods, the former serving as a model for the latter.[10] Among the most useful of such symbolic trade goods were specialized ceramic wares.

Fortunately, such pottery preserves well and has been carefully studied. Upham finds that the patterns most closely fit a "prestige chain" exchange model (Renfrew, 1975, 1977) " . . . in which the elite of widely separated polities are managing the regional flow of materials and gaining preferential access to commodities the distribution of which is restricted to the general population" (Upham, 1982, p. 137). Ritual knowledge traveled along with these prestige/symbolic goods. Restricted access to this knowledge allowed the elite to maintain their position, ostensibly because it allowed them to control natural forces, but also because it gave them access to trade networks that could supply necessary goods in times of need. Central control was necessary at the local level to administer these complex exchanges and the production processes that supported them.

Several important conclusions follow from this analysis. First, it argues for central control, the existence of an elite, and elaborate regional trade systems. Second, it follows from this that the sociopolitical organization of those Pueblo societies that survived to the time of Spanish contact were greatly simplified versions of these earlier, more complex systems. Three, the western Pueblo collapse " . . . can be understood as a series of failures, either in agricultural production or in political management, that had a *domino* effect on the remaining polities in the system" (Upham, 1982, p. 201, emphasis in original). Among other things, those areas that were most peripheral to the regional system (Hopi, Zuni, Acoma) were the very settlement areas that did not go down with the entire system, although their extent was restricted (Upham, 1982, p. 106).

Upham's work is paralleled in some ways by recent papers by Minnis (1984) and Pailes and Reff (1980, 1985) on Casas Grandes. Minnis recognizes local and regional structures and interactions, yet claims that the evidence demonstrates neither the presence or absence of regional integration. Pailes and Reff (1980, 1985) document significant regional trade centered around Casas Grandes. They argue that it was the lack of regional integration via induced dependency on trade goods that ultimately led to its collapse. Plog et al. (1982) make a similar argument for the Mogollon region.

Prehistoric Incorporation

All of the above discussions can be drawn together in a model of a pre-capitalist world-economy. The point of clarifying the model is not to correct or force-fit the archaeological data, but to sharpen the model so that the fit between the model and the data can be more precisely assessed. On the one hand, the weakness of the Mesoamerican connection affords an opportunity to assess the lower limits of the incorporation process. On the other hand, it offers at least some assessment of how the emphasis on the effects of European expansion might have distorted overall comprehension of the processes of incorporation.

There has been a tendency to identify these trade models with world-system models. Pailes and Reff (1980, 1985) argue that transportation technology did not allow the tight integration of either trade or political control throughout the Mesoamerican–Southwestern world-economy: "But in the New World the only transportation was by foot, and the peasants' feet are as good as the elites'" (Pailes and Reff, 1980, p. 10). Their point is that there are effects that are predictable. They argue that the core region initiates sufficient trade in those goods that it produces efficiently, that local production of competing goods is destroyed, engendering dependency on the core. Transportation technology, and the ease with which productive technologies spread meant that dependency could not be initiated at any level: either between the Mesoamerican core and the Casas Grandes semi-periphery or between Casas Grandes and its peripheral hinterland. This is precisely why the Casas Grandes system could not produce the strong integration that Minnis (1984), De Atley and Findlow (1982) and Plog et al. (1982) demonstrate did not exist.

World-system models are models of processes and relations. The

Southwest may indeed be the "periphery of the periphery" (McGuire, 1983, p. 5), or even the "hinterland of a periphery" (McGuire, 1986, p. 246), but still may have the same processual relations of a peripheral area to a core area. The various Mesoamerican states were core areas; the Southwestern outposts, Casas Grandes, Chaco Canyon, Snaketown, and possibly others, were semi-peripheries; and the villages surrounding these trade centers and, where applicable, neighboring nomads constituted the periphery. The semi-peripheral areas may have traded with each other occasionally, but more typically would have been competitors, especially when they dealt in the same good or goods. Such competition can be multidirectional. Semi-peripheral areas strive to maintain a monopoly over the receipt of core-produced goods that can be exchanged for valuable raw materials in their peripheral hinterlands. At the same time they strive to maintain a monopoly over the production of goods that can be traded to the core. Goods received from peripheral areas and goods traded to the core may be different, or they may be the same. For instance, Chaco Canyon may have collected raw turquoise through its periphery and manufactured turquoise chips, amulets or whatever, which were then traded to both the periphery and the core: to the periphery because the nomads or subsidiary villages did not have (or were prevented from obtaining or using) the technology for the processing of turquoise; to the core because processed turquoise was lighter and easier to transport than raw turquoise. Whether this, in fact, actually occurred awaits further archaeological research, but it does illustrate the type of system such a model would describe.

One consequence of such a system is that it would give rise to "prestige chains" (Upham, 1982; Renfrew, 1975, 1977; Pailes and Reff, 1985) and a solar rather than a dendritic trade pattern.[11] In a sufficiently complex world-economy, one with many competing semi-peripheries scattered over long distances, trade among them would resemble down-the-line trade—a system where goods are passed from one place to another, with each handler taking out a portion for his own use (Renfrew, 1975, 1977).

This analysis may shed some light on the southwestern population collapse in the thirteenth and fourteenth centuries. When the periphery and semi-periphery are in volatile, yet marginal environments, the entire system is subject to severe disruption. Even when droughts or erosion were relatively localized, if there were enough simultaneous local failures, the entire system would collapse. The effects of the collapse would then follow the trade chains. The system is also subject to disruption from the core. If the core suffers an economic downturn—for whatever reason—the supply of elite goods to the semi-periphery could be severed, undermining the basis of its regional position. This could

cause a far more severe collapse in the periphery than the original decline in the core. This is all the more possible if the core has alternative
sources of raw materials, since the loss of one peripheral area would not
be disastrous to the core.

Note also that incorporation into a regional world-economy would
promote a more complex set of political and economic developments in
the peripheral and semi-peripheral areas than might otherwise have
occurred. This could happen through simple transfer of technology.
Once the technology for making copper bells and/or raising scarlet mac-
aws was transferred to the semi-periphery, the controllers of that technological monopoly could parlay it into a regional elite position. Not the
least of resources that could contribute to more centralized control and
elite aggrandizement are the knowledge and connections necessary to
conduct trade with the core. If the local elite were somehow destroyed,
core traders might find it easier to use an alternative source, rather than
establish new relationships with hitherto unknown trading partners.

Once trade networks were established, and local elites formed, it is
highly probable that local elites would seek to imitate core elites. That
such imitation might be crude, and not fully comprehensible, is understandable. According to Upham (1982), this occurred among the western Pueblos. McGuire's (1983, 1986) claim that the Kachina cult spread
as a crisis cult among Pueblo societies is similarly plausible.

Despite the controversy a few points can be asserted with confidence.
First, state incorporation had occurred in prehistoric times. Furthermore, whatever the cause, the collapse of the southwestern regional and
Mesoamerican world-economies had occurred before the Spaniards arrived in Mexico. Second, intersocietal relations were clearly in a state of
flux at the time of Spanish contact. If there was any direction or shape to
the change, it was in the direction of decreasing complexity. There was
both inter-village competition and cooperation among Pueblo societies.
The Pueblo villages on the edge of the Plains seemed to be on the rise. It
is intriguing, though, that Pecos Pueblo was the most feared of the
Pueblo villages in Coronado's time (ca. 1540; see Kessell, 1979), and that
it was on the edge of the Plains with superior access to trade with bison-
hunting nomads. Trade relations with the Athapaskan bison hunters,
and possibly others, were beginning to form, but hardly seemed to have
stabilized. Whether they ever would have stabilized will probably remain
a moot question.

While the effects of the hypothesized Mesoamerican incorporation
will remain problematic for some time, the effects of Spanish incorporation are clearer. Spain was a far stronger state than any Mesoamerican
society, and there is no doubt that Spaniards visited, traded, and con-

quered indigenous peoples. Somewhat surprisingly, they had more difficulty with the "wild" nomads than they did with the "civilized" agrarian
and horticultural peoples, as will be seen in the following chapters.

NOTES

   1.   The definition of the region and description of its physical geography are
drawn from the following sources: Beck (1962); Lipe (1978); Willey (1966);
Woodbury (1979); Meinig (1971); and Lavender (1980). Willey and Woodbury
have cogent summaries of the definitional debates among archaeologists and
anthropologists.
   2.   Jorgensen (1983), in his smallest space analysis of many descriptive factors
of southwestern societies, finds that there is considerable covariation of social
organization and economy with such zones, but not a direct correspondence.
Culture and physical environment each serve to limit the other. He finds that at
any given level of technology only some zones are habitable, but which of the
habitable ones are used is primarily a function of culturally defined preferences
and values.
   3.   The best summaries of the literature on each of these groups may be
found in the Newberry Library Bibliographical series: Dobyns and Euler (1980)
on Pueblos, Yumans, and "rancheria peoples"; Melody (1977) on Apachean
groups; Iverson (1976) on Navajos; Stewart (1982) on Utes, Paiutes and
Shoshonis; and Hoebel (1982) on Plains Indians including Comanches. Volumes
9 and 10 of the *Handbook of North American Indians,* edited by Alfonso Ortiz
(1979, 1983), are thorough compendia on southwestern groups.
   4.   More than one critic of European ethnocentrism has observed that Europeans all speak different languages, whereas natives speak dialects. To give some
solidity to these terms, the differences between, say, Italian and Spanish, or
between German and Dutch, are of the same order as those between Navajo and
Western Apache. The difference between any Indo-European language and any
of the language families of the Southwest are of the same order as the differences between English and Chinese. Still, note that there are no universally
agreed upon criteria for distinguishing dialects, languages and language families
from each other.
   5.   The name of this linguistic group is spelled a variety of ways: Athapascan,
Athabaskan, Athabascan, or Athapaskan, the latter two being the most common.
I follow the *Handbook of North American Indians* and use Athapaskan. Sources for
this account are Young (1983); Hale and Harris (1979).
   6.   This section draws on Willey (1966, Ch. 4), Lipe (1978), Longacre (1970a,
1973), Martin and Plog (1973), Ortiz (1972), Ford (1972, 1983), Schroeder
(1972), Ford, Schroeder and Peckham (1972), D. Gunnerson (1974), Wilcox
(1981a, 1981b), and Volumes 9 and 10 of the *Handbook of North American Indians.*
The following accounts in Volume 9 (Ortiz, 1979) have been used: Woodbury,
Irwin-Williams, Woodbury and Zubrow, P. Martin, Gumerman and Haury, Di
Peso (1979a, 1979b), Schroeder (1979b), Plog, Cordell, J. Gunnerson, Hale and
Harris, and Brew; in Volume 10 (Ortiz, 1983) Opler, Ford, and Brugge were
used. Maps V.1 and V.2 indicate the locations of most of the groups discussed in
this section.

7.   The derivation of the meaning of these terms is in itself interesting. Anasazi (Plog, 1979, p. 108) is a variant of a Navajo word meaning "the ancient ones." Mogollon is the name of a mountainous region in south-central Arizona–New Mexico, named for an early New Mexican governor. Hohokam (Lipe, 1978, p. 344) is a Pima word meaning "all used up." Hakataya is the name for the Colorado River in the Yuman language (Willey, 1966, p. 229).

8.   Sources for this account are: J. Gunnerson (1979), Opler (1983), Brugge (1981, 1983, 1984), Young (1983), Hale and Harris (1979), Eggan (1983), Wilcox (1981a, 1984), Schaafsma (1981). The reader interested in this controversy is well advised to begin with Wilcox's paper (1981a) and the comments by Brugge (1981) and Schaafsma (1981), plus subsequent emendations by Wilcox (1984) and Brugge (1984).

9.   The "Mesoamerican connection" is discussed in Pailes and Whitecotton (1979), Whitecotton and Pailes (1979, 1983, 1986), Pailes and Reff (1980, 1985). These authors are most strongly associated with such models of trade between Mesoamerica and the Southwest. Baugh (1982a, 1982b, 1984a, 1984b, undated) has made an analogous model of Plains–Pueblo trade. McGuire (1983, 1986) employs a similar model, albeit critically. Plog et al. (1982), Upham (1982), Weigand (1982a, 1982b, 1982c) and Weigand et al. (1977) all use versions of world-system/world-economy models. All of these accounts rely on Kelley and Kelley (1975) and Di Peso (1974). Others have addressed the trade connections between Mesoamerica and the Southwest. Riley (1976, 1978, 1982), Riley and Manson (1983), Hedrick, Kelley and Riley (1974), Riley and Hedrick (1978), Woodbury (1979), Schroeder (1979a), McGuire (1980), and Hinton (1983) are among the more prominent. Blanton and Feinman (1984) discuss the general application of world-system models to Mesoamerica. The latest accounts are collected in Mathien and McGuire (1986). Whitecotton and Pailes (1986), McGuire (1986), and Wilcox (1986) provide especially useful essays. The American Anthropological Association meetings in Denver, November 1984, included a day-long session on the topic. I am indebted to Joseph Whitecotton and Richard Pailes for lively reports of that session.

10.   There is, of course, no reason why the above sequence could not be reversed: that real exchanges give rise to symbolic exchanges that serve to keep the channels of commerce open and smooth, so that in time of need they would operate efficiently.

11.   A solar trade pattern is one that radiates outward from a central location. A dendritic trade pattern has multiple branches, much like a tree or shrub. See C. Smith (1976) and Renfrew (1975, 1977).

CHAPTER IV

The Formation of Spanish Frontier Policy and the Cycle of Endemic Warfare

We came here to serve God and the King, and also to get rich (Bernal Díaz del Castillo, in J. H. Elliott, 1963, p. 53).

The expansion of the frontier into the northern deserts with the discovery of silver at Zacatecas created a situation for which the Spaniards were ill-prepared. They were legatees of a problem which the sedentary tribes before them had never managed to solve (Alistair Hennessy, 1978, p. 61).

It seemed that enslavement, at least during the 1570's and early 1580's, was the main answer to the problem of soldier recruiting—without the hope of Indian slaves to sell, an adequate soldiery on the frontier would have been even more difficult to maintain than it was (Philip W. Powell, 1952, p. 111).

Early Spanish frontier experience set the tone for the subsequent three centuries of Spanish policies in northern New Spain. These policies originated in the particular conjuncture of Spanish social structure, the colonial social structure it produced, aboriginal social structures and contact and conflict among these groups. The forging of the Spanish state led to the closing of the Moorish frontier and the opening of the American frontier in 1492. These nearly simultaneous events have deep roots that shaped the subsequent growth of the Empire at home and overseas. The easy conquests of the Aztec and Inca empires in the Americas gave shape to policies that were found wanting when the Spanish *conquistadores* encountered nomadic groups throughout their farflung empire. The fact that the rising Aztec empire had not conquered the northern nomads in New Spain might have suggested to a careful observer that the task would be difficult. Even had the *conquistadores* known what is now known about the extent of the various Mesoamerican empires, past experience in both the New and Old Worlds, the lure of riches, the lack of alternative paths to glory and military hubris would have led them to proceed undaunted. This kind of closed-mindedness combined with a particular balance of class forces and conflicts made subsequent policies all but inevitable.

SPAIN AND THE CONQUEST OF THE INDIES[1]

Spain was created by the union of two kingdoms, Castile and Aragon. Aragon had strong commercial interests in the Mediterranean and consequently a relatively large and significant bourgeoisie that was involved in the cloth industries. Castile had a weak bourgeoisie, was more concerned with war, and had long specialized in pastoralism. Castile was the stronger kingdom. Aragon was squeezed between expansionary designs of Louis XI of France and Catalonian rebellions. These differences were to remain after the marriage of their future monarchs, Isabella of Castile and Ferdinand of Aragon (1469), and after the ascents to their respective thrones (1479). If there was a unity in their political marriage, it was in their drive to assert state control over the aristocracy. The European trend of conflict between kings and aristocracy, the former frequently in alliance with the bourgeoisie (urban merchants and artisans) (Pirenne, 1937; Miskimin, 1969), necessarily took on different forms in the various regions of what was to become Spain: in Aragon the bourgeoisie was significant, in Castile it was not.

The legacies of Castile are most significant for the development of New World policies, since the Indies were to be the possession of Castile alone—at least in Isabella's intent, if not finally in practice. The Reconquest of Spain from the Arabs had given rise to the warrior tradition in Castile. There was a demand for luxury goods on the part of knights who were eager to display their prominence. Combined with a lack of industry and the needs of the public treasury, this led to a cycle of inflation and debasement of coinage in the thirteenth and fourteenth centuries. Reliance on the wool trades at a time when the demand for wool in both Italy and Flanders was rising solved these problems. Pastoralism gradually replaced agriculture and set the conditions for permanent food shortages. At the time of the formation of Spain, Castile had the highest population density of any province. This was reversed in subsequent years as sheep displaced humans from the countryside of Castile.

Fighting among noble houses for control of the state and land accompanied increasing urbanism and the redistribution of what we today would call ethnic minorities.[2] Property changed hands rapidly but became more stable during the reign of Isabella and Ferdinand. Spanish society was composed of over 80% peasants; 10–12% urban workers, including *conversos* and Jews; 3–5% in an urban middle class of merchants and ecclesiastics; and an aristocracy of about 2% (Vicens Vives, 1969, p. 293). The elite owned 97% of the land, nearly half of which was in the hands of a few families.

This situation did not change under Isabella and Ferdinand, but was stabilized and institutionalized by the continuing conflict between the Crown and the aristocracy. The Act of Resumption (1480) returned to the Crown concessions granted in 1464, but Isabella and Ferdinand concentrated their attacks on the political authority of the aristocracy. In 1505 the Laws of Toro confirmed and extended the right to establish *mayorazgos*, "the right of hereditary transmission which entailed property of the firstborn of a family" (Vicens Vives, 1969, p. 296; Elliott, 1963, p. 101). Charles I (of Spain) further rationalized the ranks of the nobility in 1520 by dividing them into categories of titled nobility, *segundones* (the younger sons of the great houses), and the lesser nobles, *hidalgos* or *caballeros*. The *segundones* "possessed no title of their own, and were generally victims of the *mayorazgo* system which reserved the bulk of the family wealth for their elder brothers" (Elliott, 1963, p. 103). They tended to serve in the army, the Church, or the royal bureaucracy. The lesser nobility was a variable group composed of rich and poor, urban and rural, ancient and recent, who played a major role in the conquest and colonization of the New World. While these changes tended to stabilize the ranks of the aristocracy, certain avenues of mobility were opened.

Wealth and education were the primary means of entering the nobility from the bourgeoisie. Education could lead to service in the royal bureaucracy. Such untitled bureaucrats " . . . were the main instrument of royal power" which " . . . was formed from the new caste of *letrados*" (Hennessy, 1978, p. 35). Their increasing role in the administration of the Empire led to increasing status for them (McAlister, 1963, p. 351; Elliott, 1963, p. 105; Vicens Vives, 1969, p. 296). Still, viceroyalties and high military offices were given to titled nobility (Vicens Vives, 1969). Wealth offered two avenues of entrance to the nobility: marriage or purchase. After 1520 titles could be bought, a common fundraising technique in Europe. For poorer nobles, marriage to wealthy members of the middle class, including Jews, was a path to increased respectability, more so in Aragon than Castile (Elliott, 1963, p. 105).

These paths to mobility and the stabilization of wealth helped consolidate the power of the Crown against the aristocracy, but also promoted immigration to the Indies and consequently shaped social and administrative practices in the colonies. The exploration and colonization of new territories were a consequence of (1) the vitality of Castilian society; (2) the tension between a centralized authoritarian administration and an increasingly submerged nobility; (3) the "nomadic concept of life" that was a legacy of the Reconquest; (4) desire for material wealth; and (5) a missionizing spirit (Vicens Vives, 1969, p. 315–316; see also Haring, 1947, p. 36–37). These factors are all essentially class forces or reasons of state.

The closing of the Spanish frontier, the place of pride held by conquest in Spanish culture and the increasing entailment of estates by the *mayorazgo* all provided a willing class of adventurers. The Indies did not hold as much attraction for the upper aristocracy because they "played no part in the conquest and tended to look askance at projects for emigration which would take labourers from its estates" (Elliott, 1963, p. 52). The new lands opened in 1492 offered immense opportunities for mobility at first for the lesser nobility, and later for the middle classes and *letrados*.

The first emigrants, the *conquistadores,* mainly from Andalusia and Extremadura, were younger, unmarried sons with some military experience. Cortés, the conqueror of the Aztecs, was from this group, as were 25% of the 168 men who accompanied Pizarro to Peru. These were men imbued with a strong sense of the ideal of the *hidalgo*, " . . . a man who lived for war" (Elliott, 1963, p. 20). Bishko (1963) traces the roots of their spirit to the Reconquest and the preference for pastoral nomadism over agriculture in Castile. He argues that this tradition shaped the "frontier" spirit of Spanish colonists and is the origin of the predominance of ranching over agriculture in New Spain.

As the administrative structure of the Indies grew, more *letrados*, craftsmen and merchants emigrated. Middle-class emigration increased especially in the latter half of the sixteenth century as the Castilian bourgeoisie declined in Spain, victims of the price revolution—rising prices in the sixteenth century that undermined the economic position of all except the great landowners who could capitalize on the increasing value of land leases—that was itself a consequence of the wealth returned from the Indies (Vicens Vives, 1969, pp. 337, 339, 377–384).[3] While solid data are lacking, the best estimates are that about 120,000

Spaniards, mostly Castilians, went to the Indies in the first half of the sixteenth century (Vicens Vives, 1969, p. 317). By 1600 most of the territory eventually controlled by Spain was explored and over 300 frontier towns had been established (Hennessy, 1978, p. 47).

The key issue shaping the colonial policies of the Spanish Empire was the continuing drive to maintain and expand central, authoritarian control at the expense of the aristocracy. This implied not only Crown control of exploration and conquest, but also continued vigilance lest a new aristocracy grow in the newly won colonies. This concern was paramount in the negotiations for Columbus's voyage.

The contract, or *capitulación,* with Columbus "was to reserve certain rights to the Crown in newly conquered territories, while also guaranteeing to the leader of the expedition due *mercedes* or rewards for his services" (Elliott, 1963, p. 47). It set the tone for all subsequent *capitulaciones* granted to would-be *conquistadores.* Columbus requested that he be made governor general and viceroy in perpetuity of any lands discovered. Instead he was granted the hereditary title of Grand Admiral and the right to one-tenth of all merchandise and produce of the new territories. The Crown retained sovereignty over the new territories (Elliott, 1963, p. 49).

In an effort to control trade with the newly discovered lands, the *Casa de Contratación* (House of Trade) was established in Seville in 1503. It was modeled after the *consulado de Burgos,* a merchant guild established to supervise the northern wool trade. Later in the sixteenth century a *consulado* was established in Seville. Between the *Casa de Contratación* and the *consulado,* trade with the Indies was effectively monopolized by the Crown (Gibson, 1966, pp. 100–102; Haring, 1947, pp. 317–320; Elliott, 1963, pp. 109–111). Still, foreign traders, especially the Genoese, dominated this trade for some time. Later, Italian, Flemish and French merchants gained control (Vicens Vives, 1970b, pp. 97–98). The mercantile approach to trade shaped many subsequent changes.

In addition to the issues of state control over territory, religious zeal played a major role in the colonization of the Indies. While the Crown succeeded in imposing controls over the Church in the New World, the drive to achieve an earthly paradise of converted, complacent Indians remained a theme throughout the Empire (Wolf, 1959, pp. 164–175; Hennessy, 1978, pp. 36–43, 54–60). The drive was aided by the respectability of religious service as a channel for achievement and advancement for younger sons of the nobility, and for rising middle classes who had neither money nor military ambitions.

The establishment of the Empire in the Americas was not without its effects on Spain. The infusion of gold, and especially silver, brought about dramatic changes in Spain and the rest of Europe. The price revolution is one of the most discussed consequences. Emigration to the Americas also drained Spain of its most energetic and enterprising citizens (Vicens Vives, 1970b, p. 97), and created a climate of negative attitude toward a Spain that afforded little opportunity for advancement in comparison to America (Kamen, 1978, pp. 28–29). The men who left for America in the service of the trinity of King, God and Gold took with them the conflicts engendered in Spain and gave rise to a peculiar colonial structure.

SPANISH COLONIAL SOCIETY[4]

As the *conquistadores* brought new territory under the Spanish flag, the colonial bureaucracy attempted to administer the new territories for the benefit of the royal treasury and itself. There was little local interest in long-term development. Even the *conquistadores* viewed their gains as stepping stones back to Spain for themselves or their sons. To block local bureaucratic entrenchment and the formation of a local elite, officials were rotated through various regions and offices every few years, contributing to a sojourner orientation, and slowing the accumulation of the detailed knowledge necessary for development. This problem was especially severe on the frontiers far from the amenities of the administrative centers.

Few Spaniards came with the intention of working. Rather they expected to have Indians work for them in their mines, on their plantations or in textiles (Palmer, 1976). All three spheres required an extensive labor force disciplined to steady work. At first these needs were met by the mass of Indian peasants captured with the defeat of the Aztecs, Zapotecs, Mayas and other peoples. This labor force was rapidly depleted by the high toll of European diseases (Barber, 1932; Borah, 1951; Borah and Cook, 1963; Lang, 1975; McNeill, 1976; Dobyns, 1966, 1976). High transportation costs, low return in salable exports and higher prices for slaves in other markets eventually eliminated the importation of African slaves (Palmer, 1976).

It is well known that the younger sons of the nobility, poor *hidalgos*, priests seeking salvation of souls, and bureaucrats staffing the colonial administration all went to the Indies. What is less well known is who else went. There were many unlicensed emigrants from Spain who arrived with the merchant fleets. They were mostly male artisans and peasants (Mörner, 1967, p. 16). Unfortunately little is known about them.

Within a few years of the conquest, cattle and horses had so multiplied that no Spaniard need worry for meat or walk. All could try to pass as *hidalgos*. It was in no one's interest to undermine such pretenses. Spaniards were so few in number, compared to the native populations, that the line between the conquering minority (less than 1% of the population, about 100,000 by mid-sixteenth century) and the native majority was sharply drawn even at the expense of blurring distinctions within the minority's ranks. In particular the line between noble and non-noble, especially with respect to the wealthy bourgeoisie, became less distinct than in Spain. In the Indies possession of wealth counted for more than the means by which it was attained (Mörner, 1983, p. 351). Indeed, the ease with which wealth was attained, compared to Spain, was for many the major attraction to the Indies. Thus, the social structure that emerged in the Americas, and in New Spain in particular, was different from that of Spain.

Two sets of distinctions are of direct concern here. First are the distinctions among the bureaucracy, civil and ecclesiastic, and the structures of ethnic and class groups. Second are regional differences, especially between southern and central New Spain on the one hand, and the northern provinces on the other.[5] All of these evolved in a rapid, intertwined way. It is useful to begin with an overview of the bureaucracy and social structure and then comment on regional differences.

The Bureaucratic Structure of the Indies

The dominant theme in the administration of the Indies was maintenance and extension of Crown control that was expressed in civil and religious administration, in exploration, and in control of social patterns. This approach engendered the opposition of divergent local and specialized groups, shaping the bureaucracy that remained in place for over 200 years. "Under the Spanish Hapsburgs, the colonial bureaucracy was a broker between local elites, the Indian communities, and the Crown" (Lang, 1979, p. 210).

The central administrative apparatus of the Americas was the Council of the Indies, established in 1524. The Council was generally composed of appointees with extensive experience in the Americas. It supervised the drafting and enforcement of laws for the Indies (subject to royal approval), approved papal bulls, influenced appointments to bureaucratic positions, was the court of highest appeal, conducted periodic reviews of colonial administrations (called *visitas*), and reviewed the performances of various officials upon completion of their term of office (called *residencias*).

Under the Council were the viceroyalties of New Spain (1535) and

Peru (1542); others were added in the eighteenth century. The appointment of the viceroy, the highest colonial official, was reserved to the king. Only titled nobles were chosen. The viceroy had considerable discretion, subject to the level of the king's confidence in him. The term of office was nominally three years, but often longer. Antonio de Mendoza served from 1535 to 1550, and received an annual salary of 6,000 ducats. Luis de Velasco served from 1550 to 1564, and received an annual salary of 10,000 ducats (Haring, 1947, p. 126). The viceroy was responsible for enforcing the *cedulas* (decrees) of the Council and the Crown and reported to both. The phrase *"obedezco pero no cumplo"* (I obey but do not comply) was a common indicator of discretionary deviation from official regulations. The viceroy's most severe limitation came from the *audiencia*.

The *audiencia* was primarily a judicial unit, but also served as a legislative consultant. It was headed by a captain-general or *presidente* who oversaw royal revenues, nominated minor officials both civil and ecclesiastic, and had responsibility for the welfare of Indians, and for the reallotment of vacant *encomiendas*.[6] When an *audiencia* was the seat of a viceroyalty, the viceroy served as the captain-general and the *presidente*. The *audiencia* was the most stable governmental structure in the Indies, smoothing the transitions between viceroys (Gibson, 1966, pp. 94–97). It was composed of a council of judges, *oidores*, who were professional bureaucrats with training in law. Appointment was made on the basis of "some combination of academic distinction, previous experience, and family connections" (Lang, 1975, p. 32). The senior *oidor* supervised the collections of revenues, which, after administrative and military expenses had been removed, were forwarded to Spain. *Oidores* were to be disinterested agents of the Crown with no commercial or marital ties to residents of the *audiencia*. This was honored mostly in the breech. The *oidores* could correspond directly with the Crown and the Council about all matters, including the conduct of the viceroy. Occasionally *audiencia* officials were given secret instructions from the Crown or the Council. The *audiencia* was parallel, not subordinate, to the viceroy. This structure was the source of much bureaucratic bickering. The centers of the independent states of Spanish America correspond, at least crudely, to former *audiencias*.

Under the *audiencia* were two levels of local government, provincial and municipal. Provincial government might be headed by a *gobernador*, or a *corregidor* or an *alcalde mayor*, depending on the territorial extent of the province. *Gobernadores* occasionally had military authority in their district—as was to be typical of isolated New Mexico. These officials were appointed for three-year terms. If the official was not a lawyer, he was given an assistant who was. Seldom were the salaries of *corregidores* sufficient to cover their expenses, which included making a general tour of their province. Their corruption and exploitation of Indians are well known. The *ayunamiento* or *cabildo* was the local, town unit of government. It consisted of a council of *regidores* composed of *vecinos* (property-owning citizens), who elected the *alcaldes* (magistrates) annually. These officials were drawn from the local population, as opposed to the *audiencia* officials who usually came from Spain.

Given the great distances and slow communications involved in the administration of the Indies, and the Crown's concern with the maintenance of central authority, two techniques for policing the administration were instituted. The *residencia,* typically conducted by the official's successor, was of limited effectiveness. The second, the *visita,* could focus on one official or region, or could be general. The latter was conducted by a *visitador-general,* who was usually a high-court official or member of the Council of the Indies who was highly trusted by the Crown. He had the power to examine anyone, and make general recommendations for personnel or policy changes. The *visitador-general* was expected to conduct his reviews with discretion, and was to serve as a mediator. While promoting the interests of the Crown he was also to avoid provoking conflict (Lang, 1975, p. 42). Such periodic visits served to reform administrative policy, though frequently only in the short term.

The Church in the New World was under Crown control. Secular priests were under direct government supervision. The sacred orders, Dominicans, Augustinians, Franciscans and Jesuits (after 1572), were the missionaries who had extensive contact with Indians. Unlike secular priests, these priests took a vow of poverty and hence held no personal property. The order, however, held large estates, usually entailed and gained from wills, although sometimes by purchase. Many of these priests were drawn from the nobility. The orders generally saw themselves as instructors and protectors of Indians. The Church constituted a parallel, and sometimes competing, bureaucratic structure. This institutional structure was cross-cut by an equally complex social structure.

The Social Structure of New Spain

Description of the social structure of early New Spain is problematic. The sixteenth century was an age of rapid change; most available information focuses on the elites; most summaries generalize over the entire colonial era (e.g., McAlister, 1963) or all of the Americas (e.g., Mörner, 1983; Lang, 1975, 1979; Haring, 1947), or deal with special topics (e.g.,

Mörner, 1967, 1973). The elite in New Spain was composed of the *conquistadores* and other first settlers who were granted *encomiendas* for their service to the Crown. The Crown, always jealous of its control and fearful of creating another aristocracy in the New World, required vassalage and military service from *encomenderos,* but did not grant land— only the right to Indian labor and tribute. By the end of the century they were largely supplanted by a professional army. The upper class consisted of owners of *haciendas, estancias* (grants of grazing land for cattle or sheep), mines and other enterprises and the upper levels of the civil and ecclesiastic bureaucracies.

The lower levels of nobility shaded into the local middle class of merchants, artisans and middle-level bureaucrats. As in Spain, the two groups mixed as wealth and nobility supported each other. *Encomenderos* were concentrated in this group. The lower classes consisted of the less affluent merchants and artisans, laborers and vagabonds. The latter were poor people who roamed the frontiers taking what work was available (Israel, 1975, see pp. 11–12, 77–78). They were *vaqueros* (cowboys), miners, soldiers, or bandits as circumstances warranted. Indians were at the very bottom of the status hierarchy.

As New Spain developed, a rift grew between those born in the colonies (*criollos* or Creoles) and administrators sent from Spain (*peninsulares*). In time *criollos* began to see themselves as permanent residents in the New World whose interests slowly diverged from those of the *peninsulares. Criollos* amassed large land holdings and gradually gained considerable control over local affairs. The *criollo–peninsulare* conflict became incessant. The role of Indians in colonial society was one locus of conflict. *Criollos* viewed Indians as a source of cheap labor, to be used in whatever manner suited their needs. *Peninsulares,* especially Church officials, were interested in the salvation of Indian souls and sought to protect them from *criollo* exploitation.

The rift grew deeper and more complex as more "sojourners" became permanent residents. Crown officials, especially *oidores* and *corregidores* from the northern provinces, married their children to locally prominent and wealthy *criollos*—with or without Crown approval—in an attempt to circumvent rules about acquisition of property (Chevalier, 1963a, Ch.5). In the seventeenth century, with the spread of the venality of offices to the New World, more *criollos* bought into the nobility and the bureaucracy, further entrenching their hold on the local economy and undermining the Crown's control (Lang, 1975, pp. 42–43).

The other great cleavage in the society of New Spain was between Indian and Spaniard. As a conquered people, Indians owed tribute to their new lords and were subject to their control, including the prohibition against bearing arms, wearing Spanish clothes or riding horses. The vast majority of Spanish immigrants to New Spain were male artisans and peasants (Mörner, 1967, p. 16; Israel, 1975, p. 12). The problems generated by the constant molestation of Indian women led the Crown to import white female slaves to prevent Indian–Spaniard unions (Mörner, 1967, p. 37; Davidson, 1961, p. 46). The shortage of Spanish women led to considerable interbreeding, and even some intermarriage. As early as 1501 orders were issued to prevent mixed marriages unless both parties were agreeable. The *casta* system grew out of reactions to the consequent population of individuals with mixed backgrounds (Mörner, 1967; Israel, 1975, pp. 60–66).[7] Purity of blood remained as issue throughout the Spanish era (McAlister, 1963, p. 35) and was another component of *criollo–peninsulare* competition.

Spanish and Indian societies interacted in other ways (Israel, 1975, Ch.I). First, local Spanish elites formed alliances with erstwhile Indian leaders (so-called *caciques*),[8] in administering and extracting tribute from local communities. Local leaders used their external connections to insure their position in the local community. The Indian, now frequently a peasant, paid tribute but to a different master (Wolf, 1982, pp. 145–146). Second, Spaniards used local groups of Indians as exemplary colonists for nomadic Indians in northern areas (Wolf, 1982, Ch. 5; Simmons, 1964). Third, Spaniards used Indian allies as auxiliaries in military campaigns against hostile groups. This technique was first used in the conquest of Mexico under Cortés in 1521. In all these actions the Crown sought to fragment Indian societies and consolidate control of the colonies.

Several factors contributed to the precipitous decline of the native population in the sixteenth century. The conquest destroyed the indigenous food redistribution systems and weakened the native populations (Wolf, 1982, pp. 133–135). Cattle originally imported by Spaniards escaped, multiplied rapidly and severely disrupted native food supplies (Chevalier, 1963a; Baretta and Markoff, 1978). The destruction of crops led to grain shortages, weakening Indian populations and making them more vulnerable to new European pathogens (Barber, 1932; Borah, 1951; Borah and Cook, 1963; Lang, 1975; McNeill, 1976; Dobyns, 1966, 1976). The consequent sharp decline in native population was a significant factor in a number of changes in New Spain.

The New Laws of the Indies in 1542 were issued after some epidemics had occurred but before they had run their full course (Simpson, 1966; Lang, 1975; Haring, 1947; Gibson, 1966). According to these laws Indians were free vassals of the Crown and could not be forced into involuntary labor. They could not be held as slaves, even as prisoners of war.

There were to be no more *encomiendas*, especially for secular clergy, public servants or religious institutions. Current *encomiendas* would revert to the Crown upon death of the holder. Officials would be appointed as protectors of the Indians.

The New Laws were met with uniform opposition in the New World. The *cabildo* of Mexico City sent a delegation to Charles V to protest the laws, and the viceroy of Peru was killed in a rebellion. In a discretionary compromise Indian slavery was abolished, except as punishment for rebellion; *encomiendas* were extended for one generation (and subsequently for more), but the granting of new *encomiendas* was significantly curtailed.

The sources of these changes are complex. One source was the agitation of Bartolomé de Las Casas on behalf of the rights of Indians as children of God. This, of course, was entangled with the emperor's struggle with the pope for authority over the Church within the Empire. The curtailment of the *encomienda* helped block the formation of a hereditary aristocracy in the New World, and brought in revenue through the reversions of *encomiendas* to the Crown. The drop in native population made it increasingly clear that the *encomienda* system was unworkable.

The New Laws were enforced with considerable discretion, but they were a major factor in the shift in labor systems.[9] *Corregidores* who administered the *repartimientos* were poorly paid, giving rise to much abuse. The New Laws sped the change from direct labor in tribute (*encomienda*), to paid labor under levee (*repartimiento*), to wage labor and eventually to debt peonage and enserfment (*hacienda;* see Lang, 1975; Mörner, 1973; Bauer, 1979a, 1979b; Loveman, 1979).

The North[10]

Colonial society was different in the north. The search for a passage to the Orient and mines drew Spaniards north and west of the Valley of Mexico. Nuño de Guzmán explored the northwest area between 1529 and 1536, founding several towns, and wreaking havoc among the Indians with his slave raiding. He founded the province of Nueva Galicia, which was made an *audiencia* in 1548.[11] The need for grazing land, the need to quell attacks from the north and the desire to missionize Indians all pushed the Spaniards northward. Viceroy Mendoza distributed *encomiendas* to adventurers who agreed to found settlements and defend the region.

These advances disturbed the Indians, and eventually produced the Mixton War (1540–1541), a rebellion centered among the Cazcanes, the northernmost sedentary Indians. It took two years, the direct leadership of Viceroy Mendoza, 30,000 Aztec and Tlaxcalan auxiliaries and a number of vigorous *encomenderos* to suppress the rebellion. The experience of the Mixton War convinced Spanish colonists and the viceroy that the northern nomads were a serious threat. The role of the *encomenderos* in the war spurred discretionary granting of *encomiendas* in the region even after the promulgation of the New Laws.

Both Spaniards and Indians were different north of the Valley of Mexico (Chevalier, 1963a, Ch.1; West, 1949, p. 4; Wolf, 1959, p. 9). The high-plateau country was not amenable to agricultural exploitation, and the nomadic Indians were not suitable for forced labor. Two commodities were useful in the north: grazing land and silver.

Mines were discovered at Compostela in 1543, Zacatecas in 1546, Guanajuato in 1548 and other neighboring areas in the 1550s and 1560s. The mines of Parral were opened nearly a century later in 1631. Until the Parral mines opened, the Zacatecas mines were the richest in New Spain. The founding of the town of Zacatecas is credited to four men, Cristóbal de Oñate, Juan de Tolosa, Diego de Ibarra, and Baltasar Temiño de Bañuelos, all of whom became prominent and wealthy.

Supply of labor for the mines was a problem. Black slaves and captive nomadic Indians proved intractable. Wage labor provided the solution. Vagabonds could be induced to work for a suitable salary, as could sedentary Indians seeking to escape *encomienda* or *repartimiento* labor. For many a Spaniard, mine work was a way to start his own mine and gain personal wealth (West, 1949, Ch.III; Bakewell, 1971).

Mines, however, needed supplies. Miners had to be fed. Horses and mules were needed for hauling. Leather was required in large amounts. These needs spurred the development of both agricultural and pastoral *haciendas*. *Estancias,* or cattle ranches, had substantially different structures from the agricultural establishments to the south due to the low demand for labor, and the amount of land needed to graze cattle. This gave rise to a frontier that attracted *castas,* vagabonds and escaped slaves (Chevalier, 1963a,Ch.5; Baretta and Markoff, 1978).

Transportation of material to and from the mines required roads— hence, the founding of *El Camino Real,* which eventually extended to Santa Fe, New Mexico. The traffic on the roads attracted Indian raids in retaliation for disruption of their territory and to acquire horses and cattle. Almost everyone was armed because of the presence of hostile nomads. Vagabonds were ready recruits for the armies of *encomenderos.* They could as easily turn to banditry or smuggling if the situation dictated.

In general, the frontier was far more fluid and far less subject to official control than the central and southern areas. The greater social mobility in status in the north attracted fortune seekers and assorted marginal persons (Hennessy, 1978; Baretta and Markoff, 1978). The social structure of northern Indian societies also differed sharply with that of the south.

THE "CHICHIMECAS"

Both *criollos* and *peninsulares* considered conquered peoples vassals, lower in rank than artisans and commoners and destined to serve as peasants. Spanish ethnocentrism notwithstanding, understanding the bewildering array of indigenous groups found in northern New Spain presented a formidable task to the most careful observer. Spaniards referred to the nomads north of the Valley of Mexico collectively as "Chichimecas," a term taken from their sedentary neighbors meaning "dirty, uncivilized dogs" (Powell, 1952, p. 33). The term "the Chichimecas" introduces distortions. They were not a tribe, nor even a group of tribes. Rather they were several groups of band societies, primarily hunters and gatherers, and a few simple rancheria groups. Their boundaries were quite fluid. Leaders were typical "big men":

> For such leadership as they had, each *rancheria* elected its own captain, invariably the one considered the bravest in battle . . . . Lack of over-all leadership among the Chichimecas was one of the greatest handicaps faced by the Spaniards in trying to arrange definitive peace treaties on this frontier (Powell, 1945, pp. 333–334).

Likewise, social organization, lines of political authority, and kinship bonds are virtually coextensive. Production, compensation for losses, organization of raids and wars were largely kin matters. The single most serious cause of intergroup conflict was raiding or the death of a kinsman, either of which would give rise to retaliation.

Such retaliatory raids could result in the taking of captives, usually women and children, who served as menials. Not infrequently women became wives, and children were adopted as full members of the group.[12] Adult males were typically killed (Driver, 1969, Ch.18). Captives could be traded either within the group, or to other bands in the same linguistic community, or to outsiders. The fate of a captive was largely a function of the particular circumstances of the captor. Raids were also conducted to gain prestige or to acquire material goods.

While subsistence economies produce little that could be traded, this did not mean that trade among the various societies was nonexistent or inconsequential. Trade in captives pre-dates Spanish contact. Considerable trade had long passed through the Gran Chichimeca, as the territory occupied by these groups was called. What role these band societies played in this trade is not known. It is likely that these groups already had a long history of contact with state societies. The Spaniards brought a new type of state, new technologies, but initially probably intensified old patterns of state–nonstate relations.

Powell (1945; 1952, Ch.3) divides the Chichimecas into several "nations" with "tribal" subdivisions. Specific "tribes" were named by the Spanish either for a renowned leader or for their geographical location. In general these groups varied from sedentary rancheria people in the south to hunters and gatherers further north. They also varied in their propensity to fight, and apparently spoke several different languages. Because they were subsequently absorbed into the mestizo population in later centuries little is known about them. Early ethnohistorical information is scarce (Griffen, 1983a; Hinton, 1983). The Spanish documents used by Powell are transparently ethnocentric, and full of exaggerations aimed at enhancing viceregal and Crown support. Thus, the following description is sketchy.

Powell describes four major groups ("nations"): Guachichiles, Guamares, Zacatecos, and Pames.[13] The Guachichiles, centered in the mountains of what is now the state of San Luis Potosí, were thought to share a distinctive language, were the largest group in terms of territory and population, and were reputed to be the fiercest fighters. Since they lived in rough terrain on the fringes of the mining area, their territory was penetrated relatively late by the Spaniards. They were known to form alliances with peoples further north and east. Under Spanish pressure they developed "tribal" alliances to a greater extent than other Chichimeca groups. The Guamares were centered around the Guanajuato mountains, south of the Guachichiles. They were known for their "confederations," which occasionally included some Guachichile groups.

The Zacatecos occupied territory to the west of the Guachichiles, and roamed as far west as modern Durango. Many of their groups were sedentary. They are known to have fought against neighboring Guachichile and Cazcane groups. They had allied with the latter in the Mixton War. They were rapidly integrated into Hispanic society and were used as auxiliaries against other groups.

The Pames lived east of Guachichile–Guamare territory. They were the least warlike groups of the Chichimecas. They had apparently learned some horticultural and other practices from the Otomis, their sedentary southern neighbors. Their incessant raids on cattle and horse herds were more of a nuisance than a threat to Spaniards.

The Cazcanes may or may not have been Chichimecas. They were primarily settled peoples, their languages were intelligible to the agriculturalists south of them (the Mexica Indians). They supposedly had been subdued by the Mixton War, but their subjugation was frequently in doubt throughout the second half of the sixteenth century. They were attacked by the other Chichimeca groups, in large part because of their role as auxiliaries in Spanish operations.

Their favored mode of fighting was the ambush. Male captives were tortured and killed. Reports of their extreme cruelty to captives are exaggerated, but based on a factual core. First, many of their practices were very likely learned from the Aztec and other state groups that had raided them for slaves in pre-Hispanic times. Second, Spanish atrocities spurred further cruelty. Furthermore, exaggeration of cruelty was used to solicit viceregal and Crown support. This, however, backfired, as it also increased the fear of the Chichimecas and drove up labor costs and made the recruitment of soldiers more difficult.

The foraging life-style also made these peoples more difficult to subdue than sedentary peoples. They could move readily, making use of wide and diverse territories. Their principal foods were mesquite beans, small game, and "tunas"—prickly pear cactus fruit and leaves. Occasionally they grew maize. They manufactured a native alcoholic beverage from the prickly pear fruit, and used peyote (*Lophophora williamensii*). With the advent of the Spaniards, cattle became a major meat source and a favorite prey, and hence a major enticement to raiding.

Little is known about their religion, and what little is reported is highly colored by Hispanic preoccupation with the machinations of the devil. Powell seems persuaded that the martyrdom of missionaries was part of religious reaction to the Spaniards. He seems to be confusing two processes. Since missionaries were frequently the "point men" of contact and subjugation, it could be expected that they would be resisted strongly. Second, band societies typically have animistic religions, and imbue all actions with a religious aspect, especially vital activities such as raiding and warfare. The latter are surrounded by rituals, frequently using psychoactive substances. Thus, their fighting was not the "work of the devil," or "religious warfare," but more-or-less standard behavior for band peoples resisting encroachment on their territory.

The encounter with these nonstate, nomadic Indians was a new and different experience for the Spaniards in New Spain. These encounters shaped frontier policies for dealing with nonstate societies.

SPANISH–INDIAN CONTACTS NORTH
OF THE VALLEY OF MEXICO

Spanish experiences with both the Aztec and Inca states had led to the expectation that all Indians could be subdued easily. This expectation was dashed by the encounters with the Chichimecas. In the 1540s missionaries and miners began to spread into the territory of the nomads. With the opening of the mines, especially Zacatecas in 1546, traffic to the region increased. In the late forties *El Camino Real* was opened to carry supplies north and silver south between Zacatecas and Mexico City (350 air miles). The movement of Spaniards into the region drew Indian attacks because of the desirability of Spanish goods, the taking of slaves and the disruption caused by the appropriation of Indian resources. Thus, the Chichimeca Wars were "the longest and most expensive conflict between Spaniards and the indigenous peoples of New Spain in the history of the colony. Its cost in cash and in men was to be far greater than that of Cortés' conquest of Anahuac" (Bakewell, 1971, p. 22).

Raiding continued throughout the 1550s. In 1561 there was a concerted attack by Zacatecos and Guachichiles against the new towns, San Martín and Sombrerete, and neighboring *estancias*. This attack was repulsed, but fighting continued in an episodic fashion. In 1566 peace negotiations failed. In 1567 a royal *cedula* required the *audiencia* of Nueva Galicia to mount a campaign to protect the region. The Crown was to pay one-third of the cost, the miners and settlers the remaining two-thirds. Under these circumstances, booty, primarily captives, was used to recruit soldiers and defray costs, thereby insuring that the wars would continue. Fighting remained endemic until 1585 when Viceroy Villamanrique changed policies from war to "peace by purchase," a system of supplying Indians with necessary goods in return for peace. He reduced the number of soldiers and freed captives. This policy worked. The 1590s marked the end of the Chichimeca Wars. Peace freed Nueva Galicia from hostilities, cemented the links with central Mexico, allowed the attraction of sedentary natives from the south, and generally benefitted the entire region.

How disruptive the wars were is questionable. Bakewell (1971, p. 31) reports no correspondence between decreases in silver production and in raiding. How much more silver might have been produced in the absence of hostilities is indeterminate, but it is nearly certain that the capital spent on warfare might have been more profitably invested in mines. The cost was onerous for certain leading citizens. Cristóbal de Oñate, a founder of Zacatecas and once reputed to be one of the richest men in New Spain, died in poverty (Bakewell, 1971, p. 10).

Peace allowed further development, including the last major northward thrust of the Spaniards—the founding of the New Mexico colony in 1598 by Don Juan de Oñate, son of Cristóbal. When he left for the new territories he took with him legacies of these initial encounters with nonstate societies, and thus it is that the analysis of the Chichimeca Wars is vital to the analysis of social processes in New Mexico.

The new mines required both workers and food supplies. The supply of Negro slaves was insufficient to fill the demand. Indian slaves were both undisciplined and unskilled for mine work, and were only useful as helpers (West, 1949, Ch.III; Bakewell, 1971). The labor shortage became so severe that "mining operations were outrunning the supply of labor, and the operators were in such vigorous competition with each other that they were boosting pay to the point where a maximum wage had to be set for free workers" (Powell, 1952, p. 14). Not surprisingly the Indians living in the vicinity of the mines or the roads from the mines to Mexico City were easy prey for many of the unscrupulous frontier adventurers (Powell, 1952, p. 13).

Before long the Indians began to retaliate by attacking miners and supply caravans. Any Spaniard would satisfy the need for revenge. Thus innocent Spaniards were drawn into the conflicts. Since the Spaniards, including government officials, understood neither the social organization nor the motivation and necessity for revenge, punitive expeditions frequently struck innocent groups. The ready market for booty and slaves, men for mine work, women as concubines and wives, and children as domestic servants, did not encourage those leading punitive raids to be very particular about their choice of targets. The cycle of raid and counter-raid quickly developed into a state of endemic warfare.

This cycle spread almost as rapidly as Spanish explorers. As early as 1539 northern regions of New Spain in what is now the Mexican states of Sinaloa and Sonora were being disrupted by slave raids (Riley, 1976, p. 12). The disruption was mainly the work of vagabonds and desperados scratching out a living on the frontier. There were even bands of escaped Negro slaves who raided throughout the southern reaches of the Gran Chichimeca (Powell, 1952, p. 62). The continuous fighting was the result of the combination of the social structure, economic and demographic shortages and total misunderstanding of the social organization of band societies. As long as these conditions persisted, frontier fighting remained endemic.

The fighting could only be stopped if the viceroy brought in an organized army to protect Spanish subjects from "barbaric" Indians. The Spanish Empire was hard-pressed to find sufficient fighting men and armaments for the marginal northern provinces of Mexico (Powell,

1952, p. 126). The viceroy needed to balance the costs of protective armies against revenue collected from the mines.

Two new military techniques were developed during the Chichimeca Wars. First, "flying companies" of highly mobile, lightly armored soldiers were formed. These companies could move quickly in pursuit of roving nomads. When all else failed they could penetrate the heartlands of the nomads and destroy food supplies, either their meager maize fields, or their "tuna" harvesting areas. Second, forts, or presidios, were established between Indian territories and frequent raiding targets. These presidios housed the "flying companies," and facilitated rapid reprisals for Indian raids. Such techniques, however, carried with them incentives for continued fighting.

The Spanish system required each soldier to supply his own horses, armor, and weapons. Frequently armament and supplies exceeded the annual salary of a soldier (Powell, 1952, pp. 64, 91, 98, 111, 124). Under these conditions there was considerable pressure to use booty to supplement pay. In forays against subsistence-producing Indians there was little in the way of material goods to seize, except captives (Powell, 1952, p. 111).

The New Laws of 1542 forbidding Indian slavery were circumvented by mock trials. "Treasonous" Indians were sentenced to 20 or more years of indentured labor (Powell, 1952, p. 94). Such occurrences:

> . . . strengthened [Viceroy] Villamanrique in the conviction that the greatest continuing cause of warfare in the Chichimeca country was the Spanish soldiers (the regularly enlisted as well as those recruited for specific entradas) who seemed to be fighting or raiding for slaves, with little or no thought for the larger importance of a genuine pacification. They provoked war by raiding peaceful natives, who then took the warpath for vengeance; they did not want the war to come to an end, for it would mean an end to their salaries from the royal treasury. (Powell, 1952, pp. 186–187).

Punitive attacks on Indians were not the only source of captives. As the Spanish advance displaced one group after another, inter-group fighting accelerated. This fighting generated many captives who could be traded to Spaniards who would ask no questions and pay in horses and guns—although this was in direct violation of official policy. As both raiding and trade increased, more and more horses and guns came into Indian hands, making formidable foes of formerly annoying attackers and intensifying inter-group fighting. Horses and guns became vital necessities for any group that wished to remain safe and free.

Where horses and guns could not be acquired by direct capture, they had to be acquired through trade. For subsistence-producing bands, the only items available for trade were captives (Spicer, 1962, p. 38). Thus, the demand for captives intensified inter-group fighting. Spaniards learned to exploit this rivalry by buying captives from all sides. Horses, guns and promises of a share of the booty, especially captives, bought new allies who were used as auxiliaries in subsequent campaigns. This technique remained a basic strategy throughout the Spanish era.

These early Spanish experiences led to the peace-by-purchase strat-
egy. Viceroy Villamanrique (1585–1590) used this policy with Chichimeca groups. He removed most of the military forces from the region to reduce the irritations to the Indians, and save the Crown between 200,000 and 300,000 pesos annually. But it was necessary to supply the Indians with food and clothing—items that they could only obtain by raiding, or trading captives.

Villamanrique's successor, Velasco (1590–1595), continued these policies and added two additional techniques. First, he introduced a colony of sedentary Tlaxcalan Indians from the south to serve as models of sedentary living for the various Chichimeca groups (Simmons, 1964; Powell, 1952; Bakewell, 1971; Israel, 1975, pp. 14–15, 31–35). Second, he furthered the Spanish missionary policy, *reducción*, in "which they expected to bring their variety of civilization to the Indians of New Spain" (Spicer, 1962, p. 463).

Reducción required gathering scattered rancheria groups into compact settlements run by missionaries. The *reducción* policy worked with differential success throughout northern New Spain. It proved to be the most effective in areas where aboriginal patterns approximated village life. Thus those groups that lived in horticultural bands most readily adapted to the mission system (e.g., Yaquis, Mayos, Opatas), whereas those groups that were nomadic or transhumant resisted efforts to settle them (Spicer, 1962, p. 463ff). In the Gran Chichimeca, *reducción* in combination with the other techniques was so successful that "it took slightly more than a decade of an intelligent peace by purchase policy to achieve what four decades of warfare had been unable to accomplish" (Powell, 1952, p. 203).

One of the benefits of the Chichimeca Wars was increased Spanish sophistication in dealing with nomadic Indians; "as the Spaniards became better acquainted with their enemy they acquired some facility in ascertaining which were the strategic tribes, which were the important chiefs, and what it was that most appealed to the natives as reward for peace agreements" (Powell, 1952, p. 204–205). However, the increased understanding of nomadic Indians did not prevent 40 years of

Chichimeca warfare, nor did it diffuse very well through time or space within the Spanish bureaucracy.

THE PROCESS OF ENDEMIC WARFARE

The dynamics underlying the fundamental misunderstanding of Indian relations, and the consequent chaotic policies may be seen even at this early stage. At the ideological level there was a pronounced Spanish ethnocentrism, evidenced by the view that only Spaniards were civilized, and therefore organized. Hence there was little or no attempt to discern order of any type among band-level groups. Consequently, there was little or no understanding of the fluid nature of band organization, and especially of the kin-based nature of raiding. Ethnocentrism was not a Spanish monopoly, and by itself does not constitute an adequate explanation for the pattern of misunderstanding.

Spanish ethnocentrism was exacerbated and reinforced by both bureaucratic and class structures. The constant rotation of officials slowed the accumulation of knowledge about frontier conditions. The practice of leaving detailed written instructions for successors mitigated this tendency, but bureaucratic infighting, class competition, and personal promotion also colored reports. The frequent lack of overlap between administrations all but eliminated the possibility of oral briefings.

The central feature, though, in explaining Spanish policy is the clash of interests among various frontier classes. Bureaucratic officials had to balance interests of development, including costs of administration versus revenue generated by tribute and taxes, with personal interests of improving bureaucratic position and increasing personal wealth. Miners and settlers were interested in safe acquisition of territory and cheap labor. Soldiers and labor contractors were interested in acquiring slaves to supply both miners and farmers, and avoiding government control. On the one hand the Church was the guardian of morals and the saver of souls; on the other hand it was the major assimilative agency for the Spanish state. Like the state, the Church had to balance increased costs of mission operations against revenue generated by the agricultural activity of missionized ("reduced") Indians. The Church desired the protection of the military for its missionaries, yet at the same time deplored many military actions, especially those designed to generate captives. The Church sought to administer missions in the interest of saving souls and generating revenues; the state sought to use missions as agents of state policy.

While bureaucrats, miners and farmers—the latter two as frontier producers and sellers—were interested in minimizing Indian–Spanish conflict, soldiers, labor contractors, miners and settlers (the latter two as employers and colonists) were interested in opening new territory and cheap labor. The Church sought both to protect and use Indians: it also needed military assistance in programs of *reducción,* while opposing excessive military operations. These conflicting interests produced an erratic frontier policy that shifted with the fortunes of various classes, with changes in personnel, and with the fortunes of various officers. Erratic policies drained the royal treasury and created and maintained a state of endemic warfare. War and the frontier advanced together.

CONCLUSIONS, QUESTIONS, SPECULATIONS

Clearly much of the social change that accompanied incorporation into the Spanish Empire was a product of interaction among the three sets of societies: Spain, colonial society, and indigenous societies. Politics and trade were also important factors in change. Spanish politics directed that the colonies should be profitable and support, rather than undermine, Crown power and authority. The political struggles between the Crown and the Church, and especially between the Crown, through its bureaucracy, and its subjects shaped colonial society. These conflicts pushed for steady expansion of a frontier almost continuously in a state of war with indigenous populations.

War, subjugation, and trade of, and with, Indians produced numerous changes. The introduction of new pathogens was probably the single most dramatic source of change in Indian society, within a century reducing native population to about one-tenth of its former extent. New social roles were developed, especially those of military auxiliaries and exemplary colonists. Spaniards introduced the extraction of resources for export rather than conspicuous display. The role of auxiliaries gave native peoples access to otherwise unavailable Spanish technology, especially guns and horses.

As a result of the new situation, pressure developed on indigenous political structures. Policy was consciously directed toward fragmentation of the native state societies, and unwittingly toward centralization of nonstate societies. A second major effect was increased dependency on Spaniards. The imperfectly limited access to Spanish technological goods fostered dependency for both sedentary and nomadic groups. For the sedentary peoples on the frontier, Spanish arms were necessary to cope with the raids of nomads. For nomadic peoples, horses and guns were vital for protection from Spaniards, from sedentary Indians, and from competing nomadic groups. Without detailed knowledge of how extensive similar effects of Aztec and other native states might have -been, the novelty and the intensity of the Spanish effects cannot be thoroughly assessed, although their intensity was assuredly greater.

   This analysis underscores the interactive nature of incorporation. First, native actors played an active role in the process, whether as collaborating *caciques,* auxiliaries, or exemplary colonists. Second, the effects of Spanish actions varied with the type of indigenous society encountered. State societies were fragmented politically, whereas nonstate societies became somewhat more centralized, or at least more broadly organized. Among sedentary peoples, conflict and war decreased, except for that directed and supervised by Spaniards. Among nomadic frontier peoples conflict and war increased as trade in captives and dislocations caused by Spanish expansion increased.

   In addition to the class competition and conflict transferred from the homeland, new conflicts arose and old conflicts were expressed in different ways. Missionaries, miners, and would-be *encomenderos* and *hacendados* all depended on the Empire, but sought to use it in different and often conflicting ways. These complicated interrelations helped prolong the Chichimeca Wars, and in general contributed to a chaotic administration that consistently honored official policy by violating it. *Encomiendas* were granted after the New Laws forbidding them were promulgated. Trade in captive nomads increased after the enslavement of Indians was banned.

   This analysis supports Wolf's claim (1982, p. 76; 1984) that there is no pristine past to which ethnographers can turn to understand social structure and social change in their "pure" forms. How extensive is fighting among band societies in the absence of states? More to the point, how much of the structure of the societies of the Gran Chichimeca is the product of repeated interaction with Mesoamerican state societies? Clearly the taking or sale of captives in the 1530s was significantly different than such activities in the 1580s. The former probably would be an unprecedented event (and "legal"), the latter, a recurrent (and "illegal") event, occurring in a situation laden with a variety of conflicting precedents.

   This conflict-ridden situation, exacerbated by competing lines of authority in the bureaucratic structure, opened the door to byzantine manipulations of information. Hence, official documents must be interpreted with extreme caution. The social position of the writer and the intended audience need to be carefully evaluated. A report on the torture of captives taken by Chichimecas is subject to exaggeration. There is almost no reason to expect such reports to understate the severity of torture. While perceived dangers might attract some nobles, they probably would have made recruiting ordinary soldiers more difficult.

The unravelling of the processes of incorporation will be advanced by following the evolution of these frontier policies as they were extended and modified in the northernmost province of New Spain. As noted before, it was significant that New Mexico was colonized in 1598 by Don Juan de Oñate, son of Cristóbal de Oñate, a veteran of the Chichimeca frontier.

NOTES

1. This section draws on Elliott (1963) and Vicens Vives (1969, 1970a, 1970b). Wallerstein (1974b, 1980) provides a world-system interpretation of these events.

2. Jews, *Conversos* and *Moriscos* (the latter two had converted to Catholicism, usually under duress) were subject to exclusion and confiscation of property. In 1502 all Muslims in Granada and Castile were nominally converted to Catholicism, then in Aragon in 1525. In 1609 all *Moriscos* were expelled (Vicens Vives, 1970b, pp. 77, 165; 1969, pp. 297–299; Elliott, 1963, pp. 95–99).

3. See Vicens Vives (1969, pp. 377–384), Elliott (1961), Kamen (1978, 1981), Israel (1981) and Wallerstein (1974b, 1980) on the price revolution.

4. This section draws on Lang (1975, 1979), Chevalier (1963a, 1963b), Haring (1947), Simpson (1950), McAlister (1963), Mörner (1983), Wolf (1955, 1959, 1982) and Israel (1975).

5. Chevalier (1963a), Simpson (1966), Haring (1947), Lang (1975, 1979), Baretta and Markoff (1978), Wolf (1955, 1959) and Edwards (1982) all see the seeds of subsequent conflicts in the early social structure of New Spain. Furthermore, all see a clear distinction between central and southern Mexico and the north.

6. An *encomienda* was a grant to an *encomendero* who was entitled to both tribute and labor from Indians assigned to him as part of the *encomienda* (Simpson, 1950).

7. A *casta* was a person or group of persons of mixed racial or ethnic ancestry. In theory it was a caste system, but in practice it was quite fluid (Mörner, 1967).

8. "*Cacique*" is an Arawak word for a leader akin to a "chief" and is used in Spanish in the same broad way that chief is used in English, thus it is a source of much confusion about indigenous forms of leadership.

9. Under the *repartimiento* system Indian communities supplied a specified quota (initially 2% of the adult population) of workers per week to the *repartimiento* holder (Simpson, 1950, Ch. 10; Lang, 1975, pp. 19–20).

10. This section draws from Powell (1945, 1952), Bakewell (1971, Chs. 1 and 2), West (1949), Chevalier (1963a, especially Ch. 5) and Wolf (1955, 1959).

11. Other provinces were founded as follows: Nueva Vizcaya (New Biscay, approximately modern Durango and Chihuahua) in 1562, Nuevo Leon in 1579, New Mexico in 1598, Coahuila in 1687, Texas in 1718, Sinaloa in 1734, Nuevo

Santander (approximately modern Tamaulípas) in 1746, California in 1767 (Haring, 1947, p. 81).

12.   Such menials, frequently called "slaves," were subject to control and whim of their master. The term "slave," however, is not a particularly useful label for captives in societies with little or no surplus production.

13.   The Guachichiles are sometimes spelled "Hauchichiles" in Powell's earlier writings; Cazcanes are sometimes spelled "Caxcanes." Powell (1952) and Bakewell (1971) both give general maps of the locations of these groups.

CHAPTER V

Endemic Warfare and Ethnic Relations on the Spanish Frontier: The Formation of a Region of Refuge[1]

These acts of treachery and violence sharpened the age-old hostility between the Apaches and the inhabitants of the settled areas. Inspired by a growing hatred and emboldened by new methods of warfare made possible by the horse and new weapons, the nomads began an increasingly bitter war of attrition against the Hispano–Indian settlements. The Spaniards in turn seized upon these attacks as an excuse for new campaigns and to the vicious circle thus created there was no end (France V. Scholes, 1935a, p. 85).

Two major forces propelled New Spain on its northward expansion: the desire for wealth and pre-emptive colonization. The salvation of "heathen" Indian souls was an important secondary theme in the early years of expansion. Pre-emptive colonization eventually dominated as the reason for continued Spanish occupation of the territories now comprising northern Mexico and the Southwestern United States. The entire region was at best marginal to the economies of both Spain and New Spain, draining more from them than it ever put back. Nonetheless, the region did supply slaves, sheep, wool, piñon nuts, and a few other local products to the northern silver mining regions of Parral, Santa Barbara, Saltillo, and Zacatecas (West, 1949; Moorhead, 1958; Bloom, 1935). Spaniards also introduced the horse to the aboriginal American West.

When viewed from a modern perspective in which California and Texas play major roles in the American economy, it is difficult to con-

75

ceive of them as secondary, pre-emptive colonies, founded late in the northern expansion. Although the Coronado expedition explored much of the territory as early as 1540–1542, the first successful colonizing effort did not occur until 1598. The primary motive behind this effort was fear of English encroachment on the unsettled territories, engendered by the news of Sir Francis Drake's landing somewhere on the northern coast of California in the late 1570s (Bannon, 1974; Beck, 1962; Bolton, 1929). Likewise, fear of French expansion from Louisiana prompted establishment of missions in eastern Texas in the latter part of the seventeenth century and permanent colonization in the first quarter of the eighteenth century. The systematic exploration of California began in the early eighteenth century, but serious colonizing efforts were not made until 1769 when news of southward expansion of Russian fur traders reached Madrid and Mexico City (Bolton, 1929). Throughout the Spanish era New Mexico was the most populous of the three provinces. Both New Mexico and Texas straddled territories inhabited by Comanches and Apaches. Hence policies toward those groups were split between two jurisdictions whose only path of communication was through the viceroy in Mexico City some 1,500 miles from either governor.

The era of Spanish domination may be broken up into three periods. The first period is one of initial colonization, which lasted from Oñate's arrival in 1598 until the Pueblo Revolt in 1680. The second period lasted from Vargas's reconquest in 1693 until the inspection of *Visitador General* José de Gálvez in 1765 when the Bourbon reforms finally penetrated the northern frontiers. The third period lasted from the Bourbon reorganization of the frontier until Mexican independence in 1821. Each of these periods is marked by different dynamics of ethnic relations and social change. The events of the first two periods are described in this chapter. The events of the third period are described in the following two chapters.

1. Oñate (1598) to Pueblo Revolt (1680)
2. Vargas reconquest (1693) to Gálvez (1765) reforms
3. Bourbon reforms to Mex ind (1821)

THE SEVENTEENTH CENTURY

Aboriginal Relations

New Mexico was inhabited by many indigenous groups (see Maps V.1 and V.2). There were between 110 and 150 functioning Pueblo villages at the time of Spanish contact (Forbes, 1960, Ch. VII; John, 1975, p. 87; Schroeder, 1968, 1979c). Pre-Hispanic Pueblo villages fought and traded with each other and nomadic groups (Spicer, 1962; John, 1975;

Forbes, 1960; Riley, 1976, 1978, 1982; Riley and Manson, 1983; Baugh, 1984a, 1984b; Wilcox, 1984; A. B. Thomas, 1935; S. Tyler, 1973). Reports from the Coronado expedition indicate that ruined Pueblo villages were encountered that had been destroyed in recent conflicts. Coronado destroyed a few more during his expedition.

Pre-Hispanic artifacts from Plains groups have been found at Pecos Pueblo (Kenner, 1969). According to Pedro de Casteñeda, chronicler of the Coronado expedition, Plains-dwelling Indians, the Teyas, had tried to sack Cicuye (Pecos) in about 1525 without success. They had destroyed some Pueblo villages west of Pecos in the Galisteo basin. At the time of Coronado's arrival Cicuye held sway over both the Teyas with whom they traded, and the neighboring Galisteo Pueblo villages (Kessell, 1979, pp. 20–21). There is still considerable controversy over who the Teyas were, but evidence leans strongly toward Caddoan peoples and not Apaches (Baugh, 1984a; Wilcox, 1981a, 1984; cf. D. Gunnerson, 1974, pp. 17–74). Forbes (1960) argues that sedentary–nomad conflict may have occurred occasionally in pre-Hispanic times, but inter-Pueblo conflict had probably been more common. The arrival of Spaniards led to increased sedentary–nomad conflict (Kessell, 1979; Wilcox, 1984; Scholes 1935a, 1937–40). Support for frequent nomad–sedentary conflict in the early Spanish records may be a reflection of Spanish culture that held such conflict to be natural in human affairs.

Founding of the New Mexico Colony

The move to New Mexico has roots in the early years of exploration by Spanish *conquistadores* who were searching for wealth and adventure (Hammond, 1956). The first accounts of any part of the region that was to become part of the American Southwest were from Alvar Núñez Cabeza de Vaca, who spent many years travelling overland to Mexico from a shipwreck on the coast of what is now Texas. He arrived in New Spain in 1536 with tales of the north inhabited by many Indians. These tales kindled Spanish hopes of riches in the north. Viceroy Mendoza took advantage of the presence of Cortés in Spain to encourage exploration of the north. Cabeza de Vaca refused to lead an expedition. About that time Fray Marcos de Niza, a veteran of many parts of the Spanish Indies including Peru, came to Mexico from Guatemala and agreed to lead an expedition. He left for the north in 1539 guided by Esteván/ cio, Cabeza de Vaca's erstwhile slave and companion. Esteván/ cio arrived at the Zuni villages ahead of the main party. His arrogant behavior prompted the Zunis to kill him. Word of Esteván/ cio's death discouraged Fray de Niza from entering any Zuni villages, but he did go close enough

Map V.1. Locations of Indigenous Groups at Contact, ca. 1540–1598

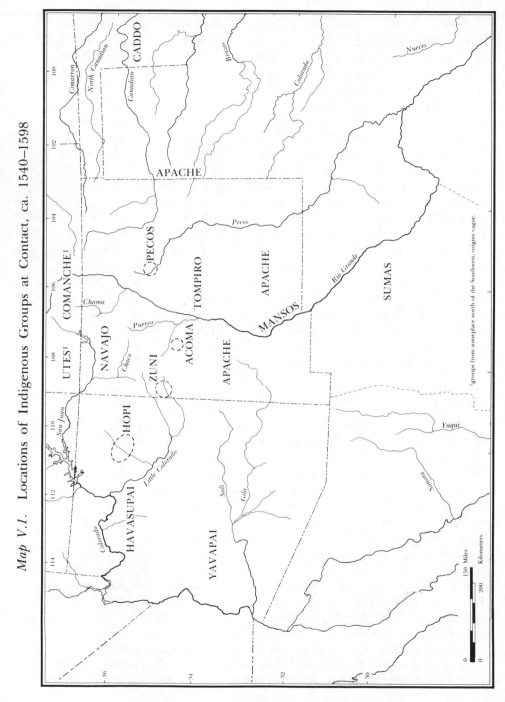

CADDO

APACHE

PECOS

COMANCHE¹

TOMPIRO

UTES¹

NAVAJO

ZUNI

ACOMA

APACHE

MANSOS

APACHE

SUMAS

HOPI

HAVASUPAI

YAVAPAI

Nueces

Cimarron

North Canadian

Canadian

Brazos

Colorado

Pecos

Rio Grande

Chama

Puerco

Chaco

San Juan

Little Colorado

Colorado

Salt

Gila

Yaqui

Sonora

100

102

104

106

108

110

112

114

36

34

32

30

¹groups from someplace north of the Southwest, origins vague.

see Map V.2 for locations of Pueblo groups.

150 Miles

200 Kilometers

0

0

Sources: Schroeder (1968:293, 1979c); see Map V.2 for locations of Pueblo groups.

Map V.2. Pueblo Groups at Contact, ca. 1540–1598

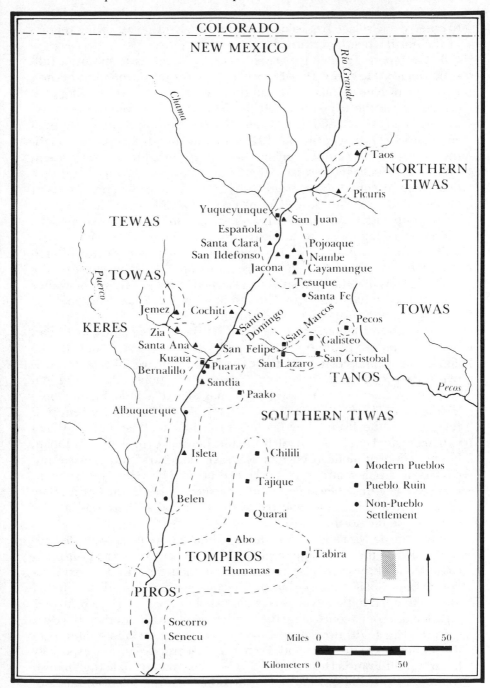

COLORADO

NEW MEXICO

Río Grande

Chama

Taos

NORTHERN
TIWAS

Picuris

Yuqueyunque

San Juan

TEWAS

Española

Santa Clara

San Ildefonso

Pojoaque

Nambe

Puerco

Jacona

Cayamungue

TOWAS

Tesuque

Jemez

Cochiti

Santa Fe

KERES

Zia

Santo
Domingo

San Marcos

Pecos

TOWAS

Santa Ana

San Felipe

Galisteo

Kuaua

San Lazaro

San Cristobal

Bernalillo

Puaray

Pecos

Sandia

TANOS

Paako

Albuquerque

SOUTHERN TIWAS

Isleta

Chilili

▲ Modern Pueblos

Tajique

■ Pueblo Ruin

Belen

● Non-Pueblo
Settlement

Quarai

Abo

Tabira

TOMPIROS

Humanas

PIROS

Socorro

Senecu

Miles 0   50

Kilometers 0   50

Sources: Schroeder (1968:294, 1979c)

to observe one village from a distance. Fray de Niza gave glowing reports of the north when he returned to Mexico City.[2]

These reports further persuaded Viceroy Mendoza to mount a full-scale *entrada*. He chose Don Francisco Vásquez de Coronado, the new governor of Nueva Galicia, to lead the expedition. After receiving official approval, the expedition left in 1540 with 230 mounted men, 62 infantrymen, about 800 Indian auxiliaries, cattle and other supplies (Bannon, 1974, p. 17; Bolton, 1949). In July an advance party fought their way into the Zuni settlements. Groups explored to the west, reaching the Hopi villages and later the Grand Canyon. During this time a delegation to Zuni (Cibola) from Cicuye (Pecos) arrived. The reports of villages to the east encouraged a small party to explore in that direction. This group passed Acoma, the Tiguex villages in the vicinity of modern Albuquerque, and went on to Cicuye. Coronado moved the entire party to Pecos for the winter to be in position for an early spring expedition to find "Quivira." Quivira was a supposedly wealthy city somewhere on the buffalo plains that the Spaniards had learned about at Pecos. The winter was unusually harsh and the impositions of the Spaniards on their "hosts" strained relations between them.

The story of the journey to Quivira is a fascinating study in Indian manipulation of Spanish greed and gullability. An Indian dubbed "the Turk" was supposed to lead the expedition. Quivira, like many such places described by Indians to the Spaniards in hopes of luring them away from their territory was "poco más allá" ("a little further on") (Bannon, 1974, p. 12; Hammond, 1956). As the explorers ventured further into the Plains they became suspicious of "the Turk." When Quivira turned out to be a small horticultural village (probably Caddoan, in the vicinity of modern Wichita, Kansas), "the Turk" was pressed into confessing his lies and summarily executed. The party returned to Cicuye so late that they spent another winter there. In the spring they returned to Mexico, and reported to the viceroy that there was little of value in the far north.

While the de Niza and Coronado expeditions were underway, de Soto was exploring the Mississippi region and others explored the California coast. None of these areas were occupied immediately. Rather, exploration in New Spain centered on the regions just north of the Valley of Mexico and led to the silver strikes discussed in Chapter IV. No further mention or actions concerning the north took place for another 40 years.

In the late 1570s two sets of forces converged to rekindle interest in the far north. On the one hand, French and British expansion, especially the travels of Francis Drake in 1578–1579, began to trouble the Spanish (Bannon, 1974; Bolton, 1929). On the other hand, Franciscan missionaries were eager for new converts among the settled Indians of the far north. Thus, in 1581 Fray Agustín Rodríguez and Captain Francisco Sánchez Chamuscado received permission to the explore the territory. They left and returned with reports that only mildly interested Viceroy Conde de Coruña. The Franciscans, however, were greatly concerned that three friars had stayed behind without military protection. The following year (1582) the wealthy Antonio de Espejo, who was in Nueva Vizcaya at the time, heard of the situation and agreed to finance a rescue mission. The would-be rescuers found that all the friars had been killed, but they explored what is now central Arizona and found several potential mines.

The news of possible mines, of Indians "more advanced" than the Chichimecas, and fears that the British were about to penetrate and possibly control the rumored northwest passage, encouraged the Spaniards to colonize the region. In spring of 1583 the viceroy received permission to launch a campaign of conquest and occupation — at no expense to the Crown. Bureaucratic obstacles and local in-fighting stalled the expedition. While official channels were moving slowly, two unauthorized expeditions took place; both were conducted with the hope that if sufficient wealth were found, the Crown would grant retroactive permission. In 1589 Gaspar Castaño de Sosa took an expedition north. The viceroy had the entire party chased down and arrested. In 1593 Francisco Leyva de Bonilla and Antonio Gutiérrez de Humaña led an expedition north, possibly as far as modern Kansas. Leyva was killed in a quarrel with Bonilla, and most of the men were killed by Plains Indians.

The name "Nuevo Mexico" reflected the hope that the new area would be another Mexico, full of mines, Indians and wealth. The boundaries of the new province were never carefully specified, since the founding of the province was in effect Spain's claim to the north country (Scholes, 1935a, p. 72). Permission was granted to Juan de Oñate, son of one of the founders of Zacatecas, to lead a colonizing expedition to New Mexico. In return for conducting the *entrada,* Oñate was to receive an *encomienda* for three generations and the right to bestow *encomiendas* on others. A change in viceroys led to renegotiation of Oñate's contract. A colonizing party consisting of 129 male heads of household, some 600–700 people (Bannon, 1974, p. 36; O. Jones, 1979, p. 119) and probably a few Tlaxcalan Indian colonists (Simmons, 1964) finally left in January, 1598. They were "a rabble too unruly to be tolerated any longer in New Spain, short of supplies, and doomed by untimely departure to reach New Mexico too late to plant crops that year" (John, 1975, p. 39). They went "to get rich quick," and viewed their investment in the colony as "a stake in a gambling enterprise" (Beck, 1962, p. 55).

In the first year of the colony the perennial conflict between church and state emerged. To protect and support themselves, the colonists found it necessary to "requisition" supplies from Pueblo villages that had sworn vassalage to the king of Spain, generating hostility. However, Oñate and the colonists were obligated to Christianize the Indians that required their friendship and cooperation. Such church–state conflict was not unique to New Mexico, but rather reproduced conflicts common in Mexico (Israel, 1975).

The following year one of Oñate's lieutenants, Juan de Zaldívar, after being refused supplies by Acoma Pueblo, forced the issue and was ambushed while supposedly being led to the granary. In retaliation Vicente de Zaldívar sacked the entire village at the cost of several-hundred Indian lives. All adult male survivors lost a foot and all other survivors were condemned to 20 years of slavery and sold. Actions such as this (this was only the most extreme) kept Pueblo–Spanish relations unsteady. Many Pueblo dwellers fled to friends among various Athapaskan-speaking bands (no doubt families with whom they had trading partnerships). Spanish officials saw such flights as the result of plots among nomads. These plots were thought to be the cause of raids against converted Pueblo Indians and Spaniards. The lack of wealth in the province and the growing frequency of raids discouraged many colonists who consequently wanted to return to Mexico. The discouraged settlers, and the priests whose apostolic work was endangered by the increasingly hostile relations, were apparently quite successful in convincing higher officials of the seriousness of the problems of New Mexico.

Reports of Oñate's excesses, "coupled with the important fact that he had failed to contribute any wealth to the royal coffers" (Forbes, 1960, p. 111), convinced the king to remove and try him for his excesses. He was convicted and fined. Indeed, Madrid determined to abandon the colony altogether, but was persuaded not to by church officials worried about the souls of Indian converts. In 1609 Pedro de Peralta became governor, and more soldiers were sent to New Mexico. They blocked abandonment of the colony, but they did not relieve its problems. Typically, the soldiers came to New Mexico seeking wealth through precious metals or Indian workers. In 1608 Viceroy Luis de Velasco had written, "No one comes to the Indies to plow and sow, but only to eat and loaf" (Forbes, 1960, p. 112). The Crown took over administrative responsibility for the province, paying over one million pesos in missionary expenses to maintain the colony over the next 75 years (Beck, 1962, p. 61). In 1610 the capital was moved from San Gabriel, near San Juan Pueblo, to the newly built town, Santa Fe.

The familiar cycle of endemic warfare arose. The usual collection of frontier officials rotated through the various governorships in New Mexico—only a desperate man would purchase so unprofitable an office (Simmons, 1968). Once in office, the only two sources of wealth were Pueblo tribute and trade, and especially trade in slaves with the southern mining districts. Both activities constantly antagonized church officials, leading to a steady flow of charges and counter charges between Santa Fe and Mexico City. The supply arrangements for the colony exacerbated the conflict (Scholes, 1930). The missions were supplied by tri-annual caravans that took six months to journey to New Mexico, remained there six months distributing supplies and collecting wool, sheep, hides, piñon nuts, and assorted other local products, then returned south (Moorhead, 1958; Bloom, 1935). In practice the caravans were irregular; sometimes seven years elapsed between arrivals. New church and state officials also arrived with the caravans. Since the church controlled the caravans, state officials were dependent on the missionaries to conduct their frequently illegal trade.

Church officials complained constantly about the excesses of state officials to higher authorities in Mexico City. These complaints were used to convict many governors of assorted crimes during the *residencia*. The only way to avoid a detrimental result to the *residencia* was to bribe the incoming official (see Scholes, 1936–1937, 1937–1940). Those governors who escaped fines or jail left office poor, having spent the profits of their administration in avoiding prosecution. This state of affairs was well known, and gave further incentive to governors to use the power of their office to pursue avenues of wealth vigorously. Thus church officials, by the very actions that were intended to control the excesses of state officials, further exacerbated their exploitive tendencies.

Indian Relations

Spanish internecine fighting shaped relations with and between the various Indian groups. To disentangle these effects it is necessary to analyze the inter-Indian relations. Forbes (1960, pp. 98–99) reports that in 1598–1601 there was no fighting between Athapaskans and Pueblos. Trade between the two groups usually took place in individual homes in Pueblo villages (Snow, 1973, 1981), indicating it was not market exchange, but trade between kin groups. This pattern is consistent with general patterns of nonmarket trading (Polanyi, 1944; Polanyi et al., 1957; Dalton, 1968). Such trade is more than mere economic exchange, it is an enduring relationship among kin groups.

When the exactions of Spanish tribute were severe, as they often were in the early years, Pueblo families fled to their nomadic trading partners until the Spaniards' demand for tribute abated. This strain should not be overstated. Snow (1983) has argued that the tribute demands on the Pueblo population were relatively small, yet large enough to be critical to the Hispanic population's survival. This is because Pueblo population was approximately 20 times larger than the Hispanic population in the early seventeenth century. Nevertheless, tribute did constitute a new drain on the economies of Pueblo societies. Spanish officials tended to view these actions as attempts to plot against them, and took steps to discourage such flights. In later years Spanish governors went so far as to consolidate various Pueblo villages into larger villages. According to the Spanish officials, this was done to simplify defense of villages. It also facilitated administrative control. The flight to nomadic trading partners solidified the alliance between some nomadic bands and certain Pueblo families. For other Pueblo individuals, the way to lessen Spanish demands was to ally with them against either nomadic groups or other Pueblos. Christianized Pueblos used this tactic. Enmity developed rather quickly between those fleeing Spanish exactions and those who allied with the Spaniards.

Various trade partnerships cross-cut nomad enmities. For those Pueblo individuals who understood both the languages and customs of the surrounding nomads, the distinction between friendly, hostile, and neutral bands was generally clear. The actions of various nomadic bands were not erratic, but consistent. But patterns of pre-Hispanic relations were strained and deformed under Spanish pressures. As Spanish tribute undermined the trading capability of many Pueblo families, nomads could no longer obtain desired or necessary goods by trade, but only by raiding. If a former trading partner stole property from a factional enemy within the village, the Pueblo partner would not always be inclined to see such acts as reprehensible. If the raid were conducted against a hostile Pueblo village, so much the better. These raids increased rapidly and steadily, raising the number of war-related deaths and captives, and adding vengeance to the causes for raiding.

As various Pueblo groups were coerced into alliances with the Spaniards, they accompanied the Spaniards on counter-raids more frequently (O. Jones, 1966). As the demand for slaves grew, peaceful nomadic groups would be attacked, and Pueblo auxiliaries, as much as the Spanish main forces, became targets of vengeance raids (Kenner, 1969, p. 14; Forbes, 1960, Ch. VI). As the cycle continued, raiding nomads found that " . . . to distinguish between Spanish and Pueblo (friend and foe) was impossible because the two were so closely interlocked" (Reeve, 1957, p. 42). This drove Pueblo groups into a closer alliance with the Spaniards that carried the twin costs of increased tribute and increased enmity of the nomads. As this process continued, more Pueblo villages were abandoned due to raids or Spanish attempts at consolidation. By 1643 the number of occupied Pueblo villages had shrunk to 43 (Forbes, 1960, Ch. VII; John, 1975, p. 87; see Map V.3). Schroeder (1968, 1979c), however, attributes many abandonments to aboriginal inter-group hostilities and to ecological factors, such as the drought of the late sixteenth century (1968, p. 296). Still, many of these changes were an indirect result of Spanish actions, through both increased ecological pressure and intensified trading–raiding competition.

Slave trading had other far-reaching effects on intergroup relations. No doubt the role of the Pueblo villages as trade centers increased the number of vengeance raids to which they were subjected. A Pueblo Indian who traded for a slave earned the hatred of the slave's group. As the demand for slaves increased, interband warfare and the taking of captives increased, leading to more vengeance attacks. When a Spanish slaving party arrived to trade for captives, nomads had the choice of trading captives taken elsewhere or being taken captive themselves (e.g., Scholes, 1935a, 1936–1937; Kenner, 1969, pp. 17–18). Such events only insured further attacks on Spaniards and their Pueblo allies.

Apaches had acquired horses by 1607, and probably as early as 1601, primarily through escaped captives who had been used as herders (Forbes, 1960, p. 110). As horses became more common, nomadic raiders became far more formidable. Horses also increased the buffalo-hunting efficiency of nomads, which increased the hides available for trade. This put further demands on Pueblo villages for supplies and on Spaniards for horses.

Improved transportation, made possible by horses, facilitated the development of more centralized leadership among Plains Apache groups (Secoy, 1953, p. 25). Indeed, Apaches took over almost all features of Spanish warfare except guns, which the Spaniards attempted to keep to themselves. Apaches used the lance (now tipped with metal, especially sword points, acquired in trade or raids), and the Spanish saddle that facilitated its use. They increasingly used leather armor, which Spanish soldiers had developed during the Chichimeca Wars. This armor was light yet effective against arrows shot from Indian bows. It was not, however, effective against guns. As long as there were relatively few guns on either side and most fighting was done in brief sorties, this armor proved effective. The vast difference in the penetrating power of guns (even early crude ones) versus arrows accounts for the seemingly preposterous feats of arms of a few Spanish soldiers.

Groups without horses were subject to attack and displacement by groups with horses. Their women and children became captives sold into the Hispanic market. Captives were the primary good, along with buffalo hides, that nomadic groups could trade for horses. The only alternative was raiding for horses. Thus a "horse frontier" gradually spread outward from New Mexico, creating a gradient of horses controlled by various groups. In the 1680s both La Salle and de Tonty reported seeing horses among groups in what is now eastern Texas and Missouri (Worcester, 1944). Conflict and trade between groups increased as horses spread.

By mid-century revolts of allied groups of Pueblos and nomads were becoming serious threats in New Mexico. For a while these were contained by Spanish superiority in arms. Furthermore, Spaniards enlisted opposing groups as allies for counter-attacks by promising shares in the booty collected. Nonetheless, the increasingly severe raids had dire effects on the province. Between 1661 and 1671 the southern Tompiro villages were permanently abandoned due to the combination of drought and Apache raids (Schroeder, 1968, p. 297). The surviving members of these Pueblo groups melted into other groups. Raids on Taos Pueblo were so severe that many of the residents fled to the Plains where they built a new village, El Cuartelejo (Schroeder, 1968, p. 297; Scholes, 1936–1937; see Map V.3). Due to increased intergroup fighting on the Plains, the Taoseños of El Cuartelejo petitioned the governor to be brought back to Taos in 1660.

In 1664 Governor Peñalosa forbade the entrance of nomadic Indians into any Pueblo village, ostensibly to prevent further Pueblo–nomad hostility. Clearly, though, Peñalosa was trying to ensure a middleman role for Spaniards in the increasing Plains trade (Kenner, 1969, p. 17; Forbes, 1960, Ch. VIII). This ruling did not stand for long because there were too few Spaniards to enforce the rule or to conduct the trade. The ban did serve to accelerate the transfer of trading from Pueblo villages to the Plains. As more trade moved to the Plains, there were fewer reasons for Plains dwellers to refrain from raiding in New Mexico. Thus, raiding increased further.

The Pueblo Revolt, 1680[3]

As the raiding increased steadily throughout the century, so did the feuding between church and state. Public statements against one faction by the other, increasing familiarity with Spanish ways, acquisition of horses and a few firearms lessened Indian fears of Spaniards. There were a number of rebellions between 1645 and 1675, most of which had been easily suppressed. Spaniards were able to capitalize on both inter-Pueblo

Map V.3. Indigenous Locations, 1598–1680

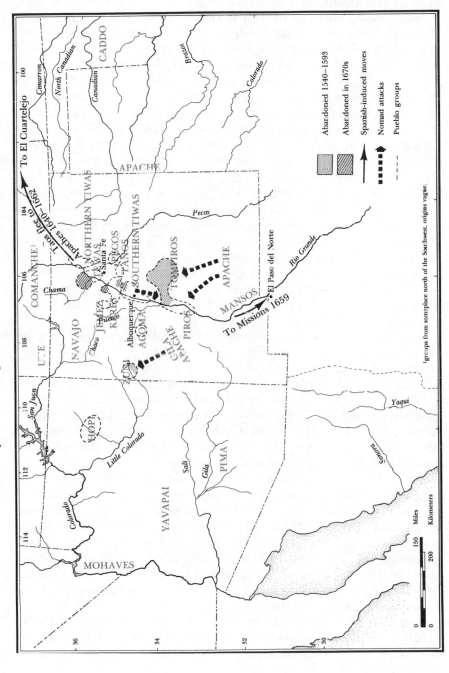

To El Cuartelejo

Apaches 1640–1697

Taos flee 1640–1661

CADDO

APACHE

NORTHERN TIWAS

COMANCHE[1]

Cimarron

North Canadian

Canadian

Brazos

Colorado

Pecos

Chama

TEWAS
Santa Fe
PECOS
TANOS
SOUTHERN TIWAS

TOMPIROS

UTE

NAVAJO

JEMEZ
KERES
Puerco

Albuquerque

ACOMA

GILA
APACHE

PIROS

APACHE

MANSOS

El Paso del Norte

To Missions 1659

San Juan

ZUNI

HOPI

Little Colorado

Rio Grande

Yaqui

Salt

Gila

PIMA

Sonora

Colorado

YAVAPAI

MOHAVES

[ ] Abandoned 1540–1593
[ ] Abandoned in 1670s
→ Spanish-induced moves
⇢ Nomad attacks
‐‐‐ Pueblo groups

[1]groups from someplace north of the Southwest, origins vague.

Miles
Kilometers

0   150
0   200

Sources: Schroeder (1968:305, 1979c)

hostility and Pueblo fear of nomad raids. In 1675 residents of some Pueblos openly returned to their traditional religion. In retaliation 47 "shamans" were arrested and brought to Santa Fe. Four were hanged, the rest were flogged publicly. They were released when a large number of Pueblo warriors threatened Governor Treviño with attack.

Popé, a religious leader from San Juan and one of those flogged in 1675, began to organize a concerted rebellion. He allied with residents of other Pueblos who held traditional offices. The rebellion was planned over several years in the kivas using secret societies (the only extant inter-Pueblo organization; Dozier, 1970a, p. 56). In 1680 the specific date of the revolt was communicated by a series of knotted ropes. Spanish officials heard about the rebellion one or two days in advance from captured messengers. Word got back to the leaders, and the revolt was begun immediately. Within a few days all Spaniards in New Mexico were either killed, captured, or forced to retreat to Santa Fe or Isleta Pueblo. A successful attack on the surrounding Indians allowed Governor Otermin to lead the Santa Fe refugees south. They later joined the group from Isleta, and met a supply caravan coming north. They all withdrew to El Paso. The Spaniards were accompanied by a number of Indians, especially from Isleta Pueblo (Ellis, 1979a), who feared retribution for their aid to the Spaniards.

Two major causes are consistently advanced for the revolt: religious repression and the church–state conflict. A third cause, not as widely cited, is economic oppression (Sando, 1979, p. 196; John, 1975, pp. 98–100; Dunbar Ortiz, 1980, pp. 37–38). Reeve (1957, p. 51) and John (1975, pp. 98–100) combine these three elements in a political explanation that sees the revolt as a reaction to exploitation. Others cite cultural domination as the source of revolt (Beck, 1962; Hackett, 1942; Bannon, 1974; Sando, 1979, pp. 194–197). Spicer (1962, pp. 160–164) and Garner (1974) provide more detailed analyses.

In the 1660s, under Governor Lopez, restraint of Pueblo religious ceremonialism was relaxed, only to be reasserted later in the decade. Between about 1667 and 1672 there was an extended drought, followed by famine in 1670 and 1671, and an epidemic in 1671. Nomadic raiding increased in 1672 (Spicer, 1962; Hackett, 1942, pp. xx–xxii). Religious repression also increased, leading to the floggings in 1675 under Governor Treviño. The growing emphasis on conformity was a consequence of both religious assertion and a response to the numerous, yet easily suppressed, uprisings of these decades.

Garner (1974) criticizes the interpretations of Chavez (1967), Forbes (1960) and Scholes (1936–1937). He interprets Chavez's emphasis on the role of Popé, a Taos mulatto, as an extension of Scholes's view of

Indians as childlike, implying that only *mestizos* could lead a revolt. He criticizes Forbes for seeing Pan-Indianism where it did not exist. He argues that Scholes exaggerated church–state conflict in New Mexico, not sufficiently allowing for biases in the historical documents. Garner asserts that the relations between *encomenderos* and friars were interdependent, and that governors were no more avaricious than colonial officials everywhere in the New World. The problem was that governors were outsiders with no local political power base, and that there were few resources they could exploit that did not upset either local *encomenderos* or the friars, or in the worst cases, both. As the seventeenth century progressed and the Pueblo Indians became more acculturated and "syncretism" (Garner's term for acculturation) proceeded, they came to understand the Spaniards better and see their weaknesses. After the Spanish failed to correct the disasters of the late 1660s and early 1670s, it became clear to the Pueblo leaders that continued collaboration with them was not profitable. This set the conditions for accumulated grievances to erupt in rebellion. That the revolt achieved its twin goals of ending missionizing and eliminating Spaniards supports this analysis (Spicer, 1962, p. 163).

Dozier (1970a, pp. 55–60) underscores two additional points. First, Popé, Tupatú and Catiti, the major organizers of the revolt, all held traditional leadership roles within Pueblo societies. They used traditional Pueblo mechanisms to organize the revolt, such as secret meetings held in the kivas. Since the only common inter-Pueblo form of cooperation was through these secret societies, it is not surprising that this mechanism was used. This also helps account for the success of planning the revolt for several years without Spanish knowledge. Second, the Franciscans used military force to back their missionary efforts after about 1630. According to Spicer (1962) Jesuits were far better at learning and using native languages than Franciscans. Thus, opposition to Catholicism among the Pueblo Indians was as much a matter of the method as the content of the religion. These various strands may be combined into a broader explanation for the revolt.

The Spanish presence in New Mexico had disrupted the precontact political-economy of the region drastically. There were massive changes in population, abandonments, and consolidations of living areas (see Map V.3). New surplus was extracted from the region in the form of tribute. Although Snow (1983) has argued that this was not severe, he docs acknowledge that even limited tribute could be critical in times of stress—which was the case in the 1670s. The introduction of the horse and other livestock greatly disrupted the ecology of the region. At the time of the revolt the Spanish population of New Mexico was about

2,900 (O. Jones, 1979, p. 119), while Pueblo population was on the order of 30,000 (Simmons, 1979, p. 185; Spicer, 1962, p. 162; Zubrow, 1974).[4]

Since the day-to-day confrontation between Spaniard and Pueblo took place in the mission setting, since the horticultural Pueblo societies organized their views of the world in religious terms (Dozier, 1970a, *inter alia*), and since Pueblo social organization, especially at the inter-Pueblo level, was along religious lines, it is not surprising that the rebellion was organized in religious terms. This, however, is not the same as a revolt against religious repression. Rather, it was a rebellion against economic, political and cultural oppression, which was manifest in the dominant idiom of both sets of cultures—religion. Traditional mechanisms were used to build a movement. The revolt was organized in the kivas, traditional Pueblo religious symbols (e.g., Pohe-Yemo) were employed, and churches and friars were special targets for destruction during the revolt. Those people who had the most experience with Spaniards, and consequently the strongest grievances, organized the rebellion. Hence, mestizos had the knowledge and motivation to lead the rebellion.

The revolt brought a new unity, but it lasted scarcely a decade. The fragility of Pueblo unity was due to a combination of factors. First, charismatic leadership which is not supported by institutional structure is inherently dependent on the personal qualities of the leader, and subject to individual failings. The leader, Popé, tried to set himself up in the role of the Spanish governor and exact tribute, but he did not have the coercive power to do so (Beck, 1962, p. 68). Second, given the level of Pueblo technology, the environment was not adequate to support a large state structure without external resources, as Spanish administrators had previously discovered. Third, although the raiding cycle cooled during the Spanish absence, the surrounding nomadic groups still posed a threat. Fourth, with the flight of the Spaniards there was no external pressure sufficiently strong to force unity from the various traditional factions. The absence of Spaniards also meant a loss of vital economic connections, and constituted a major disruption to the extensively transformed indigenous groups (see Map V.4). Nonetheless, the Spaniards learned a lesson never to be forgotten: the extreme danger in the unification of numerically superior enemies.

THE EIGHTEENTH CENTURY

After several abortive attempts and 13 years of dismal waiting at San Lorenzo (near modern El Paso) Diego de Vargas mounted a successful reconquest of New Mexico. During the period of waiting, the former

Map V.4. Indigenous Locations Between the Revolt and the Reconquest, 1680–1706

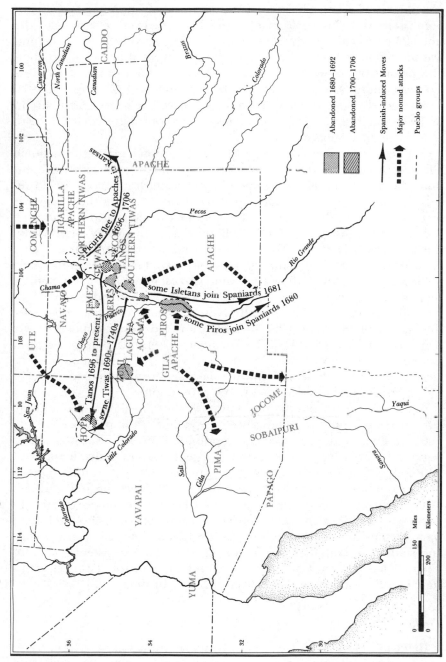

Sources: Schroeder (1968:306, 1979c)

New Mexicans were subject to continuing raids from nomadic Indians. Some settlers went south abandoning hope of ever returning to the north. The salvation of the souls of the Christianized Indians left behind was the rationale for the reconquest, but the threat of French usurpation and possible invasion of the silver-producing regions of northern Mexico was more salient (Bolton, 1929; Bannon, 1974, pp. 86–91). Wounded Hispanic pride and a number of willing applicants ready to seek glory and reward in service to the Crown contributed to the drive to recolonize New Mexico.

The reconquest proceeded rapidly. Vargas capitalized on the factional alliances between various Pueblo societies and villages and different nomadic bands that had developed in the Spanish absence. Pueblo resistance to reconquest fragmented during the 13 years the Spaniards were absent from New Mexico. Executions carried out after Santa Fe was retaken aroused a series of rebellions that were quickly quashed. By the late 1690s New Mexico was again under Spanish control. Many recalcitrant Keresans fled their homes and stayed at Acoma in the early 1690s. In the late 1690s they left Acoma and established Laguna. Shortly thereafter they made peace with the recently appointed governor of New Mexico (Ellis, 1979b, p. 438). Nomadic raids resumed soon after the return of the Spaniards. Indeed, they had never stopped in the provinces directly south of New Mexico: Sonora, Nueva Vizcaya, Coahuila, and Nuevo Leon. Concomitant with the resumption of raids were military forays against the nomads and resumption of trade in hides, horses, captives and, to a lesser extent, guns.

Beck claims that from the reconquest to the arrival of the Americans " . . . there was little of significance happening in the province" (Beck, 1962, p. 89). He draws no connection among the semi-isolation of the region, the French presence and the consequences of endemic warfare. The connection is to be found in the particular role that frontier regions play in empires. The territory was of marginal importance to the affairs of New Spain. It was significant primarily as a pre-emptive claim to northern territories. It consumed royal funds in the incessant Indian wars. Defensive colonization brought the familiar emphasis on missions and soldiers in both Texas and New Mexico. The consistent failure of missions led to a shift in emphasis to military control. Thus, church–state conflict was gradually resolved in favor of the state.

Trade

In terms of local structures of dependence, trade was divided into two main spheres: trade for manufactured goods coming north from

Chihuahua and trade with the various nomadic Indian groups surrounding the region. When New Mexico was resettled, supplies at first came through reorganized mission caravans. Slowly Chihuahua merchants gained control of the supply caravans (Moorhead, 1958, p. 41). Because of the lack of specie in New Mexico they were able to devise complex systems of valuation of goods, increasing profits (Moorhead, 1958, p. 49). Trade within New Mexico had been reduced to barter (Moorhead, 1958, pp. 50–51). Presidio commanders frequently conspired with the merchants to defraud soldiers by withholding pay supposedly to purchase goods in bulk. This was a consistent source of irritation to the troops throughout the century (Moorhead, 1961; Warner, 1966).

Although New Mexico did not supply funds for the royal coffers in Mexico City or Madrid, it certainly enriched the purses of the merchants in Chihuahua. They were able to capitalize on their privileged position as middlemen in the Mexico City–Santa Fe trade (Moorhead, 1958, p. 29). Chihuahua remained the major northern trade center until Mexican independence. Thus, New Mexico, and to a lesser extent Texas, occupied a dependent role relative to the economic and class structure of northern New Spain, although it was expensive to maintain. As is typical of a region of refuge (Aguirre Beltran, 1979), the province served to channel funds of the Empire into the hands of a particular class, especially the Chihuahua merchants, and to a lesser extent the New Mexican elite. This was done primarily through the presidio supply system (Moorhead, 1961).

These trade conditions made New Mexican officials more than willing to ignore viceregal regulations against trade with foreigners and to accept both French traders and French goods that appeared at Taos (Beck, 1962, p. 98). However, the indirect effects of the French on the Plains trade were stronger. French traders were superior to other Europeans in trading with nomads, since French interests were primarily commercial and not religious or political. These traders had begun penetrating the Plains from the north, coming south from Quebec through Illinois, and from the south, coming north from Louisiana (Eccles, 1974). It was the Plains trade that alerted New Mexican officials to French presence on the Plains.

In 1699 Apaches reported French on the Plains, and brought back European goods they had acquired (A.B. Thomas, 1935, p. 14). In 1720 Governor Valverde sent Lieutenant-general Pedro de Villasur to the Plains to investigate. The Villasur expedition ended in disaster when some Pawnees joined the French in deceiving the Spanish soldiers and killed nearly all of them (A.B. Thomas, 1935, p. 39). In 1739 the Mallet brothers arrived in Santa Fe seeking to open trade with New Mexico. The French desired to enter the potentially lucrative New Mexican market and wanted to assess the practicality of assailing Spanish mines (Bolton, 1917; A.B. Thomas, 1935, 1940).

The French also contributed to major changes among Plains groups. Groups with guns had military superiority over those that did not. Guns spread from northeast to southwest, while horses spread from southwest to northeast. When these two frontier gradients crossed, the effect was truly explosive. The groups that were able to obtain both horses and guns had a massive advantage over groups that had only one of the two.

Some time in the late seventeenth or early eighteenth century various Shoshoni-speaking groups began to move southeast from the Rocky Mountains. Precisely when and why is not known (Wallace and Hoebel, 1952; Hagan, 1976). As they acquired horses through trading and raiding, they competed more intensely for access to Plains buffalo-hunting grounds. Comanches first appeared in New Mexico records early in the eighteenth century, by which time they had already mastered the use of the horse. The name "Comanche" is a corruption of a Ute word for "enemy" (Wallace and Hoebel, 1952).

Comanche bands were able to wedge into the area north of Apache-controlled territory and gradually expand at Apache expense for several reasons. Most significant, Apache seasonal agriculture made them easy targets for highly mobile, fully nomadic Comanche groups. While Apache groups were able to slow the acquisition of horses by groups to their north and east, their continual raiding on these groups for captives provoked counter-raids. Spaniards fought with and raided them from the opposite direction. The middle position of the Comanche groups provided them access to French guns, either indirectly through the Pawnee via trade and/or raids or directly as the French sought to penetrate the "Comanche barrier" to gain access to New Mexico. Thus, Apache bands were beleaguered on all sides. Comanches, on the other hand, were able to take advantage of their central position and trade horses and captives east to the French for guns (Secoy, 1953, p. 92; Lowie, 1954). The French were a steady outlet for captives until 1763 when they lost control of Canada (Eccles, 1974, p. 149). They could also trade captives and guns in New Mexico. Indeed, more than once Spaniards traded horses to Comanches at the Taos fair for French guns (Kenner, 1969, p. 38; Moorhead, 1958, pp. 55–56).

The crossing of the horse and gun frontier had dramatic effects on social organization of nearly all groups on or surrounding the Plains (Secoy, 1953; Lowie, 1954). Comanche bands became the "Lords of the South Plains" (Wallace and Hoebel, 1952) and the scourge of New Mexico for much of the eighteenth century. Utes were a lesser threat, since they had a lower level of access to guns. Navajo bands were forced into relative peace during the middle of the eighteenth century (Reeve, 1959) due to the scarcity of guns and the consequent need for Spanish protection from Ute and Comanche raiders.

The intensification of conflict increased the dependence of nomadic groups on European goods. This dependence, in turn, encouraged nomads to produce more buffalo products (primarily hides) and captives to trade for the now necessary goods. The Plains trade was conducted primarily at annual trade fairs held at Pecos and Taos Pueblos, and at other local centers. The goods gained at these fairs, including captives, were a major source of items exchanged in Chihuahua (Kenner, 1969, p. 40). The Plains trade was an economic mainstay of many of northern New Mexican villages (Swadesh, 1974). The trade was so extensive that several drovers ventured across the Mississippi in the eighteenth century to trade for horses that were subsequently delivered to buyers in the American colonies (Bolton, 1929, p. 33).

While the Plains trade was important primarily in the local economy, it did supply some of the goods that were traded to the south, and conversely many southern-supplied goods were used in the Plains trade. As the century progressed, the role of captives in trade changed. In the seventeenth century they were traded to the mining centers in the south; in the eighteenth century they were retained for use in the local economy.

The Feudal Character of New Mexico

Many writers have described the New Mexican economy as feudal (Francis, 1976; Gonzalez, 1969; Lamar, 1970; Meier and Rivera, 1972; Zeleny, 1944, p. 69), but the evidence is weak. Others deny its feudal character (Ríos-Bustamante, 1976b, p. 359) or deny that there were strong class differences (O. Jones, 1979, p. 131). The term "feudal" is seldom used with any historical specificity with respect to New Mexico. It implies a stagnant economy transplanted wholesale from Spain (see Beck, 1962, p. 89), which prompted Ríos-Bustamante's objection to the use of the term.

Land tenure in the Spanish Empire was complicated. There were a variety of landholding practices (Knowlton, 1963, 1967, 1976; Simmons, 1968, 1969; Van Ness, 1979; Mosk, 1942, pp. 36–37; Chevalier, 1963a, 1963b; Brading, 1978; Wolf, 1955). All land was the property of the king (O. Jones, 1979, p. 8), who could, by means of different types of grants, convey ownership. Most important in New Mexico was the community land grant.

> When the grant was awarded, the village site was first laid out with plaza, church site, and residential lots delineated. House sites and irrigation land were distributed by lots. Each member family received a title to its residential site and irrigated land plus the right to graze livestock and to cut timber upon the village commons (Knowlton, 1963, p. 201).[5]

A second type of grant was given to an individual who pledged to attract settlers and supervise the new settlement. "This type of grant was frequently made in areas exposed to Indian raids" (Knowlton, 1963, p. 201). A third type of grant was made to a prominent individual in return for state services. The individual had to settle on the land to acquire hereditary title.

During the various periods of heavy nomadic raiding, village and service grants would be made, abandoned, reopened, regranted, abandoned, and so on. Many settlements were encouraged as buffers to keep raiding nomads from more populated areas (Swadesh, 1974). The histories of such grants are quite complicated (e.g., A. T. Smith, 1976). These types of grants and settlements were most common on the northern frontiers of New Mexico.

Settlements in New Mexico were concentrated in two general areas, in the north around Santa Fe, and 270 miles south around El Paso (O. Jones, 1979, p. 164). The northern area from Socorro to Taos was "divided into the Río Arriba and Río Abajo districts, with the boundary just north of Bernalillo" (O. Jones, 1979, p. 164). Most settlers lived in the Río Abajo and near Santa Fe (O. Jones, 1979, pp. 110–112). The larger estates were concentrated around El Paso or in Río Abajo since north of Bernalillo the Rio Grande narrows, and agriculture is restricted to narrow valleys where there is insufficient land to support large estates. Also, the northern settlements were more subject to raids and competed with Pueblo villages for arable land and trade with Plains nomads.

In addition to geographical differences there are important historical differences. In the first period of Spanish settlement:

> Thirty-five *encomiendas* were made in the seventeenth century, mostly for defensive purposes, since the royal government could not defend the region effectively and there was no presidio in New Mexico until after the Pueblo revolt. *Encomenderos* were permitted to collect tributes in the form of labor, grain crops, or cotton cloth from their Indians, and were obli-

gated to participate with their arms, horses, and Indian subjects in the defense of the realm from the marauding Apaches (O. Jones, 1979, pp. 136–137).

In the seventeenth century a small aristocracy "based upon family ties, service to the crown, and material possessions" (O. Jones, 1979, p. 132) did develop but did not survive the Pueblo Revolt. After the reconquest Vargas was given a personal *encomienda,* but it was never put into operation (O. Jones, 1979, p. 137). Thus, the "feudal tradition" that was transplanted from Spain did not survive the Pueblo Revolt.

The northern region, especially the Río Arriba area, was settled mainly on community grants, which came and went with the tide of nomadic raids. Such settlements could be made only with official permission (O. Jones, 1979, p. 8). Settlers were granted special favors for extending the realm, typically tax exemptions and, on frontiers, the right to possess firearms (O. Jones, 1979, p. 9), but were not allowed to leave their grants without official permission (O. Jones, 1979, p. 147). When raiding increased in the later eighteenth century, the number of vagabonds increased: Indians travelling without passports were subject to lashing; Spaniards to jail terms (O. Jones, 1979, p. 163). There was a general tension on the frontier between the state drive to control the population and to restrict movement—conditions reminiscent of feudalism—and the need to encourage settlement and occupation of the land.

Many of these northern villages served as buffers against the raids of nomads, and were centers for legal and illegal trade with nomadic groups. The membership of these villages was fluid due to the constant raiding. Some settlements were not villages, but small collections of houses spread out over large territory (Simmons, 1969). This was against Spanish policy, but facilitated contraband Plains trade. Scattered settlement both hampered official surveillance and aided the formation of trade partnerships with particular nomadic bands. Small settlements could be easily identified by nomads, thereby avoiding mistaken vengeance raids (Swadesh, 1974, p. 196). Much of this Plains trade took on the aspect of a local division of labor, resembling many systems of trade between nomadic and sedentary peoples (Barth, 1969).

There were two sources of settlers for villages. First were Spanish commoners who wanted their own land. Second were the *genízaros,*[6] detribalized Indians who were drawn from assimilated captives and ostracized Pueblo individuals (Chavez, 1955, 1956, 1979; Horvath, 1977, 1979; Gutierrez, 1980, pp. 108–109). Many young captives were raised by Spanish families and married into the Spanish community. Others, freed at age of majority, remained servants. Still others moved to special communities of *genízaros* (Zeleny, 1944, pp. 31–32). Individual Pueblo residents were sometimes exiled for becoming "overly assimilated into the settler culture" (Swadesh, 1974, p. 23). They, too, joined *genízaro* communities. *Genízaros* readily accepted land grants on the hostile frontiers in return for freedom (Swadesh, 1974, p. 39).

As noted, northern New Spain was significantly different from southern New Spain (Chevalier, 1963b; Edwards, 1982; and Chap. IV). The entrenched "semi-feudal tradition" (Chevalier, 1963b, p. 95) of the northern provinces was constantly undermined by the policy of making village grants to resettle vacant lands (Chevalier, 1963b, p. 103). The constant threat of nomadic raiders required that the peons be armed, which weakened landlord control of the large estates (Chevalier, 1963a, 1963b). The shortage of labor pushed toward debt peonage as a system of labor control, but this was undermined by the relative abundance of arms and ease of exit from any one settlement. The number of frontier settlements made it possible—if dangerous—for individuals to escape obligations by leaving. In New Mexico such villages were typical in the Río Arriba area, while the few estates were in the southern Río Abajo area.

Even the *haciendas* of New Mexico generally were not large, but extended-family dwelling units (Gonzalez, 1969, p. 35; Simmons, 1969). Still, there remained some feudal-like conditions. Labor, while formally free, could not relocate without permission. To become a vagabond on the frontier was to risk the wrath of Spanish officials and hostile nomads. Land shortage was due to the presence of the hostile raiders, who effectively policed the frontier. On the frontier, villages shaded into small freeholdings with some corporate defense obligation to the state. In the central and southern areas of New Mexico conditions more or less approximated feudalism tempered by degree of military activity and local market conditions (Zeleny, 1944, p. 61).[7]

In summary, the term feudal, with due caution, may be applied to seventeenth-century New Mexico. In the eighteenth century it loses salience. Ríos-Bustamante's (1976a, 1976b) point that New Mexico was not static is well taken. There was considerable growth in the province in the eighteenth century. Most of it was due to local natural increase (O. Jones, 1979, p. 130). Vargas brought 100 soldiers and 70 families with him in 1693 (O. Jones, 1979, p. 122). By 1790 the province had a population of about 16,081 Spanish-speaking residents and 9,544 Indians (Tjarks, 1978, pp. 60–61, Table 2). Albuquerque was founded in 1706 with 35 families comprised of 252 individuals. In 1745 the population had grown to 600, and it remained relatively stable until 1776 when it reached 763. By 1790 it had grown to 1,155 (Ríos-Bustamante, 1976b, pp. 363–364, and 380, Table 1), and had a clear hierarchial social structure of landowners and workers (Ríos-Bustamante, 1976b, pp. 379–380). Its social structure was shaped by the ever-present nomadic raiders.

Pressures for Social Change

Pressures for change came from several interrelated sources. The Spanish intentionally used military and diplomatic pressure, and produced stronger, if sometimes unintended, pressures through trade. The French likewise, in the east and north, brought trade pressures. The infusion of horses and guns had dramatic effects, giving rise to the entire Plains warrior complex. Pressures also came from various groups that were displaced by the activities of Europeans further to the east and north. Most significant for New Mexico, though, were the pressures brought by the southward migration of Comanches onto the Plains.

As they moved southward, Comanches steadily displaced other groups before them. Spaniards encouraged Comanche bands to attack Apache groups, in the hope of subjugating or destroying the Apaches. As the century wore on, Apache bands were displaced further and further to the south, where they became a constant irritant in the provinces of Nueva Vizcaya and Sonora (see Map V.5). Comanche bands gradually replaced Apache bands as the most severe threat to the stability of New Mexico. They raided and traded throughout the northern provinces. Comanche movements disrupted intergroup relations and intensified fighting among all groups. The lessons of the Chichimeca Wars had to be relearned in the New Mexican context.

Again Indian "nations" were identified on the basis of linguistic similarity, or shared appellation bestowed by enemies (e.g., "Comanche," or "Navajo"; see Reeve, 1958). Retaliations for the actions of a particular band were directed at entire "nations," insuring further vengeance raids (Swadesh, 1974, p. 25). Reeve (1958, pp. 224–225) attributes this confusion, with regard to Navajos, to "their inchoate political society," rather than Hispanic lack of understanding of the social organization of band societies. Various indigenous leaders, however, did comprehend both the Spanish misunderstanding and the political utility of the knowledge of that misunderstanding. As the century progressed, various band war chiefs learned to deflect blame from themselves by leaving evidence behind that would lead Spaniards to suspect that the raiders were from a different group. This helped keep the frontier in a state of endemic warfare, and to keep a steady supply of captives flowing into the province.

The trade in captives not only insured further vengeance raids, but

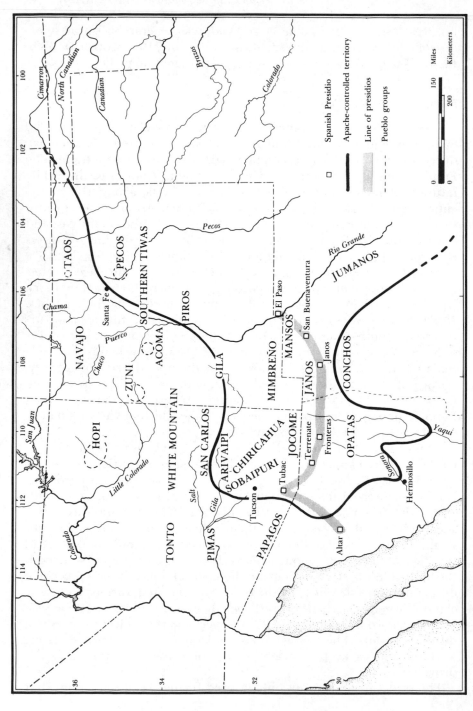

Map V.5. The Apache Corridor, 1700–1886

Spanish Presidio □
Apache-controlled territory ▬
Line of presidios ▨
Pueblo groups ┄

Miles
Kilometers

Source: Spicer (1962:237, Map 15)

augmented the state policy of encouraging war among the "heathen nations." Thus, " . . . relations of peace and trade alternated with periods of intensive raiding and counterraiding. A period of peace with one group often meant a period of warfare with another, since viceregal policies favored keeping the Indians at odds with one another" (Swadesh, 1974, pp. 23–24). These relations were further complicated by the tendency of various frontier communities to form particularistic trading partnerships with specific bands. Swadesh (1974, p. 17) recounts how Abiquiú—a *genízaro* village populated mainly by outcast Pueblos— suffered many raids due to both its own raiding and its extensive and intensive trade relations with several Ute bands. This was not without its benefits for both because the nearby Utes were neither raided, nor did they raid Abiquiú. Such relations were not uncommon, but varied from village to village. Spanish officials, appointed by the viceroy, oriented to the administrative centers in Santa Fe and Mexico City, were blind and insensitive to these local variations. This was due to their ethnocentric attitude toward Indians and settlers, who were viewed as rustic, uncouth and obstinate (Swadesh, 1974, p. 25), and to the villagers' interest in keeping their extensive, but economically necessary, contraband trade out of view of prying officials. Thus, there were many important changes in the organization, adaptation and relations of the various groups occupying the territory.

ETHNIC ORGANIZATION AND RELATIONS IN LATE EIGHTEENTH-CENTURY NEW MEXICO

In addition to discussions about the "feudal" character of Spanish New Mexico there are debates about its similarity to Latin America. Burma (1954, p. 4) asserts that New Mexico was, and remains, "an extension of Latin America into United States territory." Gonzalez (1969) amends this to a comparison with northern Mexico. Knowlton (1961) emphasized the unique, but variable, characteristics of the region. Much of the village study literature tends to take a narrow ethnographic perspective and does not address the character of the region. Van Ness (1979) places the special character of New Mexican Hispanic villages in a wider Latin American context. The appropriate comparison for New Mexican social organization is other regions of refuge (Aguirre Beltran, 1979). Here, there are many similarities: preservation of older forms of social organization, a relative isolation from outside influences, persistence of local ethnic stratification, strong maintenance of indigenous cultures—if in modified form—and a local elite dependent for its power on its position as middlemen between the central state and local citizens (e.g., appointed officials). In these ways New Mexico is very similar to much of Latin America, but only to other Latin American frontiers (Hennessy, 1978; Baretta and Markoff, 1978).

Considerable passing back and forth of individuals between ethnic communities is typical of regions of refuge (Aguirre Beltran, 1979; Collier, 1975). Swadesh (1974, p. 14) reports that Spaniards who deserted the colonies assimilated into various local communities (both nomad and Pueblo). Nomads and Pueblos were absorbed into the Spanish community both through adoption of captive youths, and through gradual absorption of the *genízaro* communities. There were also religious cults that bear a strong resemblance to the saint cults found in other parts of Latin America (Burma, 1954; O. Jones, 1979, p. 147).

Among the lower strata were the *genízaros* who lived in communities made up of "detribalized" Indians—individuals who had been sufficiently assimilated to Spanish life that they could not return to their native societies, but were not yet fully accepted as Spanish (Chavez, 1979; Horvath, 1977, 1979). These communities were frontier buffers between the Spaniards and nomadic bands. They also served as middlemen in trade. Their more successful members married and assimilated into the Spanish community (Swadesh, 1974). Their communities were spatially and ethnically transitional between the various Indian societies and Spanish society.

Pueblo societies in the eighteenth century established a symbiotic relationship with their Spanish conquerors (Gonzalez, 1969, p. 37; Zeleny, 1944, p. 69; O. Jones, 1966). There was extensive cooperation regarding defense and trade. There were even some intermarriage and godparent (*compadrazgo*) relations between the Spanish and Pueblo communities (Swadesh, 1974, p. 22). Pueblo societies maintained their cultural distinctiveness by ostracizing their more assimilated members who then were absorbed either directly into the Spanish community, or more typically, indirectly after a few generations' sojourn in *genízaro* communities (Spicer, 1962, p. 493). At the same time Pueblo societies became increasingly resistant to outside cultural influences. Pueblo societies were able to absorb new ideas and practices and to keep their ceremonial system "pure" by a process of "compartmentalization," which served to keep native and Spanish ceremonial systems isolated (Dozier, 1961, pp. 150–151, 175–178; 1970a, pp. 24–25). Compartmentalization was fully in place by the latter part of the eighteenth century, but its roots are found in seventeenth-century Spanish attempts to suppress Pueblo traditions, especially religious practices. This same mechanism was also a major source of the celebrated demographic and cultural stability of Pueblo societies (Swadesh, 1974, p. 52; Zubrow, 1974).

Of the four major groups of nomads surrounding the sedentary population—Utes, Navajos, Comanches, and Apaches—the latter two were most troublesome during the eighteenth century. Utes and Navajos played minor roles. Ute bands formed symbiotic relationships with some of the northern villages (Swadesh, 1974), due in some cases to the intense competition and fighting with Comanches, and some Apaches, over access to buffalo-hunting grounds and horses. Like other groups, they were transformed by acquisition of horses. Bands were made more mobile, more fluid in organization, more dependent on hunting buffalo, and increased their level of raiding with the acquisition of horses. Utes were frequently used against Apaches, Comanches and Navajos.

Knowledge of Navajo organization is scant for the eighteenth century due to their remote location and the lack of clear distinction from Apache bands. The blurry line between Apaches and Navajos reflects both limited Spanish understanding of local ethnic structure (Reeve, 1956), and to some extent, less than total separation of Navajo bands from linguistically related Apache bands. During the time between the Pueblo Revolt and the reconquest, many Pueblo leaders fled to live among various Navajo groups (Forbes, 1960). The use of Navajo territory as refuge in times of danger persisted into the eighteenth century. During this time the Navajo acquired horses, and more importantly sheep, which formed the basis of a pastoral society and economy that developed among the Navajo. The shift to sheep pastoralism pushed the Navajo bands into increasing quasi-symbiotic relations with the Spanish community (Reeve, 1958, 1959). As their flocks increased, the need to raid Hispanic communities decreased, but their need for protection from raiding Utes, Comanches, and others increased. Navajos were more strongly affected by the fighting than were Spaniards since many Navajos were taken captive.

Comanche and Apache bands suffered the most dramatic effects of fighting. The Comanche bands came to dominate the southern Plains where they adapted successfully to buffalo hunting as a primary means of subsistence (Wallace and Hoebel, 1952). Living in a large, flat, relatively undifferentiated territory, they developed great skill at rapid movement, and a tremendous ability to disband and reassemble in a short time. They were able to congregate in large numbers when the occasion warranted, although they typically lived in small, dispersed settlements. Like many large game hunters they were very nomadic, seldom staying in one spot for a long time. Thus they were very difficult to locate and attack, but highly skillful at hit-and-run raids. Leadership was typical band "big man" leadership, with a separation between peace chiefs and war-party leaders. The latter held authority only over those warriors who chose to accompany the raiding party, and then only for the duration of the raid (Wallace and Hoebel, 1952). Successful adaptation to buffalo hunting and raiding enabled them to displace competitors. Their central position at the nexus of the horse and gun frontiers gave them the advantage of both these new goods to maximize their own territory and to develop trading relations with the groups surrounding them (Secoy, 1953). They built and maintained extensive trading connections in New Mexico, and to a lesser extent, with the French and with other more easterly Plains dwellers. Their effects on New Mexico were dramatic (Kenner, 1969).

Comanche bands caused significant alterations in the organization and settlement patterns of Pueblo societies, New Mexicans, and Apache bands. They threatened and ultimately caused the abandonment of several Pueblo villages (Schroeder, 1968, 1979c) in their constant retaliatory raids for trading with Apaches. They were a major source of trade goods, and yet were also major raiders. They caused many outlying settlements to retreat toward Santa Fe. Their most important effect, though, in this era, was the displacement and transformation of Apache bands.

Apaches were in constant retreat from the Comanche onslaught. This situation was exacerbated by the consistent Spanish policy of encouraging Comanche attacks on Apaches and a ready willingness to buy Apache captives. Those Apaches who had either practiced horticulture aboriginally or had adopted it later were forced to abandon the practice because of constant Comanche attacks. Earlier, when Apache groups were at the top of the Indian horse gradient on the Plains, seasonal horticultural villages facilitated the formation of large raiding groups and promoted supra-band leadership (Secoy, 1953, p. 92). After Comanches obtained guns, seasonal horticulture became a liability (Secoy, 1953, p. 88). Even seasonal sedentary villages were easy targets for the highly mobile, fluidly organized Comanches. Furthermore, Comanches came to form a barrier between Apache groups and both Spanish and French traders, hindering Apache access to horses and guns. As Apache bands were displaced southward, they were moved further and further from the Plains, and concentrated more in the highly diversified Basin and Range Province.

In that environment ecological pressures pushed to make bands smaller, and forced a more crucial foraging existence. The prime "game" of Apache hunters became Spanish horses and cattle (Worcester, 1979).

Indeed, the natural carrying capacity of the environment in the southern territories could not have supported the Apache population by hunting and gathering alone. Supplement was required. Apaches adapted well and developed an efficient raiding mode of production. This had been developing from first Spanish contact, but was pushed to full efflorescence by Comanche pressure. It is estimated that as early as 1693 one Apache band had stolen upward of one hundred thousand horses in Sonora (Worcester, 1979, p. 14). Because of the number of Apache captives taken or bought by Spaniards, Apaches reserved a special hatred for them. In the early part of the eighteenth century, raiding escalated, several missions were destroyed and several promising mines in what is now southern Arizona were abandoned.

As with Ute bands, various Apache bands would maintain peaceful trading relations with specific villages or regions. These arrangements would bring peace to one Spanish village at the expense of others.[8] A pattern of raiding and taking captives and loot in one region and selling them to Spanish settlers in another region developed. Although Apache bands seemed to be less successful than Comanches, they adapted so successfully to their territory that they became the scourge of northern New Spain. Apaches contributed to the contraction of the sphere of Pueblo occupation, and caused the abandonment of Piro and Tompiro Pueblos (John, 1975; Schroeder, 1968, 1979c). Still, the retreat of Apaches under Comanche pressure continued.

CONCLUSIONS, QUESTIONS, SPECULATIONS

While the detailed mechanisms are at times obscure, changes in the wider "world-system" had important impacts on the Southwest, both directly and indirectly through the Spanish Empire as illustrated by the reasons for initial colonization, and subsequent recolonization of New Mexico. It was originally colonized in pursuit of a "new Mexico" containing riches, converts, and personal fortunes, and in fear that the British might find the northwest passage first. The colony was maintained primarily for religious purposes, and later in the seventeenth century, to preempt French claims to the interior of North America. These same factors, albeit in a different mix, plus wounded Hispanic pride, led to the recolonization of the province after the Pueblo Revolt. The concern with foreign claims was shaped largely by the politics of Europe and the effort to protect the mines of northern Mexico. Whether seventeenth century Mexican silver contributed to or delayed a problematic decline in Spain or New Spain (Kamen, 1978, 1981, 1982; TePaske and Klein,

1981, 1982; Israel, 1981, 1982), those responsible for policy decisions considered the silver vital to the well-being of the state. Whether their decisions were reasonable, and whether their information was correct are questions that will probably remain unanswered. Nevertheless, the fiscal concerns of the Empire and the viceroy, and the complicated politics of New Spain (Israel, 1975) played significant roles in decisions concerning the administration of New Mexico.

During the seventeenth century the mixed motives of salvation and preemptive control set the conditions for a precarious balance of power between church and state within the province. Since only one missionary order occupied the area, the state could not manipulate internal factionalism within the church. The governor, physically and psychologically far from the capital in Mexico, had no natural allies in the province and was too isolated to use his connections effectively. Furthermore, the general poverty of the province forced him to augment his salary in ways that conflicted either with church interests or settler interests, or in some cases both.

The perennial viceregal concern with the cost of the province meant that it was chronically underfunded, especially in times when either New Spain or the entire Empire was under pressure elsewhere. The state never really used its muscle to tip the balance of power within the province toward the governor. Thus, seventeenth-century New Mexico has aptly been called "troublous times" by Scholes (1937–1940). While the Spaniards learned some expensive lessons, the effects on the various Indian groups and their inter-relations were more profound (Schroeder, 1968, 1979c).

In the first phase of colonization, the *encomendero* system created a feudal structure in New Mexico. The *encomenderos* were able to use Pueblo villages as tributary dependencies. In return for the tribute, they were required to defend the region. As horses spread to surrounding nomads this defense became increasingly vital, if inadequate. Because the *encomenderos* owned neither the land nor the inhabitants, the social system was not feudal in the classic sense. The trade that occurred was directed at consumption, not capital accumulation. Hence, the social structure was feudal in a vital sense (see Banaji, 1976). After the reconquest the state tried a different strategy, employing permanent troops, though not in sufficient numbers. This effectively destroyed the base for recreating a feudal structure, but insured a state of endemic warfare, since fiscal concerns kept the province perpetually underfunded and short of soldiers. New Mexico was clearly dependent on New Spain for maintenance. Even after the reconquest when growth was largely endog-

enous, supplies and governmental, military, and fiscal support were vital
to the maintenance of the colony.

Changes among the indigenous societies were even more dramatic. As
Apache bands and other groups acquired horses the nature of nomadic
social structure and interrelations changed. The Plains became a viable
habitat. Buffalo could now be hunted with considerable success, and the
Spaniards were a ready market for surplus hides. Plains Apache groups
combined into larger living units based on seasonal horticulture and
buffalo hunting. Occasional exchanges of captives became a steady flow.
Later, Ute, Navajo, and Comanche bands obtained horses. The crossing
of the horse and gun frontiers enabled Comanches to develop a very
fluid social structure adapted to effective raiding. The shift to reliance
on the buffalo, raiding and trading enabled them to displace the seasonally sedentary Apache. This forced Apache groups to disperse, become
smaller and generally abandon horticulture. Navajo and Ute bands were
similarly kept from full access to the Plains.

The impact of the Spaniards on the Pueblo societies was also dramatic,
but significantly different. There was a general population decline as
disease took its usual toll. Pressure to consolidate villages was offset by
fear of producing large centers of population. Tribute and trade introduced many technological innovations and new social relations to Pueblo
societies. The constant pressure to adopt Spanish religion increased
Pueblo secrecy concerning spiritual practices, a tendency that remains
strong today.

In the eighteenth century, Pueblo societies were increasingly forced
into a symbiotic relationship with the Spaniards. Because captives could
be traded for guns in the east and there were sufficient horses on the
Plains to reproduce without imports from Mexico, Plains competition
and warfare did not stop, while raids on the sedentary groups surrounding the Plains continued. The role of the outlying Pueblo villages as
trade centers for the various Plains groups increased. Their level of
interaction with surrounding nomads, whether for trade or for raiding,
was greatly increased.

All groups, nomadic societies, Pueblo societies, and Spanish colonists,
were trapped by the need for trade both with Mexico and with their
neighbors. Inadequate funding kept warfare endemic, which in turn
made two types of habitation viable: large centers capable of defending
themselves against raiders, and small, relatively isolated settlements that
facilitated participation in the contraband Plains trade.

Despite the endemic warfare the province grew in fits and starts.
Thus, any two "snapshots" of New Mexico bear a strong superficial

resemblance, giving an illusion of stagnation or chaos which made it all too easy for invading Americans, and some historians, to describe New Mexico as backward.

Still, many issues remain problematic. How varied were the social classes? How closely were spurts in growth associated with either relative lulls in the nomadic raids or with changes in Mexico or the Empire? How and when were villages founded and abandoned? What were the relative densities of the various types of living arrangements, and who lived where? How much and how important was the trade with Mexico, to Mexico and to New Mexico? How centralized and/or dispersed were the various band societies at different times? How large were their living groups? How did they vary by season? How much planting did they do? Some of these questions will remain unanswered. A few may be unanswerable. But for some, outlines of answers are sketched in the following chapter.

NOTES

1.   Herbert E. Bolton was one of the first to put the northern borderlands, from Florida to California, in an international perspective (1929). Bannon (1964, pp. 3–19) summarizes Bolton's life work (1964) and Spanish expansion into "the borderlands" (1974). O. Jones (1979) provides a detailed account of the settlements of northern New Spain. John (1975) and Forbes (1960) give thorough accounts of Spanish–Indian relations through the end of the eighteenth century. France Scholes, writing mainly in the *New Mexico Historical Review* (1930, 1932, 1935a, 1935b, 1936–1937, 1937–1940), is the classic source on the seventeenth-century history of New Mexico. Garner (1974) criticizes Scholes for uncritical acceptance of seventeenth-century documents and Forbes for being strongly anti-Spanish. Israel's account (1975) of central New Spain provides valuable background to events in New Mexico. Sando (1979, pp. 194–197; 1982) gives an Indian interpretation of the history of New Mexico. Spicer (1962), Beck (1962) and Lavender (1980) provide general histories of New Mexico and the Southwest. Kessell (1979) tells the story of the Southwest from the perspective of Pecos Pueblo. Dunbar Ortiz (1974, 1980) concentrates on land tenure systems.

2.   Bannon (1974, p. 240, note 7) summarizes the controversial literature on the de Niza report. Undreiner (1947) provides a systematic and sympathetic analysis of it.

3.   This account is based on the following sources: Bannon (1974, pp. 80–86), Beck (1962, p. 74ff), Chavez (1967), Dozier (1970a, p. 55ff), Dunbar Ortiz (1980, pp. 35–38), Forbes (1960, Ch. VIII), Garner (1974), Hackett (1937, 1942), John (1975, pp. 97–105), Reeve (1957), Sando (1979), Silverberg (1970), Simmons (1979), and Spicer (1962, pp. 152–169).

4.   Scholes (1935a, p. 96) estimates Spanish population at less than 2,500. Garner (1974, p. 61) estimates it at about 2,800. Spicer (1962, p. 162) estimates Pueblo population in the villages of the Rio Grande drainage at between 25,000

and 30,000. Garner (1974) discounts such high estimates since church records show 16,000 and the Santa Fe *cabildo* estimated 17,000 Pueblo Indians. If the area is restricted to the near Rio Grande Valley, then 16,000 seems reasonable.

5. Knowlton's works focus on the late nineteenth and early twentieth centuries, yet these distinctions are widely used. After the manuscript for this book was completed, an excellent summary of northern New Mexican land grant practices appeared. See Briggs and Van Ness (1987), especially Chapters 1 and 2.

6. *Genízaro* refers to a detribalized Indian, generally nominally christianized, living under Spanish control. Various authors attempt to restrict the meaning to only one of the various sub-types. I use the term in a general sense.

7. O. Jones (1979), Algier (1966), and Van Ness (1979) all underscore extreme regional variability in village organization, which remains an obstacle to generalization.

8. The lack of documentation is only in part an artifact of preservation. Long experience had taught villagers to be suspicious of officials who promised to end raids. Hence few records of such relations were kept.

CHAPTER VI

Frontier Peace:
Policies and Strategies
of Pacification in the Last Years
of Spanish Control

In view of the destruction wrought on the more densely populated and inaccessible interior provinces, it might be but little exaggeration to conclude that had there been no Comanche peace in New Mexico, there might have been no New Mexico (Charles Kenner, 1969, p. 77).

Without the military assistance of the Comanches, Ugarte could never have accomplished his remarkable, although temporary, pacification of most of the Apache tribes (Max Moorhead, 1968, p. 169).

The quality of ethnic relations changed drastically in northern New Spain with the Bourbon reforms, the establishment of the intendency system and the organization of the *Provincias Internas* (see Map VI.1).[1] These changes began to affect the Spanish frontier with the work of the *Visitador General,* José de Gálvez, and the military inspection of Marqués de Rubí in 1765. Their recommendations led to the establishment of a lasting peace with Comanches in New Mexico under Governor Anza in 1786, and a subsequent, if more precarious, peace with most Apache bands under Commandant General Ugarte. The relative peace, which prevailed until approximately the turn of the nineteenth century, led to important changes in ethnic relations. This chapter examines the regional structures and processes that led to the frontier peace, and their important consequences for the social organizations of various indigenous groups.

110

Map VI.1. The Provincias Internas of New Spain

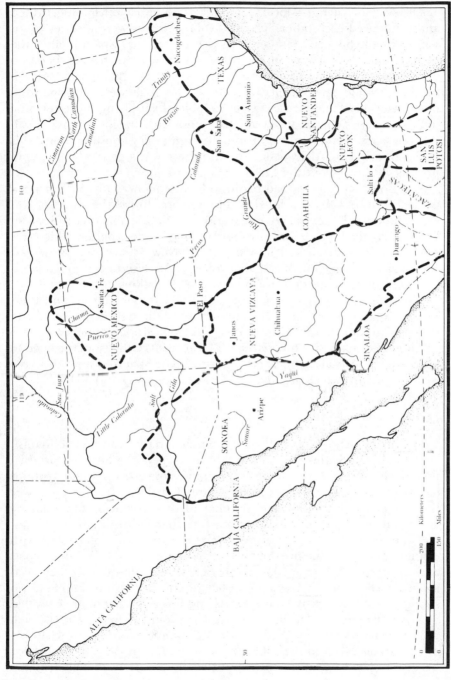

Sources: John (1975:490–491), Nasatir (1976:147), Meyer and Sherman (1979:259), Simmons (1968)

All levels of change—local, regional, state and global—intertwined and influenced each other. The Bourbon reforms were a series of attempts by the Spanish state and the viceroys of New Spain to alter the political and economic relations within the frontier provinces: between the frontier and the administrative center of New Spain, and between the Empire and Spain itself. In general, the goals were to organize a more centralized and efficient state capable of supplying more revenue to Spain. Part of that goal was to curb, if not stop, the loss of revenue in frontier wars. Tempered by various foreign policy considerations, this goal was at least partially achieved, and there was a general increase in prosperity throughout the Empire (Lang, 1975).

The Bourbon reforms had profound consequences for the northern provinces, especially New Mexico. The relationship of the entire northern frontier to the central administrations of New Spain and the Spanish Empire changed. Peace and prosperity came to the frontier, which was more tightly incorporated into the state. New Mexico, in particular, became a more dependent region of refuge. Analysis of these changes is crucial to understanding subsequent transformations of the region.

The chapter begins with a description of frontier policies and their implementation strategies. The interactions of these strategies both with the trade in Indian captives and with the ecological adaptations of various groups are examined. This analysis of local events establishes the need to articulate these local changes with changes in the Spanish Empire and the world-economy, which are discussed in Chapters VII and VIII.

POLICY GOALS[2]

Three major factors shaped the Indian policy in the last years of Spanish control of New Spain. First was the drive for peace to facilitate production of revenues from the region. Second was the attempt to use frontier bands as buffers against foreign intrusion. Third was the effort to lower the cost of administration and defense of the provinces. The mixture and relative weights of these three factors changed throughout the last half century of Spanish control with changes in world politics and with changes internal to the provinces. The resultant policy varied in its goals and processes. Three major strategies were continuously balanced against each other. First was the policy of enticing groups into Spanish subjugation by means of assorted gifts and favors—what might be called Spanish "tribute" or "bribery" to Indian groups (Chapa, 1981). Such gifts were used to engender dependency upon Spaniards for the supply of various necessary or desirable items. Second, a divide-and-conquer or balance-of-power strategy was modified by a variety of alliances designed to pit one group, acting as Spanish auxiliaries, against other hostile groups. Finally, there was considerable pressure on various groups to form more centralized political structures. This began a process of building clear identities and clear political organizations from groups of associated bands. All of these strategies were implemented in differing ways, with differing results, against the various Indian groups in the Southwest.[3]

While the success of the peace policy was less than total, under governors Anza (1778–1788) and Concha (1788–1794) "mines opened, ranches dotted the landscape, and a lively profitable trade emerged among the peoples of New Mexico" (August, 1981, p. 142). The Hispanic population of New Mexico grew from 21,000 in 1786 to 34,000 in 1793 (O. Jones, 1979, pp. 125–129; Ríos-Bustamante, 1976a, 1976b; Aragon, 1976). From 1790 until 1830 Sonora and Arizona experienced "an unparalleled era of peace and prosperity" (Worcester, 1979, p. 33; Voss, 1982, Ch. 1). From 1790 through 1810, the entire northern frontier "enjoyed considerable respite from hostilities and an opportunity to develop economically" (Moorhead, 1968, p. 289). During this time several trails were blazed connecting Louisiana with Texas and New Mexico, (John, 1975) and New Mexico with Sonora and the Californias (Moorhead, 1968, p. 278).

Peaceful relations with the various bands contributed to, and grew out of, foreign policy considerations. When Governor Anza made peace with Comanches in 1786, one of the conditions was the exclusion of all non-Hispanic Europeans from the eastern Comanche settlements (Moorhead, 1968, p. 144). Comanche friendship was considered essential for the Spanish to arrive at the territorial headwaters of the Missouri before the British (John, 1975, p. 512). Comanches were being forced into closer contact with New Mexico and Texas throughout this time. The end of the French and Indian War (1754–1763) caused many pro-French Indians to move onto the Plains, eliminating the supply of French trade goods from the north and east. Thus Comanches had fewer supplies, and faced more competition from Osages and Pawnees. After the American Revolution, formerly pro-British Indians were displaced across the Mississippi, putting further pressure on the Plains (John, 1975, p. 590–591; Secoy, 1953, Ch. VII). In 1806 fear of American invasion of Texas led to a massing of Spanish troops on the eastern border of that province. Large numbers of escaped slaves and American deserters crossed the Mississippi to Arkansas. A territory of neutral ground was established in eastern Texas. This area was filled with "criminals, robbers, and smugglers—who raided and robbed in both provinces" (Faulk, 1964, p. 125). Thus, the requirement that Comanches deal exclusively with Spaniards, converted them into a particularly fear-some border patrol.

Fiscal considerations shaped Indian policies. The cost of warfare caused Commandant General Croix to consider a policy of conciliation over a policy of war (August, 1981, p. 142). Cost considerations kept the presidios small and few. Supply contracts were important economic prizes. Requests for more men or supplies were routinely reduced or denied. Indeed, the entire reorganization of the presidio system had been done in an effort to cut the costs of frontier defense (Simmons, 1968, Ch. III; Voss, 1982, Ch. 1; Moorhead, 1975a, Pt.I). The old Span-ish custom of requiring soldiers to supply their own equipment (Sim-mons, 1968, p. 139), combined with insufficient funding of military operations, encouraged the taking and selling of captives. A soldier could not marry without permission and proof of ability to support a family independent of his pay (Simmons, 1968, p. 123). This, too, pro-moted corruption within the supply system. The combination of contra-band trade in supplies and captives was counterproductive to the intent of reducing the cost of frontier administration. These practices virtually guaranteed continual renewal of the cycle of fighting. The net effect of the various economizing moves was to hamper the peace policy, to limit economic development of the region, and to preserve much of its char-acter as a region of refuge. Still, the region did experience some devel-opment, and did become more closely tied to, and more dependent on, New Spain. These changes made New Mexico significantly, if not dra-matically, less a region of refuge, and more a periphery of New Spain.

STRATEGIES OF PACIFICATION

Induced Dependency

Two separate but complementary funds supported the efforts to in-duce dependency: the *fondo de aliados* and the *fondo de gratificación*. The *fondo de aliados* (fund for allies) was a special fund to supply gifts and rations to Indian allies. The *fondo de aliados* was sometimes called the *fondo de paz y guerra* (fund for peace and war). The *fondo de gratificación* was an officer's reserve fund for a military unit which was "a catch-all fund to provide for any financial crises arising during the course of the year" (Simmons, 1968, p. 143). As a supplement to the *fondo de aliados,* it was used to supply gifts and rations to peaceful nomads during negotia-tions. The two separate funds were frequently used for the same pur-poses. The *fondo de gratificación* amounted to approximately 500 pesos annually. The *fondo de aliados* amounted to approximately 2,000 pesos annually. It continued into the Mexican era. This fund was explicitly designed to engender dependency:

> The interest in commerce binds and narrows the desires of man; and it is my wish to establish trade with the Indians. . . . They should be made accustomed to the use of our foods, drinks, arms, and clothing, and they should become greedy for the possession of land. Even if in the beginning we are not successful in achieving these ends, as they require much time, this course will put us on the path to eventual success (Viceroy Bernardo de Gálvez in Worcester, 1951, p. 42).

In 1779 the Crown had directed Commandant General Croix to follow this policy over a war of subjugation. It was even directed that the Apaches "be given firearms for their hunting and defense, in the hope that they would lose their skills with their aboriginal weapons and thus be subject to control by the simple expedient of cutting off their gunpowder when necessary" (John, 1975, p. 530). Commandant General Croix objected since he knew from field experience that some Apache bands could manufacture gunpowder (John, 1975, p. 530). When Spain declared war on Britain in 1779, funds and military hardware for that conflict had the highest priority, and the dependency strategy became dominant.

Dependency was encouraged in other ways. Commandant General Ugarte hoped to convince Comanches to become farmers, dependent on crops—and Spaniards (Moorhead, 1968, p. 153). In 1787 a portion of the Jupes band of Comanches petitioned Governor Anza to construct a farming settlement for them. Built at an expense of 691 pesos, it was occupied for four months. When the wife of a prominent man died, the village was abandoned in accord with Comanche custom (Moorhead, 1968, pp. 161–163). When climatic conditions brought about an extended drought on the Plains at this same time, other Comanche bands were forced to give up raiding Apaches and to petition in Santa Fe for rations. Governor Concha used government funds and donations from citizens of Santa Fe to supply corn and other food (August, 1981). The dependency, however, cut both ways. Annual expenditures of up to 4,000 pesos were also a major stimulant to the local New Mexican economy which supplied the bulk of the goods for Indian "gifts" (Simmons, 1968, p. 147).

Divide and Conquer and the Formation of Alliances

The policy of dependency was augmented by a concerted Spanish effort to form alliances with some nomadic groups against others. The

Jack August

divide-and-conquer strategy was an explicit policy (called a "balance-of-power" strategy by August [1981]). In some cases Spaniards initiated conflicts, but more typically they capitalized on existing rivalries, or put to good use the cycles of revenge fueled by the use of Indian auxiliaries in their campaigns. The divide-and-conquer strategy, like the induced-dependency strategy, resulted in part from the Spanish commitment of arms, men and money to the war with Britain in 1779. This approach was to remain a key strategy in Spanish dealings with frontier problems.

Viceroy Gálvez (1785–1786) preferred to try to settle the Apaches, and to use dependency to stop their raiding. The push toward dependency could be furthered by constant pressure from other tribes attacking Apaches (Worcester, 1979, p. 23). On the frontier, Commandant General Ugarte argued that allies among other nomads were necessary to subdue hostile Apaches. Spanish soldiers could not track and defeat Apache raiders. Nomadic allies, primarily Comanches, were far more successful and efficient in inflicting casualties on Apaches (Moorhead, 1968, p. 273). Commandant General Ugarte required Apache bands who asked for peace to take to the field against other Apache bands who remained hostile. This strategy remained in force throughout the *Provincias Internas*. Commandant General Pedro de Nava (1792–1800) wrote to Governor Muñoz of Texas on May 4, 1796:

> One of the maxims that should always be observed on our part, with respect to the nations of Indians, is to allow them to make reciprocal war on each other in order in this way to bring about a diminuation of their forces, to energize their mutual hatreds, and to avoid their union and alliance; we should, however, take the lead in keeping them constantly in our friendship and in our debt (cited in Faulk, 1964, p. 68).

Four general types of Indian allies were involved in the fighting in the last years of Spanish control. Scouts and interpreters were drawn from the *genízaro* population. They were granted the privilege of bearing particular arms, and were supplied with mounts at the expense of the royal treasury (Simmons, 1968, p. 130). Pueblo Indian units, *genízaro* units, and nomadic bands made up the other three types of allied fighters. By the early nineteenth century both the Pueblo Indians and *genízaros* were organized as separate units (Horvath, 1977, 1979; O. Jones, 1966). According to O. Jones (1966) the continual use of Pueblo auxiliary units after the reconquest led to mutual dependence, and facilitated Pueblo assimilation to Hispanic culture. In 1808 *genízaros* no longer served as members of the Hispanic militia, but under their own commanders. These units were highly regarded; "because of their warlike nature, they proved formidable soldiers in battle and were useful as scouts and interpreters since they held little fear of the savage plains tribes" (Simmons, 1968, p. 151).

At the time when *genízaros* were forming their own units, the Pueblo Indians became less and less auxiliaries, and more and more part of the general citizenry subject to militia service. Pueblo Indians had long been used by Spaniards as auxiliaries,[4] but their organization as separate units under their own war leaders was a new development in the early nineteenth century (O. Jones, 1966). This marked the beginning of the acceptance of Pueblo Indians as citizens in a broader sense.

Nomadic fighters, on the other hand, were always classified as auxiliaries. They were valuable, and frequently necessary, allies, but always somewhat suspect and in need of close supervision. Apaches, Utes, Navajos and Comanches all played auxiliary roles at one time or another. They were most effective when they were enlisted against one or another traditional enemy. On some occasions auxiliaries were recruited both to present a united front to an enemy and to keep nomadic warriors under close surveillance (Simmons, 1968, p. 155). Thus, after about 1790 the term "auxiliary" generally refers to nomadic allies, while Pueblo and *genízaro* troops are designated by name. These alliances began with the development of the Comanche peace.

Comanche Peace.[5] In the late 1770s and early 1780s, Governor Anza succeeded in delivering several severe blows to Comanche enemies and then forging a diplomatic alliance with them. He proceeded to reconcile the various Comanche bands with their traditional Ute enemies and persuaded both Utes and Comanches to ally with Spaniards against Navajos. This severe pressure on Navajo bands broke up their brief (fifteen year) alliance with the Gila Apaches. Navajos were subsequently enlisted in campaigns against their erstwhile allies. By 1786 the Spanish involvement in the American Revolution had ended and new and better weapons began to reach the frontier (August, 1981, pp. 142–143). The Jicarilla Apaches, caught between Comanches, Utes, and Spaniards, were forced into alliance with the Spaniards to safeguard their survival (August, 1981, p. 149). The possibility of peace on the frontier now appeared realistic. These conditions coincided with the reorganization of the *Provincias Internas* and the appointment of Bernardo de Gálvez as viceroy over Governor Concha of New Mexico and Commandant General Ugarte. The perennially troublesome Apaches were pursued with the aid of the nomadic allies, especially Comanches.

The high esteem in which the Spaniards held Comanches provoked jealousies on the part of other allies, especially Utes and Jicarilla Apaches. These two frequently combined to raid Comanche camps. Governor Concha maintained the frontier peace by reminding all that continued Spanish favor rested on peace among all of the king's allies. He threatened to withhold gifts and rations and to wage war against those who broke the peace. He also played the role of mediator in cases of intergroup raiding, and thus was able to hold the alliance together (August, 1981; John, 1975). The combined pressures of the new alliances began to bear fruit as early as 1781 when some Apache bands began to ask for peace (August, 1981, p. 153).

✘ *Apache Peace.*   Apache attempts at peace caused difficulty for the Spaniards among their allies. Comanches wanted no part of an Apache peace, for they held all Apache bands as implacable, permanent enemies. Comanches were still expanding onto the south Plains, and had no interest in allowing competitors to hunt buffalo (Secoy, 1953). This animosity endangered the entire alliance system in Texas several times (John, 1975, Ch.19,20). Commandant General Ugarte forbade peace treaties with eastern Apaches in New Mexico, although they were at peace in Texas and Coahuila (Moorhead, 1968, p. 161). At first Viceroy Flores (1787–1789) approved, but then reversed his policy and instructed Governor Concha and Commandant General Ugarte to accept Apache peace overtures, but with severe restrictions. For a time, several Apache bands maintained the peace.

Ugarte was able to regroup them in smaller territory, and begin introducing farming techniques, by means of *establecimientos de paz* (peace establishments). This approach worked for a number of years, and reached its peak in the mid-1790s. At least two factors contributed to the decline in its effectiveness. One was the refusal to accept any new rancherias (extended families) of Apaches at existing *establecimientos de paz* in the mid-1790s. This decision was an attempt to balance risks of raiding with the costs of peace by subsidy. Apaches who surrendered were ordered to return to their home territory and keep the peace. This lowered the cost of rations (Griffen, 1983c, n.d.).

Another factor in this decline was the precarious nature of the band-by-band peace agreements with Apaches. Viceroy Flores was in fact quite suspicious of Apache bands who requested peace. They frequently sought peace as means of respite from the attacks of their enemies, especially Comanches. Other short-term goals of peace were access to Spanish trade goods, food rations when game was scarce and information on troop movements against kinsmen (Moorhead, 1963, p. 275). Commandant General Ugarte, nonetheless, held that such temporary peace was preferable, for peace allowed dependency on Spaniards to develop. The combination of dependency and alliances was vital to the relative success of frontier pacification (Moorhead, 1968, p. 169), but it could backfire. Simmons (1968, p. 155) reports that various nomadic groups would attach themselves to Spanish expeditions either in times of need, or to be in a better position to supply themselves with desired goods by theft. Thus, peace and raiding were alternative Indian strategies for obtaining desired goods. In general, exigencies of the moment dictated choice of strategy.

Three major sets of factors contributed to the propensity of Comanches to choose peace and Apaches to choose raiding. First was the effect of centralization. Second, trade in captives continued to play a significant role in the frontier economy. Third, the groups occupied different ecological niches (in both social and biological senses). Political centralization cross-cut the other strategies.

Political Centralization and the Formation of Tribes

Spanish administrators had considerable trouble understanding and dealing with band societies, but some frontier officials, such as governors Anza and Concha or Commandant General Ugarte, were particularly adept at it. But even for astute frontier diplomats the fluidity of band organization created problems. In much of the historical literature a collection of linguistically related bands is referred to as a "nation" or "tribe," giving a false sense of a unified polity.

Groups in which leadership and boundaries change easily, and often without benefit of institutionalized markers, do not mesh well with bureaucratic organizations. Spanish officials attempted to institutionalize leadership by giving staffs of office, medals and other insignia to Indian leaders big men), to mark them as official vassals of the Spanish king (John, 1975; Powell, 1952; Forbes, 1960; Moorhead, 1968). They also tried to combine bands into larger groups. *Reducción* (literally, "reduction," meaning sedentarization), as noted earlier, did not work on the northern frontier. Nomadic foragers were more difficult than semi-nomadic horticulturalists to convert into farmers. Furthermore, frontier location kept the possibility of flight to the hinterlands a viable option for restless nomads.

Officials constantly sought leaders with whom to negotiate (Swadesh, 1974, p. 25), creating pressures for political centralization. This pressure was applied, discontinuously and with varied results, to all frontier nomadic groups: Apaches, Comanches, Navajos and Utes. It was even applied, with mild success, in California (Phillips, 1975). In Sonora and Sinaloa the policy was successful when applied to the horticultural Yaqui and Mayo Indians, who became centralized tribes and formidable adversaries for the Spanish (Voss, 1982, Chs.2,3; Spicer, 1962).

The pressure to centralize is illustrated by the treatment of Lipan

Apaches who requested peace of Governor Cabello of Texas in 1778. Lipan Apaches were being hounded by both Comanches and "Nations of the North," or *Norteños*.[6] Cabello required that "the Lipans must choose among themselves one great chief whom all would obey, because it was not good that so many chiefs had to be dealt with. Cabello would give the cane to the man of their choice and name him Great Chief of all the Lipans" (John, 1975, p. 550). When four Lipan chiefs (big men) appeared and requested that the governor select a paramount chief, he refused. He required that their chief be elected by all members of the group, not only those camped nearby. These terms were agreed to by the four Lipan leaders, but never completed.

Pressure for political centralization was applied most consistently and forcefully to Comanche organization (August, 1981; John, 1975, Chs. 19, 20, 21; Moorhead, 1968, Ch. VII; Simmons, 1967). Comanche raiding increased while Spain was preoccupied with the American Revolution. Comanches gained the upper hand in both Texas and New Mexico in the early 1780s. With peace in 1783 the commandant general (first Croix, then Philipe de Neve as commandant general *ad interim*) succeeded in persuading the *Norteños* in Texas to apply considerable pressure on the Comanches, who were cut off from Louisiana trade and subjected to severe losses. In New Mexico all trade with Comanches was banned. By 1785 many Comanches and their leaders were arriving in both Taos and San Antonio seeking peace. Governors Cabello and Anza offered similar terms: end of hostilities, peace with all Spanish subjects, release of Spanish captives, exclusion of other Europeans, conformity to Spanish declarations of peace and war, war against Lipan Apaches, travel in Coahuila to pursue Apaches only on the Texas governor's permission, and annual gifts. Governor Anza, at Ugarte's urging, added the further requirement that all Comanches agree in unison.

Comanche Tribalization. The Comanches complied with Governor Anza's requirements. Early in 1786 Ecueracapa (Leather Jacket), a major leader of a main branch of Comanches, the Buffalo-eaters (Cuchantica or Cuchanec), arrived in Santa Fe ready to comply with the terms. Ecueracapa became leader with Spanish support and agreed to a reconciliation with the Utes. After the agreement was reached (with Ute participation) Governor Anza opened the annual Taos trade fair. He also published an official price list to protect the new allies from Pueblo and Spanish traders.

Commandant General Ugarte approved of Anza's actions: Most important of all, Ugarte wanted Anza to induce the new council to elect one of its members as superior chief and to cloak him with absolute control over the affairs of the entire nation, especially over those matters pertaining to the terms of peace (Moorhead, 1968, p. 149).

Ugarte was trying to coordinate the efforts of Anza in New Mexico and Cabello in Texas. In 1786 Governor Cabello of Texas had concluded a similar treaty with the "Orientales," or eastern branch of the Cuchantica or Cuchanec Comanches. He wanted a paramount chief capable of ruling all Comanches, and thus favored the election of Ecueracapa, based on the reports about him that he had received from Anza. He achieved his goal to a limited extent but the Comanche peace in Texas remained fragile compared to that in New Mexico.

The Comanche treaty was finalized in April 1787 (Moorhead, 1968, p. 159; John, 1975, p. 716) when Governor Anza met with Yupe, Yamparica and Cuchantica (Cuchanec) leaders. Ecueracapa was granted an annual salary of 200 pesos (to be paid in kind), and a salary of 100 pesos for a subordinate chief. Comanches were granted some autonomy in their own affairs. Ugarte, noting the importance of respect for law to government, ordered that the New Mexican government make it known among Comanches that there would be no granting of asylum to Comanches fleeing tribal law—even in cases where Spanish law was less harsh. Efforts to feed Comanches during a drought a few years after the election of Ecueracapa cemented the peace. By these actions the Spanish clearly sought to create a dependent, vassal group (John, 1975, p. 710). The Comanche peace became the one outstanding success of Spanish frontier diplomacy.

It is difficult to overrate the importance of this accomplishment. Indeed, Kenner (1969, p. 77) holds that it is "little exaggeration to conclude that had there been no Comanche peace in New Mexico, there might have been no New Mexico." Peace brought an end to raids and created allies who played a vital role in subduing other nomadic groups. The peace lasted well into the American era (John, 1984). It served as a model for other negotiations. In 1786 Anza was able to persuade both Utes and Navajos to elect one chief and to negotiate treaties with each group. The pressures for tribalization were not as strong, nor as long lasting, among Navajos as among Comanches. When the Navajo chief, El Pinto, died, his son temporarily succeeded him, but could not hold the bands together (John, 1975, p. 762). When Ecueracapa died, a replacement was elected by an encampment of some 4,500 Comanches (John, 1975, p. 762; Simmons, 1967, p. 31). It is significant that both chiefs died of wounds received in campaigns against Apaches.

The Comanche peace had important effects on Comanche social organization and on their ultimate survival. The succession of a paramount chief is an indication of the degree of tribalization of Comanche bands. Of all the nomadic groups Comanches became the most centralized, but even they did not achieve a permanent tribal organization (Wallace and Hoebel, 1952). This degree of centralization had immediate and short-range positive effects on Comanche survival. Interaction and trade with Spaniards was improved; communication and cooperation among the bands increased, facilitating the organization of raiding and war parties (Wallace and Hoebel, 1952). Differences in Spanish policy with respect to tribalization account for the different effects on Comanches and Apaches.

Effects of Spanish Pacification on Apache Organization.   As noted, the subjugation of Apaches was a band-by-band process. The divide-and-conquer strategy was applied among Apache bands, as well as between Apache bands and other groups. However, when four Apache bands were simultaneously forced to surrender, there appears to have been no effort exerted to force them to elect or name a senior chief. The four leaders were subjected to the same terms (August, 1981, p. 154). They were, moreover, required to restrict their living area, and were encouraged to take up farming. These latter restrictions constituted a military, rather than religious, attempt at *reducción.* The next year (1791) Governor Concha attempted to combine all the Apache settlements in southern New Mexico. This worked for a few years, then various Apache groups abandoned the settlement at Sabinal (August, 1981), one of several *establecimientos de paz.* By 1793 there were eight such *establecimientos* in northern Sonora and southern Arizona (Worcester, 1979, p. 27; Moorhead, 1975a, Chs. V,X).

Historians disagree about the utility and accomplishments of the *establecimientos de paz.* Moorhead (1968, p. 289; 1975a, pp. 112–114) holds that they strained relations considerably. They were costly in terms of supplying seeds and tools and provisioning the presidial troops required to patrol them. Constant vigilance was a major source of irritation to the resident Apaches who were accustomed to wandering freely throughout their territory. In 1786 one band of Chiricahuas living at Bacoachi fled at the approach of presidial troops. Even after being offered full pardon for fleeing they refused to return (Worcester, 1979, p. 25). Both previously settled Indians and Hispanic settlers resented the favors shown to recently pacified Apaches.

Worcester (1979) and Griffen (n.d.) disagree. In Worcester's view (1979, p. 34), "it was always much less expensive for the Spaniards to feed peaceful Apaches than to wage war against them." Both hold that the *establecimientos de paz* were responsible for maintaining relative peace from 1790 until 1831. There were, of course, occasional attacks by various unsettled bands. Still, conditions allowed considerable economic growth in northern Sonora and southern Arizona. In August's (1981) view the peace held for a much shorter time, breaking down in the late 1790s. The resolution of these differing interpretations would seem to lie in the factual history of events, but this is only partially the case. Rather, all four writers are correct in their respective presentations of facts, but fail to piece together the larger puzzle to which they all supply parts.

The confusion emanates from two sources, the temporal and regional variability of these events,[7] and the roles of slave trade and regional ecology in intergroup relations. Griffen (1983a, 1983b, 1985, n.d.) reduces some of the confusion surrounding the effectiveness of the *establecimientos de paz*. He agrees (1985) with Moorhead (1975a, Ch.X) that the *establecimientos de paz* were forerunners of later American reservations, but notes that unlike the American reservations, they did not have precise boundaries, nor was there a legal implication of local sovereignty. They constitute the only instance in the history of Mexico that the military had primary responsibility for the administration of Native Americans. Griffen's accounts of the Compá Apache family are exemplary of the many threads woven through this discussion. The father, El Compá, established peace with the Spaniards in 1786, and remained an effective ally all his life. His leadership passed in succession to his two sons, Juan Diego and Juan José.

El Compá died of old age; his sons were killed in the famed Johnson "Massacre" of 1837. John Johnson, an American trader, tricked several Apaches, including the Compá brothers, into coming to his camp to trade.[8] While they were examining goods, he opened fire on them, scalped those killed, and used the scalps to prove his efforts on behalf of the Mexicans. He received a reward of 100 pesos from Mexican authorities.

In recounting the history of the Compá family, Griffen traces the career of the son, Juan José, who could read and write Spanish. Some of his correspondence has been preserved in the Janos archives. It is clear from these accounts that the local presidial commander was looking for a chief, but became increasingly disenchanted with Juan José. Juan José had decreasing influence with other Apaches. He was distrusted and suspected of being either a Spanish agent or using his position for his own gain. Still, the local commander sought someone to replace Juan José as "general of the Apaches," although the search was never successful.

What emerges from the account of the Compás is the very complicated interactions among Apaches, among Spanish settlers, among Spanish officials at various levels, between Spanish settlers and officials, and between the Spanish and Apaches. The great variety and volatility of local relations serves to obscure regularities of Hispanic-Apache relations. These regularities only become intelligible when they are examined at a regional level, focusing attention on the slave trade and local ecology.

THE NATURE OF PACIFICATION, SLAVE TRADE, AND ECOLOGY

At a somewhat more abstract level of analysis the concept of peace is problematic. Is peace a property of the local community, of the province, or of the entire *Provincias Internas?* While the use of inter-Indian differences by Spaniards has been discussed, the complementary use by native leaders of inter-Spaniard differences has not been emphasized. The problems of trade in captives and the disposition of prisoners of war are recurrent motifs in the larger picture. All of these issues are intertwined.

Peace may be localized both in time and space. When fighting is largely a matter of revenge, as is generally the case for band societies, and especially was so for Apaches, the issue of peace is not simple. It was quite possible for an Apache leader to negotiate peace with one group of Spaniards in good faith, only to attack a more distant Spanish settlement at the first opportunity. Even if one band completely stopped raiding, another band might travel considerable distance either to avenge a past wrong, or to obtain necessary but scarce supplies. Temporally, what constitutes peace? One raid per year? per decade? none? The record is not clear. Surely, less frequent and smaller attacks constitute the more peaceful conditions. The larger the region for which such conditions held, the more general the peace. One source of the contradictions among historians is lack of overlap in time and space in the locus of discourse. August (1981) focuses on the administration of two New Mexican governors (1786–1794). Moorhead (1968) focuses on the entire *Provincias Internas* during the term of office of Commandant General Ugarte (1769–1791). Griffen (1983b, 1983c, 1985, n.d.) concentrates on the region surrounding Janos Presidio in what is now northern Chihuahua. Worcester (1979) deals with the entire period of Spanish-Mexican domination (and subsequent Anglo domination), but concentrates on Apaches in southern Arizona and New Mexico, northern Sonora, and parts of Chihuahua. There is more to the contradictions than the incomplete overlap of historical focus.

At the immediate level, there is the lack of attention to Indian organization. As Worcester notes, "'Apache,' too, became the generic term for enemy Indians" (1979, p. 33), although the Spaniards eventually came to know the separate Apache bands, and to designate them by names still used today. While this tendency emerged from an ethnocentric approach to political organization, it also accurately emphasized the feature all "Apaches" shared—hostility with Spaniards. There were, however, other sources of confusion in the identity and relations of various nomadic Apache groups. First, some bands would split and become hostile. The group of Chiricahuas who split from the main band at Bacoachi later returned to attack those who remained, to punish them for their loyalty to the Spaniards (Worcester, 1979, p. 34). This was not unusual. Second, throughout the *Provincias Internas,* both hostile nomads (John, 1975, p. 416) and frontier vagabonds and bandits (Simmons, 1968, p. 183) disguised themselves as Apaches, or left behind signs indicating that their attacks had been made by Apaches. Thus, Spanish administrative ethnocentrism was used to the detriment of Spaniards, Apaches, or both.

On the Spanish side, a parallel process of local competition occurred. Villages or settlements would buy peace from Apache bands by purchasing from them captives taken elsewhere. A village that was known as a regular purchaser of captives or booty would be spared attacks. Spanish settlers and Utes in northern New Mexico exhibited a similar symbiotic relationship (Swadesh, 1974). The major difference was that the captives sold in the south were as often as not Spanish, whereas in the north the trade was in captives from distant nomadic groups. In part this was the result of Spanish administrative structure. It was possible for a band to make peace with the governor of one province. but not the adjacent governor. "This practice gave them both a safe refuge and an opportunity to trade their loot. But it also gave the Spaniards of each province an opportunity to purchase peace at the expense of other provinces" (Worcester, 1979, pp. 25–26; see also Griffen, 1983c, n.d.). Viceroy Flores sought to end this problem by forbidding local truces.

The viceroy's intent was to break the cycle of raiding that prevailed on the frontier. Nomads from refuges in northern Sonora attacked villages in northern Chihuahua and the Rio Grande Valley. As a result of this policy against local truces, those bands that had settled in Chihuahua were pushed to resume raiding, re-igniting further hostility, and increasing the Spanish reputation for treachery among Apaches. Thus the continuing Apache wars were enmeshed in multiple levels of administrative conflict: local settlement with local settlement, province with province, province with viceroy, commandant general of the *Provincias Internas* with the viceroy, Apache with Comanche, Navajo, and Ute, and Apache with Apache. The continuing trade in captives exacerbated the administrative, aboriginal, and social organizational sources of conflict.

Slave Trade[9]

Spanish administrators discussed and tried many strategies and tactics for subduing Apaches. However, "the possibility of making peace with the Apaches by restoring those held as slaves apparently never occurred to Spanish officials; warfare with the Apaches and enslavement of Apache captives were accepted as unquestioned facts of life on the northern frontier" (Worcester, 1979, p. 22). Indeed, policy went in quite the opposite direction. The *reglamento* of 1772 ordered that unruly Indians be removed altogether from the *Provincias Internas,* and shipped to Mexico City where the slaves might be christianized (Moorhead, 1975b). Those who escaped and returned north so intensified Apache hatred for Spaniards that the policy of deporting Apaches to Havana to obviate return gradually came into practice. This practice also failed. Many Apaches (including a group of 80 women) escaped while being transported to Veracruz. Those Apaches shipped to Cuba were so troublesome that the Cuban governor protested the practice to the viceroy of New Spain (Archer, 1973). This was not the major irritation to Apaches; rather it was the constant local demand for captives.

One of the requirements of the Comanche peace was that all Apache captives under age 14 be given to the Spaniards. A few years later Governor Concha extended this policy to adults (August, 1981, p. 146). The local economy could use the input of servile labor. Spaniards, however, were not the only outlet for captives. Both Comanches and *Norteños* traded captives, who included not only Apaches, but other Indians and Spaniards, to the French, and later, the Americans (Faulk, 1964, p. 58; Secoy, 1953).

The demand for captives, the convenience of raiding poorly identified local Apache groups, and the practice of blaming all attacks on Apaches made them a ready source of slaves. But slaving continually renewed the cycle of fighting. In 1796 retiring Apache campaigner Colonel Cordero complained that the Apache wars might have been caused by the "trespasses, excesses and avarice of the colonists themselves . . . " (in Worcester, 1979, p. 29). Griffen (1983c, 1985) notes that as raiding resumed, Apaches became middlemen in trade among Mexican villages, and between American traders and Mexican villages. This trade was uneasy, and readily turned into attacks, especially after events like the Johnson "Massacre" (Strickland, 1976). While the Spanish administration had changed its policy toward the Apaches over the years from one of destruction to one of conciliation and settlement, " . . . Spanish citizens had not, for they continued to sell Apache captives into slavery" (Worcester, 1979, p. 29).

The Apache peace was self-contradictory. Under peaceful conditions the economy prospered, increasing the demand for labor and for captives. The acquisition of captives, either directly or through middlemen allies, undermined the peace. This treatment of Apaches by Spaniards is in marked contrast to the treatment of Comanches. The differences were not a consequence of primacy in treaty signing, but due to differences in the social and biological ecology of the two groups.

Ecological Considerations

Horses were the single most significant factor in the ecological adaptation of all nomadic groups (Secoy, 1953):

> Once the Utes had horses, they could go to the plains for buffalo. They could also escape when enemy Indians from the plains invaded Ute territory. Suddenly it became possible, and even necessary, for the bands to live together in the large camps not previously feasible. Men formed large hunting parties to bring meat and hides from the plains for the whole band. The greatest war leaders headed the band camps, exercising authority hitherto nonexistent among Utes. Suddenly the scale of Ute life had exploded: their subsistence, warfare, and social organization. But everything hinged upon plenty of horses (John 1975, p. 119).

What was different for Utes, Comanches, and Apaches was the physiographic features of the environments they came to occupy after adopting the horse.

The Comanches moved onto the Plains and mastered the art of mounted buffalo hunting quickly. They were so successful that they were able to hold Utes closer to the mountains in the west, and to drive Apaches south into Basin and Range territory. The vast, largely undifferentiated area of the Plains facilitated rapid movement, fluid organization, coalescence and dispersal of large numbers of people. The presence of buffalo and the difficulty of agriculture on the Plains all but forced an exclusive dependence on hunting, and later trade, for a livelihood. The more differentiated territories occupied by both Utes and Apaches made amassing large numbers of people more difficult despite the acquisition of horses. Under identical environmental conditions mounted peoples can amass larger numbers, more often and more easily, than those groups restricted to foot transportation. Given equal mastery and availability of horses, peoples living on plains may congregate more readily (and disperse) than those dwelling in mountains, deserts, or other highly differentiated environments. Comanches were located in an environment most suitable to mounted hunting and fighting. Once so located they were able to hold off all potential usurpers—until the buffalo herds were destroyed in the late nineteenth century.

Comanches held a distinct advantage in terms of biological-ecological adaptation, Apaches had a further disadvantage in terms of social-ecological location. Comanches, Navajos and Utes were on the borders; Apaches were within the frontiers. Apache bands occupied lands between settled areas: northern New Mexico and Chihuahua, New Mexico and Sonora, Texas and Chihuahua, and Texas and New Mexico. The latter area was shared with Comanches, but its occupation was disputed. In short, Apaches were obstacles to Spanish commerce. In addition, the biological capacity of their territories was more severely strained by human occupation. Most territories occupied by Apaches did not support buffalo herds. Gardening was restricted to mountain meadows and a few river valleys. Game was generally scarce. Apaches were in direct competition with Spaniards for the best locations. Thus, Apaches were forced to raid for subsistence (see Maps V.5 and VI.2). A mutually predatory relationship developed between Spaniard and Apache. Apaches raided Spaniards for food; Spaniards raided Apaches for workers to produce the food.

One way of breaking the predatory cycle was to settle the Apaches on farms (John, 1975, p. 752). But a strategy of settlement could not work. The Spanish demand for slaves was too high. Comanche leaders objected strenuously to Spanish treaties with Apaches because they "would then have no enemies on whom to make war and would consequently become effeminate!" (Moorhead, 1968, p. 160–161). Probably the loss of captives as trade goods was more important than the egos of warriors, but prestige should not be discounted. Furthermore, the border location was a major advantage for Comanches, and to a lesser extent for Utes and Navajos.

Groups located on the extreme borders of the Spanish Empire, were, by virtue of their location, middlemen in the transmission of cultural information and goods from the agrarian empire to band-organized societies. Although they faced superior enemies on one side (an empire), they faced weaker enemies on the other. Hence they could maintain control over their territory (Secoy, 1953). As noted, Comanches combined this advantage with the benefits of the trade value of buffalo products and captives to establish a profitable, symbiotic relationship with Spanish and Pueblo traders (Kenner, 1969). Utes and Navajos lacked this latter advantage, and could not capitalize as extensively on their border location.

Apaches, by contrast, were in dire straits indeed, for they were caught between the rock of Comanche aggression and the hard place of Spanish

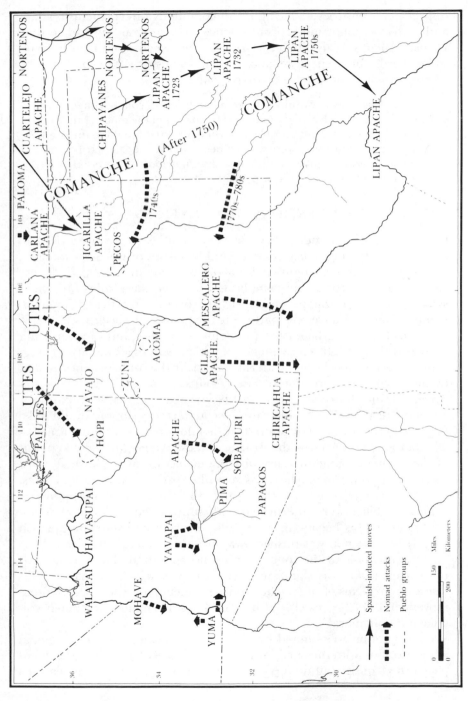

Map VI.2. Indigenous Locations in the Late Spanish Period, 1706–1820

COMANCHE

CUARTELEJO NORTEÑOS
PALOMA

CHIPAYANES NORTEÑOS

NORTEÑOS

LIPAN APACHE 1723

LIPAN APACHE 1732

LIPAN APACHE 1750s

COMANCHE

COMANCHE (After 1750)

104 CARLANA APACHE

JICARILLA APACHE

PECOS

1740s

1770s–780s

LIPAN APACHE

106

MESCALERO APACHE

UTES

UTES

ACOMA

ZUNI

NAVAJO

108

GILA APACHE

CHIRICAHUA APACHE

UTES

PAIUTES

110

HOPI

APACHE

SOBAIPURI

112

WALAPAI HAVASUPAI

YAVAPAI

PIMA

PAPAGOS

114

MOHAVE

YUMA

36

34

32

30

Spanish-induced moves

Nomad attacks

Pueblo groups

Miles

Kilometers

0   150

0   200

Sources: Schroeder (1968:307, 1979c)

oppression. Centuries of facing harsh conditions forced them to adapt and perfect a raiding mode of subsistence. "Because raiding had become virtually their sole livelihood, Apaches now relied almost entirely on stolen herds for their sustenance . . . " (Worcester, 1979, p. 15). The raiding mode of subsistence proved viable:

> . . . the Apaches successfully resisted all attempts to conquer them from the early seventeenth century until the last quarter of the nineteenth. They avoided pitched battles if possible, but when cornered fought to the death. As guerrilla fighters they were without peers; unlike the Plains tribes, they could not be starved into submission by extermination of the bison or any other animal (Worcester, 1979, p. xviii).

CONCLUSIONS, QUESTIONS, SPECULATIONS

Clearly, Spanish frontier policy was very complex. It involved the balancing of competing policy goals, sought by means of various strategies, under conditions of changing political organization in New Spain. These circumstances were further complicated by a less than full comprehension of the organization and structure of the societies being confronted—an ignorance only partly due to Spanish ethnocentrism. Logistic difficulties exacerbated the problems of muddy and/or competing lines of authority. The consequence of various strategies was also strongly influenced by local trade patterns, especially the trade in captives, and by the ecological adaptation of local groups.

Overall, the Bourbon reforms achieved their goals, at least partially. Frontier revenues were increased, economic development did take place, costs were at least shifted, if not lowered, and the French— whether as allies or foes—the British, and the Americans were kept out of the territory. Some measure of frontier peace was established, most successfully with Comanches, less so with Apaches, Navajos and Utes. The various Pueblo groups came more fully into the Spanish sphere.

Local changes were intertwined with supra-regional social changes. The frontier was becoming more fully incorporated into the Spanish Empire. The region was pushed away from the "marginal," toward the "peripheral" pole of the continuum of incorporation. This change was not extreme, but was significant, which is precisely what makes it interesting. In terms of the ratchet-and-pawl metaphor, there was definite movement, but the "pawl" did not "click"—the changes remained volatile and ephemeral.

Incorporation was limited by the need to balance effective regional administration with the needs of Empire. In particular, Spaniards had to pacify the frontier but do it economically. The net effect of the various economizing moves was to hamper the peace policy, to limit economic development of the region, and to preserve much of its character as a region of refuge. Even slight increases in incorporation produced changes in indigenous groups. Two sets of contrasts are pertinent here: the comparison of the effects of these policies on nomadic and sedentary groups and comparisons among nomadic groups.

Among nomadic groups, Comanches and Apaches form an interesting contrast. Both were reduced to peace by the Spanish at approximately the same time, but with divergent results. In the short term, Comanches benefitted and Apaches suffered. While reliable statistics are impossible to locate, there is no doubt that the number of Apaches was reduced by the constant attacks directed at them, yet they prospered in times of peace. Comanches, allied to the Spanish, not only survived but thrived under the alliance. They supplied necessary goods to the local economy, protected the borders from both Indian and European intruders, became the "Lords of the South Plains" (Wallace and Hoebel, 1952) and forced Apaches into the Basin and Range area. These differences are due to the acquisition of new productive technologies (the horse and gun), adaptation to local ecological conditions, and location in the social ecology of the region.

Apache groups had had an initial advantage over other groups due to their differential access to horses. As they were forced into the Basin and Range territory, horticulture was abandoned, except for occasional planting in mountain meadows, for a more mobile life-style. Basin and Range territory does not readily support large groups of foragers, especially those with big horse herds. The necessity of both conducting and avoiding raids required the maintenance of relatively large horse herds, and hence a nomadic life-style became the only viable option.[10]

The role of raiding in Apache life differed somewhat from its role in Comanche life due to differences in the social ecology of the two groups. Comanches were on the edge of the frontier, and were purposely used as buffers between Spaniards and outsiders. By contrast Apaches were a barrier to regional unity, disrupting commerce. The buffer-versus-barrier position carried other consequences as well.

Comanches were in a better position to engage in mutually profitable trade with New Mexicans. They brought valuable goods from outside the region—buffalo hides, jerked meat, and especially captives. The Comanche position also gave them ready access to guns through other Plains groups and European traders. Even when they raided in Texas, Spanish administrative structure was such that this produced little problem in New Mexico. Apaches were raided by Comanches, and could generally raid only Spanish villages. Thus, Apache trade was at best local, and always dangerous because they inevitably played one Spanish community against another. Thus they were subject to constant, and frequently treacherous, retaliation. Furthermore, they had low access to guns since all guns had to come from Spaniards, who tried to keep firearms from them.

Apaches also competed with Spaniards for resources, hunting territories and grazing lands. As Griffen (1983c, 1985) suggests, the initial early peace probably led to a population growth that overshot the carrying capacity of the region. Thus, Apaches were forced to raid for resources. When some groups were settled in *establecimientos de paz,* they provoked local jealousies because they received resources that local Spanish settlers thought were rightfully theirs. Furthermore, the fluid nature of Apache social organization caused Hispanic settlers to suspect that "pacified" Apaches aided or even conducted raids attributed to "wild" Apaches. Thus, the combination of environmental and social ecology trapped Apaches into a raiding mode of subsistence.

These differences between Apaches and Comanches show in the relative success of the Spanish-appointed central leaders. Wolf (1982, Ch.6) argues that local "big men" frequently benefitted from being appointed "chief" by Europeans. By virtue of their position they gained differential access to European goods, especially guns, which could be used as gifts, tools for hunting, or weapons—all of which helped widen their influence and power. Ecueracapa was able to use Spanish recognition to unite many Comanches and maintain an effective peace with New Mexico. No Apache leader was able to do this. Griffen's (1983b, 1985) account of the Compá family shows the extreme fragility of such Apache leadership.

Utes and Navajos, like Comanches, were on the fringes of the frontier, and free of the pressures experienced by Apaches. However, they were not able to capitalize on a middleman role in trade as the Comanches did, though they did conduct raids as far as California. Thus they experienced less severe pressures for change than Apaches or Comanches.

While many of these changes were obviously shaped by local conditions, the impulse came from sources outside the region. To understand the subsequent changes in social relations, it is necessary to examine some of the higher level political and economic relations between the Southwest and the wider world. The following chapters examine the origins and consequences of the Bourbon reforms for the articulation of the Southwest with Mexico City and the world.

NOTES

1. The northern provinces of New Spain were frequently referred to as *Provincias Internas,* or interior provinces, since they were located toward the interior when viewed from Mexico City. See Map VI.1.

2. This account draws from the following works: John (1975), Moorhead (1968), August (1981), Kenner (1969), Simmons (1968), and Worcester (1979). A. B. Thomas (1932, 1941) provided much of the archival materials for the aforementioned works, and for this chapter.

3. O. Jones (1966, pp. 30–31) lists five major strategies for pacification of nomadic groups: (1) diplomacy to induce sedentary life; (2) missionary efforts; (3) exemplary colonization by other indigenous groups; (4) subsidy; and (5) use of auxiliaries. He notes that only exemplary colonization was not used in New Mexico. This list differs only slightly from the one proposed here. The use of gifts is a combination of his subsidy and diplomacy strategies (1 and 4). The divide-and-conquer strategy is a combination of diplomacy and use of auxiliaries (1 and 5). The third strategy, political centralization, while not explicitly on his list, is implicit in diplomatic and missionary attempts to induce sedentary life-styles (1 and 2), which inherently meant pressure toward more centralized political structures. The lists differ mainly in their relative emphases on constituent components.

4. O. Jones (1966) remains the best source on Pueblo Indian auxiliaries. His fine-grained analysis highlights the variability and volatility of the general patterns discussed here.

5. John (1984) presents further evidence supporting the argument of this chapter, though it is not expressed in the terms used here. She presents instances of "inter-tribal" alliances. Her account of early nineteenth-century Comanche relations highlights the subtlety of these processes.

6. The phrase "Nations of the North" or "*Norteños*" refers to a number of groups, mostly horticultural villagers who occasionally hunted buffalo on the Plains, and who lived in the river valleys of what is now northern Texas, Oklahoma and Kansas. Prominent among these groups were the Tonkawas, Wichitas, Tejas, Bidais, Taovayas, Tawakonis, Caddos and others. "*Norteño*," like "Apache" and "Chichimeca," referred to a poorly differentiated mass of groups who lived outside the sphere of Spanish control.

7. Griffen states, "Over the long haul, it [Nueva Vizcaya] was more important with regard to the peace establishments . . . " (personal communication, Dec. 23, 1984). He notes further that differences between Nueva Vizcaya and Sonora are still not well understood. This, of course, underscores the point being made here: variability and lack of evidence make generalizations problematic.

8. Voss (1982, p. 71, note 20) points out that Strickland is responsible for correcting older accounts of this event that were based on the exaggerations of American traders. Strickland (1976) provides both an improved account of the event and a history of its interpretations.

9. The most complete source on Navajo slaves and captives is Brugge (1985). He gives far more detail than can be presented here.

10. In a very persuasive article, Lindner (1981) argues that precisely the opposite conditions led the Huns to abandon the use of horses after invading Europe west of the Carpathians. The movement from open plains to forested areas made horses a liability and promoted a sedentary life-style. Lindner's account is interesting in that it illustrates these same principles, but under almost opposite conditions.

CHAPTER VII

Bourbon Reforms, Mexican Independence and the Advent of the Gringo: Transformations of a Region of Refuge

The winds of economic change blew persistently across all of Mexico in the years that followed her independence from Spain, but they buffeted the far northern frontier with special fury, upsetting old structures and spinning the frontier economy around. Prior to 1821 the economic lifelines of the Far North ran southward, to the markets of Chihuahua, Durango, and Mexico City.... Provinces in northern New Spain, such as Chihuahua, were exploited by the central provinces, and they, in turn constituted a colonial dependency of Spain. Spain, meanwhile, had become economically dependent on France and England. Indians, whom the Mexican frontiersmen exploited, probably occupied the bottom of this pyramid (David Weber, 1982, pp. 122–124).

... local products were purchased at a fraction of their actual use and exchange value in north and central Mexican markets. But it was not the merchants of Chihuahua who realized the greatest gains. Just as the local New Mexican merchants were indebted to the Chihuahua merchants for credit and goods, so they were indebted to the great merchant houses of Mexico City which in turn were indebted to Spanish merchant houses which paid English or merchant houses in hard currency made of Mexican silver (Antonio Ríos-Bustamante, 1976b, p. 377).

Between 1765 and 1846 New Mexico, and the entire northern frontier of New Spain, received several complex, interrelated and overlapping shocks. With the imposition of the Bourbon administrative reforms came increased peace, increased trade, increased discontent and in-

134

creased dependence. The Bourbon reforms throughout Hispanic America, and in New Spain in particular, were both a response to *criollo* unrest and a major cause of the wave of revolt that swept through the colonies (Lang, 1975; Simpson, 1966; Stein and Stein, 1970). In New Spain this wave first crested in 1810 with the Hidalgo revolt, and finally broke under Iturbide's guidance in 1821. The independence of Mexico and the consequent internal chaos of the state allowed the northern reaches, particularly Texas and New Mexico, to slip back to the relative isolation and autonomy of the early eighteenth century.

With Mexican independence the Santa Fe Trail opened, goods began moving across the Plains, Santa Fe began to displace Chihuahua as a trade center and port of entry, Spanish and nomadic Indian social organizations were altered, and the preconditions for an American conquest were set. Texas was transformed from a sleepy, out of the way, if noisome, province to a growing, rebellious, and ultimately independent state and a threat to Mexican and New Mexican security. The changes that occurred in these 81 years give the impression of chaos because this was a time of transformation—the denouement of the Spanish era and the ascendancy of the American era. Incorporation into the Spanish Empire was loosening, while incorporation into the American state was beginning. Thus, the conventional indicators of change are somewhat arbitrary: Mexican independence in 1821 and the American conquest between 1846 and 1848.

This chapter examines the Bourbon reforms, then looks at the changes that took place during the period of Mexican independence, including the flourishing of the Santa Fe Trail trade, the transformations of New Mexican social structure, and the breakdown of frontier peace. The complicated changes in internal organization of indigenous groups and their changing relations with various levels of Spanish and Mexican bureaucracy, described in Chapter VI, form the backdrop for this discussion. These two chapters set the stage for an analysis of changes in the world-economy and the Spanish Empire that shaped the course of the Mexican state and the annexation of its northern half by the United States.[1]

BOURBON REFORMS: THEIR ORIGIN AND NATURE

The Bourbon reforms in Spain were intended to build a stronger, more centralized state, patterned after France. Spain implemented the intendency system early in the eighteenth century, reorganizing its political and economic administration (Herr, 1958). These reforms were introduced by Philip V (1700–1746), successor to Charles II (1665–1700). His ascent to the throne had been contested in the War of Spanish Succession (1702–1713). The Peace of Utrecht (1713) affirmed his right to the throne, but far more importantly, Britain won the *asiento,* which granted British traders the right to supply Spanish America with slaves, and incidentally opened the door to extensive contraband trade. The Seven Years' War (1756–1763), an unsuccessful military attempt to abrogate British trade rights, resulted in the Peace of Paris in 1763 that brought massive changes to North America. Quebec was ceded to the British, Louisiana to the Spanish. The Family Compact, a new French and Spanish alliance, was made in anticipation of further conflict with Britain. The French strongly supported Spanish colonial reforms to improve both the collection of revenues and mutual defense. The reforms were primarily fiscal, but included bureaucratic and commercial components:

> The effectiveness of the royal bureaucracy was to be counted in the treasury and not measured in heaven: Pesos-usurped salvation. In America, Bourbon reform became Bourbon despotism. Bourbon policy represented the assertion of centralized state power against the forces of regionalism and local identity (Lang, 1975, p. 72).

Commercial reform, the institution of *comercio libre,*[2] was highly variable in its effects throughout America. By opening additional ports to trade in both Spain and America, Madrid hoped to meet the challenge of British competition. These reforms were initiated in 1765, extended in 1778, and finally included New Spain and Venezuela in 1789 (Herr, 1958, pp. 120–123). The effect on trade was dramatic:

> At the end of the seventeenth century, only about 15% of the products shipped to America were Spanish. By 1798, the figure was closer to 50%. The proportion of Spanish national goods imported into New Spain continued to rise. In 1804, the consulado of Veracruz recorded the value of imported Spanish goods at 10,412,000 pesos, while foreign products imported through Spanish middlemen had dropped to 4,493,000 pesos (Lang, 1975, pp. 75–76).

The trade undermined colonial industries and favored new commercial centers that competed with older viceregal capitals of Lima and Mexico City (Lang, 1975, p. 83).

In New Spain these changes favored *criollo* merchants in the new centers (Veracruz and Guadalajara) over the *peninsulares* who had been supported by the older monopolistic practices. The older merchants either went bankrupt or shifted their capital to mining and commercial agriculture, which underwrote increased silver production in the late eighteenth century. The economic competition between *criollos* and *peninsulares* was exacerbated by the restriction of *criollos* "to not more than one third of all posts in American *audiencias*" (Lang, 1975, p. 86; Brading, 1971, p. 37), a policy intended to improve royal authority in the administration of the Empire.

Two *visitadores* were dispatched to the New World to investigate administrative conditions—José de Gálvez to New Spain in 1765–1771, and José Antonio de Areche to Peru and La Plata in 1777–1782. Both found bureaucracies dominated by local *criollos* who pursued self-interest at the expense of the Crown. Gálvez was appointed Minister of the Indies, and began instituting reforms intended to restore control of revenue to the Crown, and replace unreliable *criollos* with more trustworthy *peninsulares*.

Immediate control of revenue involved the elimination of tax farming, and tightening the royal monopolies on tobacco, silver, mercury and gunpowder. Revenues from the sales tax (*alcabala*) jumped from 1.5 million pesos in 1775 to nearly 3 million pesos in the 1780s. The tax on *pulque*, a locally produced alcoholic beverage, nearly doubled from about 470,000 pesos to 810,000 pesos in the same time period. The tobacco monopoly generated some 177 million pesos between 1765 and 1809. Silver production quadrupled in the eighteenth century; in the 1770s it rose from 12 to 18 million pesos annually. In 1789 Crown revenue from silver was 5 million pesos despite tax reductions to miners. Indian tribute increased from nearly 600,000 to 960,000 pesos between the 1760s and 1779. In short, the reforms met with initial fiscal success, both in Spain and in the colonies (Vicens Vives, 1969; Lang, 1975, p. 86). Revenues from New Spain increased from 6 million pesos in 1765 to 19 million in 1782 (Brading, 1971, p. 53).

Fiscal reforms were accompanied by administrative reforms. The intendency system replaced the older system of *corregimientos*, local administrative units which varied considerably in both size and importance (Lang, 1975, p. 89). In the Bourbon view, this was an attempt to restore order and integrity to colonial government. In the *criollo* view, these reforms were an attempt by *peninsulares* to usurp their privileges and wealth.

Because the viceregal and *audiencia* structure was left in place, there was bureaucratic conflict between the new superintendent and the viceroy over control of the treasury in New Spain. Resolution favored the viceroy. The office of superintendent was abolished, the viceroy regained control of the exchequer, and became the intendant of the viceregal district. Still, feuding continued with intendants of the outlying districts. This feuding was particularly troublesome in New Mexico and Texas, where logistic problems multiplied the effects of bureaucratic haggling.

Increased military presence served twin purposes of defending against a potential English invasion and providing means to control a restless population. Between 1758 and 1800 the military in New Spain increased from 3,000 to over 29,000. Here, too, *criollo* advancement was systematically blocked (Lang, 1975, p. 89). The insistence on augmenting special benefits for the military (called *fueros*)[3] furthered conflict between church and state, sharpening the *criollo–peninsulare* distinction. Thus, the reforms alienated every significant colonial group: merchants, bureaucrats, clergy, and landlords, most of whom were *criollos,* who "paid the salaries of the men who picked their pockets" (Lang, 1975, p. 87).[4] They also had tremendous direct and indirect effects on the course of social relations in the *Provincias Internas,* especially New Mexico.

Bourbon Reforms in the Provincias Internas

The reports issued by *Visitador* Gálvez and Inspector Rubí led to the total restructuring of the political organization of the northern frontier of New Spain. Gálvez recommended two reforms in 1769. First was the establishment of an intendency system. This was delayed until 1786. He also recommended the establishment of a *comandancia general.* Implemented in 1776, this latter recommendation grew out of "the all-embracing problem of the Apache barrier [which] was indeed of such magnitude that the Crown was contemplating a drastic overhaul of the administrative as well as military structure of the entire northern periphery" (Simmons, 1968, p. 6).

Rubí's inspection had produced more immediate results. He had found the frontier in disarray. Presidios were scattered haphazardly across the frontier. The 24 units lacked coordination. Morale among the soldiers was low due to lack of clear enlistment regulations and the corrupt practices of presidio commanders (Moorhead, 1961, 1975a). He recommended that the 24 presidios be consolidated to 15 presidios strung along the 30th parallel, with an exception for New Mexico. He urged moving the El Paso garrison south to Carrizal—El Paso's 5,000 residents being capable of defending themselves—and establishing a new garrison at Robledo, north of El Paso. He further recommended taking a more skeptical attitude toward peace overtures made by Indians, and demanding better assurances of peace in negotiations with their leaders. These recommendations resulted in the issuance of the *Regla-*

mento of 1772 and the appointment of Hugo O'Conor as commandant inspector of presidios at a salary of 8,000 pesos annually. He was to be assisted by two adjutants at 3,000 pesos annually each. By 1776 the new line of presidios was established, but problems remained (see Map V.5). As presidial commanders took their troops further afield against hostile Indian groups, other groups would raid, depleting the presidial horse herds. This problem was so severe in New Mexico in 1775 that Viceroy Mendinueta approved the purchase of 1,500 horses as replacements (John, 1975, pp. 481–482).

It was at this time that Teodoro de Croix was appointed commandant general at a salary of 20,000 pesos annually. He was to inspect all presidios annually, determine and coordinate military campaigns, and initiate peace negotiations, subject to viceregal approval. "Prisoners were to be treated kindly, and any officers, soldiers, or civilians who abused them were to be severely punished" (Simmons, 1968, p. 8). It was hoped that these reforms would pacify the region, allow economic development, and enable the interior provinces to pay a portion of their expenses.

The commandant general was the highest official in the *Provincias Internas*. He was responsible to the king, through the minister of the Indies, but was to keep the viceroy informed of his actions. Since both had comparable status within the bureaucracy, and the new Commandant General exercised jurisdiction over territory formerly controlled by the viceroy, feuding was all but guaranteed. According to Simmons (1968, pp. 9–10) there are grounds for suspecting that the feuding between Commandant General Croix and Viceroy Bucareli involved some personal factors. A structural explanation appears more tenable. Such feuding was common throughout Spanish America after the institution of the Bourbon reforms (Lang, 1975; Stein and Stein, 1970). Simmons shows (1968, p. xvii; see Figure VII.1a) the commandant general as subordinate to both the viceroy and the Audiencia of Guadalajara. He was subject to two masters. When the commandant general was, for a time, directly subordinate to the king and the Council of the Indies, he held a position comparable to the viceroy. This effectively demoted the viceroy to the level of the commandant general (see Figure VII.1b). In either case, the chain of command was multistranded, a structure that generated conflict.

Attempts were made to remedy other frontier problems. Commandant General Croix was instructed to build a mint at Arizpe, Sonora, to relieve the specie shortage that was retarding commerce (Simmons, 1968, p. 10; Radding de Murrieta, 1977). Revenues were generated from royal monopolies on gunpowder, tobacco, salt, mercury, playing

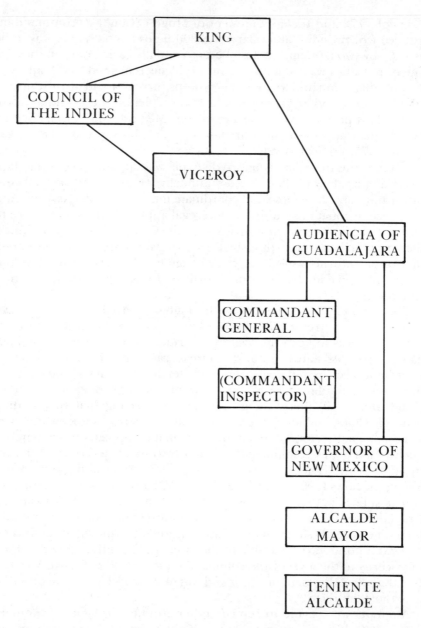

Version A*

Diagrams VII.1A and VII.1B: The Spanish Colonial Chain of Command

Sources: *Simmons (1968:xvii)
**This volume

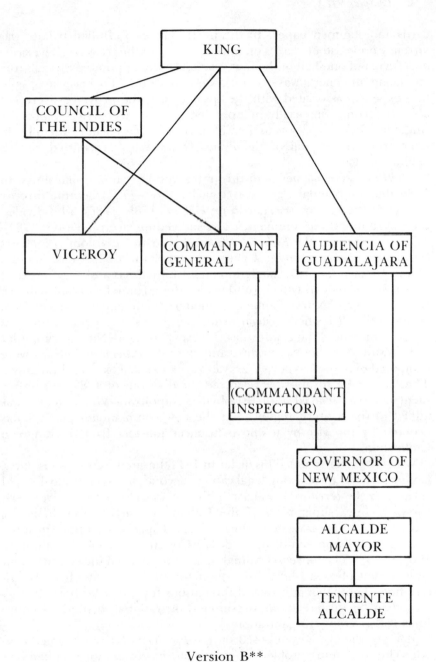

Version B**

cards and stamped paper. In the north, however, Indian tribute was virtually nonexistent. Taxes on mining added to the treasury. The *media anata*, a tax of one-half of the first year's salary of appointed officials (the commandant general was exempt), was also useful. Still, because of military expenses associated with the Indian wars, the provinces were not able to become financially independent of the viceroyalty. When the threat of other Europeans to the Californias decreased and Indian problems grew, the capital of the *Provincias Internas* was shifted east to Chihuahua City.

The *Provincias Internas* went through several organizational shifts. In 1786 the commandant general (Ugarte, 1786–1791) became directly subject to the viceroy (Bernardo de Gálvez, 1785–1786), who divided the region into three commands. The succeeding viceroy (Flores, 1787–1789) reorganized the *Provincias Internas* into two divisions: *Provincias Internas del Poniente* (under Ugarte) included the Californias, Sonora, Nueva Vizcaya (approximately modern Chihuahua) and New Mexico; *Provincias Internas del Oriente* (under Ugalde) included Texas, Coahuila, Nuevo Leon and Nuevo Santander (modern Tamaulipas). This division lasted until 1791 when a royal order reunited the provinces under a single command. The Californias, Nuevo Leon and Nuevo Santander were restored to the viceroyalty, and the new *Provincias Internas* were composed of Sonora, Nueva Vizcaya, New Mexico, Texas, and Coahuila. Then in 1804 a royal order re-sorted the divisions of 1787, but implementation was delayed until 1812 by the Napoleonic Wars. Sinaloa was added to the western region, and the new commandant general was ordered by the viceroy to move his headquarters from Durango to Chihuahua.

When the viceroy issued his order in 1814, he cited four reasons. First, Chihuahua was the existing legal capital. Second, it was centrally located relative to the territorial capitals. Third, it was closer to the frontiers, allowing closer supervision of the Indian campaigns. Fourth, it was much closer to New Mexico, which required special attention since the United States apparently had "designs on the province" (Simmons, 1968, p. 45).[5] The move to Chihuahua inconvenienced the commandant general, but pleased Chihuahua merchants and residents. It is also interesting to note that only one of the reasons for the order bore directly on Indian–Spanish relations, presumably the rationale behind the entire *Provincias Internas* reorganization.

Many of the changes imposed on the *Provincias Internas* seemed chaotic. The continuing problem of gubernatorial corruption resulted in a royal order in the 1790s withholding one-fifth of a governor's salary as an advance on fines that could be expected to be levied against retiring governors by the *residencia*. Then in 1805 the viceroy moved the annual Chihuahua fair (the main source of New Mexican supplies) some distance to the south. In response, the New Mexican governor petitioned for a new fair in El Paso. Such a fair had existed in the early Mexican period; its date of origin is uncertain (Simmons, 1968, p. 74). Also, efforts were made in the late eighteenth century to concentrate settlers for improved defense. Fray Morfi, writing in the 1780s, attributed the tendency toward dispersed settlements to desire on the part of colonists to escape state scrutiny. This allowed settlers to engage in contraband trade with nomadic bands, and gave them a free hand in the *punche* trade—a tobacco substitute of considerable importance in the local economy (Swadesh, 1974; Kenner, 1969; White, 1943; Kinnaird, 1946). But the role of dispersed settlements in protecting villagers from misdirected vengeance raids should also be noted (Swadesh, 1974, p. 196; see also Chapter V above).

Many of the problems that continued to plague the frontier regions were in fact engendered or exacerbated by the changes in policies. The constant shuffling and reshuffling of *Provincias Internas* administration guaranteed continual bureaucratic turmoil. The local governors were frequently either caught in the middle, or sought to get in the middle of such squabbles to manipulate them. At times when the *Provincias Internas* were split into districts, Texas and New Mexico fell into separate jurisdictions. This rendered coordinated Apache and Comanche policies all but impossible. The *Provincias Internas* continued to drain the royal treasury. New Mexico alone cost at least 55,000 pesos annually (Simmons, 1968, p. 88) to administer. Still, the Bourbon reforms were a tremendous force for social change for the next century.

FRONTIER PROSPERITY: POPULATION AND TRADE

The Bourbon reforms were part of a complex temporal and causal chain of social change during the century after their introduction. They helped establish relative peace on the frontier, facilitating growth of population, the local elite and trade, especially with Americans. At a wider level of analysis, they contributed to the Mexican independence movement. The weak Mexican state and the heavy Plains traffic led to a resumption of raiding by nomads except Comanches (John, 1984). These changes prepared the region for the American conquest in 1846. While all of these events are not direct consequences of the Bourbon reforms, they are connected to them at least indirectly.

The increased prosperity of the *Provincias Internas*, while certainly a product of frontier peace, was also part of the general success of the Bourbon reforms throughout the Spanish Empire (Brading, 1971; Nadal, 1973; Vicens Vives, 1969, pp. 540–551). Likewise, the independence movement must be tied to the general economic decline of Spain in the last decade of the eighteenth and first several decades of the nineteenth centuries. This decline "placed Britain at the head of world powers and relegated Spain to the role of a second rate power" (Nadal, 1973, p. 540). Of all the effects of the Bourbon reforms, two are basic: frontier peace and the regional increase in prosperity.

As problematic as census and population data are for the frontier regions of New Spain, there has been some effort to collect the figures (O. Jones, 1979; Ríos-Bustamante, 1976a, 1976b; Aragon, 1976; Tjarks, 1978; Gutierrez, 1980). The reliability and accuracy of the various sources are questionable, but the general patterns are quite clear: from the time of the reconquest the population grew steadily, increased rapidly in the closing decades of the eighteenth century, and slowed somewhat during the period of Mexican independence (O. Jones, 1979, p. 129; Gutierrez, 1980; Tjarks, 1978; Ríos-Bustamante, 1976b). Table VII.1 summarizes the New Mexican data and shows that the increase in population was most rapid while the Bourbon reforms were having their strongest effect on frontier peace. This was a period of very low immigration (O. Jones, 1979, p. 130). By 1790 the populations of both Albuquerque and la Cañada (now Santa Cruz) exceeded the population of Santa Fe for the first time (O. Jones, 1979, p. 127). Furthermore, by 1817 the population of any one of these three settlements outnumbered the total population of Texas, Baja or Alta California, or northern Sonora (O. Jones, 1979, p. 129; and Table VII.2).

With the Bourbon reforms and the attendant frontier peace, production and trade with nomadic groups and Chihuahua accelerated. New Mexico became increasingly dependent on Chihuahua for "ironware of all kinds—but especially tools and arms—domestic and imported fabrics, boots, shoes, and other articles of dress, and such delicacies as chocolate, sugar, tobacco, and liquors" (Moorhead, 1958, p. 49). Articles exported to the south were

> . . . almost entirely the produce of the soil and a few crude manufactures. In addition to sheep, raw wool, hides (of buffalo, deer, and antelope), pine nuts, salt, and El Paso brandy, there were a few Indian blankets, and occasionally, some Indian captives of war destined to slavery in the Hacienda of Encillas or the mines of Chihuahua (Moorhead, 1958, p. 49).

The articles traded south were of very low value, whereas the imported items were expensive.

Table VII.1. Spanish and Sedentary Indian Population (Pueblo and Genízaro) of New Mexico, 1746–1817[1]

Year	New Mexico			El Paso District			Total		
	Spanish & Caste	Indian	Total	Spanish & Caste	Indian	Total	Spanish & Caste	Indian	Total
1746–1748T	4,100	3,080	7,180	1,080	475	1,555	5,180	3,555	8,735
1750T	3,809	10,568	14,377	1,556	1,484	3,040	5,365	12,052	17,417
1760T	7,666	8,783	16,449	3,528	1,453	4,981	11,194	10,236	21,430
(1760B)	7,666	9,104	16,770	3,588	1,394	4,982	11,254	10,498	22,080
1776T	9,742	8,602	18,344	NA	NA	5,100	NA	NA	23,444
1790T2	16,081	9,544	25,625	5,244	1,296	6,540	21,325	10,840	32,165
1800J	19,181	8,173	27,354	5,311	825	6,136	24,492	8,998	33,490
(1799B)	18,826	9,732	28,558	4,943	637	5,580	23,769	10,369	34,138
1817J3	27,791	8,788	36,579	NA	NA	NA	NA	NA	NA

[1]For all the "Indian" figures, populations refer to settled peoples, either Pueblos residing in their own villages, Genízaros in their own villages, or Pueblos, Genízaros, or Apaches, Utes, Comanches, or Navajos living in settlements. Nomadic populations are not estimated or included. Sources for these figures are indicated as follows: T: Tjarks (1978: Table 2); J: O. Jones (1979:119–129); and B: Bancroft (1889:279).

[2]These figures differ from those supplied by Tjarks for El Paso and total, due to an apparent arithmetical error in the original.

[3]Jones gives conflicting figures on p. 122 and 129; those on 122 are reported here. In neither case are the errors significant in terms of general trends. This is also the case in comparing Tjarks's figures for 1760 with Bancroft's figures for 1760. The same is true for Jones's 1800 figures compared to Bancroft's 1799 figures.

Table VII.2.   Population of the Ten Interior Provinces of New Spain
in the Era of the Bourbon Reforms

	Year			
Province	1760–1800	(date)	1815–1821	(date)
Nuevo Santander	30,450	(1795)	38,000	(1815)
Nuevo Leon	20,523	(1760)	26,000	(1815)
Coahuila	15,272	(1787)	50,600	(1815)
Nueva Vizcaya	228,000	(1780)	190,504	(1815)
Sonora & Sinaloa	87,644	(1783)	123,854	(1815)
Baja California	500	(1790–1800)	800	(1821)
Alta California	1,000	(1790–1800)	3,270	(1821)
New Mexico	30,953	(1790)	36,579	(1817)
Texas	2,992	(1792)	4,015	(1815)
	417,334		473,718	

Source: Jones (1979: 240–241, Tables 13 and 14)

Pedro Bautista Pino, a native New Mexican, was the official representative to the Spanish Cortes in 1812. In his delegate's report he claimed that the annual trade with Chihuahua involved purchases of 112,000 pesos and sales of 60,000 pesos, for a net deficit of 52,000 pesos (Moorhead, 1958, p. 64; Simmons, 1968, p. 72).[6] This deficit continually drained the province of specie, which allowed the Chihuahua traders to maintain various fictitious accounting schemes. Even the annual government payroll of 38,000 pesos, the only source of specie, could not alleviate the deficit (Moorhead, 1958, p. 64). Chihuahua "profited from rich mining operations that supported approximately 30 smelters and a mint that stamped out more than 500,000 pesos' worth of coin a year" (Moorhead, 1958, pp. 64–65). Pino no doubt exaggerated the shortage of currency to gain sympathy. "From the evidence which remains in civil and ecclesiastical archives, the concern over the lack of hard currency in New Mexico was exaggerated, made with the explicit intent of gaining attention for New Mexico's marginal economic pursuits" (Gutierrez, 1980, p. 378). Simmons (1968, p. 72, note 67) agrees, but holds that the shortage was real. Still, growing trade and increasing deficits maintained a steady pressure for further production of export goods which, in turn, led to intensified local production and increased trade with nomadic groups.

Sheep production flourished at this time. During the last decade of Spanish control, "about 200,000 head were driven annually to the southern markets; indeed, it is asserted that, during the most flourishing times, as many as 500,000 were exported in one year" (Gregg, 1844, in Moorhead, 1954, p. 134). J. F. Chavez, a territorial delegate in the 1870s, claimed a million sheep a year had been exported in earlier times. Still, "even if these estimates were somewhat exaggerated, the happy condition of the sheep industry was perhaps the most remarkable attestation to the success of Spanish Indian policy in New Mexico" (Kenner, 1969, p. 66). In 1800 merchants took advantage of an official visit to the south by the governor to send along 18,784 sheep and assorted other goods. This occurred again in 1807 when 15,000 head of sheep were also shipped south (Moorhead, 1958, p. 45). Pike estimated that 30,000 sheep a year were shipped from New Mexico in 1806 (Pike, 1889, p. 305). While the exact extent of the sheep flow is unknowable, it is certain that it was both extensive and important to the local economy.

Trade was also a major stimulant to the economy of the more northerly communities "The vast rangelands of the Upper Chama Valley and the extra margin of opportunity offered by the (contraband) Ute trade provided doors to prosperity for impoverished young men of good family" (Swadesh, 1974, p. 148). Commandant General Ugarte had sought to make such trade part of the peace policy by instituting fairs where trade could be regulated. Unregulated trade could be detrimental to peace, since wronged parties would frequently "raid" for return of misappropriated goods, initiating a cycle of raiding and counterraiding (Swadesh, 1974, p. 167). Trading expeditions, for horses, hides, and captives, took village traders from northern New Mexico as far afield as northern Utah and Yellowstone (Hill, 1930; Swadesh, 1974; p, 169; Ulibarri, 1963, p. 70).

While the flourishing sheep industry, the expansion of Plains and intermountain trade, and the growth of population do not irrevocably establish the success of the Bourbon reforms, they collectively lend credence to the claim that the last years of Spanish control of the Southwest were years of prosperity. This prosperity and attendant trade were major factors in altering class relations in New Mexico.

THE TRAIL TO SANTA FE

The Santa Fe Trail trade altered New Mexico's relationship to Mexico, accelerated the growth of class differences, and began the process of incorporating the region into the American state. The sources of this trade are found in a continuing American interest in the Southwest. By the 1790s some frontiersmen were annoying Spanish officials in Louisiana. American pressure in part caused Spain to cede Louisiana to

France, in hopes that the stronger French state would keep the Americans at bay and protect the *Provincias Internas*. The French kept the boundaries of the territory intentionally vague (Ulibarri, 1963, p. 27). This plan backfired when Napoleon sold Louisiana to America in 1803.

Jefferson used the vague boundaries to initiate several exploratory expeditions. In 1806 General Wilkinson, governor of Louisiana, commissioned Lieutenant Pike to explore the new territory. Ulibarri (1963, p. 33ff) argues that Pike was under orders to get to Santa Fe by allowing himself to be captured in Spanish territory. This he did—whether by intention or not is of little moment.[7] Pike made the first of many attempts to draw Comanches away from Spain toward the United States (Ulibarri, 1963, pp. 33–34; John, 1984). He and his men were captured by the Mexican army and taken to Santa Fe, then to Chihuahua, where they were released a year later after some diplomatic maneuvering.

In 1810 Pike published an account[8] of his journey which described the trade imbalance between New Mexico and Chihuahua. His account encouraged several trade expeditions between 1810 and 1812. These traders, too, were imprisoned, several until 1821 (Moorhead, 1958, p. 59). Interest in the Southwest waned until negotiations for the Adams-Onís (or Transcontinental) Treaty began in 1819. The United States officially gave up all pretensions to the Rio Grande as the western boundary of the Louisiana territory to gain Florida and Oregon from Spain (Pletcher, 1973; see Map VII.1). But after Mexican independence in 1821, the United States sent Joel Poinsett to negotiate for the purchase of any or all of the Southwest territories: Texas, New Mexico or the Californias. Such negotiations continued until the Gadsden Purchase in 1853 (Ulibarri, 1963, Ch.XIII).

Economic interest in New Mexico increased with the opening of the Santa Fe Trail. In the fall of 1821, while on a trading expedition from Missouri to Comanche territory, William Becknell and his party met a detachment of New Mexican soldiers. They were guided to Santa Fe where they learned that Mexico was now independent, and that Governor Melgares welcomed further commercial ventures. Thus, the Santa Fe Trail trade opened.

The distance from Independence, Missouri, to Santa Fe was approximately 770 miles by the shortest route and took about eight or nine weeks to complete (Moorhead, 1958, p. 102) (see Map VII.1). From Santa Fe it was another 330 miles to El Paso del Norte. The additional 250 miles to Chihuahua usually took another 40 days. Santa Fe and El Paso were of comparable size, with populations of about 4,000 each. Chihuahua was considerably larger, with a population of some 12,000 to 15,000 (Moorhead, 1958, p. 117). From Chihuahua it was another 400

Map VII.1.   The Santa Fe Trail

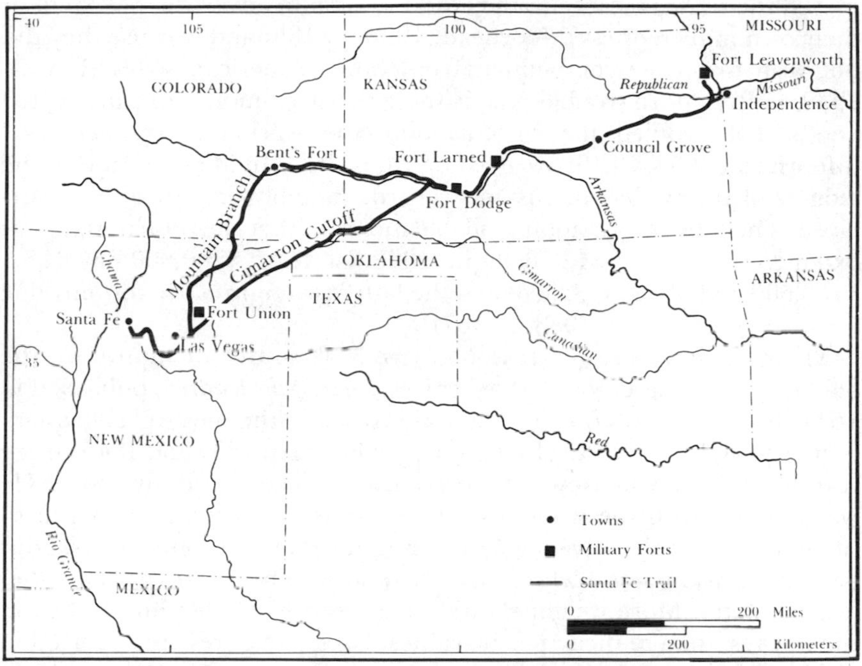

Source: Sunseri (1979:70)

miles to Durango, an additional 170 miles to Zacatecas, and another 65 miles to Aguascalientes (Moorhead, 1958, p. 116). The entire distance from Aguascalientes to Independence was nearly 2,000 miles.

Moorhead intended to assess the economic significance of the Santa Fe Trail trade when he began his research for *New Mexico's Royal Road* (1958), but he found that "the volume and value of the trade which wrought these changes can never be accurately measured" (Moorhead, 1958, p. v). Mexican custom-house figures have several defects: the trade cycle of annual caravans did not coincide with the fiscal reporting year; several years are missing; the tariffs levied varied according to category of goods; and, the entire schedule shifted from year to year. Finally, New Mexican officials used the records to justify "the amount of revenue which it actually sent to the national treasury" (Moorhead, 1958, p. 125), rather than for accurately recording trade.

American consuls at Santa Fe and Chihuahua made no effort to re-cord the amount of the trade. No export duties were collected in the

United States, so there are no records there. Missouri newspapers down-played the trade, because traders did not wish to advertise the extent of their own indebtedness (Moorhead, 1958, p. 185) and because they did not wish to attract competition from other American states (Loyola, 1939, p. 27). More troublesome is the extensive amount of unreported goods that avoided the customs house by various "arrangements" (Moorhead, 1958, Ch. 6; Swadesh, 1974, p. 163). In Missouri, few of the ledgers of the traders or customs records (notably on specie) have survived. The little information available indicates that the return trade was extensive: in 1824, $180,000; in 1829, at least $200,000; in 1832, $100,000 and in 1834, $200,000—the latter two figures are for only one company (Moorhead, 1958, p. 187).

There is, however, one reasonably reliable source of figures on the Santa Fe Trail trade, Josiah Gregg's *Commerce of the Prairies*, published in 1844. In Moorhead's opinion these figures are "the most reliable quantitative analysis available" (1958, p. 185).[9] Between 1831 and 1840 Gregg travelled to and from New Mexico as a trader, taking extensive notes. He was familiar with the trade, its ins and outs, its ruses, and its practitioners. He had the advantage of basing his estimates on conversations with traders, and not solely on written reports. The figures are nonetheless estimates. More weight should given to the changes and trends in the figures, than to their specific values. Gregg's figures are reported in Table VII.3.

Several trends are readily apparent in Table VII.3. Size of loads increased in value and bulk. The latter is indicated by the number of wagons used. There is a general decrease in the number of proprietors and a corresponding increase in the number of men employed. The dollar value of goods per proprietor increased. Initially the profits on the trade were over 100%. Later they fell to about 50% of the value of the outgoing cargo, although the rate was quite variable from year to year (Ulibarri, 1963, p. 5). The overall value of the trade is more difficult to assess, but it "netted about a half million dollars annually," excluding both trade with other provinces and smuggling (Ulibarri, 1963, p. 85). While the value of this trade is quite small when compared to total foreign trade, or even total trade with Mexico (see Table VIII.6), it was of considerable importance to both New Mexico and Missouri.

THE SIGNIFICANCE OF THE SANTA FE TRAIL TRADE

On the New Mexican end of the trail, the combination of the need for cheaper goods and the shortage of tax revenue to run the province served to encourage trade (Loyola, 1939, p. 11; Sunseri, 1979, p. 83; Ulibarri, 1963, p. 79; Zeleny, 1944, p. 80). On the Missouri end, the frontier economy was weak and lacking in cash (Moorhead, 1958, p. 59). Both sides were eager to do business, and the needs of New Mexico were more important locally than the desires of the central Mexican government to exclude foreigners (Zeleny, 1944, p. 81; Weber, 1982, Ch.7). Thus the mutually profitable trade began. American mountain men also entered the area. Most of them operated out of Taos (Zeleny, 1944, p. 85ff; Ulibarri, 1963, pp. 56, 141–142; Weber, 1972). They left few records since most of their activity was illegal under Mexican law. They helped blaze trails to California, and conducted trading expeditions to the Great Basin and California for horses and Indian captives.

Of the goods returned to the United States specie was the most significant. The cash imported from New Mexico was so vital to the Missouri economy that for years Mexican pesos were accepted at local land offices as legal tender at the rate of one peso for one dollar (Ulibarri, 1963, p. 83ff). The infusion of New Mexican goods in 1821 saved Missouri from financial collapse (H. Anderson, 1939–1940). The same was true of the Panic of 1837. Thus, "the importance of the Santa Fe trade to the economic development of Missouri can scarcely be overestimated" (Dorsey, 1936, p. 135).

For New Mexico, Missouri displaced Chihuahua as the major source of manufactured goods, since American goods were "of both better quality and lower price" (Moorhead, 1958, p. 65). American merchants also opened stores in Chihuahua, and conducted large wholesale operations there. The American interest in these markets is seen in the attempts to find other overland routes to Mexico and to eliminate the Missouri middlemen (Moorhead, 1958, p. 78). Some traders went to New York, Philadelphia, Liverpool or Hamburg to buy goods at wholesale (Moorhead, 1958, p. 77).

The main items shipped to Mexico were cotton goods grown in the South, manufactured in the North and shipped from the West (Ulibarri, 1963, p. 86ff; Zeleny, 1944, p. 82). Mules and specie were the major return goods. Mules were used in Missouri for breeding stock and supplied the farms of the West and South (Ulibarri, 1963, pp. 88–89). They were also used extensively in the trade since they could eat the native grasses while oxen could not. The increasing capitalization of trade is reflected in the spread of the trade into wider networks, in the increase in the ratio of workers to proprietors, the amount of goods per proprietor, and the proportion of goods shipped to Chihuahua (see Table VII.3). Still, the overall significance of the Santa Fe Trail trade is difficult to assess precisely. The trade gave the United States an access to

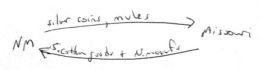

Table VII.3.   The Value and Volume of the Santa Fe Trail Trade[1,2]

Year	Total Value of Merchandise $	Number of Wagons	Total Number of Men	Number of Proprietors	Men[6] per Proprietor	Value[6] per Proprietor $	Value to Chihuahua $	Chihuahua[6] as Percentage of Total
1822	15,000	—	70	60	1.2	250	9,000	60.0
1823	12,000	—	50	30	1.7	400	3,000	25.0
1824	35,000	26	100	80	1.3	438	3,000	8.6
1825	65,000	37	130	90	1.4	722	5,000	7.7
1826	90,000	60	100	70	1.4	1,286	7,000	7.8
1827	85,000	55	90	50	1.8	1,700	8,000	9.4
1828	150,000	100	200	80	2.5	1,875	20,000	13.3
1829	60,000	30	50	20	2.5	3,000	5,000	8.3
1830	120,000	70	140	60	2.3	2,000	20,000	16.7
1831	250,000	130	320	80	4.0	3,125	80,000	32.0
1832	140,000	70	150	40	3.8	3,500	50,000	35.7
1833	180,000	105	185	60	3.1	3,000	80,000	44.4
1834	150,000	80	160	50	3.2	3,000	70,000	46.7
1835	140,000	75	140	40	3.5	3,500	70,000	50.0
1836	130,000	70	135	35	3.9	3,714	50,000	38.5
1837	150,000	80	160	35	4.6	4,286	60,000	40.0
1838	90,000	50	100	20	5.0	4,500	80,000	88.9
1839	250,000	130	250	40	6.3	6,250	100,000	40.0
1840	50,000	30	60	5	12.0	10,000	10,000	20.0
1841	150,000	60	100	12	8.3	12,500	80,000	53.3
1842	160,000	70	120	15	8.0	10,667	90,000	56.3
1843	450,000	230	350	30	11.7	15,000	300,000	66.7
1844[3]	200,000	90	175	—	—	—	—	—
1845[4]	342,000	—	—	—	—	—	—	—
1846[4]	1,000,000	363	750	—	—	—	800,000[5]	78.0

[1] Taken from Moorhead (1958: 63–64), originally from Moorhead (1954) edition of Gregg (1844).

[2] See Ulibarri (1963: note 84, p. 99) for original Gregg figures.

[3] From Moorhead (1954: 344, note 19).

[4] From Moorhead (1958: 75).

[5] Estimated from number of wagons going to Chihuahua, 315 out of 363.

[6] Ratios and percents calculated by author.

Mexico not open to British traders. Thus, it lent an overall "helping hand" to American development, but its impact on New Mexico was much stronger.

The Impacts on New Mexico

As the Santa Fe Trail trade increased, flooding the New Mexican market, the dependence of New Mexico on Chihuahua reversed:

> Now the New Mexicans were demanding hard money in the south for their own produce in order to buy their needs from the Americans. They even purchased beyond their own requirements and resold the surplus at handsome profits in Chihuahua and other southern markets where formerly they had gone into debt (Moorhead, 1958, p. 65).

New Mexico gained control of a significant proportion of the trade, possibly half (Zeleny, 1944, p. 84). Many of the leading families in New Mexico "became even wealthier by investing in this new trade route" (Horvath, 1979, p. 112).

According to Gutierrez (1980, Ch.7), the effects of the trade produced a complex transformation of wealthy New Mexican families, the so-called *ricos*[10] in New Mexico. The peace of the late eighteenth century had fostered population growth, leading to increased pressure on the land and "morselization of many patrimonial estates due to the lack of primogeniture" (Gutierrez, 1980, p. 360; see also Ríos-Bustamante, 1976b; Aragon, 1976). The aristocracy went into decline (1800–1839) for several reasons. First, land was scarce because of continued nomadic raiding. Second, the land was of marginal quality, the environment unstable, and Hispanic settlers were in competition with their Pueblo allies for its use. Third, there were only limited opportunities for diversification. These waxed and waned with the flow of trade and tides of nomadic raiding. Furthermore, their own aristocratic pretensions slowed the use of the limited commercial opportunities available to them.

During this period (1800–1839, but especially 1820–1839) some non-aristocratic families were able to move into a middle class position by participation in trade, and some *rico* families were able to stabilize or enhance their position by participation in the trade and marrying with Anglo traders (Gutierrez, 1980, p. 352). It is precisely because class lines were unclear that claims to nobility increased, either by those defending an old patrimony, or by upwardly mobile families trying to add a "name" to their wealth. These efforts caused major modifications of marriage patterns, including significant shifts in illegitimacy rates and increasing requests—and grants—for dispensation to marry within the boundaries of "incest" as defined by the Catholic Church in the nineteenth century. Premarital pregnancy appears to have been a conscious strategy to force the Church into granting such dispensations (Gutierrez, 1980, Ch.6).

Thus, the *ricos* involved in the Santa Fe Trail trade were in a curious position: they were able to consolidate wealth and power locally but only at the price of dependence on foreign trade. This situation represents an unusual coincidence of two classes typically found in dependent economies: a traditional landed elite and a local comprador capitalist (Chirot, 1977; Wallerstein, 1974a, 1974b).

Although dependent on the American traders, the *ricos* competed with them. The local traders, connected through culture and kinship to the customs officials, had considerable advantage in negotiating duties and making "arrangements" in regard to evaluation of goods. But the financing of the government depended on customs (Zeleny, 1944, p. 83) that also gave American traders considerable leverage in negotiating the duties they paid. The tension between the need for revenue and the dependence on trade led Governor Armijo—himself an active trader—to convert the customs duty to a flat $500 per wagon in the late 1830s. This system was advantageous to all traders for it effectively lowered the tax—but it also lowered state revenues and had to be abandoned (Moorhead, 1958, p. 127). About that same time the municipal government of Santa Fe levied a sales tax to finance a war against the Navajos, who were beginning to raid extensively again. When native merchants were exempted, complaints were raised with the governor. These complaints noted that the new regulations violated the United States–Mexican trade treaty of 1831. The governor was persuaded to exempt naturalized citizens from the tax, if they could show proof of service in the emergency. Foreign merchants were only given right of local appeal in "a deliberate attempt to drive Americans from the New Mexican trade" (Moorhead, 1958, p. 128).

Following an aborted invasion by Texans in 1841 (Texas had become independent from Mexico in 1836), Governor Armijo seized the opportunity to harass American traders further, successfully driving many from the province (Moorhead, 1958, pp. 132–133). Many were trappers and small traders who left for California (Ulibarri, 1963, p. 119; Minge, 1965, Ch.1; Weber, 1982, pp. 195–196; 1972, p. 9). This was Armijo's intended effect. Still, the New Mexican *ricos* were never able to monopolize the trade, because of competition from Chihuahua merchants, but especially because of their dependence on American trade. They were, however, able to capitalize on their profits.

The *ricos* used their new wealth to increase land holdings *via* land grants (administered by the governor), debt collection, and purchase (Zeleny, 1944, p. 74). This led to the development of debt peonage as a means of labor control. The rapidly expanding sheep industry surpassed agriculture as a leading industry in New Mexico in the early nineteenth century (Gonzalez, 1969, p. 43; Zeleny, 1944, p. 60; Gutierrez, 1980, pp. 404–406), and led to a distinctive form of debt peonage, the *partido*:[11]

> The owner supplied a breeding herd to his tenant. The renter agreed to return twenty lambs for every hundred ewes in the herd at the end of an agreed-upon period—usually one year. The tenant further contracted to rent rams from the owner, sell his lambs and wool through the owner, and stand responsible for all operating expenses and losses. The renter was also required to return upon demand a breeding herd of the same size and age as that originally handed over to him.
>
> In exchange, the tenant was entitled to all the wool, all the lambs in excess of the twenty-per-hundred ewes, and the right to graze his own sheep on the owner's land along with the rented sheep. However, he paid for these grazing rights at a specified rate (Gonzalez, 1969, p. 47).

An occasional *partidario* (a *partido* shareholder) would build his own herd and become an owner himself. This was a rare occurrence since the key ingredient, land, was scarce and expensive, and owners were loath to sell it unless forced to do so.

Gregg (1844), Kenner (1969), Moorhead (1958) and Gutierrez (1980) all agree that the sheep trade was a major factor in the growth of the *rico* class. Gonzalez (1969, p. 46), Leonard and Loomis (1941), and Swadesh (1974, p. 148), however, claim there was no land shortage. Both sets of writers are correct, but only at certain times. In the late eighteenth century the Bourbon reforms and the Comanche peace fueled the growth of patron–peon relations. The opening the Santa Fe Trail accelerated that growth. Still, the expansion of the *ricos* was concentrated in the more heavily populated areas of New Mexico (Swadesh, 1974, p. 59). On the frontiers servile laborers could not escape to open lands because of the presence of hostile nomadic groups. As relative peace came to the frontier, flight became an option. New settlements were founded on the northern frontier, and even advanced onto the Plains. For this time, Gonzalez, Leonard and Loomis, and Swadesh are correct: there was no severe shortage of land. Several new towns were founded early in the nineteenth century: Estancia (1819), Manzano (1829), Las Vegas (1835) (Gonzalez, 1969, p. 43; Knowlton, 1980, pp. 12–14). Anton Chico, founded about 1822 in the Pecos valley, "remained the eastern gateway to the province until the Civil War" (Kenner, 1969, p. 63). Many of these towns were populated by *genízaros* who were excluded from Hispanic towns (Kenner, 1969, p. 63; Horvath, 1979, Ch.VI).

Trade on the Plains frontier had begun in the early years of colonization. Although illegal, it was a major source of livelihood for frontier settlers (Swadesh, 1974, p. 163). Contraband trade with Americans and Comanches was conducted by frontier villagers and Pueblo individuals. The main trade items carried by *comancheros*[12] were baked bread, iron for arrow and lance points, and associated trinkets. The return items were hides, captives, guns, livestock and meat (Kenner, 1969, Ch.4). Significantly, until after the American conquest the main flow of guns was from Comanches to New Mexico (Kenner, 1969, p. 85). Many of the goods supplied by Comanches were the booty of raids conducted in Chihuahua, Durango, Texas and other interior Mexican provinces (Kenner, 1969, p. 93; R. Smith, 1963). There are few records of this trade.

After Mexican independence, trade policy fluctuated considerably. There were arrests for trading in 1827, encouragement to contact Comanches in 1828, and orders of restraint in 1831 (Kenner, 1969, pp. 79–80). In the 1830s and 1840s American traders began to appear on the Plains, breaking the New Mexican monopoly. They had a cooperative-competitive relation with the *comancheros*, which gradually evolved more toward the competitive side. Initially paralleling the *comancheros*, and subsequently blending in with them, were less scrupulous traders, both Americans and *rico*-backed New Mexicans, who sold whiskey and guns to Comanches and other Indians (Kenner, 1969, pp. 96, 97). The trading relations between Comanches and *comancheros* aggravated the hostile relations between Texas and New Mexico from the time of Texan independence (1836).

Both the *comanchero* and the Santa Fe Trail trade contributed to changes in the class structure and the rise in power of those *ricos* involved in the trade. These changes, in turn, altered the local economic structure, especially the *partido* system. The spread of the *partido* system heightened class stratification (Mosk, 1942, p. 38). On the other hand, the *comanchero* trade helped maintain egalitarian class relations on the edge of the frontier (Swadesh, 1974, p. 58). Thus, this period of transitions gives conflicting impressions of the changing social structure of New Mexico.

Feudalization in New Mexico

The applicability of the term "feudal" to New Mexico has been the cause of considerable controversy. Views differ sharply (cf. Zeleny, 1944,

p. 69, and Ríos-Bustamante, 1976a, p. 352). The dispute has less to do with social structure than with ideological connotations of the terminology used. The term "feudal" conjures notions of "traditional," which in turn suggests the idea of "stagnation" or "backwardness." In eras when "progress" is a guiding beacon, such labels carry negative evaluations and connotations. Such terms are readily associated with thinly veiled rationalizations for imperialism in which a "progressive" people "helps" a "backward" people. Because of these associations many scholars take strong exception to any use of the term "feudal." These concerns are legitimate, but can create conceptual and theoretical confusion.

After Mexico opened its borders to foreign trade, comments on the "feudal" nature of New Mexican society appeared in the writings of American travelers. Weber (1979, pp. 295–307) traces the sources of American attitudes toward Mexicans to two major roots, the persistence of the "Black Legend" (the myth among English-speaking peoples of the autocratic and vile nature of Spaniards, especially the conquerors of the New World) and American fears of miscegenation. He also notes (1979, p. 307, note 52) that such attitudes rationalized imperialist intentions.

Still, the obvious contrast with American society prompted continued use of the term, which sometimes led to the uncritical acceptance of inaccurate assumptions:

> At nearly every point of contact, the insulated character of the culture re-enforced institutional authority. "Peonage," wrote Josiah Gregg [1844], "acts with terrible severity upon the unfortunate poor, whose condition is but little better, if not worse indeed than that of the slaves of the south." And peonage could no more be avoided than the power of the Church, for the nomadic Indians were the most efficient constabulary that despotic authority could desire. No prison was ever guarded more effectively than the Utes, the Apaches, and the Comanches "guarded" New Mexico (McWilliams, 1949, p. 66).

While McWilliams is generalizing, Gregg was describing the New Mexico he visited as a trader between 1831 and 1843. It is ironic that the "feudal" character of New Mexico is attributed to its isolation, enforced by nomads, when in fact it was a result of relative peace with nomads and increased trade and contact with outside regions.

Feudalization developed shortly after Gálvez's inspection in the 1760s and continued until after the American Civil War. Chirot (1975) cites three conditions necessary for feudalization: a potential class of large landlords, labor shortage, and labor-intensive technology. Only the first condition is problematic with respect to New Mexico. On the surface, the early colonizers who held *encomiendas* would seem to fit Chirot's criteria for the formation of such a class controlling servile agricultural labor (Chirot, 1975, p. 67), but settlements in New Mexico seem closer to small-holdings than large estates. Haciendas were little more than extended family dwellings (Gonzalez, 1969, p. 35). Conquered nomads could not be converted readily to agricultural workers. *Reducción* was a consistent failure in the *Provincias Internas*. Thus, while the potential for formation of an elite class was there, the actual process had not gone very far.

Another path to feudalization is found in concentration of land ownership and an increase in landless rural population (Chirot, 1975, p. 68). This in fact began to occur in the period of the Bourbon reforms (Greenleaf, 1972, pp. 104–105). Given the precarious nature of New Mexican agriculture, it was all but inevitable that many would be forced to sell their land and become entrapped in debt servitude. One aim of the Bourbon reforms had been to reverse this trend. Several royal decrees issued between 1805 and 1820 were aimed at such redistribution (Greenleaf, 1972, p. 105; Gutierrez, 1980, pp. 385–390). Large tracts of land were sold throughout the region, but the prices were such that the landless could not afford to buy, and the wealthy saw the prices as "ridiculously cheap" (Greenleaf, 1972, p. 105).

Land concentration was made possible by the relative frontier peace and the attendant increase in trade. During the peace, villagers could sell their land and colonize new lands. The trend toward concentration accelerated due to the decrease in central control during the wars of independence. The evidence for such land concentration remains weak, but data presented by Gutierrez on land holding for several New Mexican villages (1980, pp. 391–393), household structures (1980, p. 400), and occupational stratification in Santa Fe and Santa Cruz de la Cañada (1980, p. 403) are congruent with the analysis presented here. Development of the peonage system accompanied land concentration.

There was some similarity in form to feudal Europe, but the sources of the similarity were different. European feudalism was an outgrowth of isolation and the absence of money; New Mexican feudalism was the result of trade and a dependence on imports, not exports. Thus, the "feudal" character of New Mexico was not being eroded slowly by American contact, but was a consequence of it. Its "feudal-like" character was *not* due to "stagnation," "backwardness," or isolation, but rather due to tighter incorporation into the capitalist world-economy. This superficial resemblance to "unprogressive feudalism" made it easy for nineteenth-century Americans to believe their own propaganda about the "backwardness" of New Mexico.

However, New Mexico was distinctive because it remained a region of refuge where the processes of change were relatively mild and were shaped by the waxing and waning of nomadic raids—hence the importance of the breakdown of peaceful relations with nomadic groups.

THE EFFECTS OF THE BREAKDOWN OF FRONTIER PEACE

The frontier peace was inherently unstable. On the one hand, the trade in stolen livestock and captives persisted. On the other hand, the Americans were expanding toward the Southwest, disrupting relations among Plains groups. American–Spanish rivalry for Pawnee, and later Comanche, loyalty dates back to 1803 (Kenner, 1969, pp. 66–70). Once the Santa Fe Trail trade had begun, caravans requested protection by the United States government, first in 1824 (Ulibarri, 1963, p. 86), then again in the early 1830s. Escorts were supplied for a while, but were soon discontinued: most of the trouble occurred south of the Arkansas River in Mexican territory, and after 1834 the caravans were so large that they could defend themselves. After agitation in the Senate by Senator Benton of Missouri, a treaty was concluded with the Osage and Kansas Indians on the Plains for protection of trade caravans (Moorhead, 1958, p. 68). Then in 1835 the United States signed the first treaty with Comanches and Wichitas (Ulibarri, 1963, p. 111). It was at about this time, the 1830s and 1840s, that raids by Pawnees, Cheyennes, Arapahoes and Kiowas began to increase.

Loyola (1939, p. 24) reports that New Mexican archives show a large number of Indian attacks during the 1830s and 1840s. Swadesh (1974, p. 62) notes that Ute hostilities flared up in the 1840s and persisted for the next decade. The levying of retail taxes to finance Navajo wars in 1839 has already been noted (Moorhead, 1958, p. 128). Apache attacks increased throughout northern Mexico in the 1830s (Weber, 1981; 1982, Chs. 5 and 6), in New Mexico (Worcester, 1979, pp. 34–37), in Sonora (Griffen, 1983b, 1983c, 1985, n.d.), and in Chihuahua (Moorhead, 1958, pp. 146–147). As the fighting continued, trade could be conducted only under the protection of the large and well-armed American caravans. All of northern Mexico was devastated by Indian attacks (R. Smith, 1963). According to Kenner (1969, p. 76) the Apache attacks in New Mexico were restricted mainly to the capture of livestock. Only Comanches maintained peace, and then only in New Mexico.

Why the sudden increase in raiding by the nomadic groups bordering northern Mexico? Both the scale and the duration of the attacks indicate that the causes are general and complex. The attitudes of American traders led to actions that resulted in Indian attacks on them (Gregg,

1844, pp. 16–21; Bancroft, 1889, pp. 334–335). The trade in alcohol and guns (Kenner, 1969, p. 85) also contributed to Indian unrest.[13] The continued demand and traffic in horses and captives encouraged further attacks by various groups, in attempts to obtain goods for both trade and defense. This was merely the continuation of the old trading, raiding, slaving cycle, but with new vigor and over larger territory. Horses and captives were sought as far away as California (Ulibarri, 1963, pp. 141–142; Weber, 1981, pp. 230–231; 1982, pp. 101–102; Phillips, 1975). The local demand for captives also increased. Navajo captives were in high demand after 1830 (Swadesh, 1974, p. 170).

The steady deterioration of Mexican political and economic organization also contributed to the renewed fighting. Ute raiding that flared in the 1840s was fueled both by Mexican treachery and by the decline of gifts and tribute (Swadesh, 1974, p. 62). Indeed, in the 1840s, ". . . the Utes became so infuriated by the continuing slaving expeditions of the Mexicans that they made an attack on the New Mexican governor in his office" (D. Tyler, 1980, p. 114). The increased unrest was not restricted to Utes. The rapid turnover of Mexican officials, especially in the northern provinces, and the steady decrease in the budget for Indian gifts contributed to the increased unrest (Kenner, 1969, p. 70; Weber, 1982, Chs. 5 and 6).

Apparently a critical point for these pressures was passed sometime around 1830. Once the fighting resumed, Mexican policy only made matters worse. In Sonora and Chihuahua the governors cancelled Indian rations in 1831 (Griffen, 1983b, 1983c) and embarked on a policy of Apache extermination conducted by means of bounties offered for Apache scalps. The horrors of this "trade" are well recorded (Thrapp, 1967; Worcester, 1979; Moorhead, 1958, p. 148ff; R. Smith, 1963, p. 42ff). Events like the Johnson "Massacre" (Strickland, 1976; see Chapter VI) were not rare. This particular strategy backfired, exacerbating Apache fear of Mexican treachery and assuring their undying hatred of Mexicans.

The Mexican dictatorship of 1835, which attempted to disarm the rural population in an effort to prevent liberal revolt, left the region virtually defenseless against Apache and Comanche attacks (R. Smith, 1963, p. 34). Sonora and Sinaloa were assailed by well-organized Mayos and Yaquis to the south, and Apache raiders to the north, severely disrupting local development and trade (Voss, 1982). Within New Mexico, local disorder also caused trouble. Kenner (1969, p. 75) reports that a war with Arapahoes began when Governor Armijo ignored an Arapaho request to buy back some captive kinsmen who had been sold in New Mexico.

The Texas revolution in 1836 and the New Mexican rebellion against Governor Perez in 1837 were symptomatic of the generalized state of disorder in the northern provinces (see Voss, 1982; and Chapter VIII). The growing, complex rivalries between Americans and Mexicans in the Southwest led to attempts by both to woo Comanches to their respective sides. New Mexicans continued to use Comanches as buffers against intruders, including the Americans (Kenner, 1969, p. 97).

Probably the most significant, though least obvious, source of renewed fighting was the constant population pressure on the region, both politically and ecologically. At the most elementary level the heavy Santa Fe Trail traffic put pressure on grazing and interrupted buffalo migration patterns on the Plains (Weber, 1981; 1982, pp. 100–103). The American advance from the east was displacing more easterly Plains Indians to the west. This heightened Plains competition and warfare increased the need for horses and weapons, and generated the captives to trade for them. Kenner (1969, pp. 75–76) has noted how during this time the Arapahoes, Cheyennes, and other *Norteños* became increasingly troublesome. While there were some direct attacks on New Mexico, their main effects were indirect, via increased pressure on Comanches and Apaches, and on the buffalo herds. Pressure on the buffalo herds also came from New Mexican buffalo hunters, the *ciboleros*. Hunting buffalo on the Plains was an old practice in New Mexico, but as population increased and the herds decreased, the *ciboleros* came into greater conflict with the various Plains groups. This competition sometimes flared into open hostility, but more frequently only resulted in some sort of tribute being exacted for the privilege of hunting buffalo on a group's territory (Kenner, 1969, p. 106).

Last, ecological pressures contributed to the hostilities. The growing population of New Mexico strained local land resources:

> A hundred years ago, Mexico was beginning to realize that overgrazing was a problem on the Rio Grande. In 1827, the stock-raisers of Sante Fé and Albuquerque had two hundred and forty thousand head of sheep on the tax rolls—twice the number that can be supported on that range now [i.e., 1935] (Fergusson, 1935, p. 334).

Given the general underreporting of taxable wealth in New Mexico, the herds were probably larger, and the ecological pressure no doubt extreme. Expanding sheep production and a growing population required more land. Hispanic settlers, Pueblo villagers, and *genízaros* directly or indirectly displaced nomadic groups from the fringes of their domains. Game was becoming scarcer, hunting parties had to travel further and longer. Chance encounters, and the consequent conflict, increased. Griffen (n.d.) argues that the upsurge in attacks in southern Arizona and northern Sonora-Chihuahua may have been due to population pressures generated by natural increase in Apache population during the relatively peaceful years, exacerbated by a corresponding increase in Spanish population. Thus the region was overhunted, forcing Apaches to raid for food, especially after rations were cancelled in 1831. Meanwhile, on the Plains, population increases due to migrations were leading to overhunting of the buffalo herds.

As the fighting increased, and warfare again became endemic, escape to the Plains became more difficult for New Mexican villagers. The precise nature of ecological pressures varied from location to location, but everywhere growing populations were severely taxing productive technologies. Competition with both American Plains traders and Indian buffalo hunters drove the village frontier back toward the Rio Grande Valley. These trends made it easier for *ricos* to hold their laborers and made the *partido* system seem more palatable to its participants.

CONCLUSIONS, QUESTIONS, SPECULATIONS

The Bourbon reforms are causally connected, directly, indirectly or covariantly, with a number of significant changes in the Southwest. The reforms at first contributed to an increase in prosperity of the region indirectly through the establishment of frontier peace, directly through fiscal reform, and covariantly with the rise in prosperity throughout the Empire. These changes led to a tighter incorporation during the late eighteenth and early nineteenth centuries, moving the region away from marginality in the direction of full-blown peripherality. As that movement started, Mexican independence led to political and administrative chaos that loosened the degree of incorporation. As this occurred, trade with Americans via the Santa Fe Trail opened, and rapidly transformed the region again. Incorporation again tightened, but this time the dependence was on American trade.

Dependence on American trade was multifaceted. The local government, now nearly autonomous due to the disorder in the Mexican central government, depended on tariff revenues for its support. Likewise, local economic improvement was dependent on trade, both for its direct benefits, and for the indirect benefits of being a regional entrepôt. The major indirect effect of trade was continued growth and prosperity of the *ricos* who used trade profits to acquire land to build large sheep herds through the *partido* system. The resumption of nomadic raids and population growth combined to make land more valuable. Thus, the local ruling elite became dependent on trade to maintain its position.

Clearly, all of northern New Spain was affected in complex and divergent ways by changes occurring outside the region. In this sense it remained a "region of refuge," an arena of more than marginal interest to New Spain and Mexico, but never fully incorporated, never becoming a full-blown periphery. These changes were not extreme, but remained reversible, and varied considerably by location.

They altered the local stratification system. There was an apparent rise of servitude—conditioned by intensity of nomadic raiding and hence the availability of new land. The *rico* class was gradually transformed from a nobility in pretensions only, to an increasingly powerful aristocracy. They began to resemble comprador groups found elsewhere. Locally they were important and powerful, but only because of their role in helping outsiders. Two consequences for local social structure arise from this situation.

First, to outsiders especially, the system appeared to be "feudal," but only if conditions of origination and connotations of "stagnation" or "backwardness" are ignored. Still, even this mild case is significant because it follows general patterns seen elsewhere. The resemblance to classical feudalism facilitated an interpretation of New Mexico as "stagnant" or unchanging. This is clearly a false interpretation. If anything the region has been marked by incessant social change since before Coronado.

The second consequence of the peculiar conditions of this frontier was the beginning of an ethnic stratification system, which placed Indians at the bottom, and various types of mestizos, especially *genízaros,* above them. Both were superseded by Hispanic villagers. A small group of *ricos* dominated the entire system. While locally powerful, the *ricos* are most impressive for their relative weakness compared to nobles in other systems. There were hints of the *Ladino, Mestizo, Indio* distinctions that became common throughout Latin America, but the system never developed fully.

At a somewhat broader analytic level the Bourbon reforms played a part in the independence movement in Mexico. For northern New Spain, and then northern Mexico, a major consequence of independence was the arrival of American traders, who in effect conducted an economic preconquest of the region. To understand fully how these local changes shaped the American conquest and subsequent social, ethnic, and class relations, it is necessary to shift to yet a wider level of analysis. The next chapter focuses on changes in state economies and changes in the world-economy and struggles for dominance within it.

NOTES

1. Lang (1975) and Brading (1971) are major sources on the Bourbon reforms. Gutierrez (1980), Kenner (1969), Moorhead (1958), A. B. Thomas (1932, 1941), Ulibarri (1963) and Weber (1972, 1973, 1979, 1982) are major sources on the Southwest in this era. Max Moorhead (1954) provides the definitive edition of Josiah Gregg's *Commerce of the Prairies* (1844).

2. *Comercio libre* was an attempt to combat British trade by opening more ports in both Spain and America. Literally it means "free trade," but does not carry the connotations that that term has today.

3. A *fuero* (literally, right) was "a privileged judicial jurisdiction or court which functioned independently of ordinary civil tribunals" (Simmons, 1968, p. 221). Simmons glosses *fuero* as "jurisdiction," typically a special or privileged court (1968, pp. 101–102, especially note 8).

4. The cleavage between *criollos* and *peninsulares* is problematic in the literature. Lang (1975) holds that this cleavage began early and lasted for the entire colonial phase. Stein and Stein (1970, p. 66) see the split arising in the seventeenth century along with the rise of large landowners. Brading (1973) disputes these interpretations and sees the rift arising in the last quarter of the seventeenth century and becoming acute just before independence. McAlister (1963) ties the distinction to the Hispanic preoccupation with blood purity, as evidenced in the elaborate *casta* system (Mörner, 1967). Both Israel (1975) and Wolf (1955) present strong evidence that similar rifts existed in New Spain from the sixteenth century. In any case, all agree that the split became acute and was a factor in the various Latin American independence movements. Whether the underlying mechanism was one of relative or absolute deprivation (Brading versus the rest) does not affect the analysis put forward here.

5. Louisiana had been sold to the United States in 1803, and Pike had entered New Mexico via the Plains in 1806.

6. Further details of New Mexico's trade are supplied in the report of Don Pedro Bautista Pino written in 1812 for the Spanish Cortes. This report has been translated and annotated by Carroll and Haggard (1942, especially Ch. XIV, pp. 106–127). For most of the early nineteenth century one peso was worth one dollar (Turlington, 1930).

7. Ulibarri (1963, Ch.II, especially note 65, p. 48) reviews the literature on this controversy. The point here remains that Pike: (1) entered New Mexico, and (2) reported back on the riches of New Mexico, stirring further American interest. Whether this was by overt planning or a fortuitous accident does not change the analysis presented here.

8. The preface to the 1889 edition (Pike, 1889, pp. v–xii) summarizes the report's publication history through 1889.

9. Throughout this work "Gregg (1844)" refers to the Moorhead (1954) edition.

10. The Southwest literature abounds with references to *ricos:* Gonzalez (1969, pp. 44–46), Moorhead (1958, pp. 71, 109, 111, 194), McWilliams (1949, pp. 68, 69, 70, 75), Mosk (1942, pp. 38–40), Simmons (1968, pp. 94, 99, 152), Swadesh (1974, pp. 26–27, 59), Zeleny (1944, pp. 69, 74), Gutierrez (1980, Chs. 7,8), Dunbar Ortiz (1980, Chs. 3,4), Weber (1982, Ch.11).

11. *Partido* has several meanings: (1) a district or territorial division, (2) the jurisdiction of a *teniente alcalde* (Simmons, 1968, p. 222), or (3) a shares agree-

ment between an owner and a contractor to raise crops or livestock for a fixed percentage of the yield. A *partidario* is a "sharecropper or shareherder" (Swadesh, 1974, p. xx). Gutierrez (1980, pp. 404–406) gives essentially the same definitions.

12.   A *comanchero* was a "trader, licensed or unlicensed, who traveled out on the buffalo Plains to trade with Comanches and other nomadic tribes" (Swadesh, 1974, p. xvii).

13.   Lamar (1977) sees traders as making valuable contributions to the frontier through their role as cultural brokers, as opposed to farmers who had no use for indigenous populations. While Lamar's point is well-taken, traders were also the point men of social change, much of which proved to be detrimental to its recipients. Traders, per se, are neither beneficial or harmful, but rather must be seen in a wider social context.

CHAPTER VIII

The Sources of the American Conquest of the Southwest

– how US, Mexico, and SW (TX, NM, CA) contributed to inevitably of Mex–Am War

Prior to 1846, Mexico itself was not prosperous, populous, powerful, or stable enough to people its frontier, neutralize nomadic raiders, and create tight commercial and political links between the periphery and the metropolis. In a larger sense, the Mexican frontier is best understood as the periphery of an aspiring nation that was itself peripheral to the world's capitalist system. During the nineteenth century, while the United States made the transition from a peripheral agrarian state toward becoming one of the core nations of the industrial world, Mexico remained a peripheral state in the world capitalist system. . . . The relative underdevelopment of the Mexican frontier, then, cannot be understood by looking only at conditions on the frontier, or by pointing to the supposed "indolence" of the pobladores. Mexican frontiersmen responded to many forces beyond their control and those can only be understood when the Mexican frontier is viewed from a broad perspective (Weber, 1982, p. 282).

Poor Mexico, so far from God and so close to the United States! (Porfirio Díaz)

The origin of the American conquest of the Southwest—like any major imperial undertaking—is complex. Several levels of change occurred simultaneously. Each level contributed to the final result. On the global level Britain dominated the world-economy, establishing a "Pax Britannica" and hegemony over world trade. On the national level American and Mexican paths of development diverged radically. The United States began to grow, and came to compete, if at first only in a small way, with Britain for Latin American and Asian trade. As the United States began to industrialize, the seeds of conflict between the industrial North

167

and the agrarian South matured toward conflict. Western farmers changed their roles with shifting patterns in world trade. While the United States was industrializing, Mexico first "stagnated" then began to "underdevelop." Mexico became more and more a pawn of British financial interests. British interference in the Mexican economy helped transform the Mexican class structure and virtually insured a situation of endemic rebellion. Mexico was lurching from marginality toward full-blown peripherality.

Changes in the world-economy and the Mexican state affected the development of the various frontier provinces of Mexico and the United States. Mexican frontier regions became increasingly autonomous as central control loosened. American frontier regions struggled to overtake the North or South via trade or agricultural production for national and, later, world markets. The trajectories of change in these respective regions influenced both the timing and nature of the impending clash between the two states. The quarter century of commerce between them via the Santa Fe Trail had already prepared the way for the conquest.

To disentangle the causes of this conflict it is useful to analyze the position of each state in the larger world order, then examine the internal dynamics of each state in more detail, especially the frontier areas. This analysis begins with a sketch of the conventional accounts of the war.

CONVENTIONAL ACCOUNTS OF THE ORIGIN OF THE MEXICAN-AMERICAN WAR, 1846–1848[1]

A great deal has been written about the Mexican–American War, much of it tainted with the political agenda at that time, or of today, or of both. American accounts of the war can be placed in the following broad categories: the "slave-power conspiracy" thesis, the "Polk-Democratic" thesis, the "Whig thesis," and a variety of synthetic approaches. The slave-power–conspiracy thesis holds that southwestern expansion was part of a continuing pattern designed to extend proslavery political power and the range of cotton cultivation. This theory "has largely disappeared" from contemporary history (Benjamin, 1979, p. 169). The 1850 Compromise admitting New Mexico as a territory without formal comment on slavery was achieved because all parties knew that New Mexico was not suitable for slave-based cotton production (Beck, 1962, p. 139). This knowledge was presumably available before the war, so cotton expansion can be ruled out as a motive for acquiring New Mexico. This is in sharp contrast to cotton expansion into Alabama, Mississippi, and later Texas (Moore, 1966, p. 119). Thus, the verdict that the slave-power conspiracy thesis should be abandoned seems correct. The slavery issue, however, did have considerable bearing on the immediate and intermediate effects of the war.

The Polk-Democratic thesis, in contrast to the slave-power thesis, holds that the causes of the war are to be found in Mexico. This thesis originated in Justin Smith's (1919) Pulitzer-Prize-winning account of the war (Benjamin, 1979; Brack, 1975; Graebner, 1980; T. Jones, 1975). Goetzmann (1966) and Connor and Faulk (1971) present two recent variants of this approach. Connor and Faulk (1971) find the cause of the war in Mexico's reaction to the American annexation of Texas in 1845, in Mexico's need to defend its honor against the United States, and in Mexico's internal disorganization.[2] They reject all other causes. Goetzmann (1966) argues that Polk sought to negotiate the boundary dispute from a position of strength, and thus when the Mexicans attacked, he was prepared to respond. The attack is seen as motivated by the internal dissension within Mexico, thus the United States "became the victim of Mexican internal strife" (Goetzmann, 1966, p. 57). While it is clear that internal conditions in Mexico contributed to the origin and timing of the war, the causes of these internal conditions are not addressed.

The Whig thesis explains the war as a direct result of Polk's expansionist aims. The historical Whig position blames Polk directly for the war. Stenburg (1935, 1938, 1941) and G. Price (1967) argue that Polk deliberately manipulated Mexico into war, and actively sought to "annex a war" as well as the state of Texas in 1845. This was part and parcel of Polk's pursuit of Manifest Destiny (Sellers and May, 1963, Ch.13) and his drive to acquire suitable Pacific ports. Blaming the United States for the war is a continuation of Whig party politics.

Claims by American merchants against Mexico for mistreatment and loss of goods are sometimes included as a cause of the war. American diplomats used the claims to bring pressure on Mexico to sell some of its northern territory to pay its debts. In the Polk-Democratic analysis the claims were yet another Mexican cause for the war. Loyola (1939, p. 43) argues that the claims were an excuse, not a cause. Graebner (1980, p. 408) argues that Polk used them to exert diplomatic pressure on Mexico, but doubts that he would have gone to war over them.

Other writers (Williams, 1972; Van Alstyne, 1960, 1972) see the war as the natural, imperialistic result of an expanding capitalist state. In Van Alstyne's analysis several factors combined to produce westward expansion, and specifically the Mexican war. Simultaneous to, and intertwined with, the boundary controversy surrounding Texas was the controversy

over the Oregon Territory (Pletcher, 1973). American commercial classes were seeking a usable Pacific coast port to facilitate trade with Asia
(Graebner, 1955). California was particularly suitable because it has several ports—San Francisco and San Diego—and was the primary source
of sea otter pelts, a major trade good. Once it was discovered that the
mouth of the Columbia River was not navigable, there was further pressure to acquire California.

Of these theories, some variant of the Whig thesis seems to be the most
persuasive, but it is lacking in several respects. While accounting for
American expansion, and highlighting the role of the doctrine of Manifest Destiny as a justifying ideology, the account overemphasizes the
internal American sources of the war, and in reaction to the Polk-Democratic thesis, sorely neglects the Mexican sources of the conflict. Brack's
(1975) careful critique of the Polk-Democratic thesis details how American actions steadily eroded initially friendly attitudes, and steadily exacerbated antagonisms. Indeed, it is difficult to believe that any informed
contemporary observer could have been fooled by the posturing of the
Mexican press. The bellicose statements in the Mexican press were clearly intended for domestic political purposes. Brack adequately documents the awareness of Mexican officials of Mexico's inability to win a
war with the United States.

Graebner (1980), McAfee (1980), and Brack (1975) are also somewhat
critical of the conspiracy (Whig) thesis. Graebner (1980, p. 412) argues
that G. Price's (1967) case against Polk, while laudable, remains circum-
stantial. Rather, Graebner sees a pattern—continuing to the present—in
American foreign policy of pushing a cornered adversary until he attacks in frustration. The United States responds in self-righteous defense. Brack argues that Polk's ineptitude (and that of his diplomatic
emissaries) stemmed from ethnocentrism that rendered American diplomats blind to the obvious implications of Mexican domestic politics.
The appearance of new documents (McAfee and Robinson, 1982) indicates that Polk was quite well aware of what he was doing. In a review of
those documents, Graebner (1983) sees more support for the Polk conspiracy thesis. The controversies about Polk's culpability no doubt will
continue. They cannot be settled here.

There are other gaps in the discussion of the origins of the Mexican–
American War. Van Alstyne draws some connections between internal
American class structure and interests and movements in international
trade but these are not explored fully or systematically. Benjamin notes
(1979, p. 177) that the "desire for a southern transcontinental railroad
route, as a motivation for American expansion is a seriously neglected
subject." To this might be added the general neglect of the role of the

Santa Fe Trail trade in heightening American interest in New Mexico. As seen in Chapter VII, the Chihuahua–St. Louis connections via the Santa Fe Trail, the New Mexican sheep industry, and to a lesser extent, the local class structure, all contributed to the increased interest in New Mexico. An account is needed that can examine the connections among world-market conditions and internal conditions in the United States, Mexico, and the Southwest. Various strands of these conventional accounts appear in the following synthetic account, which begins with an analysis of the American sources of the conflict.

AMERICAN SOURCES OF THE WAR WITH MEXICO[3]

American sources of the war of 1846 are found in changes in the world economic order and in the trajectory of America's advance in the world-economy. At independence the new American state began with several distinct advantages, all of which were lacking in the Spanish colonies. First, the colonial overhead, despite the propaganda of the time, was relatively light. Robert Thomas (1965) estimates that approximately 0.3% of the total income of the thirteen colonies in 1775 was lost due to British mercantile policies. In contrast, Coatsworth (1978) estimates that the cost of colonial status for New Spain was 7.2% of its total income. Second, connection with Britain gave Americans access to the most advanced technology and business methods then known, though the access was slowed by British mercantilist policies. Third, utilizing the natural advantages of harbors, timber, and location, New England merchants were able to acquire considerable experience and capital in the carrying trades before independence (North, 1966, 1974). These three advantages were incidental benefits of the relatively benign neglect experienced by the American colonies due to British preoccupation with other affairs.

For the northern colonies at least, the pattern of settlement favored a relatively egalitarian class structure consisting of many small, independent farmers. This population was more skilled and literate than the population of the Spanish colonies. This is not to deny extensive trade with Britain, but to highlight the simultaneous competition with Britain, especially in the carrying trades (North, 1966). Although the new American state started with excellent advantages for development, how and why it was able to make use of them requires explanation.

The development of the American state was a consequence of the joint occurrence of changes in the world-economy and local conditions. New England and the middle states had a significant advantage in cheap, abundant resources for ship-building. This advantage outweighed high-er labor costs typical of the colonies (North, 1966). The late eighteenth century was also a time of rapid expansion of the world-economy (Woodruff, 1973; Wallerstein, 1980; Bergesen and Schoenberg, 1980), and colonial production did not pose a strong threat to British producer interests, nor did it threaten the livelihood of those merchants spe-cialized in carrying goods from England to the colonies. Britain's preoc-cupation with France only served to widen the opportunities presented by the expanding world-economy.

Meanwhile the southern colonies had begun to specialize in plantation production. Plantations were profitable enough that nearly all slaves introduced into the British colonies went there directly or were resold there. Southern planters capitalized on the twin advantages of abun-dant, good farmland and the lack of strong indigenous resistance to occupation. The southern colonies, like all the British American colo-nies, were settler colonies. The British colonists brought their own wom-en and did not intermarry with natives, but rather displaced them west-ward (Lang, 1975). Finally, despite British efforts to the contrary, colonists began to cross the Appalachians and settle and farm in first the Ohio, and later the Mississippi valleys.

Continuing British–French rivalry finally exploded in the Napoleonic Wars (1805–1815). The fighting so disrupted Atlantic trade that the new state was able to expand its role in shipping into a major industry (North, 1966, 1974) and to expand its manufacturing sector signifi-cantly. Thus, all classes were able to benefit from the growth of the economy. After peace in 1815, the British flooded the American market with cheap manufactured goods in an effort to eliminate the American competition. The resumption of British navigation sent the American shipping trades into a decline that only ended in the 1830's (North, 1966). Thus began the class struggles that were manifest in the political maneuverings over protective tariffs (Moore, 1966).

The period 1816 to 1832 was marked by a rise in protectionism. Na-scent manufacturers were hurt by the flood of cheap British goods, and petitioned Congress for protection. The entire nation had been made painfully aware of its European dependence by the embargos associated with the War of 1812. As European agriculture recovered from the war, agricultural exports dropped, exacerbated by the passage of the last of the Corn Laws[4] in 1815. Farmers and manufacturers formed a protec-tionist alliance. Merchants were opposed to the tariffs both because they undercut profits, and because of their financial connections to London. Shipbuilders allied with merchants, since the tariffs affected the prices of several of their raw materials. However, as the trading industries declined, New England merchants began to shift capital to manufacturing, and came to support protectionism. Demand for New England manufactured goods increased,[5] so that by 1832 coarse New England cottons were able to compete with British cottons on an equal footing in the growing Far Eastern trade.

Competition with Britain did not curtail support of rebellions in the Spanish Empire. Americans supported the revolts because they were seen as attempts by co-revolutionists to throw off the yoke of European imperialism, and no doubt more important, because the United States, like Britain, saw the opportunity to expand its trade relations with the former Spanish colonies. American traders possessed certain advantages over British traders in capturing the Latin American trade. Transshipment through New Orleans was considerably cheaper than shipment from Europe. This allowed American traders to capture a sizeable portion of the Gulf trade (Graebner, 1951). In addition to the seaborne trade Americans had a virtual monopoly on the overland trade carried on the Santa Fe Trail.

During this same period, cotton was becoming a major export from southern plantations, based in part on technological improvements such as the cotton gin, invented in 1793. Westward expansion of cotton culture was further fueled by land exhaustion in the eastern plantations, especially South Carolina (Moore, 1966, pp. 119, 132). North (1966, 1974) shows a strong association between westward expansion in the South and cotton prices. Some of this expansion spilled over into the Mexican province of Texas. Cotton was the most important export from Texas. In 1834 about 7,000 bales, worth approximately $315,000, were shipped to New Orleans (Weber, 1982, p. 141).

The growth of the monocultural cotton economy began to alter the class balance against protectionism. Southern planters were directly opposed to tariffs because they derived no benefits from them and were hurt by the increased price of consumer goods imported from England. As cotton prices began to decline in 1818 due to increased world production of cotton (North, 1966), southern planters became increasingly opposed to tariffs.[6] The tariffs were used to develop transportation networks in roads and canals, but primarily in the North. Conflict over tariffs

> was largely a class conflict between core capitalists interested in creating a diversified and integrated national economy and peripheral capitalists specializing in the exchange of raw materials for European core products. These two groups contended throughout the antebellum period for the support of other politically important classes: merchants, farmers, and increasingly, workers (Chase-Dunn, 1980, pp. 210–211).

Moore (1966, Ch.III) makes much the same argument.

As long as Britain maintained tariffs against grains but not against cotton, farmers and plantation owners were on opposing sides of the protection issue. But then conflict began to develop between Northern manufacturers and Western farmers over the issue of cheap land. Manufacturers were opposed to cheap land because it undermined their labor supply and drove up labor costs (Moore, 1966, p. 127). Senator Benton of Missouri, a prime backer of the Santa Fe Trail trade, interpreted Northern opposition to cheap land as yet another subsidy to manufacturers (Forsythe, 1977; Chase-Dunn, 1980, p. 212). While cotton dominated exports from 1815 to 1861, hovering around 50% of all exports after the mid 1830s (North, 1966, 1974), after 1829 wheat began to increase in importance. With the growth in wheat exports, farm support of protectionism began to wane.[7] Andrew Jackson was elected president in 1828 with strong support from the new coalition of workers, farmers and planters. His dissolution of the National Bank marked the shift of state power away from manufacturers toward the South and West. Increased cotton sales spurred land expansion, and English capital backed plantation expansion, canal projects and railroads. The 1830s were the peak of British involvement in the American economy (see Table VIII.1).

Americans increasingly participated in the opium, tea and porcelain

Table VIII.1.   Ratio of British
General Imports into the United
States to the U.S. Realized
National Income
in Manufacturing

Year	Ratio
1821	0.365
1829	0.249
1839	0.387
1849	0.191
1859	0.241
1869	0.146
1879	0.104
1889	0.078
1899	0.039

Sources: U.S. Bureau of the Census (1975, Pt.
II:907, for British imports); R. Martin
(1939: Tables 1 and 17); after Chase-
Dunn (1980:215)

trades (Basu, 1979). Manufacturing continued to expand throughout the 1830s, but its control of the federal government based on class alliances steadily eroded. A decline in trade led workers and farmers to favor protectionism. Manufacturing recovered more quickly than either the farmers or plantation owners (North, 1966), rejuvenating the Western–Southern alliance against protectionism. In 1845, the Irish potato famine increased the demand for American agricultural products and supplied a new wave of immigrant labor. Thus, manufacturers were not as inclined to view cheap western land as an attractive alternative to new workers. Texas was annexed the same year. The following year tariffs were lowered, the Oregon Territory was acquired by treaty with Britain, and the war with Mexico began.

The northern movement into the Oregon Territory occurred at the same time as the Southwestern expansion. Wagon trains crossing the northern Plains carried the first West coast settlers. These migrations had four immediate results: they sharpened the conflict with Britain over the Oregon Territory; they presented still another reason for increasing commerce with the West; they severely disrupted Anglo–Indian relations along the migration routes; and they considerably altered intertribal relations on the Plains. The controversy and interest in Oregon Territory (which included modern Washington State) played a major role in the timing of the Mexican-American War (Pletcher, 1973).

Since the commercial classes interested in acquiring California had strong banking ties to Britain, they did not want a war with Britain over Oregon. Southern planters were also heavily mortgaged to British textile producers. The influence of these classes is demonstrated by the lowering of tariff rates early in the Polk administration in 1846. When the British Corn Laws were repealed in 1846 and the American grain trade with Britain increased, it became clear that a war over Oregon Territory would not be worthwhile (Pletcher, 1973). The 49th parallel compromise was settled in June of 1846.

Before this compromise, the Mexican government had sought to use the Americans against the British. The British owned all the principal trading firms and mines in Mexico at that time (Van Alstyne, 1972, p. 101) and had access to the California ports. For a time they even sought an alliance between Texas and Britain. The British resisted the alliance, since it was clear to their minister that the United States was striving to initiate a war with Mexico. Rather, they suggested that Mexico recognize the independence of Texas to use as a buffer with the United States and concentrate on defending California, which the British hoped to keep out of American hands (Graebner, 1980, pp. 414–416). The annexation of Texas destroyed that possibility.

According to Van Alstyne (1972), annexation of Texas was only pre-
liminary to acquiring California—hence the United States support of
Texas claims to a western boundary of the northern Rio Grande (see
Map VIII.1).

> At stake in 1845 was no mere boundary question. Texas must be kept
> coupled with California and New Mexico, and to this end the Rio Grande
> was essential. It was the wedge driven into the heart of New Mexico—
> Santa Fe, Taos, and Albuquerque, the principal towns of the province, lay
> to the *east* of the river—and New Mexico was the land bridge to California.
> The Texans, we remember, had tried to conquer it in 1841 (Van Alstyne,
> 1972, p. 105, emphasis in original).

T. Jones (1975, p. 112) argues that acquisition of California was "the
most important part" of Polk's dream of an American empire. Graebner
(1955, 1980, 1983, p. 292) sees the acquisition of California as a major
force behind American expansion. Even Connor and Faulk (1971, p. 23)
recognize its significance, although they deny it elsewhere (see also pp.
22, 27, 28, 32; see Graebner, 1980, p. 418, note 31). Finally, McAfee and
Robinson provide numerous documents indicating Polk's desire for California (1982, Ch.3, and p. 111). New Mexico was of commercial significance since its territory contained the overland routes from California to
both Texas and St. Louis, following the Old Spanish Trail and the Santa
Fe Trail.[8]

In summary, there were many factors pushing for American expansion into the Southwest. There was, indeed, a small thrust to expand
cotton production. This was offset by the Northern concern over the
expansion of slavery, and more particularly concern over further expansion of southern political control of the government. Eastern and western merchants in fierce competition with Britain wanted to expand
trade. Texas was something of a political anomaly—an independent
state, populated by Americans, not recognized by Mexico. Texas offered
an opportunity for cotton-culture expansion, expansion of southern political power, and for improved trade routes to Mexico. Finally, British–
American rivalry over the trade with Asia made acquisition of a Pacific
port highly desirable. California was of prime importance for its sea-
ports. This importance increased once the Oregon issue was settled, and
no port appeared available in the Oregon Territory. New Mexico was
important as a land bridge to California. The possibility of a land route
to California, especially an all-season, southern rail route, offered a huge

Map VIII.1. Changing Definitions of New Mexico During the Spanish and Mexican Eras

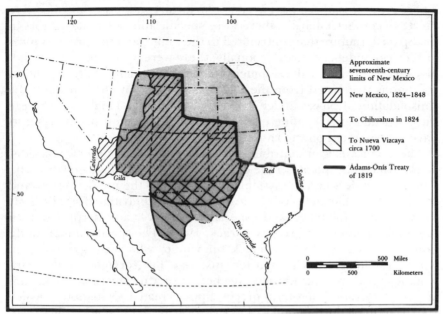

Source: Beck and Haase (1969:Map 19)

potential edge over the British in the Asian trade (Benjamin, 1979). Southern officials hoped to gain control of this region for expanding cotton culture and political power. Northerners wanted the region for the trade possibilities that would be opened. Fear of alienating Britain, the main cotton buyer, tempered the South's inclination toward war. The Northern merchants were disinclined to go to war because they feared provoking British interference, and expanding southern political control over Congress. Whig criticism of Polk was not directed at the acquisition of California, but at the use of arms to acquire it. Even while continuing their attacks on Polk, Whig congressmen continued to vote funds for the war. Overall, the forces for expansion were stronger than those for diplomacy. By this time Manifest Destiny was reaching a fever pitch (Merk, 1966, 1971, 1972). In this ideological climate the patriotism of those who opposed expansion was cast into doubt.

In addition to these factors, there were pressures within Mexico which also pushed toward armed conflict.

MEXICAN SOURCES OF THE WAR OF 1846–1848

There are at least three ways in which Mexican conditions contributed to the 1846 conflict. Globally, there were specific and systematic factors in the Spanish Empire that contributed to the timing and the circumstances of Mexican independence. Nationally, there were the changes in foreign investment, economic development, and the turbulent internal political conditions that lasted from the Hidalgo rebellion in 1810 through the consolidation of power under Porfirio Díaz in 1876. Finally, there were the particular precipitating events in Mexico. Most historical accounts have concentrated on the latter level.

The major Mexican contribution to the conflict was at the two broader levels, which also point up the causes of Mexico's chaotic government. Failure to understand the systematic reasons for the political chaos and contradictory statements of Mexican politicians contributed significantly to American diplomats', and especially to Polk's, misinterpretation of Mexican intentions and resolve (Brack, 1975). The specific initial conditions—who made the first attack on whom, who was aggressing on whose territory, which minister insulted his foreign counterpart, whether Polk wrote his war message before or after the first attack—are largely irrelevant. Long-term preconditions created a situation in which relatively small, inconsequential events triggered a major conflict.

The independence movements of former Spanish colonies share several features: they were all directed against trans-Atlantic control of the economy, and all had to address "a legacy of sectional and regional conflict" (Stein and Stein, 1970, p. 131). These conflicts focused on the competition between the old colonial capitals, which attempted to maintain "their monopolistic position in the national and international trade" (Stein and Stein, 1970, p. 133),[9] and the various subregions that were insisting on local autonomy. After independence, competition became manifest in centralist–federalist conflicts. There were elements of competition between local and national merchants, between protectionists and free-traders, and between agricultural exporters and nascent manufacturers. These conflicts were one root of the continual political instability in Mexico, and in much of Latin America. The persistence of these conflicts can be attributed to two major sets of causes: approximately balanced strength of the various constituent classes in the new states and external interference in class relations by various foreign powers, especially Britain.

At the beginning of the nineteenth century New Spain had a typical colonial economy: large indigenous, culturally distinctive populations, and trade infrastructures oriented toward export. Some sixty percent of

[margin handwritten note: argues that systematic conditions made war inevitable – immediate events irrelevant]

the population were Indians (Schmitt, 1974, p. 50) who supplied most of the labor on the haciendas and in the mines, but still maintained semi-autonomous local villages with communally owned land (Wolf, 1955, 1959; 1982, Ch. 5). The transportation system focused on the capital at Mexico City, and from there on the port of Veracruz (Pletcher, 1973, p. 33). The system was organized around direct primary extraction, mostly bullion. Acapulco was a secondary port, shipping silver to the Philippines in exchange for Asian goods.

Coatsworth interprets transportation costs as one of the two major obstacles to Mexican economic growth in the nineteenth century. If Mexico had had the advantages of the United States in terms of water transportation and low geographical barriers, "the difference in produc tivity between the Mexican and American economies would have been reduced, all other things being equal, by at least one third" (Coatsworth, 1978, p. 91). While it is surely the case that much of this difference is due to accidents of geography, it is also true that the lack of development of transportation facilities is in itself a result of colonial development. But transportation problems were only secondary in slowing Mexican development.

The prime factor retarding Mexican economic development was "inefficient economic organization . . . 'feudalism'" (Coatsworth, 1978, p. 91). Here, again, is the confusing identification of the existence of servile forms of labor with classic European feudalism. The persistence of feudalism is supposedly due to that grand bugaboo of development, tradition. For Mexico the evidence is far more complete than it is for the northern provinces, and the argument for incorporation-induced feudalization is readily made. The great estates were run economically. They were not based on formal serfdom, and their owners were not conservatives, but liberal federalists. Summarizing the results of many estate studies on the early nineteenth century, Coatsworth finds that the estate owners or operators shifted crops, experimented, and invested in equipment in an economically rational manner:

> Not one estate owner had been found who might qualify as the sort of aristocratic, prestige-oriented, economic nincompoop once thought by many to be typical of Spanish American *hacendados*. Each was greedy in the ordinary way—even managers of Church estates. . . . Every one of them demonstrated a primordial desire to maximize income and to minimize production costs (Coatsworth, 1978, p. 87).

This is certainly not descriptive of "feudal" production, but is the essence of capitalist production—economically responding to changing market conditions. The owners of these estates were understandably opposed to tariffs on imports, which lowered profits and produced no benefits; this produced their liberal, free-trade orientation, and opposition to strong central government. Their employment of labor makes the same economic sense—employing, laying off, using various forms of coerced labor.

The Spanish colonial legacy left an ideal situation for capitalist, market-oriented production: a captive work force capable of supporting itself in lean years but desperate enough that it could be forced to work for minimal wages (Coatsworth, 1978, p. 96). When conditions improved, the landowners sought to expand their estates at the expense of local villages. The only protection available to the villagers had to come from a strong central state, or from their own rebellions—hence, the alliance between "tradition-oriented" Indians and conservative Church and centralist parties (Hale, 1968, Chs.6,7).

When land is relatively abundant, and labor relatively scarce, some type of coerced labor system will typically prevail (Chirot, 1975). The form of labor coercion varies with the social context of potential laborers. If slave labor is unavailable, land owners may use debt peonage or political coercion. If there is an indigenous population that still lives in traditional communities (i.e., in a subsistence sector), and who works only part-time—either seasonally or over a lifetime—in the productive sector, indirect coercion via taxes is preferred. Indirect coercion transfers a portion of the maintenance cost of laborers to the traditional community, which is outside the capitalist economy, and thus is not a cost to the producer (Wallerstein, 1979, Ch.6). Wages may then be lower than they would otherwise need to be if the producers had to supply all the maintenance costs for workers throughout their lifetimes.

Bauer (1979a, 1979b) and Loveman (1979) note that there is tremendous regional variability in the degree and type of labor control in Mexico.[10] Still, if the labor systems prevailing in Mexico in the nineteenth century grew from the needs of capitalist agriculture, then the confusion engendered by the term "feudal" is readily resolved. It refers to conditions that are a result of incorporation, not its absence.

Table VIII.2 shows that Mexico begins the nineteenth century well behind both the United States and Britain in comparative national incomes, but ahead of Brazil. The gap widens considerably throughout the century. Mexico even falls behind Brazil, and recovers only late in the century, after the Porfirio Díaz dictatorship (1876–1911) was firmly in place. The growing gap is due to the failure of entrepreneurial practices to thrive in a hostile setting (Coatsworth, 1978, pp. 92–94; Wolf, 1955, 1959). Coatsworth hypothesizes that if the difference between Mexican

Table VIII.2. Comparative National Incomes, 1800–1910

A. TOTAL INCOME IN MILLIONS OF 1950 U.S. DOLLARS (Mexican income as a percentage of each state's income)

Year	Mexico	Brazil	Great Britain	United States
1800	438	198 (221)	2,094 (21)	858 (51)
1845	420	510 (82)	6,293 (7)	5,493 (8)
1860	392	778 (50)	8,510 (5)	10,900 (4)
1877	613	1,115 (55)	16,690 (4)	21,629 (3)
1895	1,146	1,633 (70)	27,930 (4)	50,754 (2)
1910	2,006	2,129 (94)	36,556 (5)	95,201 (2)

B. PER CAPITA INCOME (Mexican per capita income as a percentage of each state's per capita income)

Year	Mexico	Brazil	Great Britain	United States
1800	73	62 (118)	196 (37)	165 (44)
1845	56	72 (78)	323 (17)	274 (20)
1860	49	77 (64)	370 (13)	359 (14)
1877	62	83 (75)	497 (12)	430 (14)
1895	91	89 (102)	745 (12)	735 (12)
1910	132	94 (140)	807 (16)	1,035 (13)

Source: Coatsworth (1978:82)

and American economic organization were removed, there would have been no gap in their respective levels of productivity in 1800. But the gap was present, not because of persistent "feudalism," but because of increasing peripheralization.

New Spain was a source of revenue for Spain. With independence, Britain replaced Spain as the buyer of Mexican products. Mexico traded political independence for economic dependence. The basis of dependent development was formed during the Bourbon reforms and early independence (Platt, 1972). For Mexico the nineteenth century was a journey from marginality to peripherality. This shift, or rather the causes underlying it, is responsible for the increase in coerced labor forms (feudalism), and therefore for the increasing gap between the United States and Mexico. It is also the source of the political instability and endemic conflict among nearly balanced class forces.

The facile equation of landowning with feudalism, and hence political conservatism, has caused confusion concerning which classes brought about the revolt. The revolt began as a liberal movement against Spanish mercantile policies (Bazant, 1977, p. 9). The colonial elite was divided into opposing camps of *criollos* and *peninsulares*. To raise money for the war with France in the early nineteenth century, the Spanish Crown forced heavy taxes and loans on the wealthy *criollos* throughout the Empire. In New Spain the *criollos*, led initially by Hidalgo in 1810, rebelled in an attempt to establish an independent Mexico. To gain Indian support Hidalgo had abolished Indian tribute in 1809. The sacking of *peninsulare haciendas* to finance the revolution quickly spread to the sacking of all *haciendas*. When the revolt began to take on more of the character of a peasant-Indian revolt threatening all estate owners, the major landowners and the central *criollo* elite joined with the royalists to quash the rebellion. By 1815 the revolution was defeated and order restored.

When the liberal revolution took place in Spain in 1820, the *criollo* elite seized power in the name of the king under a former royalist officer, Iturbide, and declared independence in 1821 (Bazant, 1977, pp. 13–14). Despite royalist intentions, the need for revenue required continued sale of former Jesuit properties that had been seized under Bourbon rule, and enforced loans from local landowners. The royalist government failed because of the combined opposition of the merchant classes who had a vested interest in free trade, in alliance with similarly minded *hacendados* who supported the liberals. "Far from desiring a restoration of Bourbon centralism, most landowners wanted to be allowed a free hand to control their immediate surroundings" (Coatsworth, 1978, p. 97). The small capitalist class also opposed state practices that thwarted business development, although they were favorable to protection of their industries from foreign competition.

Iturbide's excesses quickly led to a revolt that established the liberal presidency of Guadalupe Victoria and the 1824 constitution. The liberals introduced reforms that undermined the revenue-generating mechanisms of the state (Pletcher, 1973, p. 43). Mexico began to seek foreign money for support of the government. Aid was sought primarily from Britain because of British wealth and because of distrust of the United States. The total debt on the loans, principal plus interest, was 32 million pesos (Schmitt, 1974; Turlington, 1930). The loans were accompanied by heavy British investment, especially in the mining industry. Gold and silver exports increased. Exports amounted to 6 million pesos in 1826 and nearly 10 million in 1827 (Turlington, 1930).

Borrowing money to run the state had the deleterious effects of distorting the class structure, heightening conflict, and opening the door to foreign intervention. When the first interest payments on the various loans could not be met, the government was again forced to sell Church lands and resort to forced loans. In 1827, and again in 1829, the government declared that all Spaniards (i.e., *peninsulares*) would be expelled and their holdings seized. This provided Spain with an excuse to attack Mexico, setting the stage for one of Santa Anna's well-timed rescues (Simpson, 1966). Conservative revolts followed, which placed Bustamante in power in 1830. Alaman, who had been a minister in the Iturbide government, was named finance minister. He sought to restore the depressed mining industry, which had suffered severe setbacks in the unrest. Alaman also sought to encourage other industries (Bazant, 1977, pp. 44–45). The British of course objected, and the proposal was dropped, partially as a result of the renegotiation of the various British loans (Turlington, 1930; Bazant, 1977).

Meanwhile, the liberals were agitating against the Bustamante policies. Gómez-Farías formed an uneasy alliance with Santa Anna and seized power in 1833. The next year Santa Anna suppressed the liberal reforms of Gómez-Farías. His efforts to assert strong, centralized control predictably incited the rural *hacendados* to rebellion: "On the entire perimeter of Mexico—in Yucatan, California, New Mexico, and Texas—opposition to centralism led to militant action as local leaders refused to accept the domination of Mexico City" (Meier and Rivera, 1972, p. 55; see also Weber, 1982, Ch.12; Voss, 1982). Of these rebellions only the Texas rebellion of 1836 succeeded.

Throughout the first 50 years of Mexican independence nearly half the annual budget was used for military expenses (Turlington, 1930). The various loans to the Mexican government virtually insured free trade, prevented protective tariffs, and tied up much state revenue in pledges for interest payments (Turlington, 1930; Pletcher, 1973, p. 33). To meet interest payments the various governments were forced to sell Church properties and levy forced loans (Bazant, 1977). The shortage of revenues is the key contradiction that insured political instability. No matter who was in power, actions intended to stabilize the government simultaneously undermined the powerholders' position. When liberals were in power the selling of Church properties would incite the conservatives; levying forced loans cut against the grain of the liberal cause, leading to dissension among liberal backers; attempts to raise tariffs encountered opposition from *hacendados* at home, and stern reaction abroad. When conservatives were in power, levying forced loans incited liberals; selling Church property cut against the conservative grain, leading to dissension among conservatives; raising tariffs, while ideologically acceptable, encountered stiff foreign opposition—opposition with its hands firmly on the purse strings of the state in the form of loans.

The liberal *hacendados* favored local autonomy and free trade. This allowed them both a freer hand in exploiting the local labor supply and a better rate of exchange in the market. Each was extremely jealous of his local power. It is this orientation, and not the primordial workings of feudalism, that explains why "the nation disintegrated into a multiplicity of regional satrapies controlled by local *caudillos*" (Coatsworth, 1978, p. 94).[11] Whenever a liberal government would begin to exert state authority to raise necessary revenues, some of the *hacendados* could be counted on to ally with the conservative faction to oust the current usurper. The conservatives, especially Church officials, could always raise an Indian army against the liberal *hacendados*, who were always eager to take over communal Indian lands.[12] Whenever the conservatives would try to impose more centralized control of the economy, the *hacendados* in alliance with liberal middle class merchants would find a champion who would rise to the occasion (Schmitt, 1974, p. 50).

 Thus the Mexican state was in perpetual revolt. "Mexican history from 1833 to 1855 constantly teetered between simple chaos and unmitigated anarchy. . . . the presidency changed hands thirty-six times, the average term being about seven and a half months" (Meyer and Sherman, 1979, p. 324). No class, or class alliance, could command sufficient power to assert its interests over those of the opposition. To take power was to invite revolt. British interference, particularly in the form of strings attached to loans, contributed to the instability. Britain manipulated governments, tax laws and tariffs to its benefit—albeit not always successfully. The United States, on the other hand, repeatedly tried to capitalize on changing conditions to arrange a deal for Texas. No leader, regardless of political leanings or opportunism, could negotiate with the United States and remain in power (Brack, 1975). This is why Polk's attempts to force negotiated land sales were doomed to failure. The territories of concern, though, were not simply passive players, but actively shaped the movement toward armed conflict.

SOUTHWESTERN SOURCES OF THE MEXICAN–AMERICAN WAR

The half of Mexico annexed by the United States from Mexico in 1848 may be divided into three major but economically different areas: Texas, New Mexico, and California (see Map VIII.1). All three areas had population-growth rates higher than those of central Mexico during this era (1821–1846), a similar frontier location, and similar reactions to Mexican administration. New Mexico grew the slowest of the three regions (Weber, 1982, p. 195), but in the late 1830s still had a larger population than Texas and California combined (see Tables VIII.3 and VII.2). The population growth of the frontier regions was not from Mexican immigration, but due to local increase and immigration of foreigners (non-Mexicans). There was little incentive for Mexicans to migrate to the frontier. There were limited opportunities, land was still available in the central areas away from the Indian wars, and the depressed economy meant there were few Mexicans with the means to undertake such migration (Weber, 1982, pp. 187–188). Northern Sonora, which did not attract foreigners, actually lost population during the Mexican era. The population of the 10 northern Mexican provinces was about 636,000 of whom some 30,000 were Americans, residing mainly in Texas (Schmitt, 1974, p. 16).

For the entire north, Mexican independence meant greater autonomy than had been the case under Spanish administration, but many patterns persisted: insufficient economic support, failure to support an adequate judiciary, insensitivity to frontier problems and consequently a series of administrations focused almost exclusively on central state concerns. Influence flowed from the central state to the frontier. The frontier had little effect on Mexico (Weber, 1982, p. 283). Local well-being frequently was more dependent on commerce with foreigners than on loyalty to the Mexican state. Consequently Mexican frontiersmen had at best a tenuous loyalty to the Mexican state. The shifting tides of Mexican politics exacerbated this ambivalence.

In the 1830s when the balance of power in Mexico shifted from the federalists to the centralists, the attempts to tighten control of the frontier provinces by appointing outsiders as administrators led to a wave of rebellions (Weber, 1982, Ch.12). Texas, New Mexico, California and Sonora (Voss, 1982) all staged revolts. Only Texas was successful, although Mexico never officially recognized the fact (Weber, 1982, p. 33). Even though frontier autonomy increased throughout the Mexican era the increase never matched expectations and there was little local resistance to the American annexation. There were considerable differences among these provinces which had significant consequences for their respective reactions to change in Mexico.

Texas

Americans had started to occupy Texas shortly after the Mexican independence (1821). Mexican fears of American expansionism were exacerbated by Pionsett's offers in 1822 to buy the "troublesome" province of Texas, and by his efforts to foment liberal revolution by organizing the York Rite Masonic lodges in Mexico (Bazant, 1977;

Table VIII.3. Population of Three Southwestern Regions, 1793–1850

Year	New Mexico			Texas			California			Total		
	Total	Mexican	Percentage Mexican	Total	Mexican	Percentage Mexican	Total	Mexican	Percentage Mexican	Total	Mexican	Percentage Mexican
1793 [j]	30,953	30,953	100	2,992	2,992	100	1,000	1,000	100	34,945	34,945	100
1810s [s, j]	36,579	36,579	100	4,000	Most	Most	3,270	Most	Most	43,849	Most	Most
1827 [s]	—	—	—	15,000	5,000	33	—	—	—	—	—	—
mid 1830s [s]	57,000	57,000	100	25,000	4,000	16	—	—	—	—	—	—
1845–46 [w]	65,000	65,000	100	—	—	—	7,300	6,620	91	—	—	—
1850* [n]	61,421	56,223	92	217,592	11,401	5.2	92,597	6,678	7	371,610	74,302	20.0

*These figures may be the result of as much as a 20% underenumeration (Nostrand, 1975:383, note 29).

Sources: [j] O. Jones (1979); [s] Schmitt (1974); [w] Weber (1982); [n] Nostrand (1975)

Brack, 1975; Loyola, 1939; McAfee, 1980; Pletcher, 1973; Schmitt, 1974). The history of the diplomatic efforts to obtain Texas is fascinating, complicated with intrigues, bribes, and secret deals, none of which worked. Still, Mexico sought to protect and increase its trade with the United States, which by 1826 amounted to some $6 million[13] in Mexican imports and nearly $4 million in exports (Schmitt, 1974, p. 43).

In spite of misgivings, the Iturbide government granted a license to Stephen Austin in 1822 to take 300 families to settle in Texas.[14] This was only one of many such licenses granted to Americans seeking new land. Mexico sought to populate Texas through the use of such land grants (Weber, 1982, Ch.9). Only the area around San Antonio remained distinctly Mexican after the beginnings of American immigration (Meinig, 1969, p. 35ff). The main activities of the early settlers were subsistence agriculture and cattle raising. Increasing cotton exports from the United States and soil exhaustion in the older cotton-producing areas created a mounting pressure for expansion of cotton production into Texas. By the 1830s cotton culture had begun to dominate eastern Texas. According to a Mexican census report for Texas in 1834 (Castañeda, 1925[15]), most of the exports from Texas were cotton (63%) and furs (28%). The total export trade was valued at $500,000, with imports at $630,000, for a net trade of $1,130,000. Unfortunately there is no way to assess the accuracy of these figures, other than noting that they appear quite large given the total volume of Mexican trade. If they are accurate, trade between Texas and Mexico on the eve of the revolt appears to be larger than the Santa Fe Trail trade for the same year, though it should be noted that Gregg's figures (see Table VII.3) are wholesale import figures.

Unrest had begun early in Texas. There had been the abortive Fredonia revolt in 1826 (Meier and Rivera, 1972, p. 58; Weber, 1982, p. 166). After this the Americans in Texas had two major conflicts with the Mexican government. The first centered around the attempt to abolish slavery in 1830. Clearly this attempt went against the interests of the growing class of cotton producers. The second conflict centered on the sporadic efforts of the Mexican government to regulate trade in favor of the Mexican state. Small holders and cotton producers had strong interest in free trade. American Texans were especially desirous of free trade with the United States. Resentment was also building against the Mexican system of justice which differed sharply from the American system. Mexican central control was most irksome when directed at regulation of the growing trade between the United States and Mexico, since lower transportation costs gave American traders a competitive advantage over Mexican traders.

The movement for independence in Texas began as a response on the part of federalist, liberal Mexicans seeking to break away from the centralist, conservative Santa Anna regime (Barker, 1943). Lorenzo de Zavala, a former minister in an earlier liberal government, was in exile in Texas and was a major Mexican organizer of the revolt (Estep, 1954). The American Texans, who by 1830 were the vast majority of the population (see Table VIII.3), backed the revolt. In 1836 the rebels defeated Santa Anna and declared Texas an independent republic. The revolt was not an ethnic conflict per se. Numerous Mexican Texans participated. Rather, American presence exacerbated intra-Mexican differences since Americans brought their own traditions of local autonomy with them to Texas (Weber, 1982, p. 255).

The Texas secession was recognized by the American, British, and French governments; the Mexican government never formally recognized the independence of Texas (Weber, 1982, p. 33). The Americans recognized Texas in March of 1837, after they were sure it could defend itself. France offered recognition in 1839. Britain held out until 1840 hoping to force the abolition of slavery, but recognized Texas without abolition in order to block American annexation (Schmitt, 1974, p. 59). The sectional controversy complicated immediate admission of Texas to the Union, so it remained an independent republic until 1845.

Texas independence was followed in 1840 by the brief Republic of the Rio Grande, which included the provinces of Tamaulipas (formerly Nuevo Santander), Nuevo Leon, and Coahuila (which had formerly included Texas; see Schmitt, 1974, p. 56: Pletcher, 1973, p. 76; Vigness, 1954; Weber, 1982, p. 266). Texas did not formally recognize the new republic, for fear of jeopardizing recognition negotiations with Mexico, but did supply many volunteers and some matériel to the rebellious provinces. Texas also fielded a small navy that operated in the Gulf during the "pastry war," the brief French invasion of Mexico over foreign debts in 1838–1839. In 1841 Texas negotiated a defensive alliance with the secessionist government of Yucatan, which used Texas warships as raiders. This independence, too, was short-lived. Yucatan signed a treaty with Santa Anna when he returned to power, yet again, after defeating the French (Vigness, 1954).

During the period of the Republic (1836–1845), Texans attempted to exert a claim to the Rio Grande as the western boundary of Texas. Polk actively encouraged the government of Texas to claim this boundary. In 1841 this led to an attempted invasion of New Mexico that was soundly repelled (Barrera, 1979; Beck, 1962, p. 140ff; Meinig, 1969; Minge, 1965, Ch.1; Sunseri, 1979, Ch.1; Weber, 1982, pp. 266–267; Zeleny, 1944, p. 91ff; see Map VIII.1). At that time west Texas was basically unknown to east Texans, and was more properly considered to be part of the New Mexico hinterlands (Carroll, 1938, pp. 101–102). Texans tried several times to intervene in the Santa Fe Trail trade and divert it south to the Gulf of Mexico, but they were always repulsed (Moorhead, 1958; Ulibarri, 1963). The New Mexicans, quite understandably, feared the Texans' imperialist aims; the St. Louis merchants had superior market connections to the east and had no desire to share the lucrative Santa Fe Trail trade with Texans. Comanches were an additional barrier between east Texas and northwestern Santa Fe and Taos trade centers since their main trading and plunder trails bisected the proposed Texas–New Mexico routes (Daniel, 1968; Richardson, 1933; R. Smith, 1963; Weber, 1982, Ch.5).[16]

Texas was a thorn in Mexico's side from the time of the revolt. Its annexation in 1845 was a major precipitating factor in the Mexican–American War. In 1845 Polk placed troops between the Nueces and the Rio Grande in south Texas to defend the new state and to push constantly on the vague boundary between Texas and Mexico. In May of 1846 there was a skirmish between Mexican and American troops. From a Mexican perspective, the troops were defending Mexican soil. From an American perspective the fight was an act of war. Mexico did not disintegrate as expected, but did lose the war. According to the proposed treaty of Guadalupe Hidalgo, America was to receive Texas, New Mexico and California in settlement, to pay Mexico $15 million, and to assume all debts owed to American citizens by Mexico, another $3 to $4 million.

Many wanted the United States to annex more, or even all, of Mexico. In 1848 Sam Houston urged rejection of the treaty and broader annexation, for "the Mexicans are no better than Indians, and I see no reason why we should not go on in the same course now and take their land" (in Weber, 1973, p. 100). Polk was disappointed in the final settlement (Weber, 1982, p. 274). The Treaty of Guadalupe Hidalgo contained provisions intended to alleviate Mexican fears of property loss at the hands of the annexing Americans. The treaty guaranteed the protection of property rights to those Mexican citizens in the territories ceded to the United States and protection of the northern Mexican border from "marauding savage Indians." (These provisions are found in Articles VIII and XI of the Treaty of Guadalupe Hidalgo; see Tate, 1970, and Weber, 1973, pp. 162–168.)

New Mexico

While the loss of Texas was already an established fact in 1846, the loss of New Mexico was new. New Mexico, of course, was of interest to the

United States because all trade with the interior provinces of Mexico passed through New Mexico and because all hopes for an overland connection to the Pacific ports in California rested on having easy passage through New Mexico. New Mexico differed from both Texas and California in several ways. First, it had large Mexican and Indian populations that had been there for centuries. Second, its population growth rate was slowest of the three northern regions, and was primarily local (Weber, 1982, p. 195). Third, it was the site of the only non-elite organized rebellion on the northern frontier.

Most of the population was centered in three towns, Santa Fe, Santa Cruz, and Albuquerque (O. Jones, 1979, p. 163). The remainder was distributed in the small villages of northern New Mexico, the Río Arriba. The larger settlements, the homes of the *ricos,* were located mainly in the south, the Río Abajo (Weber, 1982, pp. 210–212). By the 1830s and 1840s the *ricos* controlled most of the land, the majority of the sheep, and a sizeable portion of the Santa Fe Trail trade. The outlying communities were the homes of the small freeholders and small estates. Some communities were mostly *genízaros,* others were mainly poor Hispanos.[17] Interspersed along the Rio Grande and other river valleys were the surviving Pueblo villages. The northern peoples engaged in subsistence agriculture, buffalo hunting and trade with various nomadic groups. The geographical divisions of Río Abajo and Río Arriba, which were quite old, were loosely associated with class differences (Weber, 1982, pp. 280–282), but local variations make generalization hazardous (Van Ness, 1979, pp. 38–44).

Both the central and outlying groups were dependent on foreign trade, but in different ways. The *ricos* owed their continued prosperity to their position in the trade. Even while competing with Americans, New Mexican *ricos* were dependent on them. All the wealth of the province either came from the trade—in the form of tax revenues, or in profits— or was generated in the process of producing goods for the trade. Rural people were tied to the trade via production of market goods or through trade with nomadic Indians—usually both. Their position in the local class structure gradually eroded with increasing trade.

This class division generated its own conflicts, which surfaced in the 1837 rebellion (Beck, 1962; Dunbar Ortiz, 1980, pp. 86–88; Lecompte, 1985; Reno, 1965, Sanchez, 1978; Weber, 1982, pp. 262–264). This brief episode bears further scrutiny because it reveals the nature of the class structure and conflicts late in the Mexican era. In 1835 Santa Anna appointed Albino Pérez governor of New Mexico. This represented a break with local tradition in which "local government was effectively in the hands of the Río Abajo *ricos,* and gubernatorial appointments usually went to members of this group" (Reno, 1965, p. 198). Pérez had been an officer in the Mexican army. Although he did choose his administration from the local *ricos* with whom he shared ideas, he did not receive financial support from either the central government, or from the *ricos*. Consequently he could not maintain an adequate militia and was blamed for the increase in Indian raids. When New Mexico was made a department in 1836 village autonomy was decreased, and Pérez became responsible for collecting local taxes. A highly factionalized ruling class seized the opportunity to incite the northern villages against him, which was relatively easy to do because of increasing inequality (Bloom, 1914, p. 4).

A high-handed act of a local *alcalde* triggered the generally anticipated revolt (Reno, 1965, p. 199). The revolt was centered in the Río Arriba region (Weber, 1982, pp. 262–264) and was led by José Gonzales of Taos, son of a Taos Pueblo mother and a non-Pueblo, *genízaro* father (Reno, 1965, p. 197; Chavez, 1955).[18] Northern villagers and Pueblo Indians backed the revolt. Governor Pérez was killed, and Gonzales became governor. The new government set about appointing a commission to confirm its loyalty to Mexico and state its grievances. They sought to eliminate the new taxes, to restore governmental power to local village leaders and to include Pueblo Indians in councils on government policy (Reno, 1965, p. 210). "When the assembly failed to make Manuel Armijo governor, he took steps to overthrow the revolutionary regime" (Reno, 1965, p. 206).

Armijo was assisted by the *ricos* of the Río Abajo (Weber, 1982, p. 263), and by American traders who gave Armijo 410 pesos after he had seized power to aid in the "reestablishment of order in New Mexico" (Reno, 1965, p. 202). Reno notes that the Americans' "attitude toward the Gonzales government is shown by their co-operation in overthrowing it" (1965, p. 207).

This local episode, lasting only a few months, presents in a New Mexican microcosm all the features of the general state of affairs in Mexico: a local *caudillo* taking action against a group of anticentralist rebels in the name of order, but also in his own personal and class interests. But this case is unique in several aspects. First, outside intervention was by Americans, not the British. Second, the rebellion centered in Taos (the center of the Pueblo Revolt in 1680). Third, and most significant in the context of New Mexico, this was the only rebellion fomented by lower classes and not openly organized by the elite (Weber, 1982, p. 261).[19]

The uneasy partnership between the local elite and American traders worked against the interests of the local population. The New Mexican government depended on tariffs for revenues. But when forced loans (Moorhead, 1958, p. 143), arbitrary taxes on goods (Moorhead, 1958, p.

146) either by cargo or by wagonload, and special taxes to support local battles became too high, Americans complained to Washington and filed claims against the Mexican government (Minge, 1965, Chs.III and V). Foreign traders devised many ways to avoid taxes. Some formed partnerships with Santa Fe residents (Beck, 1962, pp. 114–115). Others moved to New Mexico and became naturalized citizens (Loyola, 1939, Ch.2). Still others married into various *rico* families (Zeleny, 1944, p. 91). While this group was politically important, it was demographically small. According to the 1850 census not more than 550 of the nearly 57,000 New Mexicans were of American origin (Sunseri, 1979, p. 38), and many of them fled to California in the early 1840s in response to the anti-Texas hysteria (Moorhead, 1958; Minge, 1965; Weber, 1982, p. 195).

The pattern of intermarriage is in itself revealing of relations between the two groups. Intermarriage was a matter of some resentment on the part of male *ricos*. *Rico* women, on the other hand, welcomed American suitors. The role of women in Mexican families, even among *ricos*, was one of subservience to the male head (Gutierrez, 1980). American men were more egalitarian in their approach to family roles, so they were desirable husbands (Zeleny, 1944, p. 91). Still, it should be noted that these intermarriages were both one way—American men and New Mexican women—and restricted to the *rico* class. Failure to pay attention to these class limitations led Gonzalez (1969, p. 80) to claim that the entering Americans had little prejudice against Mexicans. Weber argues that the prejudice was far stronger against Mexican men than toward Mexican women. He attributes this, at least in part, to the dearth of women among Americans in Mexico, especially in New Mexico (Weber, 1979, pp. 295–307), but the class aspect of these marriages is not brought out as strongly as it might be. Sunseri (1979, p. 95) correctly points out that prejudice is lacking only with respect to the *ricos*—many of whom were kin—and is not lacking with respect to "Mexicans" in general. In fact American traders and later immigrants took over the *rico* attitudes toward *pobres* and grafted them onto their own antiforeign prejudices.

Intermarriage also became a mechanism for acquiring trading privileges and land. In an attempt to populate the northern reaches of New Mexico and create barriers to increasing nomadic raids and encroaching Americans, Armijo made a number of land grants to Americans who had become Mexicans via marriage. Charles Bent, a former mountain man turned trader (Weber, 1972), was prominent in several of these as a silent partner. He was attempting to gain a favorable position for his trading company with respect to the Santa Fe Trail trade. These grants, made in haste and desperation, were to become the key to "legal" dispossession of New Mexicans from their land after the American conquest (Weber, 1982, pp. 190–194; Minge, 1965, Ch.IX).

Given the various types of dependence on American trade, American money, and even American arms in combatting hostile nomads, it is not surprising that New Mexico offered no resistance to Kearny's army when it invaded New Mexico. Governor Armijo led an army to meet the Americans, but fled before they arrived. Armijo's actions are readily understandable (Minge, 1965; see notes 11 and 19 in this chapter). Armijo, and the entire *rico* class, had nothing to gain and everything to lose by resisting the obviously superior American army. As there was insufficient reason to rebel against Mexico, so there was insufficient reason to resist invading Americans.

Because of the larger Mexican population, internal social-structure factors played a greater role in New Mexico than in Texas or California in the reactions of Americans. These features made a lesser contribution to the Mexican–American War in California.

California

Several factors promoted interest in California. Before the war it was known to possess many resources. Chief among these were sea otters, good ports, and fertile agricultural land (Almaguer, 1977, 1981). The ports of California were desirable both as harbors for the northeastern whaling industry and for the Asian trade. There was also considerable fear that Mexico would sell California to Britain, America's main rival in the Asian trade (Loyola, 1939, pp. 54–55). Foreigners had traded in California since the late eighteenth century for sea otter furs and supplies for whaling ships. By the 1820s California cattle products were being traded for eastern manufactured goods (Almaguer, 1977, 1981). Between 1826 and 1848 California shipped 6 million hides and 7,000 tons of tallow to Boston (Weber, 1982, pp. 138–139). Some trade was carried via an overland route in the 1830s on the Old Spanish Trail (Graebner, 1955; Ulibarri, 1963; Moorhead, 1958). San Diego was doubly desirable for its harbor and for its central role in the hide trades. The major source of interest in California was its potential to help American merchants in their drive to increase their share of the Pacific trade. Gold was not discovered until near the end of the war.

Hence trade played a major role in California's contribution to the Mexican–American War. The extensive hide trade helped form a small but not too wealthy oligarchy. Until the secularization of the missions in the 1830s (Weber, 1982, pp. 60–67), trade had been dominated by the

Franciscan missionaries. Even after that time, it was primarily by barter, not cash. The *Californios* traded at unfavorable terms, frequently buying on credit advanced against the following year's production. Hides went to Boston, and a few shoes returned. No local industry developed (Weber, 1982, pp. 135–146). The small number of *Californios* (3,320 in 1821, 7,300 in 1845; Weber, 1982, p. 206; see Table VIII.3) were from the beginning tied to capitalist trade (Almaguer, 1977, 1981).

The *Californios* chafed under central control from Mexico. Rebellions occurred in 1828, 1829, 1831, and 1836 (Weber, 1982, p. 243). The latter rebellion was the most serious. It was typical of northern rebellions, organized by the local elite to increase local control over tariffs and trade, to eliminate the importation of convicts as settlers, to improve the administration of justice, and especially to open civil and military governmental positions to the *Californios*. It was settled through diplomatic efforts. Unlike Texas, Americans played at most a minor role in the rebellion. No threat from the Mexican Army united the quarreling northern and southern factions, and there was a strong fear of usurpation by foreigners—British, French, or especially the Americans (Weber, 1982, pp. 255–260).

Again in 1842–1844, rebellion loomed. Mexican governor Micheltorena sent his agent, Castañares, to Mexico to ask for help, or even to cede California to the British to keep out the Americans. Local rebels also approached British agents to ask for protection. British agents declined both offers (Weber, 1982, p. 269). *Californio* fears of Americans were well founded. In 1842 Commodore Jones had seized Monterey in the mistaken belief that a war with Mexico had been declared. Even though Monterey was restored and apologies offered, American power and intentions had been amply demonstrated (Weber, 1982, p. 202).

It was after the secularization of the missions in the mid-1830s that large numbers of Americans entered California seeking land. Most grants of land were made in the early 1840s, with a significant proportion going to foreigners. Trade attracted settlers to coastal areas; land for agriculture attracted settlers to inland areas especially around Sutter's colony near Sacramento (Weber, 1982, p. 204–206). In 1846 this latter group staged a revolt, triggered by unrest over the American annexation of Texas and in hope of repeating the 1836 revolt in Texas. The opening of the Mexican–American War rendered the "Bear Flag Revolt" moot.

Of the three regions annexed by the United States the local population in California had the least to do with the start of the Mexican–American War. Both the Mexican and American populations there were small. Local *ricos* did not have the ambivalent loyalties the New Mexicans had. Trade and agriculture were capitalist activities. Thus, California is "the key to understanding commercial interests in expansion" (Barrera, 1979, p. 13). Clearly, all three regions contributed to the war, but in different ways that interacted with both the Mexican and American sources of war.

CONCLUSIONS, QUESTIONS, SPECULATIONS

The events leading to the Mexican–American War were part of wider changes in the world economy (Weber, 1982, p. 282). The most significant change was the transformation of the northern half of Mexico from a declining economy to a vital, expanding economy. Several distinct levels of social change must be analyzed simultaneously to understand these processes. Globally, the forces behind the rise of Britain and the decline of Spain also influenced this transfer. Nationally, the integration of the Mexican and American frontiers was a major problem. Regionally, the peculiar class structures produced by the weak incorporation of the frontier areas into their respective states shaped the course of events.

Long-term processes were involved in the gradual shift of hegemony in the growing European world-economy from the Iberian Peninsula to England via the Low Countries (Wallerstein, 1974a, 1974b, 1980). The first wave of decolonization that accompanied these shifts followed independence of the United States from Britain and of Mexico from Spain (Bergesen and Schoenberg, 1980). Britain's eagerness for wider markets led it to encourage the independence of the Spanish colonies (Stein and Stein, 1970, 1980; Platt, 1972, 1980a, 1980b; see note 9 above). Mexico suffered the typical consequences of peripherality: its people did not develop a shared sense of nationhood; the state had weak control over outlying areas and a weak hold on its various parts; there was low integration and development of trade patterns and infrastructure (Coatsworth, 1978), and a consequent high degree of internal social, cultural, and economic variability. It was Mexico's peripheral status that was the root of both its political instability and its immense internal diversity (Bauer, 1979a, 1979b; Loveman, 1979).

Changes in imports and exports, in degree of concentration in primary versus secondary exports, in stability of governments, in degree of external control of the economy, and in relative size, are reflected in population changes (see Table VIII.4). The impact of the chaotic conditions in Mexico appears in the slightly negative population growth between 1810 and 1830. The United States experienced steady growth:

Table VIII.4. Total Population of
the United States and Mexico,
1790–1845 (Population in millions)

Year	United States [1]	Mexico
1790	4.0	5.0
1810	7.2	6.1
1830	13.0	6.0
1845	20.1	7.5

[1] Schmitt estimates immigration to the United States between 1820 and 1850 to have been about 1.5 million (1974:46).
Source: Schmitt (1974:45)

population grew to over 20 million, only 1 or 2 million of which was due to immigration (Schmitt, 1974, p. 46).

In contrast to Mexico, the United States was rising in the world-economy due to continued British preoccupation with other, seemingly more profitable and important, ventures, and the vast resources the new state controlled or to which it had access. Trade fueled economic and demographic growth and encouraged geographic expansion at the expense of Native Americans. The wave of Latin American independences offered new opportunities for American traders, who used their proximity to Latin America, and especially Mexico, to advantage.

The independence and annexation of Texas was both an indicator and a cause of the final conflict. After Mexico's independence, trade with Mexico increased rapidly. By 1835 trade with Mexico was by far the most important segment of trade with Latin America. Not until the mid-to-late 1840s did trade with either Brazil or Cuba match the peak of Mexican trade, which was $9 million in 1835 (Graebner, 1951, p. 49). The impact of the growing conflict over Texas can be seen in the decline in Mexican trade after 1835 (see Table VIII.5). By 1845, when Texas was annexed, Mexican trade had declined to little more than the Santa Fe Trail trade (see Table VII.3). Before this time, the vast bulk of Mexican trade had been via Gulf commerce (Graebner, 1951).

The importance of Texas to Mexican trade is revealed in the annual figures for export of Mexican silver and gold (in both specie and bullion) to the United States (see Table VIII.6). There was a flurry of activity in 1834–1835, a precipitous decline to former levels in 1836 (the year of the Texas revolt), and a steady decline thereafter. Importing specie was vital to the Missouri economy, and it was a significant factor in transforming the New Mexican economy. Even with the exercise of due cau-

Table VIII.5. U.S. Trade with Mexico Compared to Total Trade, Cotton Trade, and Specie Imports, 1826–1845

Year	Imports[g] from Mexico	Specie[u] from Mexico	Percentage of Mexican Imports in Specie	Percentage of Total U.S. Imports from Mexico[n1]	Exports[g] to Mexico	Percentage of Total U.S. Exports to Mexico[n2]	Percentage of Cotton in Total U.S. Exports
	$	$			$		
1826	3,916,198	2,850,409	72.8	5.0	6,281,050	8.6	34.3
1830	5,235,241	4,702,716	89.8	8.3	4,837,458	6.7	41.4
1835	9,490,446	8,343,181	87.9	6.8	9,029,221	7.8	56.4
1840	4,175,001	3,458,892	82.8	4.2	2,515,341	2.0	51.6
1845	1,702,936	NA	NA	1.5	1,152,331	1.1	48.8

Sources: [g]Import and export totals (Graebner, 1951:49)
   [u]Specie from Mexico, *Niles' Register* 66 (July):342, and Ulibarri (1963:200–201)
   [n1]Total U.S. imports (North, 1966:234, Table C-VIII)
   [n2]Total U.S. exports and cotton exports (North, 1966:233, Table A-VIII)

All percentages calculated by author.

tion, allowing for extensive contraband trade (Platt, 1972, p. 59), it is clear (see Table VIII.5) that specie and bullion were major imports from Mexico.[20] The level of export is comparable to the level of specie and bullion export to Britain (Platt, 1972; Turlington, 1930). This trade itself was part of the conquest of Mexico.

Rivalry with Britain concerned not only Latin American trade but trade with Asia. Toward that end the possession of a Pacific port and a land connection to it became vital concerns. Once the Oregon issue was settled, and it became clear that there were no suitable ports in the new territory (Pletcher, 1973), interest in California increased. This interest became part of the emerging and changing politics of the new nation-

Table VIII.6.   Specie and Bullion
Imports from Mexico,
1821–1842

Year	Import Value	Index[1]
	$	
1821	80,590	0.9
1822	137,664	1.5
1823	86,169	0.9
1824	51,047	0.6
1825	2,603,108	28.3
1826	2,850,409	31.0
1827	4,005,255	43.5
1828	3,853,880	41.9
1829	4,534,946	49.3
1830	4,703,716	51.5
1831	4,463,134	48.5
1832	3,626,704	39.4
1833	4,592,892	49.9
1834	9,204,517	100.0
1835	8,343,181	90.6
1836	4,537,418	49.3
1837	4,650,978	50.5
1838	2,689,426	29.2
1839	2,253,548	24.5
1840	3,458,892	37.6
1841	1,938,083	21.1
1842	1,342,817	14.6

[1]Index based on percentage of high year (1834 =
100.0), calculated by author.
Source: *Niles' Register* 66:(July):342; also in Ulibarri (1963:200–201)

state. While Britain was a major rival, it was also a major trade partner. Britain bought southern cotton, and eventually western grains. The one relationship tempered the other for both America and Britain. If Yankee traders sought to best British rivals in Asia, they did not wish to promote their hostility. While British traders sought to undercut their American rivals by denying them access to California ports, they did not wish to do so at the price of war with either the United States or Mexico.

At this broad level, the balance of class forces in both Mexico and America tipped in favor of war. In Mexico no group could remain in power and advocate ceding land to the United States. In the United States, rivalry with Britain sufficiently tempered Whig opposition to war that it became inevitable. The ambivalence in American attitudes even surfaced in debates over how much of Mexico to annex. The Texas affair lowered trade with Mexico, hurting both general commerce with Mexico, and troubling the Santa Fe Trail trade. Texas was a serious threat to the Missouri traders, and to New Mexican *ricos*. Both groups profited from a trade route through New Mexico, rather than a shorter route through Texas.

Mexico's northern frontier was, indeed, the periphery of a periphery (Weber, 1982, p. 282). Throughout the region the same indicators of marginal incorporation appear time and again. The political and judicial systems varied from ineffective to nonexistent. Population growth, although higher than in central Mexico, was due to foreign (i.e., non-Mexican) immigration. Trade was poorly regulated and taxed, if at all. Santa Fe, the major northern entrepôt, was oriented toward St. Louis, and not Mexico. Finally, the indigenous populations were barely assimilated into Mexican culture. The various subregional units did not and could not coordinate their activities even with respect to controlling nomadic raiders. This weak integration into the Mexican state was responsible for the highly variable social, cultural and economic conditions found across the northern frontier.

The reliance on foreigners for trade goods, for money in the form of taxes, and their presence in the local society (strongest in Texas, weakest in New Mexico), accounts for the tenuous and ambivalent loyalties of local citizens. In Texas, Mexicans had fought beside Americans for independence. There were revolts in both New Mexico and California. Ultimately, there was little resistance to American annexation. While there were grounds for fearing the Americans, there was little to be lost by severing ties with Mexico.

Finally, weak incorporation and its consequences contributed to the general increase in nomadic raiding in the 1830s. As the balance of power shifted to the centralists, and the federalist-oriented northerners wrested greater autonomy from the central administration, coordination of Indian policy was lost, as were the funds to pursue it. This led to an end to rations, the issuing of bounties on scalps, and to reliance on booty and captives as payments for military services. The decline of the missions, especially in California, undercut control.

Geopolitics, too, played a role. As Americans moved west over the Oregon and Santa Fe Trails seeking trade and new land in the west, more and more Indian groups were pushed west beyond the Mississippi. The intrusion of new groups, Indian and American, onto the Plains disrupted social relations and exacerbated conflict among Plains groups. This pressure forced Comanche groups to move further south and to rely more heavily on raiding, which led to even stronger pressures on Apache groups. The latter were now denied access to the Plains, and with the end of rations, were increasingly forced to raid for subsistence. The trade in captives served to fuel the raiding, and endemic warfare again became the norm on the northern frontier.

All of these changes, as momentous as they were for local and regional conditions, were the result of relatively small changes in incorporation. Under the Bourbon reforms the northern frontier had become more tightly incorporated into Spanish administration. With Mexican independence, the incorporation again loosened. As political instability and chaos increased throughout Mexico, bonds on the frontier loosened even more. These changes pushed inexorably toward a war to make official what was already approaching an accomplished fact—the transfer of the region from Mexican to American control.

This analysis suggests that these changes must be explained by articulating disparate types of change occurring along different political, economic and temporal axes, and that such changes are a matter of degree. The history of this region under Spanish, then Mexican, and then American domination suggests the nature of the dominating state is crucial to understanding these processes, as are the natures of the societies incorporated by the state. Finally, the question remains, how typical were such changes in frontier areas?

Clearly, the conquest had tremendous impacts on local, regional and national patterns of change and development. New Mexico remained marginal to American interests, a region of refuge, but now within the dynamic capitalism of the rising American state. This partial incorporation shaped the distinctive course of development in New Mexico—as opposed to that of Texas and California—and facilitated the survival of its indigenous ethnic groups. These topics are discussed in the following chapter.

NOTES

1. Benjamin (1979), Graebner (1955, 1980), Brack (1975), and Pletcher (1973) inform much of what follows in this chapter. Brack examines the war from a Mexican perspective. McAfee (1980) provides a detailed diplomatic history of the events immediately before the war.

2. These versions (Connor and Faulk, 1971; Faulk and Stout, 1973; S. Connor, 1972, 1973, and a special issue of *Journal of the West*, 1972 [11:2(April)] edited by Faulk) amount to "blaming the victim" on a macropolitical scale, a reflection of the backlash to the antiwar movements in the 1960s. T. Jones (1975), Brack (1975), and Graebner (1980) criticize this approach.

3. This section draws heavily on Chase-Dunn's (1980) world-system analysis of the rise of the United States.

4. The various Corn Laws were enacted in England to protect the interests of the landed class against importation of cheap agricultural products. The tariffs were so high that they virtually assured that American grains would not be marketable in England.

5. There is considerable disagreement over where these new manufactures were sold. Zevin (1971) sees the demand coming from the West as production of homespun declined; North (1966) emphasizes the southern market; and Lindstrom (1978) sees most of the demand coming from the East itself. But there is no disagreement that the demand for manufactured goods, especially cotton goods, increased.

6. Chase-Dunn (1980, p. 209) shows the decline: "Cotton prices fell from 31¢ a pound in 1818 to 14¢ in 1820; 10¢ in 1826; and 8¢ in 1831." North (1966) on the other hand gives the prices as 1818, 24.0 cents; 1820, 17.0 cents; 1826, 12.19 cents; 1831, 9.71 cents (Tables A–X, p. 257). North's figures refer to average New York prices. The lack of agreement is not serious, in that the trend is the same, and the explanations proposed for the decline are similar.

7. For Chase-Dunn (1980) this convergence of economic interests grew out of both the marketing of Ohio Valley agricultural products in the South and the shared use of the New Orleans entrepôt by both Southern and Ohio Valley producers. North (1974, Ch.VI), however, finds that the western trade was primarily with the Northeast and foreign areas (including Mexico; see Graebner, 1951). This somewhat different reading, however, would seem to strengthen Chase-Dunn's case for farmer protectionism, since dependence on foreign markets leads to shared trade interests, as opposed to simply wanting protection for major buyers.

8. Weber provides excellent maps of the region, depicting the boundaries of the Mexican states in 1824 (1982, p. 23) and the various trading trails (1982, pp. 126–127).

9. Platt (1980a, 1980b) and the Steins (1980) argue heatedly, if at times tediously, over the applicability of a dependency model to early nineteenth-century Latin America. Platt argues that Latin America was not even peripheral at that time. The Steins argue the dependency model fits. Both are correct and both are in error. The confusion stems from conceptualization of dependency and incorporation as dichotomous, rather than variable relations. Platt is correct in asserting that early nineteenth-century Latin America, especially Mexico, was not a full-blown periphery. The Steins are correct in asserting that the movement toward dependency was already in progress at that time. Based on Platt's

(1972) own evidence, Latin America and Mexico were becoming more peripheral, but the process was only in the early stages at the time of the Mexican–American War.

10.   Bauer (1979a, 1979b) and Loveman's (1979) exchange conveys some of the sense of the problems of generalizing about labor, coercion, oppression and incorporation. Both writers feel that generalization is premature. Their main point is the lack of a theory to explain the extreme variability in labor forms. Thus there is no consistent terminology, and no means to decide when a specific case is anomalous or simply an uncommon combination of common factors.

11.   Wolf and Hansen (1967; 1972, Ch. 6) provide the best discussions of the *caudillo, caudillismo* and *caudillaje*. According to Wolf and Hansen (1967, p. 169, note 3), "*Caudillo* is best translated as chieftain. The term derived from the Latin *caput*, head. *Caudillaje* refers to the condition of caudillo competition and rule." A *caudillo* may be thought of as a "big man" peculiar to peripheral agrarian economies. The point is that the conditions that produced *caudillos* were systematic, even if the resulting political situation appears chaotic.

12.   Hale (1968, especially Chs. 6 and 7) discusses the tension between liberal *hacendados* and Indians. Liberals wanted Indians to become citizens and abandon communal landholding. This would presumably lead to Indian development, but actually led to *hacendado* usurpation of Indian lands. Conservatives argued for maintaining the old order including communal ownership of Indian lands. Hence, the frequent alliance between Indians and conservatives. As with much else in Mexico, this generality is riddled with exceptions.

13.   According to Turlington (1930) in the early nineteenth century one peso was worth one dollar, and five pesos were worth one British pound.

14.   Iturbide had actually granted the license to Austin's father, who died before he could organize the colonial expedition. Stephen reapplied, and was given the grant.

15.   Castañeda is the translator of a report made by Juan Almonte to Valentín Gómez Farías, Vice President of Mexico, who requested the report because of the unrest in Texas. It was in part intended to prepare for military action as well as to guide reforms. See "Translator's Note" (Castañeda, 1925, p. 177).

16.   See Weber (1982, p. 84) for an excellent map of these trails.

17.   The term "Hispano" is generally used in Southwest literature to refer to Spanish speakers, or those descended from Spanish speakers who have lived in New Mexico from the time of the Spanish conquest. They distinguish themselves from more recent Mexican immigrants. The use of this label has given rise to a great deal of controversy (Sandoval, 1982; Nostrand, 1970, 1980, 1981, 1984; Blaut and Ríos-Bustamante, 1984; Hansen, 1981; Meinig, 1984; Simmons, 1984; Chavez, 1984; and T. Hall, 1984a). Weber (1973, 1979, pp. 295–307) provides a close view of Mexican and New Mexican reactions to the conquest.

18.   Lecompte (1985, pp. 36–40) disputes the *genízaro* background of Gonzalez, and sees him as a local Hispano farmer and buffalo hunter. Either way he was definitely not a *rico*.

19.   Minge (1965) depicts Armijo as a local strongman, trying to maintain both his position and the security of New Mexico—typical activities for a *caudillo* (see note 11). Lecompte (1985), too, claims that Armijo has been unfairly portrayed by American historians. She interprets the rebellion as a democratic movement without class or racial overtones. However, her own account belies this interpretation. The rebellion appears to have been complicated by intrigues

by local notables attempting to benefit from the unrest. Thus, Reno's (1965) interpretation appears more tenable, despite Lecompte's (1985) more thorough research. None of the errors Lecompte attributes to Reno would change his, or this, interpretation.

20.   Contraband trade was also extensive: "In Mexico, the contraband trade was carried on 'with the utmost audacity.' MacGregor considered that the $8 million difference in the early '40s between exports ($20 million) and imports ($12 million) was fully covered by smuggling" (Platt, 1972, pp. 59–60).

CHAPTER IX

The Consolidation of the American
Conquest of the Southwest

The sudden leap of the nation's boundaries to the Pacific set off a process of confrontation and conflict between whites and the Indians of the Trans-Mississippi West. It was a process even then ending in catastrophe for the tribes of the eastern woodlands. Having destroyed one "Indian barrier," an aggressively westering America now faced another. In less than half a century this barrier too would be destroyed, and white civilization would reign unchallenged over the plains, mountains, and deserts of the Trans-Mississippi West (Robert Utley, 1984, p. 4).

Conquest of New Mexico by the United States unleashed some two decades of furious fighting with various Indian groups, worse than all previous hostilities. The tacticians of this warfare were people who devoutly believed in Indian extermination, and they were able to bring into service weapons much more deadly than had previously been used in New Mexico. Hispanic New Mexicans, despite General Kearny's promise that the United States government would protect them from Indian raids, were exposed more than ever before and were required to carry the brunt of the fighting in the territorial militia (Frances Swadesh, 1974, pp. 64–65).

The war with Mexico officially began on May 13, 1846, and ended February 2, 1848, with the Treaty of Guadalupe Hidalgo. The conquest of New Mexico took a much shorter time, from June 26 through August 18, 1846, and was totally bloodless. Colonel (soon to be General) Stephen W. Kearny led the Americans into New Mexico, and on to California. He instituted a new government in New Mexico, retaining local officials wherever they would swear loyalty to the new rulers. The easy conquest was a product of long-term national and international movements combined with a quarter century of trade and virtual economic dependence on American traders. It took much longer to consolidate the ridiculously easy conquest: control over Texas and California had to be affirmed, the sectional controversy and the Civil War remained to be settled, and most troublesome of all, the various warring nomadic Indian groups had to be subdued. Even so, the immediate effects of the conquest were dramatic for Texas and California. Texas continued to grow rapidly. California experienced even more precipitous growth with the discovery of gold in 1848. By 1850 California had been admitted as a free state, offsetting the earlier annexation of Texas as a slave state. New Mexico immediately became embroiled in the sectional controversy over slavery.

New Mexico was granted territorial status in 1850. The issue of slavery was to be left up to the local populace. The other parts of the 1850 Compromise relevant to the Southwest were the admission of Utah Territory on terms similar to New Mexico's admission, and the elimination of Texas's claims to the Rio Grande as its western boundary in return for the federal government's assumption of its public debt ($10 million). New Mexico was split in half in 1863 when the Arizona Territory was carved from its western part and pieces of surrounding territories (see Map IX.1).

California and Texas became states and developed rapidly, if in substantially differing ways (Barrera, 1979; Pitt, 1966; Almaguer, 1977, 1981; Murgia, 1975). New Mexico, and subsequently Arizona, remained territories for a longer period than any other region of the continental United States, a result not unconnected with their ethnic composition. The majority of the population was either Mexican or Indian. Texas succeeded in driving nearly all Indians from its territory into what was to become Oklahoma. Between disease and skirmishing, most of California's Indian population was destroyed (Cook, 1976). Apache, Navajo, and Pueblo groups for the most part remained in New Mexico and Arizona. Utes from northern New Mexico became a Colorado problem. The differences in development among the Southwestern regions are summarized in Table IX.1.

The conquest of the Southwest was not completed until new governmental structures were firmly in place and new patterns of trade and development had replaced the older patterns. As with the overlap of declining Spanish control and rising American penetration in the early parts of the nineteenth century, the conquest took nearly 30 years to complete. It coincided with the rise of distinctively American frontier institutions. With the firm implantation of capitalist democracy, an entirely new dynamic of social relations began to take shape, and the trajectory of change in New Mexico departed radically from that of California and Texas after American annexation.

The consolidation of the conquest of New Mexico brought the gradual evolution of the New Mexican Hispanic community from a relatively

Map IX.1.   Changes in Political Geography, 1853–1866

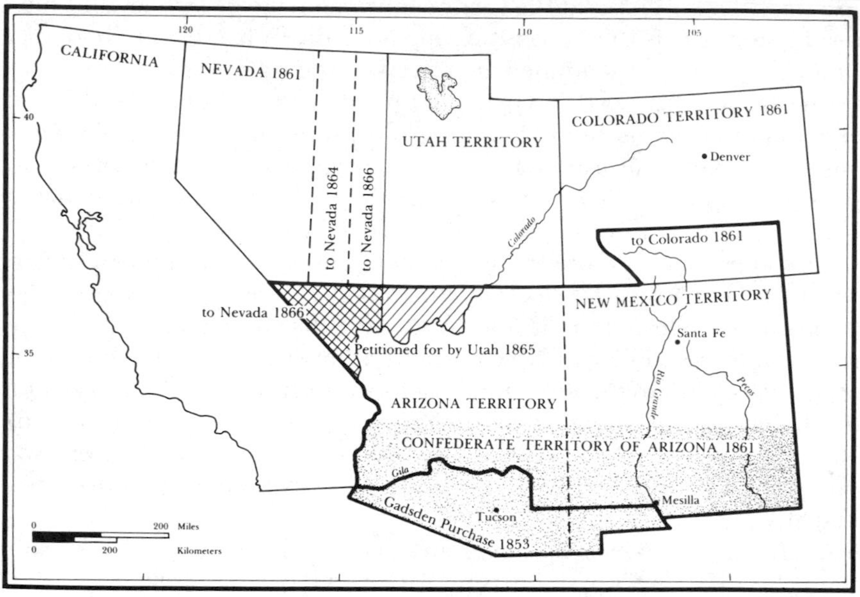

Source: Meinig (1971:21)

autonomous society to an enclaved ethnic group and ended autonomy for all Indian groups. The Hispanos of New Mexico became a political minority in their own homeland, many years before they became a demographic minority in 1928 (Lamar, 1970, p. 4). The analysis begins with an overview of the changes that occurred during consolidation, then proceeds to a more detailed description of the processes of change within New Mexico, and finishes with an account of the final subjugation of the various Indian groups. Not unexpectedly these processes are interconnected, and the distinctions drawn among them are mainly analytic.

MAJOR EVENTS OF THE CONSOLIDATION OF THE CONQUEST

No sooner had the Americans taken control of New Mexico than the intensity of Indian fighting increased and remained high for the next 20 years (Swadesh, 1974, p. 64; Zeleny, 1944, p. 109). In 1847 there was a

Table IX.1. Major Economic Developments in the Southwest, Mid to Late Nineteenth Century

Time	Texas	New Mexico	Arizona	California
1850s	Cotton Grains Cattle	Santa Fe trade Sheep	Mining (silver) Apache wars	Gold Mining Grains Cattle
CIVIL WAR 1860s	Cattle	Sheep Cattle Navajo and Ute peace	New Terr. 1863 Mining declines Ranching Apache wars	Gold Mining Grains Cattle decline
1870s RAIL- ROADS	Sheep Cattle (fences) Cotton Comanche wars	Cattle Sheep Mining (silver)	Mining resumes (copper) Commercial farming Apache wars	Grains Fruits and vegetables

Source: This table follows Barrera (1979:38, Figure 1), with slight modifications to adapt it to this discussion.

rebellion in Taos that resulted in the assassination of Governor Charles Bent and several other officials. The rebellion was symptomatic of reactions of native New Mexicans, Mexicans and Indians, to ill treatment from highly prejudiced American soldiers (Zeleny, 1944, p. 106; McNierney, 1980) and to class and ethnic pressures similar to those of the 1837 rebellion (Beck, 1962, Ch.VII). Throughout the 1850s the occupying army amounted to some 1,700 men at an average annual cost of $3 million (Lamar, 1970; Beck, 1962; Zeleny, 1944). Provisioning them was a major source of money in the region.

Shortly after the conquest, General Kearny sent Major Cooke with the Mormon battalion to mark a wagon road to California. In 1849 over 50,000 gold seekers used the road to travel to the new gold fields (Lamar, 1970, pp. 416–417). The original Mexican boundary had been too hastily drawn to allow completion of a southern rail route through American territory (Lamar, 1970, p. 110). The Gadsden Purchase was made in 1853 to gain the territory necessary to build a line to California (Loyola, 1939, p. 139ff; see Map IX.1). Support for the Gadsden Purchase increased with the discovery of copper and silver in the southern part of what was to become Arizona. The United States began subsidizing the Butterfield Overland Mail along Cooke's wagon road to California at the rate of $600,000 per year (Lamar, 1970, p. 104). Thus, the main impetus behind the acquisition of New Mexico was quickly fulfilled—a southern overland route to California.

The movement of miners into this area fueled the rivalry between the largely unpopulated western portion of New Mexico and the more heavily populated Rio Grande Valley. Petitions for the formation of a separate territory began appearing in 1856 (Faulk, 1970; Meinig, 1971; Lamar, 1970). The proposed division would have split New Mexico along the 34th parallel to form a new territory called Arizona (Confederate Territory in Map IX.1). This proposal was rejected, but agitation for a separate territory continued.

The Civil War had varying effects on different parts of the West. At first all the regular soldiers were taken from the region, exposing it to Indian attacks (Utley, 1984, pp. 67–70). They were replaced by volunteers who "brought to their task a harsh, uncompromising view of the Indian and usually preferred extermination to negotiation" (Utley, 1984, pp. 70–71). The continued military presence in the West was due to Lincoln's need for "western gold and silver and western political support for the prosecution of the war" (Utley, 1984, p. 71). Yet this military presence ebbed and flowed with the fortunes of war, upsetting relations with nomadic Indians throughout the Southwest.

When the Civil War erupted, many of the military officers in the Southwest were from Southern states and favored secession (Lamar, 1970). Chances for local control appeared to many to be better under the Confederates. The practices of holding Indian captives and debt peonage were more consistent with Confederate principles and were favored by the territorial assembly (Anonymous, 1962). Secession raised the possibility of the local elite (e.g., Armijo) returning to control. For those in the southern portion of the territory—a large proportion of whom were Texans—it offered an opportunity to realize their desires for a break from Santa Fe.

Colonel Sibley, who joined the Confederacy, and his Texas division quickly gained military control of the region. Two factors turned New Mexico pro-Union. Sibley's men lived by foraging on the countryside, alienating the local people and driving them into the arms of the Union (Lamar, 1970, p. 115). Anti-Texas feelings all but insured New Mexican opposition to the Confederacy (Lamar, 1970, pp. 77–78). There was no desire to become part of a new government that would be heavily controlled by Texans who had a long history of trying to usurp both New Mexican land and the Santa Fe Trail trade. When Colonel Canby succeeded in driving Sibley into Texas, New Mexico became firmly pro-Union.

While the allegiance of the region, along with its actual military control, was in dispute, the federal Congress organized an Arizona Territory, splitting New Mexico into eastern and western divisions. Capitalizing on New Mexican hatred of Texas, the new New Mexico Territory was to be a barrier between Texas and Arizona, blocking Confederate access to the Pacific (Lamar, 1970, p. 4). This split placed most of the nomadic Indians in the Arizona portion of the territory. Population estimates for the 1860s give totals of 40,000 to 58,000 Indians for the region, 60% of whom were in Arizona (Lamar, 1970, p. 436). Arizona appeared almost empty to Anglos. Indeed, "the government had arrived before the people" (Lamar, 1970, p. 436). The 1864 census showed only 4,187 Europeans in the entire province (Lamar, 1970, p. 437). These were mostly Mexican settlers who had drifted north from Sonora, and a handful of miners working the southern deposits. New Mexico had a population of approximately 90,000 (Zeleny, 1944, p. 126), mostly Hispanos.

This geographical division shaped the course of social change after the Civil War. New Mexico had a long history of symbiotic relations with various Indian groups. Northern villagers had dealt with Ute trading partners (Swadesh, 1974). Pueblo Indians had been Spanish–Mexican allies for well over a century. The Comanche peace was nearly three-quarters of a century old. The northern villagers and the Pueblos had long been involved in trade with Comanches. All the irrigable land had been taken up by Mexicans or Pueblo Indians. The major immigrants to New Mexico were federal officials, commercial adventurers, and agents of large-scale enterprises interested in land or mines (Lamar, 1970). The Apaches who roamed Arizona and southern New Mexico hated the Mexicans for the years of scalp hunting that had been carried out in Sonora and Chihuahua. They were rejected as allies by the invading Americans (Faulk, 1970, p. 61), especially by the miners who brought with them a conception of Indians as obstacles of progress to be removed as quickly and efficiently as possible.[1] The land was open to anyone who would settle it. Following the arrival of more miners after the Civil War, mainly southerners fleeing Reconstruction (Faulk, 1970; Lamar, 1970), and the subsequent arrival of the army to protect them, came large groups of Mormon farmers to feed them (Lamar, 1970, p. 486; Meinig, 1971, 1965). Anglos[2] quickly became the majority in Arizona, 40,000 according to the 1870 census (U.S. Census, 1975, p. 24).

The period after the Civil War was the time of the bloodiest conflicts in the Southwest, especially in Arizona. During this time the various nomadic groups were permanently settled on reservations and traditional life-styles and cultures were eliminated or tremendously modified. The adaptive strategies of the past, including the raiding-trading complex, were destroyed. Pushed outside the new economic order, the Indians' main economic function became that of welfare recipient whose presence justified the growing military and social bureaucracies.

THE SUBORDINATION OF THE HISPANOS—
THE FORMATION OF AN ETHNIC GROUP

The annexation of the Southwest—Texas in 1845, New Mexico and California in 1848—converted Mexican citizens into a subjugated political minority. They were already a demographic minority in Texas even before the revolt of 1836. After the discovery of gold in California in 1848 the territory was overrun with Americans (Pitt, 1966; Barrera, 1979), reinforcing political changes with demographic changes. Mexicans remained a demographic majority only in New Mexico (see Table VIII.3). While the 1850 figures in Table VIII.3 may be the result of as much as a 20% underenumeration (Nostrand, 1975, p. 383, note 29), it is abundantly clear that by 1850 the former Mexican citizens were less than 10% of the total populations of Texas and California, yet remained more than 90% of the population of New Mexico.[3] The latter lived primarily in the upper Rio Grande Valley (Nostrand, 1975, pp. 385–386).

Both New Mexico and Arizona remained territories until 1912. Under Spanish and Mexican control the region had been a preserve of various nonstate societies. After the American conquest these groups, mainly the nomads, were transformed at gunpoint into sedentary groups. New Mexican Hispanos now became an enclaved ethnic group, with a distinctive culture and a distinct class position within a larger structure. This transformation was accomplished by conversion of at least part of the former elite into a comprador class who served as agents of indirect colonial rule. The process of taking control of the land—the major economic resource in the region—away from the Hispanic elite and shifting it to an Anglo elite began (Dunbar Ortiz, 1980, Ch.5). Finally, the role of the *pobres* changed. No longer were the roles of middlemen in the Indian trade, or the occupation of buffalo hunters, available. Villagers reverted to subsistence farming, and were pushed out of the economy. Had it not been for the growth of the sheep industry, there would have been little economic role for them (Carlson, 1969; Mosk, 1942; Knowlton, 1980).

A *"Conquest of Merchants"*

Lamar describes the annexation of New Mexico as "a conquest of merchants" (1970, p. 63). After Kearny's takeover, the merchants continued to prosper. The $3 million a year that poured in to support the army in the 1850s became the economic mainstay of the region. After the disruption of the Civil War the flow of money resumed and remained crucial (Sunseri, 1979, p. 88; Lamar, 1970, p. 134) until the nomadic Indians were finally settled on reservations. The cash flowed mainly to Anglo traders and their *rico* allies (Sunseri, 1979, p. 90). Missouri traders had achieved their goal in the war—maintenance of their lucrative trade. In 1859 Senator Phelps of Missouri "visited New Mexico and told the inhabitants quite bluntly that the region was important chiefly as part of Missouri's economy" (Lamar, 1970, p. 108). During this phase of American control, Anglo immigration was significant economically and politically, but it was much smaller than in Texas and California.

In addition to military personnel, immigrants included "political officials, traders, contractors and a few homeseekers" (Zeleny, 1944, p. 132) and "a great number of fortune-hunters" (Zeleny, 1944, p. 147). The heavy immigration of Anglos did not begin until the 1870s, and only began in earnest in the 1880s with the coming of the railroads (Zeleny, 1944, p. 130). According to the United States Census, in 1850 there were 772 people born in other parts of the United States living in New Mexico. In 1860 there were 1,168; and by 1870, 2,780 (Zeleny, 1944, p. 126). There were, however, significant changes in the origins of immigrants during this time. Before the Civil War many of the immigrants were from the South. All the governors were southerners (Sunseri, 1979, p. 41). After the Civil War the number of southerners resident in Santa Fe declined drastically, and the number of northerners increased (D. Bailey and Haulman, 1976). It was these few immigrants who combined with the local *ricos* to make up a ruling elite.

The census manuscripts for 1860 and 1870 in Santa Fe provide some insightful evidence into the events of this period (Bailey, 1975; Bailey and Haulman, 1976, 1977). In addition to documenting the Civil War shift from southern to northern immigration, they establish that an ethnic division of labor had already formed among the elite, and that the Anglo immigrants already had substantial control of the local wealth by 1860. From Table IX.2 it is clear that Anglos were overrepresented in the class of wealth holders (defined as owning $500 or more in real property in Santa Fe). Total wealth was even more concentrated. Anglos were approximately one-fifth of the Santa Fe population, but held nearly two-thirds of all real property.

The major implication of Table IX.2 is that by 1860 Anglos had already gained considerable control of the local real property in Santa Fe. This apparently happened quickly, although it is difficult to tell how far

Table IX.2. Distribution of Wealth in Santa Fe Among Anglo and
Hispano Occupation Holders, 1860 and 1870

	1860			1870		
Percentage of	N	*Hispano*	*Anglo*	N	*Hispano*	*Anglo*
Total Population	1682	81.2	18.8	1569	77.7	22.3
Real Wealth at $500 or more	206 (12.2%)	8.5	28.5	250 (15.9%)	13.9	23.1
Total Santa Fe Wealth	$823,808	36.7	63.3	$1,251,492	33.8	66.2

Source: Bailey and Haulman (1976:13, Table 1). Their sample of the 1860 and 1870 census manuscripts included all Spanish surnamed and Anglo persons in the work force.

the process had gone before the conquest. Since a number of Anglo
traders had married into local *rico* families, the differences in distribution of wealth may be exaggerated. These marriages literally straddle
the ethnic boundary, but due to patrilineal naming customs in both
groups, most interethnic marriages were recorded in the census as Anglo households.

The occupational structure among the wealthy also reveals the social
structure. Hispanos specialized in agriculture; Anglos concentrated in
business, government, and crafts, with a significant overlap of both in
business and crafts. Again, cultural patterns may exaggerate the economic differences. Many Hispanic *ricos* no doubt gave agriculture

Table IX.3. Percentage Occupational Distribution
Among Santa Fe Wealth Holders ($500 or more),
1860 and 1870

	1860		1870	
Occupation	*Anglo*	*Hispano*	*Anglo*	*Hispano*
Agriculture	5.6	62.1	2.5	47.9
Business	32.2	15.5	25.9	11.2
Crafts	21.2	18.1	24.7	14.2
Government	15.5	0.8	19.8	3.0
Other Occupations	25.6	3.5	27.2	23.7
Total Number	90	116	81	169

Source: Bailey and Haulman (1976:14, Table 3)

(meaning owner of a *hacienda* or rancho) as an occupation even if they were also engaged in business. On the other hand, many Anglo traders who might have had at least part interest (especially those married into Hispanic families) in agricultural ventures probably would have given business as their occupation. Still, the degree of specialization is striking. Table IX.3 suggests that there was a clear ethnic division of labor in 1860, but that it was beginning to change by 1870 when Hispanos were beginning to move into other occupations.

The ethnic division of labor was not unique to the capital city. Ethnic specialization was also found in the livestock industry. Sheep grazing received a significant boost after the American conquest (Carlson, 1969; Fergusson, 1935; Gonzalez, 1969, p. 45; Lamar, 1970, p. 106; Mosk, 1942; Zeleny, 1944, p. 169). In 1850 sheep numbered about 375,000 and cattle only about 33,000 (Zeleny, 1944, p. 169). Much of the new mutton was "marched all the way to California to be consumed by the voracious argonauts there" (Lamar, 1970, p. 106). The cattle industry began a slow but steady increase at this time. It was a predominantly Anglo business. It should be noted that sheep and cattle are not compatible grazers, and require use of separate grazing ranges. Much later, economic competition over land took on an ethnic tone, based on the historic division of labor in the livestock industry (Zeleny, 1944; Gonzalez, 1969; Lamar, 1970; Larson, 1968; Beck, 1962).

The elite was composed of a group of immigrant Americans and local *ricos*. According to Lamar (1970, pp. 100–101) "Rather than parties, New Mexico had cliques, usually led by one man and generally organized for the specific purpose of winning an election or controlling patronage." This, of course, is the familiar system of *caudillos,* but in alliance with the agents of the invading Americans. *The caudillos* became compradors and linked to the American administrative elite.

This combination of local *ricos* and national administrators became known as the Santa Fe Ring (Zeleny, 1944; Gonzalez, 1969; Faulk, 1970, p. 134; Beck, 1962; Larson, 1968; Swadesh, 1974; Barrera, 1979; Sunseri, 1979; Rasch, 1972). Unfortunately, most of the literature on the Santa Fe Ring focuses too tightly on its New Mexican character. Lamar (1970, p. 459) points out that there were similar rings in all the Four Corners territories: Arizona, Utah, Colorado, and New Mexico. Each ring consisted of federal officials who used their offices to fleece both the local economy and the federal government. Such rings are typical of the territorial phase of empire building, which Lamar (1970, pp. 5–6, 16–17) labels "internal colonialism." The New Mexico ring only began to take shape in the period immediately after the Civil War, and marks the beginning of intense colonial development (Swadesh, 1974, p. 29).

The ring was focused around land, the primary means of production in New Mexico (Van Ness, 1976). Land had been granted to some foreigners by Governor Armijo. The elite were in the process of consolidating land holdings early in the postconquest era.

The key conflict was in the use-value of land to the respective occupants (Van Ness, 1976). In the northern villages, grazing lands were communally owned. Boundaries were not well marked because there was no critical need for precise boundaries. Ownership was based on use of the land as much as abstract titles (Zeleny, 1944, p. 144; Lamar, 1970, p. 139; Barrera, 1979, p. 27; Swadesh, 1974, p. 69). These vague boundaries were used by the Santa Fe Ring to encumber land titles in litigation for many years. Since court costs had to be borne by litigants (Zeleny, 1944, p. 146), many lawyers became wealthy landowners.[4] This kind of land theft ultimately eroded the wealth of the northern villages and of some of the *ricos*. But long before the land deals of the Santa Fe Ring took their final toll, the *pobres* had lost much of their economic means of survival.

The Destruction of the Plains Trade

Many of the northern villagers, and the Pueblo Indians, supplemented their farm and herding production by trade with the various nomadic tribes and by buffalo hunting. Five processes combined to destroy the Plains trade. First, after the Civil War, debt peonage and the captive trade were outlawed by the federal government in 1867 (Lamar, 1970, p. 131). General Carleton saw that continued trade in captive Navajos, which reached a peak in the 1860s (Swadesh, 1974, pp. 170, 153, 229, note 33; see also Brugge, 1985), was hampering peace efforts. The abolition of debt peonage also destroyed some of the *ricos* and forced many former peons to seek other kinds of work. Among other things, this increased the interest in ranch labor, and especially in buffalo hunting and trade with Indians.

Trade competition was the second major means of undermining northern New Mexican rural economy. American traders had been moving onto the Plains since the 1830s and 1840s (Kenner, 1969; Lamar, 1977) and now more *pobres* were joining the *comanchero* trade. Pueblo Indians are seldom mentioned in regard to this trade, probably because most Anglo observers did not bother to distinguish Hispano and Pueblo *comancheros* (Kenner, 1969). The Pueblo Indians were, however, more effective traders than the Anglos. They had better rapport with Comanches, and were more trusted (Kenner, 1969, p. 164). Accusations about which group did more to stir up Comanche and Apache raiding via the introduction of liquor, guns, and the purchase of captives abound in the literature (Utley, 1984, Ch.1; Beck, 1962; Kenner, 1969; Lamar, 1977). The issue is not who caused these changes but how and why. More traders meant better terms for Indians, increasing the incentive for raiding. More traders also meant less profit per trader, and hence lower returns. This made trade more desperate, which, in turn, resulted in the further introduction of guns and liquor and vigorous attempts to turn the ransoming of captives into a lucrative business (Kenner, 1969).

Increased buffalo hunting led to a decrease in herd size and constituted the third factor in the decline of the Plains trade. Buffalo had been the economic mainstay of the various Plains groups, both for consumption and for trade. As Anglos expanded westward, they drove many Indian groups before them onto the Plains, increasing the intergroup competition. After the American conquest, eastern Anglos hunted buffalo for their hides. Some (Wallace and Hoebel, 1952) claim that as early as the 1830s the herds had begun to shrink. After the Civil War it is certain that they did. This undermined buffalo hunting and led to increasing hostility with and among Plains Indians.

The decrease in the buffalo herds, in turn, led to the fourth factor, the destruction of the various Plains groups, especially Comanches. As Comanches and other nomads were removed from the Plains, one side of the trading partnership was gradually eliminated.

Finally, the rise of cattle production in Texas was instrumental in destroying another basis of trade. As the cattle industry grew, more and more cattle were stolen by Comanches who traded them to New Mexicans. This was simply the continuation of old patterns of Plains trade. As the buffalo herds declined, cattle raiding increased. Texas cattlemen brought increasing pressure on federal officials in New Mexico to curb the trade. They even mounted campaigns to New Mexico to recover stolen cattle (Kenner, 1969, p. 174). Governor Connelly (1861–1866) of New Mexico had refused to use the New Mexican militia to repress the *comancheros* for fear of Comanche retaliation on New Mexico (Kenner, 1969, p. 148). The cattle industry continued to expand, replacing the buffalo and displacing Indians. By 1872 Plains traffic was all but ended (Kenner, 1969, Ch.9), and the trading portion of northern New Mexican economy destroyed.

Class and Ethnic Relations in New Mexico

The class structure of New Mexico in the days of the consolidation of the conquest was peculiar. Among the Hispanos there was a small, elite group of *ricos* in alliance with a small Anglo administrative elite. Most Hispanos were poor; many had been peons indebted to *ricos,* or had been frontier tradesmen, hunters, and subsistence farmers. The sedentary Pueblos lived in semi-autonomous villages and held a status similar to poor Hispanos. Surrounding the territory were a variety of nomadic Indian groups who were considered outside the system of social relations, and who were increasingly the objects of attack and subjugation. The Anglo community consisted of a small administrative and business elite, and an equally small group of tradesmen and soldiers. The attitudes of Anglos and Hispanos toward each other have been matters of some debate.

Gonzalez holds that there was little prejudice toward Hispanos, citing the frequency of intermarriage, business and political partnerships (1969, p. 80). But intermarriage was restricted to the elite (Loyola, 1939, Chs.1,2), though other classes may have intermarried due to the unbalanced sex ratio. The *ricos* considered themselves "Spanish" (i.e., pure blooded), a view accepted by Americans. They shared and expressed the same attitudes toward the New Mexico poor as the conquering Anglos (Weber, 1973, pp. 78–81). There is much evidence demonstrating a pervasive attitude of disgust toward "Mexicans" in New Mexico (Weber, 1973, Chs. II,III; 1979, pp. 295–307; Sunseri, 1979, Ch.7). Some New Mexicans accepted offers of repatriation to Mexico because of Anglo prejudice (Zeleny, 1944, p. 115). Prejudice was a major factor in blocking New Mexico's admission to statehood for 62 years (Larson, 1968; Lamar, 1970, Ch.19; Sunseri, 1979). By contemporary standards New Mexico in 1850 had sufficient population and wealth to warrant admission (Zeleny, 1944, p. 203).

These attitudes were reinforced during the consolidation. The poorer Hispanos, especially the *comancheros,* were seen as allies of Comanches against the Anglos. When Comanches attacked a wagon train they killed all Anglos and left all Mexicans alive (Kenner, 1969, p. 123), Americans took this as evidence of Mexican–Comanche collusion. Most Anglo newcomers did not understand the nature of the long-standing trade partnerships with Comanches. When Comanches began attacking cattle ranches in the post–Civil War era, similar events occurred. Whenever the lives of Mexican ranchhands were spared (Kenner, 1969, p. 145), it was assumed that they were in league with the attacking Comanches (Faulk, 1974, p. 114). In fact, what was happening was the reenactment of two old practices: nonaggression against allies and taking from the herds for food. The conflict between sheep and cattle operations also took on an ethnic overtone (Beck, 1962, p. 161).

Prejudice against Hispanos was rooted in economic competition for land, and to a lesser extent in the need for cheap labor on ranches. Competition for federal money was another sphere of conflict. As long as New Mexico remained a territory, appointed Anglo officials would maintain control over federal money without fear of being outvoted by the numerically superior Hispanic population. In Arizona the Hispano population was small. Prejudice there was directed against Indians, who ✗ were seen as obstacles to free development of the mining industry. The differences in prejudice, and their differing competitive bases, had notable effects on the course of Indian pacification in the two territories.

THE FINAL PEACE: ANGLO "PACIFICATION" OF THE NATIVE AMERICANS[5]

The Mexican–American War brought changes in federal Indian policy:

> First, military protection had to be provided to citizens threatened by Indians. Second, Indian title to lands coveted, needed, or already possessed by whites had to be formally "extinguished." Third, now that removal beyond a Permanent Indian Frontier was no longer possible, some other humane disposition of the Indians had to be worked out (Utley, 1984, pp. 39–40).

These goals were to be achieved via the reservation policy that was intended to isolate, protect, educate and christianize Native Americans (Utley, 1984, p. 46). In brief, the reservation was an instrument of subjugation, forced assimilation, and dispossession from the land.

Indian fighting increased after the conquest (Zeleny, 1944, p. 109; Swadesh, 1974, p. 64). This was due, in part, to the continued growth of Santa Fe Trail traffic. Competing uses of land, cattle grazing versus buffalo hunting, put severe ecological pressures on older nomadic productive technologies and contributed to increased fighting. Anglo leaders "who devoutly believed in Indian extermination" exacerbated conditions (Swadesh, 1974, pp. 64–65). There was extensive use of volunteer forces whose only pay was booty—typically captives. Regular army members were underpaid (Faulk, 1974, p. 34), virtually forcing them into pursuit of booty. The increased traffic in captives insured further fighting. Ecological competition had advanced to the point that many bands, and even entire groups, had no choice but to continue raiding or to starve.

Some groups, mainly Navajos and Apaches, were predisposed to form an alliance with the Anglos against the Mexicans (Lamar, 1970, p. 92).

Such overtures were soundly repulsed. As had been the case from the sixteenth century, the actions of soldiers as often as not caused the very hostilities they were supposed to eliminate. The lull in Comanche raids during the Civil War lends credence to this proposition (Kenner, 1969, p. 137). The army indirectly encouraged fighting through its role in local economies (Lamar, 1970, p. 134, 451; Faulk, 1970, p. 134; Mosk, 1942). The influence of the military budget on local communities was not limited to creating a sentiment favorable to Indian wars. Local leaders on several occasions actually initiated conflicts where there had been none to keep the military in the area, and to keep the federal funds flowing into their pockets.

Bureaucratic bungling exacerbated conflict. Incompetent and certainly unprepared officials were rotated in and out of office before they could acquire sufficient knowledge to administer Indian affairs (Beck, 1962, p. 185). Constant feuding among various bureaucracies over who was responsible for Indian affairs heightened the effects of bureaucratic competition. Lamar (1970, pp. 107–108) notes that "after fifteen years of conquest it was not yet clear who ruled: the governor, the commander, or the Indian superintendent." These bureaucracies worked at cross-purposes, and were quick to assign blame for failures to rival agencies. Denial of blame was important to individual bureaucrats because many had hopes of converting patronage jobs into political careers.

A brief examination of the pacification of several groups will illustrate the various combinations of factors.

Navajos

Raids and counter-raids had been going on between Navajos and New Mexicans for some time. Both Governors Calhoun (1851–1852) and Lane (1852–1853) tried to stop the raiding process by preventing New Mexican attacks (Dale, 1949, p. 49), and by forcing Navajos to sign peace treaties (Faulk, 1970, p. 57). No sooner had several Navajo leaders signed a treaty, agreeing to abandon certain lands in 1855, then New Mexicans began moving into the area. Both strategies left the subdued side feeling vulnerable to attack. Insufficient manpower and money forced Calhoun to accept volunteer militia in operations against Navajos (Dale, 1949; Lamar, 1970). Volunteers were paid in booty that they captured on raids. Not until 1862 did local military commanders begin to refuse, and even curb, such volunteer raiders (Dale, 1949, p. 54).

The booty captured by volunteers consisted of sheep, women, or children, the latter to be sold as slaves (McNitt, 1972). There was a steady, increasing demand for Navajo captives who served as menials, herders, and house servants (Swadesh, 1974, pp. 153, 229; Faulk, 1974, p. 50). Both McNitt (1972, p. 441ff) and Sunseri (1979, p. 63) provide lists of slaves held in various New Mexican communities in the 1860s. These slaves were overwhelmingly Navajos, although there were some Utes and Apaches. At the time of the Civil War there were 500 Navajos in bondage in Santa Fe alone and as many as 6,000 captives throughout the territory (L. Bailey, 1966, p. 179). Considering a European population of 70,000 and a nomadic population of some 30,000, these captives constituted about 10% of the settled population or about 20% of the Indian population.

Indian enslavement was practiced extensively, since "any householder who could raise $150 . . . could purchase an Indian captive" (L. Bailey, 1966, p. 179). Furthermore, "nearly every federal officer in New Mexico held Indian menials" (L. Bailey, 1966, p. 181). The slave traffic had prompted both General Carleton and special agent Graves to pressure Congress to outlaw the practice in 1867 (Dale, 1949, p. 58). The growing sheep market steadily heightened the pressure to expand grazing land, or to acquire more sheep through theft. Many of the so-called punitive raids against Navajos, which sought to force them to come to terms by destroying their means of subsistence, also supplied the fighters with large numbers of valuable sheep.

Such attacks, even when conducted by the military under less suspicious conditions, still served to further raiding on the part of Navajos. With food supplies destroyed, there was no choice left but to raid in order to eat. Governor Lane sought to avoid the problem by feeding peaceful Indians, but Washington refused to supply sufficient funds to carry out the work (Faulk, 1974, p. 60). Again in 1861 treaties were signed with 54 Navajo headmen. Immediately afterward, several parties of New Mexicans set out on slave raids. Fighting and raiding became so rampant that a concerted effort to control Navajos was begun in 1863. General Carleton enlisted Kit Carson to help subdue the Navajos. A concentrated effort was made to destroy their means of subsistence (Dale, 1949; McNitt, 1972; Lamar, 1970; Beck, 1962; Faulk, 1974). This successful effort was aided by several groups of allies and volunteer militia, including many Utes (Beck, 1962, p. 189; Dale, 1949, p. 53; Faulk, 1974, p. 81).

Navajos were rounded up and marched several hundred miles on the "Long Walk" to a reservation Carleton had selected near Bosque Redondo.[6] He had constructed Fort Sumner to guard the Navajos and the Mescalero Apaches who had already been gathered there. Carleton's idea was to contain and guard the Indians and train them to farm. This experiment was a notable failure, and had to be abandoned only four years later in 1868. The reasons for failure are complex, but reveal the typical problems of frontier pacification.

As soon as captive Navajos began arriving, conflict with the already resident Mescaleros began. Navajos and Mescaleros were not initially on friendly terms. When the Navajo population became large, it was decided to move the Mescaleros to a different part of the reservation to make room for the Navajos. They were moved to inferior land (Dale, 1949, p. 56). The reservation as a whole proved to be inadequate, lacking sufficient firewood and water (Dale, 1949; Lamar, 1970; Beck, 1962, pp. 190–191). The resulting food shortages led to hunger, starvation, disease and renewed raiding. Between 1865 and 1866 the reservation population declined from 8,491 to 6,915 (Dale, 1949). The losses were due to both disease and desertion. Navajos left the area in some numbers to raid the *comanchero* trails east of Fort Sumner (Kenner, 1969, p. 162). Comanches retaliated and raided Navajos on the reservation, who were particularly vulnerable in their settled state. Obviously, military protection was inadequate.

Lack of adequate military support was part and parcel of general shortage of funds. Maintaining the reservation was expensive:

> From January 11, 1865, to December 5, 1865, the total cost of subsistence for the Navajo was $748,308.87. More surprising, in view of the fact that the Navajo had such large herds of sheep in their old homeland, the number of their sheep at Bosque Redondo was estimated as 1,100, which, with about the same number of horses and mules and 450 goats, constituted their entire holding of livestock. In addition to subsistence, blankets and clothing were issued to the Navajo, making the entire cost of maintaining them upon the reservation approximately $1,500,000 annually, if the expense of laborers and of the necessary military establishment were added to that of feeding and clothing them (Dale, 1949, p. 57).

These conditions were sufficiently bad, but added to them were the pressures from local ranchers who were eyeing the better grazing land on the reservation and feared continued raids from the Indians settled there. Jurisdictional disputes among competing bureaucracies further complicated the situation. The Indian Bureau, which had opposed the reservation, claimed that the military should pay its cost, since it was their project. The military claimed that it should be taken over by the Indian Bureau, since the military's mission (collecting Indians) was complete. In November of 1867 responsibility was shifted to the Indian Bureau. Only $200,000 of $600,000 requested were granted in March 1867 (Dale, 1949, p. 59). The lack of funding, the bureaucratic fighting, and the political maneuverings of local ranchers (Lamar, 1970, p. 125) led to the abandonment of Bosque Redondo in July of 1868 (Utley, 1984, p. 120). The Navajo returned to a reservation on their traditional lands.

The 8,500 Navajos taken to Bosque Redondo may have been less than half of the Navajo population living in the northern areas of New Mexico and Arizona.[7] They inhabited a wide area and were accustomed to fleeing to certain Pueblo groups in dire times. There had been insufficient military activity to round up all Navajos; only the most vulnerable ones were captured. When those who survived the four-year incarceration at Bosque Redondo returned, they rejoined lost and scattered kin and began to reestablish their pastoral economy. The land they were given for the reservation was mainly in the western portion of their traditional territory. This region was far removed from New Mexican settlements, out of the path of any travel or trade routes, on land that was thought to be unsuitable for agriculture. The Navajos entered a period of neglect.

Utes

Ute bands ranged over a wide territory. Those bands that ranged into northern New Mexico were a small part of the Ute population (Jorgensen, 1972, Ch.3). The northern New Mexican Utes were heavily intermarried and allied with some branches of the Jicarilla Apaches (Swadesh, 1974, p. 65). Superintendent of Indian Affairs James Calhoun forced a treaty on these Utes in 1849 in which they promised Anglos the right to travel across their land (these were mainly Mormons heading for Utah) and to deliver to the federal government all property taken in raids, including captives (Dale, 1949, p. 66). Ute raiding continued sporadically after this, and reached a peak in the mid 1850s. During this time Hispanic settlers were pushing northward into Ute territory. Since the Ute bands and settler communities were frequently involved in trading partnerships (Swadesh, 1974), this encroachment was not heavily resisted. Nevertheless, Ute raiding continued against Anglo wagon trains and military installations.

One such Ute attack in 1854 prompted strong retaliation (Beck, 1962, p. 186). The defeat delivered to the offending Utes led to a treaty in 1855. This was only one of several treaties Governor Meriwether concluded with some Utes, Navajos, and Apaches in 1855. All were rejected by the U.S. Senate in 1856 (Utley, 1984, pp. 56–58). Nevertheless, Utes generally maintained peace in New Mexico. As has been seen, they then became frequent participants in the war against the Navajos. This was only partially motivated by traditional enmity. At about this time the Ute slaving networks, which reached into northern Utah, began to break down as the Mormons increasingly refused to be involved in the trade (Malouf and Malouf, 1945; Sonne, 1962). The Navajo wars provided the Utes with a new source of captives to sell in New Mexico to their Hispano trading partners (Dale, 1949, p. 68). Beck (1962, p. 186) also notes that Utes were the only New Mexican Indians to be considered Union Indians during the Civil War. Once the war was over, a report reviewing New Mexican Indian policy recommended that the Utes in New Mexico join the Utes on a southern Colorado reservation. This recommendation was implemented in an 1868 treaty (Dale, 1949, p. 61). The Utes were then effectively removed from New Mexico. In Colorado they came into increasing competition with the Anglo miners flooding the state. The story of the raiding, massacres, reservations and agent incompetence (Jorgensen, 1972, p. 41ff) closely parallels, in time and processes, the Apache story.

The Pueblos

Some 20 Pueblo villages became part of the United States in 1848. Their treatment at the hands of the Anglos is almost without parallel, for they were accorded a measure of respect. This was certainly unique in the Southwest. Superintendent of Indian Affairs Calhoun recommended in 1849 that they be affirmed in their lands and that they be organized into six or seven districts. Each district was to have its own agent, and eventually each Pueblo its own subagent. He also recommended that they be issued arms to better defend themselves (Dale, 1949, p. 49). Yet Calhoun had doubts, doubts that are still expressed in regard to Indian rights today. He was concerned about whether they should be granted full citizenship; whether, pending the citizenship issue, their lands should be confirmed; whether they should be relocated (they held the richest valleys) or their land be subject to sale (Sunseri, 1979, p. 51).

Some Anglos considered Pueblo Indians superior to Mexicans, because they were less recalcitrant in accepting Anglo advice (Sunseri, 1979, p. 56). This was because the Pueblo groups sought Anglo aid in preserving their land against encroaching Hispanos. Hispano encroachment on Pueblo lands, which had occurred throughout the era of Spanish control, increased after the conquest (Carlson, 1975). As a consequence, Pueblos became political footballs in the maneuverings of *rico* and Anglo allies seeking access to Pueblo land. During the early 1850s they were granted the vote and participated in territorial elections

(Lamar, 1970, p. 93). In the mid-1850s, though, the vote was taken away from them (Lamar, 1970, p. 105). The land commission, which was set up after the conquest, but was notable for its lack of completion of claims, heard 60 claims and confirmed 30 by 1863. Seventeen of those claims were for Pueblo lands (Zeleny, 1944, p. 146). They also managed to achieve a minimal level of citizenship while retaining communal land rights and identity.

This special treatment has continued to be a matter of some jealousy between Hispanos and Pueblo residents since the time of the consolidation of the conquest. Pueblo communities have been protected by the federal government, whereas the lands of Hispanos have been subject to loss through tax liabilities, indebtedness, and other forms of forced sales (Zeleny, 1944, p. 163; Briggs and Van Ness, 1987).

The conquest destroyed the Pueblos' long-term trading relation with Comanches. From the mid-1850s the Pueblo villages became more isolated, and participated less in territorial affairs. Their right to vote was taken away, their lands had been confirmed, and trade, which had been the basis of their external relations, was destroyed. These changes, especially the confirmation of land titles, are at the root of the celebrated cultural tenacity of Pueblo groups (Sunseri, 1979, p. 56).

Comanches

The actual population of the combined Comanche bands is a matter of considerable dispute. Mooney (see Wallace and Hoebel, 1952, p. 31; Thornton, 1978, p. 12) estimated that the aboriginal population of Comanches was about 7,000 in 1690. Wallace and Hoebel (1952) estimate that in 1786 the total Comanche population was between 20,000 and 30,000, based on reports by Governor Anza and his emissary Ortiz. For the 1830s, estimates of the number of Comanche warriors range from 8,000 (Mexican government) to 5,400 (U.S. Army) to 4,500 (Osage agent). This yields an estimate of 15,000 and 20,000 total population (Wallace and Hoebel, 1952, pp. 31–32). Catlin places the population at 30,000 to 40,000 (Thornton, 1978, p. 12). Other estimates for the 1840s range from 12,000 to 20,000 total population. In 1866 Comanche population numbered about 4,700; by 1882 it was 1,382 (Wallace and Hoebel, 1952, p. 32). Comanches suffered epidemics in 1816, 1839–1840, 1861–1862, and possibly cholera in 1849 (Wallace and Hoebel, 1952). Regardless of the estimation technique, it is clear that Comanches suffered precipitous losses during pacification.

A major reason for the intense pressures against Comanche bands was their geographical location. They blocked westward expansion in Texas, they straddled the Sante Fe Trail and they were in an increasingly narrow no-man's-land between Texas, New Mexico, and northern Mexico. They were able to prosper by trading and raiding among these territories and escaping to the unmapped south Plains, but they were gradually surrounded. Their northern territory was invaded by other displaced Plains groups. Their eastern range was occupied by some of the "Civilized Tribes" relocated in Indian Territory (Oklahoma). Expanding livestock operations in New Mexico—first sheep, later cattle—infringed on their western range. Texans were constantly expanding from the southeast. Control of the south was disputed by Apaches, whom they had defeated on the Plains, but who became formidable foes in the Basin and Range territory (Kenner, 1969).

Comanches had sought to negotiate a barrier between themselves and the Texans several times. At first President Houston of Texas agreed, then President Lamar favored a war of extermination, and then Houston again favored a barrier (Wallace and Hoebel, 1952; Hagan, 1976; Faulk, 1974, pp. 91–93; Richardson, 1933). Texans constantly settled past the line of forts established as a barrier, then complained bitterly about Comanche raids. Besides glory and food, revenge for displacement was a major motive for increased cattle raiding in Texas. Stolen cattle were sold via *comancheros* in New Mexico. This trade added further fuel to the smoldering Texas–New Mexico rivalry (Kenner, 1969, p. 172; Wallace and Hoebel, 1952; Hagan, 1976, p. 42). During the early years of the consolidation, Texas began to replace northern Mexico as a major target for raids, because of increasing enmity with Texas as well as Apache competition in Mexico.

The accelerated raiding repeated, yet again, the old cycle of attack, mistaken counter-attack, and further revenge. Military officers, especially Texas Rangers, were not careful to distinguish among peaceful and hostile groups. Any Comanche would do for a counter-raid (Kenner, 1969, p. 133; Utley, 1984, pp. 55–56). Trade in captives continued. This trade was accelerated by the dilemma facing American officials in New Mexico: to ransom Anglo captives, usually from Texas, was to encourage further raiding for captives. To fail to ransom such captives was to seal their fate to be sold in Mexico or killed. Ransoming was preferable, but served to keep the raiding cycle going and intensify Texan hatred of Comanches (Richardson, 1933).

But land was not the only threatened resource. The buffalo herds were declining during this time. Plains groups hunted more intensively as they were pushed further onto the Plains. New Mexicans continued their hunting. Anglo hunters began to appear on the Plains, at first slowly before the Civil War, then in larger and larger numbers afterward. According to Wallace and Hoebel (1952, Ch.III) annual sales of buffalo hides to the Canadian and American markets in 1846 amounted to some one hundred thousand hides at $3 to $8 each. The severity of the decline is shown in the returns for buffalo robes sold by Comanches and Kiowas to their official traders during the late 1870s: in 1876 the value was $70,400; in 1877, $64,500; in 1878, $26,375; and in 1879, $5,068 (Kenner, 1969, p. 209). This final decline was all the more serious to Comanche welfare since the *comanchero* trade essentially ended by 1872 (Kenner, 1969, Ch.9). In 1871 the herds were still over four million, a steep decline from estimates of up to 100 million in earlier times. The final destruction of the herds came in the late 1870s. Between 1868 and 1881 it is estimated that the bones of over 31 million buffalo were gathered to be used as fertilizer. For groups solely, or heavily, dependent on the buffalo for maintenance and survival, this decline meant disaster.

The growing traffic in stolen cattle—which increased during the Civil War when there was less military surveillance and a large number of loose cattle—became impressive. One cattle rancher estimated that between 1860 and 1867 Comanches stole over 300,000 head of cattle (Hagan, 1976, p. 24). According to more conservative estimates, only 100,000 head were taken between the conquest and the early 1870s (Kenner, 1969, p. 174). In either case the trade was extensive. Not surprisingly the bulk of the profits from the traffic in stolen cattle went to prominent New Mexicans, both Mexican and Anglo, engaged in the cattle business. They paid the *comancheros* very low prices and sold the cattle at enormous profits (Kenner, 1969, pp. 172–174).

Congress was interested in cutting the costs of dealing with Indian problems (Hagan, 1976, p. 1). The 50th Congress estimated that it cost $1 million to kill a single Plains warrior (Hagan, 1976, p. 4). Such an estimate, no doubt, was inflated by senatorial hyperbole, but it was expensive to keep a cavalry troop on the Plains. It cost between $125,000 and $250,000 a day, including supply and support systems (Hagan, 1976, p. 4). The ubiquitous bureaucratic bickering and economy moves blocked the establishment of a separate Comanche agency, as well as the establishment of a reservation in New Mexico (Kenner, 1969, pp. 142–144). These impasses prolonged resistance since the Comanches preferred New Mexico to Texas or Indian Territory because of their old ties with New Mexico. Even after nearly all the Comanches were settled in the 1870s, they shared their agency with the Kiowas and Wichitas (Hagan, 1976, p. 138).

The council of Medicine Lodge Creek in 1867 was an attempt to negotiate treaties with several Plains groups (Utley, 1984, pp. 114–116).

It defined the first Comanche reservation (see Map IX.2). The agency responsible for Comanches, like most other Indian agencies, was grossly underfunded, and could not supply an adequate diet (Hagan, 1976, Ch.4; Utley, 1984, pp. 140–148). Comanche cattle herds that had been set up to supplement meager rations were raided by other Indians and neighboring Anglos (Hagan, 1976, p. 105). Comanches continued to raid in Texas, provoking counter-raids by settlers. The final Comanche battle was fought at Palo Duro Canyon, Texas, in 1875. After that Comanches remained on their Fort Sill reservation (Utley, 1984, pp. 174–178).

A key factor in the rise and demise of the Comanches was their rapid adaptation to a specific ecological niche, as mounted hunters and warriors. This adaptation was augmented by their social role as traders on the fringes of a state empire. When the buffalo declined, and the Comanche bands were caught between two states, both bases of adaptation were destroyed. The rapidity of their decline is illustrated in Map IX.2, which shows the territory ceded to the United States in 1865 and 1867.

Apaches

After 1869 the only Indian battles fought in Arizona and New Mexico were with Apaches (Dale, 1949, p. 113). The fact that Apaches were scattered in a large number of bands, over a diverse territory, is the major reason they were so difficult to contain, and the reason the history of their subjugation is difficult to summarize. The number of battles, treacheries, reversals and changes in policy is tremendous (Spicer, 1962, pp. 229–261; Faulk, 1974, pp. 142–197; Terrell, 1972; Thrapp, 1967; Worcester, 1979). As with the Comanches, much of the Apache situation may be explained by their social location in the wider region, a location that was significantly different from that of the Comanches. Apache bands had long formed a barrier to trade (see Map V.5), and had been in a state of endemic warfare with the surrounding state. They had developed a very effective raiding mode of production, supplying their needs by raiding the surrounding sedentary peoples, Spanish and Indian. Their raiding was supplemented by foraging and trading. Not even in their sedentary villages were they heavily dependent on any single food source. They moved freely over a vast range of territory and had no need to attack the same target frequently.

With the American conquest of the Southwest, this began to change. Competition with new settlers gradually increased. More concerted military efforts were made to control their activities. There was more regional unity, so Apache bands could not use the security of one village in return for raiding a neighboring village as they had in the past (see

Map IX.2. Comanche and Kiowa Treaty Cessions of 1865 and 1867

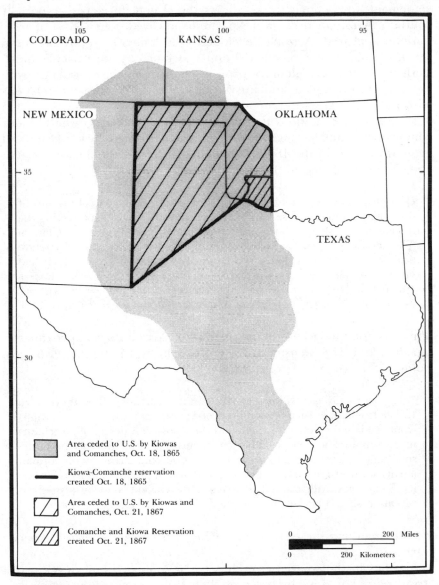

COLORADO 105 KANSAS 100 95

NEW MEXICO OKLAHOMA

35

TEXAS

30

Area ceded to U.S. by Kiowas
and Comanches, Oct. 18, 1865

Kiowa-Comanche reservation
created Oct. 18, 1865

Area ceded to U.S. by Kiowas and
Comanches, Oct. 21, 1867

Comanche and Kiowa Reservation
created Oct. 21, 1867

0   200   Miles

0   200   Kilometers

Source: Hagan (1976:22, 40)

Chapters VI and VII, and Griffen, 1983b, 1983c). To attack one Anglo settlement was to attack them all. As the region developed, especially southern Arizona where most Apache bands lived, a new kind of competition appeared. Arizona developed as a "mineral empire" (Lamar, 1970, p. 439). Miners needed supplies as much as the Apaches did—both depended on sedentary producers. Arizona was populated with newcomers, unfamiliar and unsympathetic toward symbiotic relations with Indians of any sort.

Under these conditions the military presence itself became a major source of revenue. Indian wars were necessary to keep the local capitalist economy going. In the 1860s the economic role of the military in Arizona had contributed to the hostilities:

> General Ord explained it best when he concluded at the end of his tour of duty that "hostilities in Arizona are kept up with a view of protecting the inhabitants, most of whom are supported by the hostilities." General Thomas also pointed out in a devastating report that six years of warfare against the Apache had cost the nation $15,000,000, a sum which had virtually sustained the economy of the territory. Even the *Weekly Arizonian* admitted in 1870 that many saw "the presence of the military in Arizona" as the "only inducement held out to immigration" (Lamar, 1970, p. 451).

This was at a time when the population of Arizona was approximately ten thousand (U.S. Census, 1975, p. 24). This was not a matter of economic influence, but of conspiracy:

> . . . it was good business for merchants in the Territory when there were Indian troubles. At such times more troops were sent, which meant rations would be bought locally for them and their horses. A group of merchants in Tucson were actively promoting incidents, a group known as the "Tucson Ring"; moreover, they were in collusion with many of the Indian agents to furnish substandard rations at standard prices, splitting the profits. Sometimes, with the aid of a reservation agent, they furnished no rations at all and pocketed the money (Faulk, 1974, pp. 166–168).

Before analyzing these patterns further a brief sketch of the Apache wars is in order.

Apaches in the southern reaches of New Mexico had developed a strong hatred of Mexicans based on their feelings toward the scalp hunters in northern Mexico (Faulk, 1974, pp. 142–145; see Chapters VI and VII). Superintendent Calhoun saw the inherent difficulty in the situation. The American public would not tolerate an outright annihilation of the nomadic tribes, including Apaches, who in turn had no source of surviving save raiding (Faulk, 1974, p. 147). In his annual report for 1852 Secretary of War Conrad suggested buying Apache territory at as much as quintuple its value to free the territory of raids (Faulk, 1974, p. 148). The only other alternative was for the government to feed the Indians, and funds were not forthcoming. Thus, Conrad and Calhoun were proved accurate prophets.

In Arizona, for the first few years after the conquest, conditions were generally peaceful. There were only a few raids (Dale, 1949, p. 47; Faulk, 1974, p. 147). In the mid-1850s raiding increased somewhat when southerners tried to develop mines in hopes of building a southern empire to the Pacific (Lamar, 1970, p. 111). In 1859 reports from Tubac indicated that Apaches still raided predominantly in Mexico, and ignored local targets (Faulk, 1974, p. 151). Indeed, for part of the decade, Cochise's band had a contract to supply wood to the Butterfield Overland Mail, and allowed mail carriers to pass unmolested through Apache territory (Faulk, 1974, p. 153; Lamar, 1970, p. 437). These relatively peaceful conditions did not survive the beginning of the Civil War.

With the war Apache–Anglo relations deteriorated quickly. A treacherous arrest of Cochise unleashed a cycle of raids by his band (Beck, 1962, p. 192; Lamar, 1970, p. 438; Utley, 1984, p. 65). The increase in traffic to California strained relations (Dale, 1949, p. 53). By 1862 Carson was dispatched to round up the Mescaleros, who were placed at Bosque Redondo in 1863. They remained there until food shortages (Lamar, 1970, p. 125) and the arrival of the Navajo prompted them to flee. Apaches began attacking the sedentary Pimas, Papagos and Maricopas in southern Arizona, further exacerbating conditions. Several treacherous massacres of nonhostile Apaches by miners set the southern frontier ablaze with raids (Beck, 1962, pp. 194–195; Utley, 1984, pp. 135–139). Between 1868 and 1870 more than 100 Anglo men were killed by Apaches. A three-way conflict over policy emerged from the renewed hostilities.

The army wanted to control and direct the fighting; the Indian Bureau wanted a system of reservations; local citizens wanted to raise a militia and take care of themselves. By 1865 both Tubac and Tucson were nearly abandoned due to the severity of the attacks. Bureaucratic policy fights were key to the disorder of Indian affairs (Lamar, 1970, pp. 446–447). In 1871 Governor Safford of Arizona was granted three companies of militia, despite the fact that most Apaches were on reservations by then (Lamar, 1970, p. 449). That year the militia massacred over 100 peaceful Indians at Camp Grant (Dale, 1949, pp. 95–96; Lamar, 1970, p. 449; Utley, 1984, p. 139). The public outcry in the east was so great that Colyer, a Quaker and an ardent advocate of Grant's Peace Policy, was put in charge of Arizona. He quickly placed 4,000 Apaches on four reservations (three in Arizona) and provided food and supplies for them. This outraged the local citizens. General Crook was also dispatched to Arizona to round up recalcitrant Apaches. These moves coincided with new coal and copper strikes in southeastern Arizona (Lamar, 1970, p. 462). By 1873 nearly all Apaches were on reservations, and relative peace was restored. But peace did not last.

After the pacification of 1873, short rations prompted more raids. This time the motivation was not only military presence, but removal of Apaches from their reservations to gain access to newly discovered copper deposits on the San Carlos reservation, or access to prime grazing and farming land around the White Mountain and Fort Apache reservations (Lamar, 1970, p. 473ff; Faulk, 1974, p. 170ff). Actions such as these gradually abated, but not until 1886 when Geronimo, the last Apache guerrilla, was captured.

Some of the difficulties that arose on the San Carlos reservation were the result of overcrowding. Four thousand Apaches were placed on an area that had formerly sustained 800 people (Faulk, 1974, p. 175). Some of the bands placed there had had hostile relations with each other before being relocated. These hostilities were also exploited to the benefit of the Tucson Ring (Utley, 1984, pp. 193–201). Reservation conditions prompted the flight of Victorio and Geronimo. Victorio was eventually killed by the Mexican militia in 1880 (Utley, 1984, p. 197). Geronimo was captured and imprisoned in 1886, ending the Indian wars in the United States (Utley, 1984, p. 201).

Eventually the various bands were forced to live together on reservations. No doubt, Apache survival was due to their adaptability in various and variegated living situations. The ability to form new alliances, to use multiple survival strategies, and a general ability to adapt to rapidly changing circumstances—all finely honed over centuries of practicing a raiding mode of subsistence—contributed to a resourceful approach to reservation living.

CONCLUSIONS, QUESTIONS, SPECULATIONS

The completion of the American conquest of the Southwest drastically changed the nature of ethnic relations. Nomadism was no longer a viable way of life. The actions and territories of the various Indian groups came under the jurisdiction of the state. Isolation was no longer to be explained on the two bases of geography and hostile relations. Incorporation into the capitalist market became an increasingly important consideration. These changes began with Kearny's arrival in 1846, slowed with the American Civil War, then intensified once it was over. By 1886 the last Indian war was over and the conquest that had begun with the opening of the Santa Fe Trail in 1821 was completed.

The utility of a group's resources to Americans was a major factor in the type and result of conquest. The location of externally imposed, and largely arbitrary boundaries was also significant. For the Hispanic residents of New Mexico, the local class structure was of some importance. The type and amount of resources left to a group affected its chances of survival. The compatibility of the adaptive strategy of a group with the dynamics of a capitalist state complements utility of resources as a factor in change.

For all the nomadic groups, there was a low level of compatibility with the capitalist state system. Nomadism, barter, raiding and slavery did not mesh well with more intensive uses of the resources available in the area. The carrying capacity of nomadic foraging—even when mixed with occasional gardening or herding—is low compared to that of farming or intensive pastoralism. The greater the flexibility of nomadic adaptation, the greater its ability to adjust to new conditions. Comanches were heavily dependent on buffalo; once the buffalo were gone, Comanche life was doomed. Navajo and Apache groups had more adaptable adjustments. Navajos had mastered sheep herding. Apaches were not tied to any one food source or method of acquisition. Location was equally, if not more, important. Comanches blocked expansion, especially for the growing cattle industry, onto the southern Plains. Apaches blocked some trade, and slowed mining operations. By contrast, Navajos were more of a nuisance than a threat. Their attacks were triggered by Hispanic sheep and slave raiding, and by food shortages. Utes were similar to Navajos, but had no pastoral base. Furthermore, they were pushed from the region. Apache and especially Comanche lands had fairly high utility to Anglo settlers. Navajo land had low utility. The major differences between Apache and Comanche were flexibility of adaptation—high for Apaches, low for Comanches—and degree of central organization—relatively low for Apaches and relatively high for Comanches. Apaches were able to spread out, avoid concentration and annihilation. The earlier tribalization of Comanches and heavy dependence on buffalo made them more vulnerable to quick defeat.

For the sedentary groups, the Pueblos and Hispanos, other factors are more important. Among the Hispanos, class was a major consideration. The few upper-class Hispanos who became involved in the expanding capitalist market not only maintained, but improved, their position. They were able to capitalize on their class position to become the middle-

men between the new and the traditional cultures. For the poor Hispanos, the situation was reversed. They became increasingly dependent
on their *rico patrones* as they were increasingly blocked from their usual
means of subsistence. Buffalo hunting and Indian trade were eliminated
when the nomadic groups were pacified. The spread of cattle industry
undercut sheep herding, leaving little but subsistence farming. They
could not shift to cash crops and still eat, and so were forced to stay, for
the time being, in subsistence villages. The Pueblos were even more
isolated since they did not have the *rico* connection to the market. They
were, however, fortunate to have their lands confirmed, preserving their
resource base. Their prime ecological competitors were Hispano villagers, who were prevented by state action from encroaching further on
Pueblo resources. Pueblo villages were located in places remote from
Anglo interest; their lands were suitable only for subsistence agriculture.
They, like Navajos, were left in their traditional homes with a resource
base sufficient to provide for their continued existence. Apaches and
Comanches could not continue along traditional lines, although Apaches
were able to adapt somewhat better than Comanches.

These conditions are summarized in Table IX.4. Pueblo groups and
Hispanos were sedentary farmers and pastoralists. The Hispanos were
part of a larger state organization, albeit loosely connected to it. Both
were more politically centralized than any nomadic group. Hispanos
were distinctive with respect to Plains trade because they participated in
the formal Santa Fe Trail trade and the informal *comanchero* and contraband trade. Participation corresponded crudely to class differences. En-
gaging in the capitalist market gave some Hispanics more ecological
flexibility than Pueblo groups who did not participate. The ecological
adequacy of adaptation changes in opposite directions for Comanches
and Apaches. As the buffalo declined Comanches declined; Apaches
prospered (or at least did not decline so precipitously) as they perfected
their raiding and foraging strategies. Finally, the utility of territory to
the American state was a significant factor for all groups. Comanches
initially occupied a no-man's-land, then became a barrier to trade.
Apaches at first harassed Mexican farmers, but became a major obstacle
to mineral development. Navajos and Utes were pushed into marginal
lands. Indeed, Utes were pushed out of the territory into Colorado
where they suffered as that region developed, following a different trajectory (see Lamar, 1970; Jorgensen, 1972). Pueblo groups, due to their
legal title to land, were of little interest to outsiders. The utility of Hispanic resources shifted as the territory was needed for a land bridge to
the Pacific, then used for local resources, then gradually became less

Table IX.4. Social Changes Among Southwestern Groups from Late Spanish to Early American Periods (ca. 1800 until ca. 1880)

	Nomadic Groups				Sedentary Groups		
						Hispanos	
Characteristic[1]	Comanche	Apache	Navajo	Ute	Pueblos	Elite	Poor
Sociopolitical organization[2]	Band	Band	Band	Band	Chiefdom	Region of refuge of an agrarian state	
Political centralization	High	Low	Low	Low	High	High	Moderate
Intensity of trade	High	Moderate	Low	Low–moderate[3]	High	High	High–low
Ecological flexibility	Low	High	Moderate	Moderate	Low	High–moderate[3]	High–moderate[3]
Ecological adequacy	High–low[3]	Low–moderate[3]	Moderate	Moderate	High	High	High
External utility of resources	Low–high[3]	Moderate–high[5]	Low	Low[4]	Low	High–moderate–low[5]	

[1]The evaluations of these characteristics are relative, and do not imply an absolute scale.
[2]See Chapter II for a discussion of these various terms.
[3]Indicates significant change during this era.
[4]The Utes were pushed out of the region after the Americans took over.
[5]New Mexico was of interest primarily as a land bridge. Once California was secure, American interest in the area dropped rapidly.

relevant to American state concerns. The conquest had brought about major changes for and among all the groups.

Much of the change that occurred during the consolidation of the conquest was due to the shift of the region from a floundering peripheral state to a dynamic capitalist state. Yet New Mexico remained of marginal interest to the American state; it was a means to get somewhere else, the source of a few useful minerals, and a source of irritation with its continuing Indian wars. While much changed, much remained the same.

Renewed hostilities unleashed the old patterns of fighting and raiding. The same patterns were repeated: the use of volunteer fighters, low pay for the military, use of booty and captives to supplement pay, initiation of hostile actions by locals bent on their own advancement with little or no regard for the consequences, failure to identify nomadic raiders carefully, continued bureaucratic fighting and bungling, the use of bureaucratic positions on the frontier as stepping-stones to higher office in the administrative centers. This was yet another cycle of patterns that dated from the Chichimeca Wars (see Chapter IV) and Spanish and Mexican administrations (see Chapters VI and VII). It was as if Americans had studied the Spanish archives to discover how to make the same mistakes again. These patterns repeated because the structural conditions were similar. The region was still only marginally incorporated into the dominant state. What was different with America, and what caused the age-old patterns to fade away, was the far greater strength of the American state.

Utley (1984) interprets the pervasive conflict between white Americans and Indians as resistance to the reservation system. While this is certainly true, the basis of that resistance was not only in a clash of worldviews, but was fundamentally rooted in incompatible uses of a basic resource, land. The American state, a growing capitalist industrializing state, was particularly intolerant of "inefficient" use of resources. Farming, ranching and mining all used the land more "efficiently" than foraging or gardening. There was no room for compromise, symbiotic cooperation, or even an uneasy division of labor among sedentary and nomadic technologies, as had been the case under the Spanish and Mexican states. Indians who were foragers or gardeners confronted by a capitalist state had two choices: become lower-class members of a capitalist state on marginal lands or die resisting. Many took the second option.

Still, the process of "pacification" was far from uniform. During the process many patterns common in the Spanish era reappeared, frequently with similar results. But there were two outstanding differences under American control: the incorporation of all territory into the state (the closing of the frontier), and the presence of far greater resources to enforce the will of the state, even in marginally incorporated areas.

The incorporation of all territory into the state meant there was no frontier to cross in order to avoid state actions (although the Mexican–American border served that function for some time; see Martinez, 1985). To be sure, some groups such as the Navajo experienced minimal contact due to their apparent lack of useful resources, but all groups came under American state authority. Formerly nomadic groups were located on reservations and forced to live in geographically restricted areas. The pressure for change was immense. Within 50 years Comanches were transformed from the "Lords of the South Plains" into poverty-stricken reservation dwellers on the verge of extinction. The full effect of American policies was not to come until the twentieth century, when the Indian Reorganization Act (1934) forced all reservation groups to elect tribal governments. Nevertheless, the initial conditions for subsequent twentieth-century changes were set during the consolidation of the conquest of the Southwest.

The end of Indian hostilities had other consequences. The informal Plains trade died, sheep grazing expanded, and the American conquest had changed the social environment. The destruction of the Plains trade reinforced the initial Anglo prejudices against "Mexicans." The *comancheros,* and rural Hispanos in general, came to be seen as enemies as much as Indians. The *ricos* were supported by the local Anglo administration, which preferred to deal with upper-class "Spaniards" who could deliver votes on demand. Although debt peonage was illegal, economic dependence was not, and northern villagers became almost totally dependent on the *ricos* (some of whom were their kinsmen) for jobs, either on their ranches, or for positions in the political spoils system under the tight control of the Santa Fe Ring. As the sheep trade flourished, the *partido* system grew, increasing *rico* control of large herds. The *partido* system, while somewhat servile, did offer a limited possibility of class mobility, and hence did not represent as strong an instance of feudalization as occurred during the Bourbon reforms and the Mexican era. Thus, the conquest had multiple, complex effects on all groups within the region.

For at least the period of consolidation, the homelands of these groups were in a region that was marginally incorporated into the wider economy. Neglect was the easiest action on the part of the state. For Utes and Comanches, being forced out of the Southwest was detrimental; the state was to pay more attention to them. For the other groups, the neglect associated with living in a marginal region gave them time to adapt to a new situation. New Mexico was to be a land bridge to California. Once the passage was clear, there was no need to disturb the region further. The region was a refuge, a preserve, for older social forms that had been destroyed elsewhere, a role it had played in larger state systems with varying degrees of intensity since initial European contact.

NOTES

1.   There were other sedentary groups in southern Arizona: the Pima, Papago, Maricopa and some Mojave and Yuma groups. They have not been discussed in this work. For details on their organization and history see Spicer (1962), Bee (1981, Chs.1,2), and Dobyns and Euler (1970).

2.   The term "Anglo" is used in Southwest literature to refer to Americans.

3.   Nostrand (1975) uses a variety of sources, the Seventh U.S. Census manuscripts included, to derive his population estimates. He is careful to count only resident Mexicans. He omitted transients such as the several thousand Sonorans who worked as laborers in the California mines, but who for the most part did not remain there. He also located information on the Gadsden Purchase area, included the El Paso region in the count, and obtained approximations for the lost returns from the San Francisco Bay area.

4.   Oczon (1982) provides a bibliographic introduction to the vast literature on land grants in New Mexico. See also Briggs and Van Ness (1987).

5.   "Pacification" is a common term in the history of the American West. It might be glossed as "elimination of Indian opposition to Anglo occupation of the land."

6.   The journey to Bosque Redondo and back is known in Navajo history, appropriately, as the "Long Walk." See Roessel (1973) for Navajo oral history of the Long Walk.

7.   In the 1850s, Navajo population was estimated at between 10,000 (Beck, 1962, p. 184) and 15,000 (Lamar, 1970, p. 92). Utley (1984, p. 84) estimates that the 8,000 Navajo who went on the Long Walk were about three-quarters of the entire group. Kluckhohn and Leighton (1962, p. 23) and Iverson (1981, p. 7) estimate a population of about 15,000 in 1870, just a few years after the return from Bosque Redondo. I would guess that these estimates err on the low side for three reasons. First, Navajo oral history provides many accounts of people who did not go on the Long Walk (Roessel, 1973). Second, the traditional Navajo lands are rugged, and provide many well-supplied, secluded hiding places where small groups could easily have avoided detection by a military force moving rapidly through the area. Third, the area was capable of supporting a large number of traditional Navajos even after the destruction of standing crops—especially in the years before the extensive damage due to overgrazing in the twentieth century.

CHAPTER X

Conclusions, Questions, Speculations

> Historical sociology is . . . the attempt to understand the relationship of personal activity and experience on the one hand and social organisation on the other as something that is continuously constructed in time. It makes the continuous process of construction the focal concern of social analysis. That process may be studied in many different contexts. . . . The particular context to which sociologists have chosen to pay most attention is the one I have called the transition to industrialism. But in the end historical sociology is more a matter of how one interprets the world than of what bit of it one chooses to study (Philip Abrams, 1982, pp. 16–17).

The marginality of the Southwest to the various states that have shaped its past is double-edged: while it facilitates close examination of subtle processes of change, it also means that general patterns are tenuous at best. Case studies, even long and complicated ones such as this, are limited in their generality. They are, however, useful for critiquing and extending existing theories.

SOUTHWESTERN TRAJECTORIES OF INCORPORATION

At least three levels of social change shaped the incorporation of the Southwest into the European world-system. First, the evolving world-economy brought internal changes to the states that had imperial control of the Southwest. Second, the actions of these states produced changes in the indigenous nonstate societies as they were incorporated. Third, the interaction between and among nonstate societies shaped the incorporation process.

237

Four state societies have had an impact on the Southwest, but none acted with complete autonomy. First were the Mesoamerican states that had very mild influence on Southwestern changes, yet even they drew the Southwest into wider networks. Spain experienced a long, episodic decline beginning in the early seventeenth century. Mexico entered the world-system as a peripheral state and remained there for most of the nineteenth century. The United States grew from a rising peripheral to a semi-peripheral state during the mid-nineteenth century. The Southwest was not the major arena of competition for any of these states. Hence, the incorporation of the Southwest, a "periphery of a periphery," remained relatively weak.

The effects of incorporation became steadily, if unevenly, stronger with each succeeding state. Mexico is the only exception to this pattern. The Mesoamerican states were by far the weakest in their effects on the region. Nevertheless, there seem to have been some important effects of trade and other contacts, such as the formation of local trade centers that were the foci of regional development. It is also possible that nomadic groups may have been drawn into these networks. The strongest evidence for such networks is a relatively rapid collapse of regional trade networks when the connections with Mesoamerica were severed. Such collapses do not establish external connections, but they are consistent with them.

The effects of the Spanish state were not consistent due to changes in Spanish power that were reflected in colonial policies. In the sixteenth and part of the seventeenth century, Spain waxed strong. In the seventeenth and early eighteenth centuries, Spain lost power. One of the most significant changes during this time was the adoption of guns and horses by nomadic groups. The expenses associated with the ensuing endemic warfare prompted reform-minded Bourbon rulers to reorganize frontier administration. These reforms led to Spanish resurgence, then decline as a wave of independence movements swept through Latin America.

The rebellion from Spain, the prolonged fighting, and the formation of a weak, strife-torn state loosened the ties of the northern frontier to the central state and simultaneously opened it to commercial penetration by the United States. The rebellion drained the country's resources, leaving little to spend on a northern frontier. This led to the disintegration of peace with nomadic groups. The region might have been abandoned entirely if there had been no threat of American expansion. During this chaotic era, older Spanish patterns began to erode and were gradually replaced with new patterns derived in large part from participation in American trade.

The United States changed this. It was expanding, attracting new immigrants, industrializing and developing complex trade rivalries with Britain. Americans wanted to secure their own borders for trade, to gain a foothold in the newly independent Latin American countries and to compete with the British in the Far East. At the same time, competition between and among northern industrialists and merchants, southern cotton growers and western farmers was building slowly toward war. These factors helped overpower internal opposition to expansion in the Southwest, and ultimately led to the annexation of what had been the northern half of Mexico (including Texas).

Once the American Civil War was settled, Americans applied their considerable resources to the consolidation of their western holdings. Indians throughout the West were decimated, subdued, and forced onto reservations. California and Texas developed rapidly; New Mexico and Arizona fell into relative neglect, recreating circumstances similar to those of the early Spanish and late Mexican eras, with similar results— endemic frontier warfare between nomadic and sedentary groups.

These events show that the effects of states on sedentary groups have been different from their effects on nomadic groups. In the two or three centuries preceding Spanish intrusion there had been a contraction of Puebloan living domain and considerable fluidity in group location. In a few decades after Spanish intrusion the number of occupied villages dropped precipitously. Pueblo population decreased steadily throughout the Spanish era. After the Pueblo Revolt in 1680, Hispanic settlers and the surviving Pueblo villages developed a crude alliance to protect themselves from raiding nomads. When the Americans annexed the region, the special status of the Pueblo groups was continued, although they never held first-class citizenship rights. The surviving Pueblo groups have managed to preserve much of their culture. In part, this is because they were able to expel nonconforming individuals to surrounding communities.

Of all the groups in the Southwest, the various nomads—Apaches, Comanches, Navajos and Utes—have the most complicated trajectories of incorporation. Originally groups of linguistically similar bands, these groups, *qua* groups, are products of Spanish actions. They played major roles in their own changes. They were used by, and less frequently used, the Spaniards in fights against each other. The Pueblo Revolt had taught Spanish administrators the dangers of large alliances. Once peace with Comanches was established in the late eighteenth century, other nomadic groups were locked into the role of enemy, especially the numerous Apachean bands. Some groups experienced considerable pressure toward tribalization, and others toward fragmentation. Only Comanches felt a consistent pressure to form a central political structure, and even that was very fragile. The pressure for fragmentation was strongest on Apaches. More often than not, Navajos were the victims of raids by other nomadic groups and Spanish settlers. Eventually, they were allowed to remain in what had become their traditional homeland, for the most part out of the way of state action. The Ute bands lacked pastoralism, were closer to the Plains and consequently had more intense competition with other nomadic groups. They were finally forced from the region by the Americans.

Apache and Comanche bands are a study in contrast. Both groups were a threat to Hispanic settlers, both were among the first indigenous nomadic groups to acquire horses, and both became formidable raiders. A combination of factors contributed to their divergent yet intertwined trajectories of change. Comanches were able to benefit from the crossing of the horse and gun frontiers to become powerful hunters and raiders. Apaches, with less access to guns, were gradually displaced south and west from the Plains. The New Mexican support of Comanche alliances contrasted with implacable opposition to Apaches. Comanches came close to forming a tribe; Apaches were fragmented into highly mobile and fluid bands. At first Comanches profited and Apaches lost from this arrangement, but after the American conquest, their paths reversed. The combination of inopportune location and dependence on the buffalo subjected Comanche bands to rapid losses. Apaches were able to capitalize on their differentiated territory and fluid organization to resist effectively the American onslaught.

Before turning to the analysis of incorporation, it is appropriate to underscore some general implications of this study.

LESSONS FROM THE SOUTHWEST
FOR THE STUDY OF SOCIAL CHANGE

There are a few broad lessons to be drawn from this study. First, scale is an important factor in the study of social change, both with respect to geographical location and with respect to time. Certainly from the fifteenth century, and probably from long before then, local, regional and global changes have been intertwined. To ignore any level while studying another invites error. Yet, the way to connect them is not altogether clear. A world-system approach offers one possibility. There should be others.

Second is the role of social structure in interpreting historical documents. Since various bureaucracies have different stakes in the ebb and flow of empire, many reports are written to support local bureaucratic ideology without violating superior ideology. The common expression, *"obedezco, pero no cumplo"* (I obey, but do not comply), which appears so frequently in reports of Spanish colonial officials, is a familiar, transparent example (Lang, 1975). When the competition among missionaries, miners, *encomenderos* and *hacendados* is added to bureaucratic competition and the inevitable personal competition, interpretation of historical documents becomes hazardous. It is all too easy to attribute the byzantine quality of official reports to "personality conflicts." The analysis used here strongly suggests that such "personality conflicts" are the result of structurally induced competition, and not explanations of it.

Finally, history and sociology have a complementary rather than an antagonistic relationship. As Abrams (1982) has argued, historians and sociologists do the same thing but use divergent strategies and materials. Each serves to refine the work of the other. This study will have made a contribution to that exchange if it inspires other scholars to dig for new information to settle some of the issues raised here.

SOUTHWESTERN PROCESSES OF INCORPORATION

While these lessons verge on cliches, the lessons about incorporation are both more informative and more problematic. Incorporation is problematic with respect to: (1) incorporating state or system; (2) types of incorporated groups; (3) both timing and degree of incorporation; and (4) a variety of factors that can affect the process.

First, the stronger the state the more drastic the changes that accompany incorporation. The difference between Spain in the late eighteenth century versus the United States in mid-nineteenth century illustrates the significance of state strength. With great effort and considerable cost, Spain approached peace on the northern frontier after centuries of contact. The United States achieved these goals in a few decades.

Second, the level of sociopolitical development of incorporated societies plays a role in the incorporation process, as is shown by the effects of the various indigenous groups on both Spanish and American policies toward them. Incorporation alters local intergroup relations and affects local alliances and productive patterns, even when local production is not transformed to serve the global accumulation of capital. Sedentary groups (e.g., Pueblo societies) had significantly different relations with Spanish colonists than did nomadic groups (e.g., Apaches and Comanches). The Pueblo Revolt made it abundantly clear to Spanish administrators that too much unity among native groups was dangerous.

The cost of endemic warfare made it equally clear that too little unity, as among the nomadic band societies, was also dangerous.

Incorporation involves a complex "interaction effect." The incorporation process is shaped by both the type of state system (and hence, type of world-system) and the type of nonstate society or societies (or even state societies) being incorporated. The degree to which an area or group is incorporated into a world-system sets the context within which local changes may occur. The effect of an incorporating state on an incorporated group is a function of the type of state or world-system. Conversely, these effects are also a function of the nonstate societies' sociopolitical configuration, e.g., sedentary horticultural societies versus nomadic foragers. Local actions are major factors in determining the costs of incorporation.

Third, incorporation is a variable and volatile process. Shifts in incorporation are not entirely elastic, as a region becomes more closely incorporated into the world-economy, external pressures impinge more forcefully on local groups. When such pressures are sufficiently strong, and of sufficient duration, the structure of local groups will be changed. If the transformation is sufficiently drastic, it becomes difficult to reverse—even in the event of a shift to looser incorporation, as happened when nomads adopted horses. Other changes, such as political centralization, appear to be more easily reversed. The limits of variability and reversibility of incorporation-induced changes are not clear. Still, sporadic, episodic and erratic changes tend, in net, to be in one direction. The more complete previous incorporation has been, the more difficult it is to return to the previous state. Specifying the ranges and limits of the incorporation process will require further studies of these processes in other locations with other groups.

Fourth, many factors affect the incorporation process. Location, within, on, or beyond the frontier of state control is important. In the Spanish era Comanches lived on the frontier and served as buffers and middlemen in relations with external groups. Apaches, on the other hand, blocked internal development and consequently were systematically attacked. In the American era Comanches became obstacles to internal development and were all but destroyed. Apaches were merely nuisances in a backwater area, and consequently survived in greater numbers. Only the historical accident of relatively constant transportation technology in the Southwest (the horse) makes the effects of geographical factors readily apparent.[1] These differences were reinforced by differences consequent to location in the Basin and Range Provinces versus location on the Plains, given similar levels of technology.

These processes interact to produce others. Once Apaches acquired horses they were able to displace nonmounted rivals. Their very success stimulated counterraids and emulation. Once Comanches were able to add guns to horses they could displace Apaches and other groups who did not have equal access to either horses or guns. Thus, horses and guns became increasingly vital for the survival of every group. Second, stability may result from the maintenance of specific structural conditions. As long as there was a shortage of adequate military protection, inadequate pay for soldiers, lack of control of transfrontier territory, and continued demand for captives, nomadic raiding remained endemic.

Still, endemic warfare was common at several different times: in the Chichimeca area during the sixteenth century, and in New Mexico during the seventeenth and early eighteenth centuries, the Mexican era, and immediately after the American conquest. While the structural conditions of these instances were similar, their origins were different. "Feudalization" exhibits a similar pattern. The feudalism of the *encomienda* system before the Pueblo Revolt was produced by the transmission and application of Spanish traditions to new territory. The "feudalism" of the late eighteenth and early nineteenth centuries was engendered by increased trade, and intensified during the nineteenth century by participation in capitalistic markets. Rather than being a persisting "tradition," it was a product of incorporation. Similar surface manifestations do not necessarily imply similar processes of origination.

Religious zeal and preemptive colonization were also important factors in the initial colonization (1598) and reconquest (1693) of New Mexico. That these actions also served economic purposes by supporting economic exploitation of silver resources further south is not at issue. The conflicts between and among the church, the state and the treasury all indicate that each sphere had autonomous effects on the processes of incorporation. Overall, it appears that economic considerations, especially articulation with market systems, become increasingly important with respect to politics and ideology as states become stronger.

Finally, systemic forces can be manifest at the individual level in bureaucratic wrangling. Bureaucratic structures can give rise to conflicts over jurisdictions in a variety of ways. Conflicts can be over territorial jurisdictions, as happened in conflicts between New Mexico and Texas in the prosecution of wars against nomads in the Spanish era, and in the massive reorganizations under the Bourbon reforms. Or, conflicts can be over substantive jurisdictions, as between church and state in early New Mexico, or among the viceroy, regional governors and the commandant general in eighteenth-century New Spain, and among competing war, interior, and local bureaucracies under American control. Indeed, bureaucratic conflicts engender personality conflicts rather than vice versa. Likewise, policy directives have multiple sources, many of which come from outside the area where the policy is to be imposed. Furthermore, such policies may have objectives that do not serve local interests. Securing the northern border from territorial claims by competing states was a major goal of Spanish occupation of much of northern New Spain. A secure, all-weather land route to the Pacific outweighed interest in local development of New Mexico in the immediate post–American conquest period. That the Southwest did not readily lend itself to capital-intensive agriculture also lowered interest in development of the region. Finally, resources available for pursuing policies within a region may vary with external relations. Spanish colonial vigor waxed and waned with Spain's fortunes in European wars. American efforts to pacify nomadic groups were disrupted by the American Civil War.

What does this study say about world-system theory's analysis of incorporation?

WORLD-SYSTEM THEORY AND INCORPORATION

An assessment of the world-system account of incorporation must acknowledge that world-system theory is not a "theory," but a "paradigm" in Kuhn's sense (1970, 1977). That is, it is a model for applying an analysis. The primary value of a paradigm is in posing questions that can be answered via a known strategy. Paradigms are not tested or proved, but are more or less useful. This suggests that: (1) there should be other "theories" about the interconnections of the "modern" world, since paradigms usually give rise to families of theories; and (2) the world-system model is a useful foil against which to test other theories. Indeed, one of the limits of world-system theory at present is that it has been applied primarily to the rise of capitalism. Is world-system theory, as a paradigm, really specific to this era or can it usefully be extended to "pre-capitalist" or "pre-modern" world systems, or even to relatively mild instances of incorporation early in the rise of the "modern world-system"?

World-system theory was developed to explain a fundamental change over approximately the last 500 years: the expansion of European societies and the industrial revolution. To some extent it remains harnessed to that agenda. This change has been described as the origins of capitalism, the transition from feudalism to capitalism, or the "great transformation" (Polanyi, 1944; see Abrams, 1982, pp. 16–17). Wallerstein (1974a, 1974b) argues that capitalism began in the "long sixteenth century" (1450–1650). Wolf (1982, Ch.10) and Tilly (1981,Ch.1) argue against Wallerstein for a late appearance of global capitalism, coincident with the industrial revolution. The disagreement is not over the "facts," but over the labels—or so it would seem.

The disagreement is clearest in Wolf (1982, Ch.10), who argues that capitalism consists of the transfer of control from the direct producers to the owners of the means of production. Wallerstein argues that capitalism consists of production of goods for exchange on the market—the system of production being determined by a variety of local, regional, and global factors. Wallerstein seeks to explain the recurrence of what appeared to be "pre-capitalist" social structures after the appearance of capitalism. He solved the problem in the same way that Frank (1969a, 1969b) solved it, by positing and uncovering cases where incorporation into the world-economy produced social forms that resembled pre-capitalist forms.

Several different issues are confused in this analysis. The distinction between world-empires (meaning an exchange network under the domination of a single polity) and world-economies (meaning an exchange network among more-or-less autonomous polities) is one source of confusion. Wallerstein argues (1974a, 1974b) that until the appearance of the "modern world-system," world-economies generally turned into world-empires as one polity came to dominate all the others in the system. Fundamentally, what is not clear is whether this change was primarily qualitative, meaning a new social form and new social processes have appeared, or if they are primarily quantitative, meaning that social forms and process are the same, but there have been large changes in the "variables" that constitute them. Wallerstein claims the former.

It is important not to restrict a priori the possible applications of world-system theory through an overly narrow concept and theory of incorporation, which is too tightly harnessed to capital accumulation as the only motor of incorporation. Even when a peripheral area is a net expense to a core region, there is still a tremendous impact on it. Core exploitation of peripheral areas may be a relatively late development. If "contact" or "marginal" incorporation does not contribute to the accumulation of capital, then why does it happen? One way to help discover the limits of a world-system model is to push it until it cracks. So far it has been remarkably resilient. Whether or not world-system theory proves useful to understanding Southwestern processes of incorporation, the attempt helps define its limits.

The study of the Southwest reveals major differences in the process of incorporation by Mesoamerican states, the Spanish Empire, and America. Each was more powerful than its predecessor, each produced larger effects in shorter time. If the extremes are compared, the differences in the impacts of state incorporation are stupendous. But are these differences quantitative or qualitative? Is American capitalist trade all that different from the efforts of Mesoamerican traders or is it simply far more intense? (See Schneider, 1977.) The comparison of extreme cases suggests that the differences are qualitative.

Mesoamerican traders may have introduced new religious ideas into the region, but certainly without the same depth of penetration. Even under Spain, nomadic groups were able to retain substantial autonomy, although certainly less than under Mesoamerican influence. In a few decades the American state succeeded in transforming relatively autonomous societies into dependent minorities subject to alien laws and forced assimilation to new cultural values (Snipp, 1986a, 1986b). Contemporary Native American politics revolves around issues of local control, an issue not all that different from local and regional politics everywhere in the United States—surely an indicator of rather extensive incorporation. But how does this bear on the nature of the "great transformation"?

First, the nature of ethnicity was significantly transformed during this era (see T. Hall, 1984b). In some sense the very concept of ethnic group is tied to the notion of states, an ethnic group being some type of subcomponent of a state. If the term is used in the sense of an "ethny" (van den Berghe, 1981, p. 22), or a "people," then it becomes almost synonymous with "society." In general, societies are thought to have more autonomy, politically and economically, than ethnic groups. The shift from "society" to "ethnic group" is illustrated most dramatically by the various nomadic groups analyzed in this study. But the Hispanos experienced much the same transition as a consequence of the American conquest. The *genízaros* (detribalized Indians) form an interesting case. Their social organization was a consequence of their changing frontier context. As frontier conditions changed, specifically as wars with hostile nomads slowed and finally stopped, the services of this group were no longer necessary. A fundamental change throughout this era may be the increasing salience of geopolitical context in shaping local social units.

Second is the relation of capitalism and trade. This issue is raised with respect to the Southwest by Gutierrez (1980, pp. 378, 427, note 11) in his discussion of the so-called specie shortage in northern New Spain. Gutierrez argues that capitalism arrived in New Mexico in approximately 1770 when trade with Chihuahua and other centers to the south increased. Weber (1982, Ch.13) argues that it only arrived with the Americans and the Santa Fe Trail trade. This debate would seem to be terminological, but it is a local manifestation of the Wallerstein-Wolf-Tilly debate.

The same debate surfaces between the Steins (1970, 1980) and Platt

(1972, 1980a, 1980b) over the beginning of underdevelopment, or "peripheralization," in Mexico. Platt (1980) argues, contra Stein and Stein (1970), that peripheralization did not begin in colonial times. His own trade figures (Platt, 1972), however, indicate that the process actually began during the era of Bourbon reforms. It took nearly a century for the process to come to full force. The problem is that the Bourbon reforms produced significant changes in northern New Spain, including increased trade and prosperity. These very improvements played a role in the subsequent independence movement, which, in turn, opened the gates to trade with the United States and Britain. This trade, however, was more than a reinstatement of the Bourbon patterns with new partners. The trade was harnessed to new, more dynamic states.

Wallerstein is correct in noting the major role of trade in producing local social change. Tilly and Wolf are correct in noting that there are significant differences between trade harnessed to a mercantile state (or in Wallerstein's terms, a failing world-empire) and trade harnessed to a capitalist state (or a growing world-economy). Platt is correct in asserting that full-blown peripherality or underdevelopment did not develop until the late nineteenth century in Mexico, yet the Steins are correct in asserting that the process began under mercantile Spain. From a local point of view, Weber is correct in asserting that capitalist trade did not penetrate northern New Spain, and New Mexico in particular, until after Mexican independence and the beginning of trade with Americans. Gutierrez is correct, though, in asserting that these changes began late in the Spanish era with the increase in trade attendant to the Bourbon reforms. How can such seemingly disparate and contradictory claims all be correct?

The confusion emanates from an overly narrow conception and theory of incorporation which limits the world-system analysis of it. First, incorporation begins much earlier and has stronger effects than world-system theory recognizes. While the "nominal-effective" incorporation distinction is useful and valid for the analysis of its effects on core development, it is not as useful for analyses of incorporated areas. Second, incorporated groups, especially nonstate societies, play a more active role in the process than is typically accorded them. Third, incorporation is a variable and sporadic process. The specific trajectory of incorporation of a region or group is affected by a number of factors. Fourth, the generality, variability, reversibility and limitations of the processes of incorporation in frontier (or marginally incorporated) areas remain unclear. The work of Lattimore (1951, 1962) and Wolf (1982) suggests that similar processes are quite common. Clearly, though, the stronger the incorporating state the more rapid and complete the incorporation seems to be. Finally, all this suggests that too close a concern with the imperialism thesis, that the exploitation of the periphery is necessary for core development, detracts from other processes involved in expansion and incorporation into the "modern world-system."

Whether world-system theory is sufficiently resilient to accommodate these theoretical extensions or whether a broader approach is needed remains to be seen in the analysis of other areas and other times. It is abundantly clear, however, that while peripheral areas may at times be marginal to core areas and to the system as a whole, theoretical understanding of these areas is central to any theory of the origins and functioning of the "modern world-system." Clearly, too, any theoretical account of social change, especially during the last half millennium or so, must take serious notice of the variability and volatility of incorporation processes, the critical and dynamic roles of incorporated groups in those processes, and the conjuncture of many levels of social change in the process of incorporation.

NOTES

1.   Chirot (1985) demonstrates the significance of geographical factors in the rise of the West. In general, the role of geographical factors in the operation of the world-system has not been adequately addressed, but see Agnew (1982) and P. Taylor (1981, 1982, 1985) for excellent discussion.

References

1. Citations to the *Handbook of North American Indians* (Volumes 9 and 10, edited by Alfonso Ortiz in 1979 and 1983 respectively) are followed by a date in square brackets ([]), to indicate when the final version of the article was accepted by the editor, since this was occasionally long before publication. When the dates are the same, no separate notation is made.

2. Where a book has been reprinted the first entry indicates the edition used. The original date and publisher are given in parentheses.

3. The following abbreviations have been used:

AJS	American Journal of Sociology
ASR	American Sociological Review
CSSH	Comparative Studies in Society and History
CUP	Cambridge University Press
HAHR	Hispanic American Historical Review
NMHR	New Mexico Historical Review
OXUP	Oxford University Press
SWHQ	Southwest Historical Quarterly
UAZP	University of Arizona Press
UCALP	University of California Press
UCP	University of Chicago Press
UNMP	University of New Mexico Press
UOKP	University of Oklahoma Press

Abrams, Philip. 1982. *Historical Sociology*. Ithaca, NY: Cornell University Press.
Agnew, John A. 1982. "Sociologizing the Geographical Imagination: Spatial Concepts in the World-System Perspective." *Political Geography Quarterly* 1:2(April):159–166.
Aguirre Beltran, Gonzalo. 1979. *Regions of Refuge*. Society for Applied Anthropology, Monograph No. 12, Washington, DC. (Originally, 1967, *Regiones de Refugio*. Ediciones Especiales, No. 46. Mexico City: Instituto Indigenista Interamericano.)

249

Algier, Keith Wayne. 1966. "Feudalism on New Spain's Northern Frontier: Valle de San Bartolomé, A Case Study." Ph.D. diss., Dept. of History, University of New Mexico, Albuquerque.

Almaguer, Tomas. 1977. *Interpreting Chicano History: The "World-System" Approach to 19th Century California.* Institute for the Study of Social Change, Working Papers Series, no. 101, Berkeley.

———. 1981. "Interpreting Chicano History: The World-System Approach to Nineteenth Century California." *Review* IV:3(Winter):459–507.

Amin, Samir, 1976. *Unequal Development.* New York: Monthly Review Press.

Anderson, Hattie M. 1939–1940. "Frontier Economic Problems in Missouri, 1815–1828." *Missouri Historical Review* 34:1(Oct.):38–70, 2(Jan.):182–203.

Anderson, Perry. 1974a. *Passages from Antiquity to Feudalism.* London: New Left Books.

———. 1974b. *Lineages of the Absolutist State.* London: New Left Books.

Anonymous. 1844. "Specie from Mexico." *Niles Register* 66:21(July):342.

Anonymous. 1962. "Notes and Documents: The New Mexico Territorial Assembly, 1858–59." NMHR 37:1(Jan.):77–80 (F. Reeve and P. Walter, eds.).

Appelbaum, Richard. 1970. *Theories of Social Change.* Boston: Houghton Mifflin.

Aragon, Jamie Louise. 1976. "The People of Santa Fe in the 1790s." *Aztlan* 7:3(Fall):391–417.

Archer, Christon I. 1973. "The Deportation of Barbarian Indians From the Internal Provinces of New Spain, 1789–1810." *The Americas* 29:3(Jan.):376–385.

Aronowitz, Stanley. 1981. "A Metatheoretical Critique of Immanuel Wallerstein's *The Modern World System.*" *Theory and Society* 10:4(July):503–520.

Arrighi, Giovanni. 1979. "Peripheralization of Southern Africa, I: Changes in Production Processes." *Review* III:2(Fall):161–191.

Arrighi, Giovanni, Terence K. Hopkins and Immanuel Wallerstein. 1983. "Rethinking the Concepts of Class and Status-Group in a World-System Perspective." *Review* VI:3(Winter):283–304.

Aston, T. H., and C. H. E. Philpin, eds. *The Brenner Debate: Agrarian Class Structure and Economic Development in Pre-Industrial Europe.* Cambridge: CUP.

August, Jack. 1981. "Balance-of-Power Diplomacy in New Mexico: Governor Fernando de la Cocha and the Indian Policy of Conciliation." NMHR 56:2(April):141–160.

Bach, Robert L. 1980. "On the Holism of a World-System Perspective." Pp. 289–318 in *Processes of the World-System,* edited by T. K. Hopkins and I. Wallerstein. Beverly Hills: Sage.

Bailey, Alfred G. 1969. *The Conflict of European and Eastern Algonkian Cultures 1504–1700: A Study in Canadian Civilization.* Toronto: University of Toronto Press (first published in 1937).

Bailey, David T. 1975. "Stratification and Ethnic Differentiation in Santa Fe, 1860 and 1870." Ph.D. diss., Dept. of Sociology, University of Texas, Austin.

Bailey, David T., and Bruce E. Haulman. 1976. "Patterns of Landholding in Santa Fe in 1860 and 1870." *Social Science Journal* 13:3(Oct.):9–19.

———. 1977. "Ethnic Differences in the Southwestern United States Frontier, 1860." Pp. 243–257 in *The Frontier: Comparative Studies,* Vol. I, edited by D. H. Miller and J. O. Steffen. Norman: UOKP.

Bailey, L. R. 1966. *Indian Slave Trade in the Southwest.* Los Angeles: Westernlore Press.

Bakewell, P. J. 1971. *Silver Mining and Society in Colonial Mexico, Zacatecas 1546–1700*. Cambridge: CUP.

Banaji, Jairus. 1976. "The Peasantry in the Feudal Mode of Production: Towards an Economic Model." *Journal of Peasant Studies* 3:3(April):299–320.

Bancroft, Hubert Howe. 1889. *History of Arizona and New Mexico, 1530–1888*. Volume XVII of *The Works of Hubert Howe Bancroft*. San Francisco: History Company.

Bannon, John Francis. 1974. *The Spanish Borderlands Frontier, 1513–1821*. Albuquerque: UNMP. (Originally, 1963, New York: Holt Rinehart and Winston.)

_____. 1964. *Bolton and the Spanish Borderlands*. Norman: UOKP.

Barber, Ruth K. 1932. "Indian Labor in the Spanish Colonies." NMHR 7:2(April):105–142; 3(July):233–272; 4(Oct.):311–347.

Baretta, Silvio R. D., and John Markoff. 1978. "Civilization and Barbarism: Cattle Frontiers in Latin America." CSSH 20:4(Oct.):587–620.

Barker, Eugene C. 1943. "Native Latin American Contribution to the Colonization and Independence of Texas." SWHQ 46:3(April):317–335.

Barraclough, Geoffery. 1983. "Return of the Natives." *New York Review of Books* 30:9(June, 2):33–35.

Barrera, Mario. 1979. *Race and Class in the Southwest: A Theory of Racial Inequality*. Notre Dame, IN: University of Notre Dame Press.

Barth, Frederick. 1969. *Ethnic Groups and Boundaries*. Boston: Little Brown.

Basu, Dilip. 1979. "The Peripheralization of China: Notes on the Opium Connection." Pp. 171–187 in *The World-System of Capitalism: Past and Present*, edited by W. Goldfrank. Beverly Hills: Sage.

Bateman, Rebecca. 1986. "Strouds, Deer, Wars and Breeches—Some Suggestions Toward an Economic Analysis of the 18th Century South Carolina Deerskin Trade." Paper presented at the Comparative Frontiers Symposium, Norman, OK, April.

Bauer, Arnold Jr. 1979a. "Rural Workers in Spanish America: Problems of Peonage and Oppression." HAHR 59:1(Feb.):34–63.

_____. 1979b. "Reply." HAHR 59:3(Aug.):486–489.

Baugh, Timothy. 1982a. *Edwards 1 (34BK2): Southern Plains Adaptations in the Protohistoric Period*. Studies in Oklahoma's Past, No. 8. Norman: Oklahoma Archaeological Survey.

_____. 1982b. "Southwestern–Plains Interaction: A Processual View." Paper presented at the 55th Pecos Conference, Pecos, New Mexico, August.

_____. 1984a. "Southern Plains Societies and Eastern Frontier Pueblo Exchange During the Protohistoric Period." *Papers of the Archaeological Society of New Mexico* 9:156–167. Albuquerque: Archaeological Society Press.

_____. 1984b. "Southern Plains Macroeconomy: A Changing Frontier." Paper presented at the Comparative Frontiers Symposium, Norman, OK, March.

_____. n.d. "The Southern Plains Macroeconomy: The Structure of Regional Exchange." Ms. on file with Oklahoma Archaeological Survey.

Bazant, Jan. 1977. *A Concise History of Mexico: From Hidalgo to Cardenas, 1805–1940*. Cambridge: CUP.

Beck, Warren A. 1962. *New Mexico: A History of Four Centuries*. Norman: UOKP.

Beck, Warren A., and Ynez D. Haase. 1969. *Historical Atlas of New Mexico*. Norman: UOKP.

Beckett, Patrick H., and Kira Silverbird (eds.). 1982. *Mogollon Archeology: Proceedings of the 1980 Conference*. Ramona, CA: Acoma Press.

252   *References*

Bee, Robert L. 1981. *Crosscurrents Along the Colorado: The Impacts of Government Policy on the Quechan Indians.* Tucson: UAZP.

Bendix, Reinhard. 1967. "Tradition and Modernity Reconsidered." CSSH 9:3(April):292–346.

Benjamin, Thomas. 1979. "Recent Historiography of the Origins of the Mexican War." NMHR 54:3(July):169–181.

Bergesen, Albert, ed. 1980. *Studies of the Modern World-System.* New York: Academic Press.

———. 1983. "Modeling Long Waves of Crisis in the World-System," Pp. 73–92 in *Crises in the World System,* edited by Albert Bergesen. Beverly Hills: Sage.

Bergesen, Albert, and Ronald Schoenberg. 1980. "Long Waves of Colonial Expansion and Contraction, 1415–1969." Pp. 231–277 in Bergesen (1980).

Bishko, Charles J. 1963. "The Castilian Plainsman: The Medieval Ranching Frontier in La Mancha and Extremadura." Pp. 27–46 in *The New World Looks at Its History,* edited by A. R. Lewis and T. F. McGann. Austin: University of Texas Press.

Blanton, Richard, and Gary Feinman. 1984. "The Mesoamerican World System." *American Anthropologist* 86:3(Sept.):673–682.

Blaut, J. M., and Antonio Ríos-Bustamante. 1984. "Commentary on Nostrand's 'Hispanos' and Their 'Homeland'." *Annals of the American Association of Geographers* 74:1(April):157–164.

Bloch, Marc. 1961. *Feudal Society.* 2 vols. Chicago: UCP.

Bloom, Lasing B. 1914. "New Mexico under Mexican Administration, 1821–1846." *Old Santa Fe* 2:1(July):3–56.

———. 1935. "A Trade-Invoice of 1638." NMHR 10:3(July):242–246.

Blum, Jerome. 1957. "The Rise of Serfdom in Eastern Europe." *American Historical Review* 62:4(July):807–836.

Bolton, Herbert E. 1917. "The Mission as a Frontier Institution in the Spanish American Colonies." *American Historical Review* 23:1(Oct.):42–61, reprinted in Bannon (1964, pp. 187–211) and Weber (1979, pp. 51–76).

———. 1929. "Defensive Spanish Expansion and the Significance of the Borderlands." Pp. 1–42 in *The Trans-Mississippi West,* edited by J. F. Willard and C. B. Goodykoontz. Boulder: University of Colorado Press.

———. 1949. *Coronado: Knight of Pueblos and Plains.* Albuquerque: UNMP.

Borah, Woodrow W. 1951. *New Spain's Century of Depression.* Ibero–Americana 35. Berkeley: UCALP.

Borah, Woodrow W., and Sherburne F. Cook. 1963. *The Aboriginal Population of Central Mexico on the Eve of Spanish Conquest.* Ibero–Americana 45. Berkeley: UCALP.

Bousquet, Nicole. 1980. "From Hegemony to Competition: Cycles of the Core?" Pp. 46–83 in *Processes of the World-System,* edited by T. K. Hopkins and I. Wallerstein. Beverly Hills: Sage.

Brack, Gene. 1975. *Mexico Views Manifest Destiny, 1821–1846: An Essay on the Origins of the Mexican War.* Albuquerque: UNMP.

Brading, David A. 1971. *Miners and Merchants in Bourbon Mexico, 1763–1810.* Cambridge: CUP.

———. 1973. "Government and Elite in Late Colonial Mexico." HAHR 53:3(Aug.):389–414.

———. 1978. *Haciendas and Ranchos in the Mexican Bajío: Leon 1700–1860.* Cambridge: CUP.

Braudel, Fernand. 1984. *The Perspective of the World.* Volume 3 of *Civilization and Capitalism 15th–18th Century.* Trans. Siân Reynolds. New York: Harper & Row.

Brenner, Robert. 1976. "Agrarian Class Structures and Economic Development in Pre-Industrial Europe." *Past & Present* 70(Feb.):30–75.

———. 1977. "The Origins of Capitalist Development: A Critique of Neo-Smithian Marxism." *New Left Review* 104(July):25–93.

———. 1982. "Symposium: Agrarian Class Structure and Economic Development in Pre-Industrial Europe." *Past & Present* 97(Aug):16–113.

Brew, J. O. 1979. "Hopi Prehistory and History to 1850." Pp. 514–523 in Ortiz (1979), [1975].

Briggs, Charles L., and John R. Van Ness (eds.). 1987. *Land, Water, and Culture: New Perspectives on Hispanic Land Grants.* Albuquerque: UNMP.

Bronitsky, Gordon. 1982. "Technological Assessment of Selected South-Western Ceramics: Phase 1 Research Design." Pp. 279–287 in Beckett and Silverbird (1982).

Brugge, David M. 1981. "Comments on Athabaskans and Sumas." Pp. 282–290 in Wilcox and Masse (1981).

———. 1983. "Navajo Prehistory and History to 1850." Pp. 489–501 in Ortiz (1983), [1974].

———. 1984. "The Protohistoric Among Non-Pueblo Groups of the Southwest." *Papers of the Archaeological Society of New Mexico* 9:169–175. Albuquerque: Archaeological Society Press.

———. 1985. *Navajos in the Catholic Church Records of New Mexico, 1694–1875.* Tsaile, AZ: Navajo Community College Press.

Burma, John H. 1954. *Spanish-speaking Groups in the United States.* Durham: Duke University.

Carlson, Alvar. 1969. "New Mexico's Sheep Industry, 1850–1900: Its Role in the History of the Territory." *NMHR* 44:1(Jan.):25–49.

———. 1975. "Spanish-American Acquisition of Cropland Within the Northern Pueblo Indian Grants, New Mexico." *Ethnohistory* 22:2(Spring):95–110.

Carroll, H. Bailey. 1938. "Some New Mexico-West Texas Relationships, 1541–1841." *West Texas Historical Association Year Book* XIV:92–108.

Carroll, H. Bailey, and J. Villasana Haggard (trans. and eds.). 1942. *Three New Mexico Chronicles.* Albuquerque: The Quivira Society.

Castañeda, C. E. (trans). 1925. "Statistical Report on Texas by Juan N. Almonte." *SWHQ* 28:3(Jan.):177–221.

Chapa, Jorge. 1981. "Wage Labor in the Periphery: Silver Mining in Colonial Mexico." *Review* IV:3(Win.):509–534.

Chase-Dunn, Christopher. 1978. "Core-Periphery Relations: The Effects of Core Competition." Pp. 159–175 in *Social Change in the Capitalist World Economy,* edited by B. H. Kaplan. Beverly Hills: Sage.

———. 1980. "The Development of Core Capitalism in the Antebellum United States: Tariff Politics and Class Struggle in an Upwardly Mobile Semiperiphery." Pp. 189–230 in Bergesen (1980).

———. 1984. "The World-System Since 1950: What Has Really Changed?" Pp. 75–104 in *Labor in the Capitalist World-Economy,* edited by Charles Bergquist. Beverly Hills: Sage.

Chavez, Fray Angelico. 1955. "José Gonzales, Genízaro Governor." *NMHR* 30:3(July):190–194.

————. 1956. "Tomé and Father JBR." NMHR 31:1(Jan.):68–74.

————. 1967. "Pohe-Yemo's Representative and the Pueblo Revolt of 1680." NMHR 42:2(Apr):85–126.

————. 1979. "Genízaros." Pp. 198–200 in Ortiz (1979), [1978].

————. 1984. "Rejoinder." *Annals of the American Association of Geographers* 74:1(April):170–171.

Chevalier, Francois. 1963a. *Land and Society in Colonial Mexico: The Great Hacienda.* Trans. by Alwin Eustis. Berkeley: UCALP. (Originally, 1952, *La Formation de grandes domaines au mexique. Terre et société aux XVIe–XVIIe siècles.* Paris: Institut d'Ethnologie.)

————. 1963b. "The North Mexican Hacienda." Pp. 95–107 in *The New World Looks at Its History,* edited by A. R. Lewis and T. F. McGann. Austin: University of Texas Press.

Chilcote, Ronald H. 1984. *Theories of Development and Underdevelopment.* Boulder, CO: Westview Press.

Chilcote, Ronald H., and Dale L. Johnson. 1983. *Theories of Development: Modes of Production or Dependency?* Beverly Hills: Sage.

Chirot, Daniel. 1975. "The Growth of the Market and Service Labor Systems in Agriculture." *Journal of Social History* 8:2(Win.):67–81.

————. 1977. *Social Change in the Twentieth Century.* New York: Harcourt, Brace Jovanovich.

————. 1980. Review of Wallerstein (1979) and Meyer and Hannan (1979). *Social Forces* 59:2(Dec.):538–543.

————. 1981. "Changing Fashions in the Study of the Social Causes of Economic and Political Change." Pp. 259–282 in *The State of Sociology,* edited by James Short. Beverly Hills: Sage.

————. 1985. "The Rise of the West." *American Sociological Review* 50:2 (April):181–195.

————. 1986. *Social Change in the Modern Era.* New York: Harcourt, Brace Jovanovich.

Chirot, Daniel, and Thomas D. Hall. 1982. "World-System Theory." *Annual Review of Sociology* 8:81–106.

Cipolla, Carlo M. (ed.). 1970. *The Economic Decline of Empires.* London: Methuen.

————. 1973. *The Fontana Economic History of Europe: The Emergence of Industrial Societies,* Vol. 4, Pt. 2. London: Fontana.

Coatsworth, John H. 1978. "Obstacles to Economic Growth in Nineteenth-Century Mexico." *American Historical Review* 83:1(Feb.):80–100.

Collier, George A. 1975. *Fields of the Tzotzil: The Ecological Bases of Tradition in Highland Chiapas.* Austin: University of Texas Press.

Connor, Seymour V. 1972. "Attitudes and Opinions About the Mexican War, 1846–1970." *Journal of the West* 11:2(April):361–366.

————. 1973. "Changing Interpretations of the Mexican War, 1846–1970." Pp. 203–208 in Faulk and Stout (1973).

Connor, Seymour V., and Odie B. Faulk. 1971. *North America Divided: The Mexican War, 1846–1848.* New York: OXUP.

Connor, Walker, 1972. "Nation-Building or Nation-Destroying?" *World Politics* 14:2(Jan.):319–355.

————. 1977. "Ethnonationalism in the First World: The Present in Historical Perspective." Pp. 19–45 in *Ethnic Conflict in the Western World,* edited by Milton J. Esman. Ithaca: Cornell University Press.

Cook, Sherburne F. 1976. *The Population of the California Indians, 1769–1970.* Berkeley: UCALP.

Cordell, Linda S. 1979. "Prehistory: Eastern Anasazi." Pp. 131–151 in Ortiz (1979), [1978].

Dale, Edward E. 1949. *The Indians of the Southwest: A Century of Development Under the United States.* Norman: UOKP.

Dalton, George. 1969. "Theoretical Issues in Economic Anthropology." *Current Anthropology* 10:1(Feb.):63–80.

Dalton, George (ed.). 1968. *Primitive, Archaic and Modern Economies: Essays of Karl Polanyi.* Boston: Beacon.

Daniel, James M. 1968. "The Spanish Frontier in West Texas and Northern Mexico." SWHQ 71:4(April):481–495.

Davidson, Basil. 1961. *Black Mother: The Years of the African Slave Trade.* Boston: Little, Brown.

De Atley, Suzanne P., and Frank J. Findlow. 1982. "Regional Integration of the Northern Casas Grandes Frontier." Pp. 263–277 in Beckett and Silverbird (1982).

Denemark, Robert A., and Kenneth P. Thomas. 1988. "The Brenner-Wallerstein Debate." *International Studies Quarterly* 32:1 (March):47–65.

Di Peso, Charles. 1968. "Casas Grandes and the Gran Chichimeca." *El Palacio* 75:4(Win.):45–61.

_____. 1974. *Casas Grandes, A Fallen Trading Center of the Gran Chichimeca.* Dragoon, AZ: Amerind Foundations Publications.

_____. 1979a. "Prehistory: O'otam." Pp. 91–99 in Ortiz (1979), [1974].

_____. 1979b. "Prehistory: Southern Periphery." Pp. 152–161 in Ortiz (1979), [1974].

Dobyns, Henry F. 1966. "Estimating Aboriginal American Population: An Appraisal of Techniques with a New Hemispheric Estimate." *Current Anthropology* 7:4(Oct.):395–416, 440–444.

_____. 1976. *Native American Historical Demography.* Bloomington: Indiana University Press.

Dobyns, Henry F., and Robert C. Euler. 1970. *Wauba Yuma's People: The Comparative Socio-Political Structure of the Pai Indians of Arizona.* Prescott College Studies in Anthropology 3. Prescott, AZ: Prescott College Press.

_____. 1980. *Indians of the Southwest.* Bloomington: University of Indiana Press.

Dorsey, Dorothy B. 1936. "The Panic and Depression of 1837–43 in Missouri." *Missouri Historical Review* 30:2(Jan.):132–161.

Dozier, Edward P. 1961. "Rio Grande Peublos." Pp. 94–186 in *Perspectives in American Indian Cultural Change,* edited by Edward H. Spicer. Chicago: UCP.

_____. 1964. "The Pueblo Indians of the Southwest." *Current Anthropology* 5:2(April):79–97.

_____. 1966. *Hano: A Tewa Community in Arizona.* New York: Holt, Rinehart and Winston.

_____. 1970a. *The Pueblo Indians of North America.* New York: Holt, Rinehart and Winston.

_____. 1970b. "Making Inferences from Present to Past." Pp. 202–213 in Longacre (1970a).

Driver, Harold E. 1969. *Indians of North America,* 2nd ed. Chicago: UCP.

Dunbar Ortiz, Roxanne. 1974. "Land Tenure in Northern New Mexico: An Historical Perspective." Ph.D. diss., Dept. of History, UCLA.

————. 1980. *Roots of Resistance: Land Tenure in New Mexico, 1680–1980*. Los Angeles: Chicano Studies and American Indian Studies, Centers, UCLA.

Dutton, Bertha. 1975. *Indians of the American Southwest*. Englewood Cliffs, NJ: Prentice-Hall.

Earle, Timothy, and Jonathon E. Ericson (eds.). 1977. *Exchange Systems in Prehistory*. New York: Academic Press.

Eccles, W. J. 1974. *The Canadian Frontier, 1534–1760*. Albuquerque: UNMP. (Originally, 1969, New York: Holt Rinehart and Winston.)

Edwards, Beatrice. 1982. "Articulation of the Modes of Production in Mexico." *Current Perspectives in Social Theory* 3:73–91.

Eggan, Fred. 1979. "Pueblos: Introduction." Pp. 224–235 in Ortiz (1979), [1977].

————. 1983. "Comparative Social Organization." Pp. 723–742 in Ortiz (1983), [1981].

Ekholm, Kajsa, and Jonathan Friedman. 1982. "'Capital' Imperialism and Exploitation in Ancient World-Systems." *Review* IV:1(Summer):87–109.

Elliott, J. H. 1961. "The Decline of Spain." *Past & Present* 20(Nov.):52–75, reprinted in Cipolla (1970, pp. 168–195).

————. 1963. *Imperial Spain, 1469–1716*. New York: St. Martin's Press.

Ellis, Florence Hawley. 1979a. "Isleta Pueblo." Pp. 351–365 in Ortiz (1979), [1977].

————. 1979b. "Laguna Pueblo." Pp. 438–449 in Ortiz (1979), [1977].

Estep, Raymond. 1954. "Lorenzo de Zavala and the Texas Revolution." SWHQ 57:3(Jan.):322–35.

Faulk, Odie B. 1964. *The Last Years of Spanish Texas, 1778–1821*. The Hague: Mouton.

————. 1970. *Arizona: A Short History*. Norman: UOKP.

————. 1974. *Crimson Desert: Indian Wars of the American Southwest*. New York: OUP.

Faulk, Odie, and Joseph A. Stout, Jr. (eds.). 1973. *The Mexican War: Changing Interpretations*. Chicago: Sage Books.

Fergusson, Erna. 1935. "Tearing Down the West." *Yale Review* 35(n.s.):2 (Dec.):331–343.

Forbes, Jack. 1960. *Apache, Navaho, and Spaniard*. Norman: UOKP.

Ford, Richard I. 1972. "An Ecological Perspective on the Eastern Pueblos." Pp. 1–17 in Ortiz (1972).

————. 1983. "Inter-Indian Exchange in the Southwest." Pp. 711–722 in Ortiz (1983), [1981].

Ford, Richard I., Albert H. Schroeder, and Stewart L. Peckham. 1972. "Three Perspectives on Puebloan Prehistory." Pp. 19–39 in Ortiz (1972).

Foster, Charles R. (ed.). 1980. *Nations Without A State*. New York: Praeger.

Forsythe, Dall W. 1977. *Taxation and Political Change in the Young Nation, 1781–1833*. New York: Columbia.

Francis, E. K. 1976. *Interethnic Relations: An Essay in Sociological Theory*. New York: Elsevier.

Frank, Andre Gunder. 1969a. *Capitalism and Underdevelopment in Latin America: Historical Studies of Chile and Brazil*, rev. ed. New York: Monthly Review Press.

————. 1969b. *Latin America: Underdevelopment or Revolution*. New York: Monthly Review Press.

Fried, Morton. 1967. *The Evolution of Political Society*. New York: Random House.

————. 1975. *The Notion of Tribe*. Menlo Park, CA: Cummings.

Garner, Van Hastings. 1974. "Seventeenth Century New Mexico." *Journal of Mexican American History* 4:41–70.

Genovese, Eugene. 1969. *The World the Slaveholders Made*. New York: Random.

Gibson, Charles. 1966. *Spain in America*. New York: Harper.

Godelier, Maurice. 1975. "Modes of Production, Kinship, and Demographic Structures." Pp. 3–27 in *Marxist Analyses and Social Anthropology*, edited by M. Bloch. New York: Wiley.

————. 1977. *Perspectives in Marxist Anthropology*. Trans. Robert Brain. Cambridge: CUP. (Originally, 1973, *Horizon, trajets marxistes en anthropologie*. Paris: Maspero.)

Goetzmann, William H. 1966. *When the Eagle Screamed: The Romantic Horizon in American Diplomacy, 1800–1860*. New York: Wiley.

Gonzalez, Nancie L. 1969. *The Spanish-Americans of New Mexico: A Heritage of Pride*, rev. ed. Albuquerque: UNMP.

Graebner, Norman A. 1951. "United States Gulf Commerce with Mexico, 1822–1848." *Inter-American Economic Affairs* 5:1(Sum.):36–51.

————. 1955. *Empire on the Pacific*. New York: Ronald Press.

————. 1980. "The Mexican War: A Study in Causation." *Pacific Historical Review* 49:3(Aug.):405–426.

————. 1983. "Review of McAfee, Ward, and J. Cordell Robinson, *Origins of the Mexican War: A Documentary Source Book*." NMHR 53:3(July):291–292.

Granovetter, Mark. 1979. "The Idea of 'Advancement' in Theories of Social Evolution and Development." AJS 85:3(Nov):489–515.

Greenleaf, Richard E. 1972. "Land and Water in Mexico and New Mexico, 1700–1821." NMHR 47:2(April):85–112.

Gregg, Josiah. 1844. *Commerce of the Prairies*, 2 vols. New York: H. G. Langley. See also Moorhead (1954).

Griffen, William B. 1983a. "Southern Periphery: East." Pp. 329–342 in Ortiz (1983 [1981]).

————. 1983b. "The Compás: A Chiricahua Apache Family of the Late 18th and Early 19th Centuries." *American Indian Quarterly* VII:2(Spring):21–48.

————. 1983c. "Spanish Military Administration of Apache Indians: The North Mexican Peace Establishments of the Late Colonial Period." Paper presented at the Western Social Science Association meeting, Albuquerque, April.

————. 1984. "The Spanish System of North Mexican Peace Reserves." Paper presented at American Anthropological Association meeting, Denver, CO, November.

————. 1985. "Apache Indians and the North Mexican Peace Establishments." Pp. 183–195 in *Southwestern Culture History: Collected Papers in Honor of Albert H. Schroeder*, edited by Charles Lange. Archaeological Society of New Mexico No. 10. Santa Fe, NM: Ancient City Press.

————. n.d. "Juan José Compá: An Apache Leader of the 1830's." Unpublished Ms.

Gumerman, George J., and Emil W. Haury. 1979. "Prehistory: Hohokam." Pp. 75–90 in Ortiz (1979), [1974].

Gunnerson, Dolores A. 1974. *The Jicarilla Apaches: A Study in Survival*. DeKalb: Northern Illinois University Press.

Gunnerson, James H. 1979. "Southern Athapaskan Archeology." Pp. 162–169 in Ortiz (1979), [1978].

Gutierrez, Ramon Arturo. 1980. "Marriage, Sex and the Family: Social Change in Colonial New Mexico, 1690–1846." Ph.D. diss., Dept. of History, University of Wisconsin, Madison.

Hackett, Charles W. (ed.). 1937. *Historical Documents Relating to New Mexico, Nueva Vizcaya, and Approaches Thereto, to 1773.* Washington, DC: Carnegie Inst. Collected by Adolph F. Bandelier and Fanny R. Bandelier.

———. 1942. *Revolt of the Pueblo Indians of New Mexico and Otermín's Attempted Reconquest 1680–1682.* Albuquerque: UNMP.

Hagan, William T. 1976. *United States–Comanche Relations: The Reservation Years.* New Haven: Yale University Press.

Hale, Charles A. 1968. *Mexican Liberalism in the Age of Mora, 1821–1853.* New Haven: Yale University Press.

Hale, Kenneth, and David Harris. 1979. "Historical Linguistics and Archeology." Pp. 170–177 in Ortiz (1979), [1974].

Hall, John R. 1984. "World-System Holism and Colonial Brazilian Agriculture: Critical Case Analysis." *Latin American Research Review* 19:2:43–69.

Hall, Thomas D. 1983. "Peripheries, Regions of Refuge, and Nonstate Societies: Toward a Theory of Reactive Social Change." *Social Science Quarterly* 64:3 (Sept.):582–597.

———. 1984a. "Rejoinder." *Annals of the American Association of Geographers* 74:1 (April):171.

———. 1984b. "Lessons of Long-Term Social Change for Comparative and Historical Study of Ethnicity." *Current Perspectives in Social Theory* 5:121–144.

———. 1986. "Incorporation in the World-System: Toward A Critique." *American Sociological Review* 45:3(June):390–402.

Hammond, George P. 1956. "The Search for the Fabulous in the Settlement of the Southwest." *Utah Historical Quarterly* 24:1(Jan.):1–19, reprinted in Weber (1979, pp. 20–33).

Hannan, Michael T. 1979. "The Dynamics of Ethnic Boundaries in Modern States." Pp. 253–275 in Meyer and Hannan (1979).

Hansen, Niles. 1981. "Commentary: The Hispano Homeland in 1900." *Annals of the Association of American Geographers* 71:2(June):280–282.

Haring, Charles H. 1947. *The Spanish Empire in America.* New York: OXUP.

Harris, Marvin. 1968. *The Rise of Anthropological Theory.* New York: Thomas Y. Crowell.

———. 1979. *Cultural Materialism: The Struggle for a Science of Culture.* New York: Random House.

Hechter, Michael. 1975. *Internal Colonialism: The Celtic Fringe in British National Development, 1536–1966.* Berkeley: UCALP.

———. 1978. "Group Formation and the Cultural Division of Labor." AJS 84:2(Sept.):293–318.

Hechter, Michael, and William Brustein. 1980. "Regional Modes of Production and Patterns of State Formation in Western Europe." AJS 85:5(March):1061–1095.

Hechter, Michael, and Margaret Levi. 1979. "The Comparative Analysis of Ethnoregional Movements." *Ethnic and Racial Studies* 2:3(July):260–274.

Hedrick, Basil C., J. C. Kelley, C. L. Riley (eds.). 1974. *The Mesoamerican Southwest: Readings in Archaeology, Ethnohistory, and Ethnology.* Carbondale, IL: Southern Illinois University Press.

Hennessy, Alistair. 1978. *The Frontier in Latin America History.* Albuquerque: UNMP.

Herr, Richard. 1958. *The Eighteenth Century Revolution in Spain.* Princeton, NJ: Princeton University Press.

Hill, Joseph J. 1930. "Spanish and Mexican Exploration and Trade Northwest from New Mexico into the Great Basin, 1765–1853." *Utah Historical Quarterly* 3:1(Jan.):3–23.

Hinton, Thomas. 1983. "Southern Periphery: West." Pp. 315–328 in Ortiz (1983), [1975].

Hoebel, E. A. 1982. *The Plains Indians.* Bloomington: Indiana University Press.

Hopkins, Terence K. 1979. "The Study of the Capitalist World-Economy: Some Introductory Considerations." Pp. 21–52 in *World-System of Capitalism: Past and Present,* edited by W. Goldfrank. Beverly Hills: Sage.

Hopkins, Terence K., and I. Wallerstein (eds.). 1980. *Processes of the World-System.* Beverly Hills: Sage.

_____. 1982. *World Systems Analysis: Theory and Methodology.* Beverly Hills: Sage.

Horowitz, Donald L. 1975. "Ethnic Identity." Pp. 111–140 in *Ethnicity: Theory and Experience,* edited by Nathan Glazer and D. P. Moynihan. Cambridge, MA: Harvard University Press.

Horvath, Steven. 1977. "The Genízaro of Eighteenth-Century New Mexico: A Reexamination." *Discovery:*25–102. Santa Fe: School of American Research.

_____. 1979. "The Social and Political Organization of the Genízaros of Plaza De Nuestra Señora De Los Dolores De Belén, New Mexico, 1740–1812." Ph.D. diss., Dept. of Anthropology, Brown University, Providence, RI.

Houser, Nicholas P. 1979. "Tigua Pueblo." Pp. 336–342 in Ortiz (1979), [1975].

Howe, Gary N., and Alan M. Sica. 1980. "Political Economy, Imperialism, and the Problem of World System Theory." *Current Perspectives in Social Theory* 1:235–286.

Irwin-Williams, Cynthia. 1979. "Post-Pleistocene Archeology, 7000–2000 B.C." Pp. 31–42 in Ortiz (1979), [1978].

Israel, Jonathan I. 1975. *Race, Class and Politics in Colonial Mexico, 1610–1670.* Oxford: OXUP.

_____. 1981. "The Decline of Spain a Historical Myth?" *Past & Present* 91(May):170–180.

_____. 1982. "The Seventeenth-Century Crisis in New Spain: Myth or Reality?" *Past & Present* 97(Nov.):150–156.

Iverson, Peter. 1976. *The Navajos.* Bloomington: Indiana University Press.

_____. 1981. *The Navajo Nation.* Albuquerque: UNMP.

John, Elizabeth A. H. 1975. *Storms Brewed in Other Men's Worlds.* College Station: Texas A & M University Press.

_____. 1984. "Nurturing the Peace: Spanish and Comanche Cooperation in the Early Nineteenth Century." NMHR 59:4(Oct.):345–369.

Jones, Oakah L., Jr. 1966. *Pueblo Warriors and Spanish Conquest.* Albuquerque: UNMP.

_____. 1979. *Los Paisanos: Spanish Settlers on the Northern Frontier of New Spain.* Norman: UOKP.

Jones, Thomas B. 1975. "Mexican War Scholarship: The Connor-Faulk Assessment." *Journal of Mexican American History* 5:103–121.

Jorgensen, Joseph G. 1972. *The Sun Dance Religion: Power for the Powerless.* Chicago: UCP.

_____. 1983. "Comparative Traditional Economics and Ecological Adaptations." Pp. 684–710 in Ortiz (1983), [1976].

Kamen, Henry. 1978. "The Decline of Spain: A Historical Myth?" *Past & Present* 81(Nov.):24–50.

———. 1981. "A Rejoinder." *Past & Present* 91(May):181–185.

———. 1982. "The Seventeenth-Century Crisis in New Spain: Myth or Reality?" *Past & Present* 97(Nov.):144–150.

Kay, Cristobal. 1974. "Comparative Development of the European Manoral System and the Latin American Hacienda System." *Journal of Peasant Studies* 2:1(Oct.):69–98.

Kelley, J. Charles. 1966. "Mesoamerica and the Southwestern United States." Pp. 95–110 in *Archaeological Frontiers and External Connections,* edited by G. F. Ekholm and G. R. Willey, Vol. 4 of *Handbook of Middle American Indians,* R. Wauchope, gen. ed. Austin: University of Texas Press.

Kelley, J. Charles, and Ellen A. Kelley. 1975. "An Alternative Hypothesis to the Explanation of Anasazi Culture History." Pp. 178–223 in *Collected Papers in Honor of Florence Hawley Ellis,* Theodore R. Frisbie, ed. Albuquerque: Papers of the Archaeological Society of New Mexico 2.

Kendall, Martha B. 1983. "Yuman Languages." Pp. 4–12 in Ortiz (1983), [1981].

Kenner, Charles L. 1969. *A History of New Mexican–Plains Indians Relations.* Norman: UOKP.

Kessell, John. 1979. *Kiva, Cross and Crown: The Pecos Indians and New Mexico, 1540–1840.* Washington, DC: U.S. Government Printing Office.

Kinnaird, Lawrence. 1946. "The Spanish Tobacco Monopoly in New Mexico, 1766–67." NMHR 21:4(Oct.):328–339.

Kluckhohn, C., and D. Leighton. 1962. *The Navaho,* rev. ed. Natural History Library. Garden City, NY: Doubleday. (Originally, 1946, Cambridge, MA: Harvard University Press.)

Knowlton, Clark. 1961. "The Spanish Americans of New Mexico." *Sociology and Social Research* 45:4(July):448–454.

———. 1963. "Causes of Land Loss Among the Spanish Americans of Northern New Mexico." *Rocky Mountain Social Science Journal* 1:2(April):201–211.

———. 1967. "Land Grant Problems Among the State's Spanish Americans." *New Mexican Business* 20:6(June):1–13.

———. 1976. "The Study of Land Grants as an Academic Discipline." *Social Science Journal* 13:3(Oct.):3–7.

———. 1980. "The Town of Las Vegas Community Land Grant: An Anglo-American Coup d'État." *Journal of the West* 19:3(July):12–21.

Kuhn, Thomas S. 1970. *The Structure of Scientific Revolutions,* 2nd ed. Chicago: UCP.

———. 1977. "Second Thoughts on Paradigms." Pp. 293–319 in *The Essential Tension: Selected Studies in Scientific Traditions and Change,* edited by T. S. Kuhn. Chicago: UCP.

Lamar, Howard R. 1970. *The Far Southwest, 1846–1912: A Territorial History.* New York: Norton.

———. 1977. *Trader of the American Frontier: Myth's Victim.* College Station: Texas A & M Press.

Lang, James. 1975. *Conquest and Commerce: Spain and England in the Americas.* New York: Academic Press.

———. 1979. *Portuguese Brazil: The King's Plantation.* New York: Academic Press.

Langacker, Ronald W. 1968. *Language and Its Structure: Some Fundamental Concepts.* New York: Harcourt, Brace and World.

Larson, Robert W. 1968. *New Mexico's Quest for Statehood, 1846–1912*. Albuquerque: UNMP.

Lattimore, Owen. 1951. *Inner Asian Frontiers*, 2nd ed. Boston: Beacon Press. (Originally, 1940, New York: American Geographical Society.)

———. 1962. *Studies in Frontier History: Collected Papers, 1928–58*. London: OXUP.

Lauer, Robert H. 1982. *Perspectives on Social Change*, 3rd ed. Boston: Allyn & Bacon.

Lavender, David. 1980. *The Southwest*. New York: Harper and Row.

Leacock, Eleanor B. 1954. *The Montagnais "Hunting Territory" and the Fur Trade*. American Anthropological Association Memoir 78. Menasha, WI: American Anthropological Association.

Lecompte, Janet. 1985. *Rebellion in Río Arriba, 1837*. Albuquerque: UNMP.

Lenski, Gerhard. 1966. *Power and Privilege: A Theory of Social Stratification*. New York: McGraw-Hill.

———. 1976. "History and Social Change." *AJS* 82:3(Nov.):548–564.

Lenski, Gerhard, and Jean Lenski. 1982. *Human Societies*, 4th ed. New York: McGraw-Hill.

Leonard, Olen, and Charles P. Loomis. 1941. *Culture of a Contemporary Rural Community: El Cerrito, New Mexico*. Bureau of Agricultural Economics, Rural Life Studies 1. Washington, DC: U.S. Department of Agriculture.

Lieberson, Stanley. 1961. "A Societal Theory of Race and Ethnic Relations." *ASR* 26:6(Dec.):902–910.

Lindner, Rudi Paul. 1981. "Nomadism, Horses and Huns." *Past & Present* 92(Aug.):3–19.

Lindstrom, Diane. 1978. *Economic Development in the Philadelphia Region, 1810–1850*. New York: Columbia.

Lipe, William D. 1978. "The Southwest." Pp. 327–401 in *Ancient Native Americans*, edited by Jesse D. Jennings. San Francisco: W. H. Freeman.

Lister, Robert H. 1978. "Mesoamerican Influences at Chaco Canyon, New Mexico." Pp. 233–241 in Riley and Hedrick (1978).

Lobeck, Armin K. 1948. *Physiographic Diagram of North America*. New York: Columbia University, Geographical Press.

Longacre, William A. (ed.). 1970a. *Reconstructing Prehistoric Pueblo Societies*. Albuquerque: UNMP.

Longacre, William A. 1970b. "A Historical Review." Pp. 1–10 in Longacre (1970a).

———. 1973. "Current Directions in Southwestern Archaeology." *Annual Review of Anthropology* 2:201–219.

Loveman, Brian. 1979. "Critique of Arnold J. Bauer's 'Rural Workers in Spanish America: Problems of Peonage and Oppression.'" *HAHR* 59:3(Aug.):478–485.

Lowie, Robert H. 1954. *Indians of the Plains*. Garden City, NY: Natural History Press.

Loyola, Sister Mary. 1939. *The American Occupation of New Mexico, 1821–1852*. Albuquerque: UNMP. Reprint, 1976, New York: Arno Press.

McAfee, Ward. 1980. "A Reconsideration of the Origins of the Mexican–American War." *Southern California Quarterly* 62:1(Spring):49–65.

McAfee, W., and J. C. Robinson (eds.). 1982. *The Origins of the Mexican War: A Documentary Source Book*. 2 vols. Salisbury, NC: Documentary Publications.

McAlister, L. N. 1963. "Social Structure and Social Change in New Spain." HAHR 43:3(Aug.):349–370.

McGuire, Randall H. 1980. "The Mesoamerican connection in the Southwest." *Kiva* 46:1–2(Fall/Win.):3–38.

_____. 1983. "Prestige Economies in the Prehistoric Southwestern Periphery." Paper presented at Society for American Archaeology, Pittsburgh, April.

_____. 1986. "Economies and Modes of Production in the Prehistoric Southwestern Periphery." Pp. 243–269 in Mathien and McGuire (1986).

McNeill, William. 1963. *The Rise of the West: A History of the Human Community.* Chicago: UCP.

_____. 1976. *Plagues and Peoples.* Garden City, NY: Doubleday.

_____. 1980. *The Human Condition: An Ecological and Historical View.* Princeton: Princeton University Press.

McNierney, Michael, ed. 1980. *Taos 1847: The Revolt in Contemporary Accounts.* Boulder, CO: Johnson Publishing.

McNitt, Frank. 1972. *Navajo Wars: Military Campaigns, Slave Raids and Reprisals.* Albuquerque: UNMP.

McWilliams, Carey. 1949. *North from Mexico: The Spanish-speaking People of the United States.* New York: J. B. Lippincott. Reprint, 1968, Westport, CT: Greenwood Press.

Malouf, Carling, and A. Arline Malouf. 1945. "The Effects of Spanish Slavery on the Indians of the Intermountain West." *Southwestern Journal of Anthropology* 1:378–391.

Malowist, Marion. 1958. "Poland, Russia and Western Trade in the 15th and 16th Centuries." *Past & Present* 13(April):26–39.

Mandel, Ernest. 1980. *Long Waves of Capitalist Development.* Cambridge: CUP.

Martin, Robert F. 1939. *National Income in the United States 1799–1938.* New York: National Industrial Conference Board.

Martin, Paul S. 1979. "Prehistory: Mogollon." Pp. 61–74 in Ortiz (1979), [1975].

Martin, Paul S., and Fred. T. Plog. 1973. *The Archaeology of Arizona: A Study of the Southwest Region.* Garden City, NY: Doubleday Natural History Press.

Martinez, Oscar. 1985. "Indian Use of the U.S.–Mexico Borderlands for Survival." Paper presented at Western Social Science Association meeting, Fort Worth, TX, April.

Mathien, Frances Joan, and Randall McGuire (eds.). 1986. *Ripples in the Chichimec Sea: Consideration of Southwestern-Mesoamerican Interactions.* Carbondale, IL: Southern Illinois University Press.

Meier, Matt S., and Feliciano Rivera. 1972. *The Chicanos: A History of Mexican Americans.* New York: Hill and Wang.

Meinig, Donald W. 1965. "The Mormon Culture Region: Strategies and Patterns in the Geography of the American West, 1847–1964." *Annals of the Association of American Geographers* 55:2(June):191–220.

_____. 1969. *Imperial Texas: An Interpretive Essay in Cultural Geography.* Austin: University of Texas Press.

_____. 1971. *Southwest: Three Peoples in Geographical Change, 1600–1970.* London: OXUP.

_____. 1984. "Rejoinder." *Annals of the American Association of Geographers* 74:1(April):171.

Melody, Michael E. 1977. *The Apaches.* Bloomington: Indiana University Press.

Merk, Frederick. 1966. *The Monroe Doctrine and American Expansionism, 1843–1849*. New York: Knopf.

———. 1971. *Fruits of Propaganda in the Tyler Administration*. Cambridge, MA: Harvard University Press.

———. 1972. *Slavery and the Annexation of Texas*. New York: Knopf.

Meyer, John W., and Michael T. Hannan. 1979. *National Development and the World System: Educational, Economic, and Political Change, 1950–1979*. Chicago: UCP.

Meyer, Michael C., and William L. Sherman. 1979. *The Course of Mexican History*. New York: OXUP.

Miller, Wick R. 1983. "Uto Aztecan Languages." Pp. 113–124 in Ortiz (1983), [1981].

Minge, Ward Alan. 1965. "Frontier Problems in New Mexico Preceding the Mexican War, 1840–1846." Ph.D. diss., Dept. of History, University of New Mexico, Albuquerque.

Minnis, Paul. 1984. "Peeking Under the Tortilla Curtain: Regional Interaction on the Northeastern Periphery of Casas Grandes." *American Archeology* 4(3): 181–193.

Miskimin, Harry A. 1969. *The Economy of Early Renaissance Europe, 1300–1460*. Englewood Cliffs, NJ: Prentice-Hall.

Moore, Barrington Jr. 1966. *Social Origins of Dictatorship and Democracy: Lord and Peasant in the Making of the Modern World*. Boston: Beacon Press.

Moorhead, Max. 1958. *New Mexico's Royal Road: Trade and Travel on the Chihuahua Trail*. Norman: UOKP.

———. 1961. "The Presidio Supply Problem of New Mexico in the Eighteenth Century." NMHR 36:3(July):210–229.

———. 1968. *The Apache Frontier: Jacobo Ugarte and Spanish-Indian Relations in Northern New Spain, 1769–1791*. Norman: UOKP.

———. 1975a. *The Presidio: Bastion of the Spanish Borderlands*. Norman: UOKP.

———. 1975b. "The Spanish Deportation of Hostile Apaches: The Policy and the Practice." *Arizona and the West* 17:3(Aug.):205–220.

Moorhead, Max (ed.). 1954. *Josiah Gregg's Commerce of the Prairies*. Norman: UOKP. See also Gregg (1844).

Mörner, Magnus. 1967. *Race Mixture in the History of Latin America*. New York: Little, Brown.

———. 1973. "The Spanish American Hacienda: A Survey of Recent Research and Debate." HAHR 53:2(May):183–216.

———. 1983. "Economic Factors and Stratification in Colonial Spanish America with Special Regard to Elites." HAHR 63:2(May):335–369.

Moseley, K. P., and I. Wallerstein. 1978. "Precapitalist Social Structures." *Annual Review of Sociology* 4:259–290.

Mosk, Sanford A. 1942. "The influence of tradition on agriculture in New Mexico." *Journal of Economic History* 2(suppl.):34–51.

Murgia, Edward. 1975. *Assimilation, Colonialism and the Mexican American People*. Austin: University of Texas Press.

Nadal, Jordi. 1973. "Spain 1830–1914." Pp. 532–672 in *The Fontana Economic History of Europe: The Emergence of Industrial Societies*, Vol. 4, Pt. 2. London: Fontana.

Nagel, Joane, and Susan Olzak. 1982. "Ethnic Mobilization in New and Old

States: An Extension of the Competition Model." *Social Problems* 30:2 (Dec.):127–143.

Nasatir, Abraham. 1976. *Borderland in Retreat: From Spanish Louisiana to the Far Southwest.* Albuquerque: UNMP.

Nash, June. 1981. "Ethnographic Aspects of the World Capitalist System." *Annual Review of Anthropology* 10:393–423.

Nielsen, Francois. 1985. "Toward a Theory of Ethnic Solidarity in Modern Societies." ASR 50:2(April):133–149.

Nisbet, Robert. 1969. *Social Change and History: Aspects of the Western Theory of Development.* New York: OXUP.

North, Douglass C. 1966. *The Economic Growth of the United States, 1790–1860.* New York: Norton.

_____. 1974. *Growth and Welfare in the American Past: A New Economic History* (2nd ed.). Englewood Cliffs, NJ: Prentice-Hall.

Nostrand, Richard L. 1970. "The Hispanic-American Borderland: Delimitation of an American Culture Region." *Annals of the Association of American Geographers* 60:4(Dec.):638–661.

_____. 1975. "Mexican Americans circa 1850." *Annals of the Association of American Geographers* 65:3(Sept.):378–390.

_____. 1980. "The Hispano Homeland in 1900." *Annals of the Association of American Geographers* 70:3(Sept.):382–396.

_____. 1981. "Comment in Reply." *Annals of the Association of American Geographers* 71:2(June):282–283.

_____. 1984. "Hispano Cultural Distinctiveness: A Reply." *Annals of the Association of American Geographers* 74:1(April):164–169.

Oczon, Annabelle M. 1982. "Land Grants in New Mexico: A Selective Bibliography." NMHR 57:1(Jan.):81–87.

Olzak, Susan. 1983a. "Ethnic Ties and Political Mobilization: Comment on Leifer." AJS 89:1(July):188–192.

_____. 1983b. "Contemporary Ethnic Mobilization." *Annual Review of Sociology* 9:355–374.

_____. 1983c. "The Economic Construction of Ethnicity." Paper presented at the American Sociological Association meeting, Detroit, Sept.

Opler, Morris E. 1983. "The Apachean Culture Pattern and Its Origins." Pp. 368–392 in Ortiz (1983), [1975].

Orlove, Benjamin S. 1980. "Ecological Anthropology." *Annual Review of Anthropology* 9:235–273.

Ortiz, Alfonso (ed.). 1972. *New Perspectives on the Pueblos.* Albuquerque: UNMP.

_____. 1979. *Handbook of North American Indians. Volume 9: Southwest.* Washington, DC: Smithsonian.

_____. 1983. *Handbook of North American Indians. Volume 10: Southwest.* Washington, DC: Smithsonian.

Pailes, Richard A., and Daniel T. Reff. 1980. "Colonial Exchange Systems and the Decline of Paquime." Paper presented at the Society for American Archaeology meeting, Philadelphia, May.

_____ . 1985. "Colonial Exchange Systems and the Decline of Paquime." Pp. 253–263 in *The Archaeology of West and Northwest Mesoamerica,* edited by Michael Foster and Phil Weigand. Boulder, CO: Westview Press.

Pailes, Richard A., and Joseph W. Whitecotton. 1979. "The Greater Southwest and the Mesoamerican 'World' System: An Exploratory Model of Frontier

Relationships." Pp. 105–121 in *The Frontier: Comparative Studies*, Vol. 2, edited by William W. Savage and Stephen I. Thompson. Norman: UOKP.

Palmer, Colin A. 1976. *Slaves of the White God: Blacks in Mexico, 1570–1650*. Cambridge, MA: Harvard University Press.

Phillips, George Harwood. 1975. *Chiefs and Challengers: Indian Resistance and Cooperation in Southern California*. Berkeley: UCALP.

Pike, Zebulon. 1889. *Exploratory Travels Through the Western Territories of North America*. Denver, CO: W. H. Lawrence. (Originally, 1811. London: Paternoster-Row.)

Pirenne, Henri. 1937. *Economic and Social History of Medieval Europe*. Trans. I. E. Clegg. New York: Harcourt, Brace, and Jovanovich. (Originally, 1933, *Histoire du Moyen Age*, Vol. 8, edited by H. Pirenne, G. Cohen, and H. Focillon.)

Pitt, Leonard. 1966. *The Decline of the Californios*. Berkeley: UCALP.

Platt, D. C. M. 1972. *Latin America and British Trade, 1806–1914*. London: A & C Black.

———. 1980a. "Dependency in Nineteenth-Century Latin America: An Historian Objects." *Latin American Research Review* 15:1:113–130.

———. 1980b. "The Anatomy of 'Autonomy' (Whatever that May Mean): A Reply." *Latin American Research Review* 15:1:147–149.

Pletcher, David M. 1973. *The Diplomacy of Annexation: Texas, Oregon and the Mexican War*. Columbia, MO: University of Missouri Press.

Plog, Fred. 1979. "Prehistory: Western Anasazi." Pp. 108–130 in Ortiz (1979), [1978].

Plog, Fred, Steadman Upham, and Phil C. Weigand. 1982. "A Perspective on Mogollon–Mesoamerican Interaction." Pp. 227–237 in Beckett and Silverbird (1982).

Polanyi, Karl. 1944. *The Great Transformation: The Political and Economic Origins of Our Time*. Boston: Beacon Press.

Polanyi, Karl, M. Arensberg and Harry W. Peterson. 1957. *Trade and Market in the Early Empires*. Chicago: Henry Regnery Company.

Portes, Alejandro. 1976. "On the Sociology of National Development: Theories and Issues." AJS 82:1(July):55–85.

Powell, Philip Wayne. 1945. "The Chichimecas: Scourge of the Silver Frontier in Sixteenth-Century Mexico." HAHR 25:3(Aug.):315–338.

———. 1952. *Soldiers, Indians, Silver: North America's First Frontier War*. Berkeley: UCALP. Reprint, 1975, Tempe, AZ: Arizona State University Press.

Price, Barbara. 1978. "Secondary State Formation: An Explanatory Model." Pp. 161–186 in *Origins of the State: The Anthropology of Political Evolution*, edited by Ronald Cohen and Elman R. Service. Philadelphia: ISHI.

Price, Glenn W. 1967. *Origins of the War with Mexico: Polk-Stockton Intrigue*. Austin: University of Texas Press.

Radding de Murrieta, Cynthia. 1977. "The Function of the Market in Changing Economic Structures in the Mission Communities of Pimería Alta, 1768–1821." *The Americas* 34:2(Oct.):155–169.

Ragin, Charles, and David Zaret. 1983. "Theory and Method in Comparative Research: Two Strategies." *Social Forces* 61:3(March):731–754.

Rasch, Philip J. 1972. "The People of the Territory of New Mexico Vs. The Santa Fe Ring." NMHR 47:2(April):185–202.

Reed, Erik K. 1964. "The Greater Southwest." Pp. 175–191 in *Prehistoric Man in the New World*, edited by Jesse D. Jennings and E. Nordbeck. Chicago: UCP.

Reeve, Frank D. 1956. "Early Navajo Geography." NMHR 31:4(Oct.):290–309.
———. 1957. "Seventeenth Century Navajo–Spanish Relations." NMHR 32:1(Jan.):36–52.
———. 1958. "Navajo–Spanish Wars 1680–1720." NMHR 33:3(July):205–231.
———. 1959. "The Navajo–Spanish Peace: 1720s–1770s." NMHR 34:1(Jan):9–40.
Renfrew, Colin. 1975. "Trade as Action at a Distance: Questions of Integration and Communication." Pp. 3–59 in *Ancient Civilization and Trade*, edited by Jeremy A. Sabloff and C. C. Lamberg-Karlovsky. Albuquerque: UNMP.
———. 1977. "Alternative Models for Exchange and Spatial Distribution." Pp. 71–90 in Earle and Ericson (1977).
Reno, Philip. 1965. "Rebellion in New Mexico—1837." NMHR 40:3(July):197–213.
Reyman, Jonathan E. 1978. *"Pochteca* Burials at Anasazi Sites?" Pp. 242–259 in Riley and Hedrick (1978).
Richardson, Rubert N. 1933. *The Comanche Barrier to South Plains Settlement.* Glendale, CA: Arthur H. Clark Co.
Riley, Carroll. 1976. *Sixteenth Century Trade in the Greater Southwest.* University Museum Mesoamerican Studies No. 10. Carbondale, IL: Southern Illinois University Press.
———. 1978. "Pecos and Trade." Pp. 53–64 in Riley and Hedrick (1978).
———. 1982. *The Frontier People: The Greater Southwest in the Prehistoric Period.* Center for Archaeological Investigation. Carbondale, IL: Southern Illinois University Press.
Riley, Carroll, and Basil C. Hedrick, eds. 1978. *Across the Chichimec Sea: Papers in Honor of J. Charles Kelley.* Carbondale, IL: Southern Illinois University Press.
Riley, Carroll, and Joni L. Manson. 1983. "The Cibola–Tiguex Route: Continuity and Change in the Southwest." NMHR 58:4(Oct.):347–367.
Ríos-Bustamante, Antonio. 1976a. "A Contribution to the Historiography of the Greater Mexican North in the Eighteenth Century." *Aztlan* 7:3(Fall):347–356.
———. 1976b. "New Mexico in the Eighteenth Century: Life and Trade in La Villa de San Felipe de Albuquerque, 1706–1790." *Aztlan* 7:3(Fall):357–389.
Roessel, Ruth. 1973. *Navajo Stories of the Long Walk.* Tsaile, AZ: Navajo Community College Press.
Sahlins, Marshall D. 1960. "Evolution: Specific and General." Pp. 12–44 in *Evolution and Culture,* edited by M. Sahlins and E. Service. Ann Arbor: University of Michigan Press.
———. 1961. "The Segmentary Lineage: An Organization of Predatory Expansion." *American Anthropologist* 63:2(April):322–345.
———. 1963. "Poor Man, Rich Man, Big-Man, Chief: Political Types in Melanesia and Polynesia." CSSH 5:3(April):285–303.
———. 1972. *Stone Age Economics.* Chicago: UCP.
Sanchez, Joseph P. 1978. "Año Desgraciado, 1837: The Overthrow of New Mexico's Jefe Politico Albino Perez." *Atisbos* 1(Sum./Fall):180–191.
Sando, Joe S. 1979. "The Pueblo Revolt." Pp. 194–197 in Ortiz (1979), [1977].
———. 1982. *Nee Hemish: A History of Jemez Pueblo.* Albuquerque: UNMP.
Sandoval, David A. 1982. "What Do I Call Them?: The Chicano Experience." *The Colorado Association for Chicano Research Review* 1:1:3–25.
Schaafsma, Curtis F. 1981. "Early Apacheans in the Southwest: A Review." Pp. 291–320 in Wilcox and Masse (1981).
Schermerhorn, Richard A. 1978. *Ethnic Plurality in India.* Tucson: UAZP.

Schmitt, Karl M. 1974. *Mexico and the United States, 1821–1973: Conflict and Coexistence*. New York: Wiley.

Schneider, Jane. 1977. "Was There a Pre-Capitalist World-System?" *Peasant Studies* 6:1(Jan.):20–29.

Scholes, France V. 1930. "The Supply Service of the New Mexican Missions in the Seventeenth Century." NMHR 5:1,2,4(Jan., Apr., Oct.):93–115; 186–210; 386–404.

_____. 1932. "Problems in the Early Ecclesiastical History of New Mexico." NMHR 7:1(Jan.):32–74.

_____. 1935a. "Civil Government and Society in New Mexico in the Seventeenth Century." NMHR 10:2(Apr.):71–111.

_____. 1935b. "First Decade of the Inquisition in New Mexico." NMHR 10:3(July):195–241.

_____. 1936–1937. "Church and State in New Mexico, 1610–50." NMHR 11:1,2,3,4(Jan., Apr., July, Oct.):9–76; 145–178, 283–294; 297–349; 12:1 (Jan.):78–106.

_____. 1937–1940. "Troublous Times in New Mexico, 1659–70." NMHR 12:2,4 (Apr., July):134–174; 380–452; 13:1(Jan.):63–84; 91–93; 15:3,4(July, Oct.):249–268; 369–417.

Schroeder, Albert H. 1960. *The Hohokam, Sinagua and Hakataya*. Archives of Archaeology 5. Madison, WI: Society for American Archaeology.

_____. 1968. "Shifting for Survival in the Spanish Southwest." NMHR 43:4(Oct.):291–310, reprinted in Weber (1979, pp. 239–255).

_____. 1972. "Rio Grande Ethnohistory." Pp. 41–70 in Ortiz (1972).

_____. 1979a. "History of Archeological Research." Pp. 5–13 in Ortiz (1979), [1972].

_____. 1979b. "Prehistory: Hakataya." Pp. 100–107 in Ortiz (1979), [1973].

_____. 1979c. "Pueblos Abandoned in Historic Times." Pp. 236–254 in Ortiz (1979), [1978].

_____. 1979d. "Pecos Pueblo." Pp. 430–437 in Ortiz (1979), [1973].

_____. 1982. "The Protohistoric and Pitfalls of Archaeological Interpretation." Paper presented at the 55th Pecos Conference, Pecos, NM, August.

_____. 1983. "Querchos, Vaqueros, Cocoyes, and Apaches." *Papers of the Archaeological Society of New Mexico* 8:159–166.

_____. 1984. "The Protohistoric and Pitfalls of Archaeological Interpretation." *Papers of the Archaeological Society of New Mexico* 9:133–140. Albuquerque: Archaeological Society Press.

Schroeder, Albert H. (ed.). 1973. *The Changing Ways of Southwestern Indians: A Historic Perspective*. Glorieta, NM: Rio Grande Press.

Secoy, Frank R. 1953. *Changing Military Patterns on the Great Plains (17th Century Through Early 19th Century)*. Monographs of the American Ethnological Society 21. Locust Valley, NY: J. J. Augustin.

Sellers, Charles, and Henry May. 1963. *A Synopsis of American History*. Chicago: Rand, McNally.

Service, Ellman R. 1971. *Primitive Social Organization*, 2nd ed. New York: Random House.

_____. 1975. *Origins of the State and Civilization*. New York: Norton.

Silverberg, Robert. 1970. *The Pueblo Revolt*. New York: Weybright and Talley.

Simmons, Marc. 1964. "Tlascalans in the Spanish Borderlands." NMHR 39:2(April):101–110.

_____. 1968. *Spanish Government in New Mexico*. Albuquerque: UNMP.

_____. 1969. "Settlement Patterns and Village Plans in Colonial New Mexico."
Journal of the West 8:1(Jan.):7–21, reprinted in Weber (1979, pp. 99–115).
_____. 1979. "History of Pueblo-Spanish Relations to 1821." Pp. 178–193 in
Ortiz (1979), [1978].
_____. 1984. "Rejoinder." Annals of the American Association of Geographers
74:1(April):169–170.
Simmons, Marc (ed. and trans.). 1967. Border Comanches: Seven Spanish Colonial
Documents. Santa Fe, NM: Stagecoach Press.
Simpson, Lesley Byrd. 1950. The Encomienda in New Spain: The Beginning of
Spanish Mexico. Berkeley: UCALP.
_____. 1966. Many Mexicos, 4th rev. ed. Berkeley: UCALP.
Skocpol, Theda. 1977. "Wallerstein's World Capitalist System: A Theoretical
and Historical Critique." AJS 82:5(March):1075–1090.
Smith, Andrew T. 1976. "The Founding of the San Antonio de las Huertas
Grant." Social Science Journal 13:3(Oct.):35–43.
Smith, Anthony D. 1981. The Ethnic Revival. Cambridge: CUP.
Smith, Carol A. (ed.). 1976. Regional Analysis, I: Economic Systems, II: Social Systems.
New York: Academic.
Smith, Justin Harvey. 1919. The War with Mexico. 2 vols. New York: Macmillan.
Smith, Ralph. 1963. "Indians in American-Mexican Relations Before the War of
1846." HAHR 43:1(Feb.):34–64.
Snipp, Matthew. 1986a. "The Changing Political and Economic Status of Ameri-
can Indians: From Captive Nations to Internal Colonies." American Journal of
Economics and Sociology 45:2(April):145–157.
_____. 1986b. "American Indians and Natural Resource Development." Ameri-
can Journal of Economics and Sociology 45:4(Oct.): 457–474.
Snow, David H. 1973. "Some Economic Considerations of Historic Rio Grande
Pueblo Pottery." Pp. 55–72 in Schroeder (1973).
_____. 1981. "Protohistoric Rio Grande Pueblo Economics: A Review of
Trends." Pp. 354–377 in Wilcox and Masse (1981).
_____. 1983. "A Note on Encomienda Economics in 17th Century New Mex-
ico." Pp. 347–357 in Hispanic Arts and Ethnohistory in the Southwest, edited by
Marta Weigle. Santa Fe: Ancient City Press.
_____. 1984. "Prologue to Rio Grande Protohistory." Papers of the Archaeological
Society of New Mexico 9:125–132. Albuquerque: Archaeological Society Press.
Sokolovsky, Joan. 1985. "Logic, Space, and Time: The Boundaries of the Cap-
italist World-Economy." Pp. 41–52 in Urbanization in the World-Economy, edited
by Michael Timberlake. New York: Academic Press.
Sonne, Conway B. 1962. World of Wakara. San Antonio, TX: The Naylor
Company.
Spicer, Edward E. 1962. Cycles of Conquest: The Impact of Spain, Mexico and the
United States on the Indians of the Southwest, 1533–1960. Tucson: UAZP.
Stanislawski, Michael B. 1979. "Hopi-Tewa." Pp. 587–602 in Ortiz (1979),
[1975].
Stavenhagen, Rodolfo. 1975. Social Classes in Agrarian Societies. New York:
Doubleday.
Steffen, Jerome O. 1979. The American West: New Perspectives, New Dimensions.
Norman: UOKP.
Stein, Stanley J., and Barbara H. Stein. 1970. The Colonial Heritage of Latin
America. London: OXUP.

———. 1980. "D. C. M. Platt: The Anatomy of 'Autonomy'." *Latin American Research Review* 15:1:131–146.

Stenberg, Richard. 1935. "The Failure of Polk's Mexican War Intrigue of 1848." *Pacific Historical Review* 4:1(March):39–68.

———. 1938. "Polk and Fremont, 1845–1846." *Pacific Historical Review* 7:3(Sept.): 211–227.

———. 1941. "President Polk and California: Additional Documents." *Pacific Historical Review* 10:2(June):217–219.

Steward, Julian. 1955. *Theory of Culture Change: The Methodology of Multilinear Evolution.* Urbana, IL: University of Illinois Press.

———. 1977. *Evolution and Ecology.* Urbana, IL: University of Illinois Press.

Stewart, Omer C. 1982. *Indians of the Great Basin.* Bloomington: Indiana University Press.

Stinchcombe, Arthur. 1978. *Theoretical Methods in Social History.* New York: Academic Press.

———. 1982. "The Growth of the World System." *AJS* 87:6(May): 1389–1395.

———. 1983. *Economic Sociology.* New York: Academic Press.

Strickland, Rex W. 1976. "The Birth and Death of a Legend: The Johnson 'Massacre' of 1837." *Arizona and the West* 18:3(Aug.):257–286.

Sunseri, Alvin R. 1979. *Seeds of Discord: New Mexico in the Aftermath of the American Conquest, 1846–1861.* Chicago: Nelson-Hall.

Swadesh, Frances Leon. 1974. *Los Primeros Pobladores: Hispanic Americans of the Ute Frontier.* Notre Dame: University of Notre Dame Press.

Tate, William (ed.). 1970. *Guadalupe Hidalgo Treaty of Peace 1848 and the Gadsden Treaty with Mexico 1853.* Truchas, NM: The Tate Gallery.

Taylor, John. G. 1979. *From Modernization to Modes of Production: A Critique of the Sociologies of Development and Underdevelopment.* New York: Macmillan.

Taylor, Peter. 1981. "Geographical scales within the world-economy approach." *Review* V:1(Sum.):3–11.

———. 1982. "A materialist framework for political geography." *Transactions of the Institute of British Geographers* n.s. 7:15–32.

———. 1985. *Political Geography: World-Economy, Nation-State and Locality.* London: Longman.

TePaske, John J., and Herbert S. Klein. 1981. "The Seventeenth-Century Crisis in New Spain: Myth or Reality?" *Past & Present* 90(Feb.):116–135.

———. 1982. "A Rejoinder." *Past & Present* 97(Nov.):156–161.

Terrell, John Upton. 1972. *Apache Chronicle.* New York: World Publishing.

Thomas, Alfred Barnaby (trans. and ed.). 1932. *Forgotten Frontiers: A Study of the Spanish Indian Policy of Don Juan Bautista de Anza, Governor of New Mexico, 1777–1787.* Norman: UOKP.

———. 1935. *After Coronado: Spanish Exploration Northeast of New Mexico, 1696–1727.* Norman: UOKP.

———. 1940. *The Plains Indians and New Mexico, 1751–1778.* Coronado Historical Series Volume 11. Albuquerque: UNMP.

———. 1941. *Teodoro de Croix and the Frontier of New Spain, 1776–1783.* Norman: UOKP.

Thomas, Robert Paul. 1965. "A Quantitative Approach to the Study of the Effects of British Imperial Policy upon Colonial Welfare." *Journal of Economic History* 25:4(Dec.):615–638.

Thornton, Russell. 1978. "Implications of Catlin's American Indian Population

Estimates for Revision of Mooney's Estimate." *American Journal of Physical Anthropology* 49:1(July):11–14.

Thrapp, Dan L. 1967. *The Conquest of Apacheria.* Norman: UOKP.

Tilly, Charles. 1981. *As Sociology Meets History.* New York: Academic Press.

———. 1984. *Big Structures, Large Processes, Huge Comparisons.* New York: Russell Sage Foundation.

Tilly, Charles (ed.). 1975. *The Formation of National States in Western Europe.* Princeton, NJ: Princeton University Press.

Tjarks, Alicia V. 1978. "Demographic, Ethnic and Occupational Structure of New Mexico, 1790." *The Americas* 35:1(July):45–88.

Turlington, Edgar. 1930. *Mexico and Her Foreign Creditors.* New York: Columbia University Press.

Tyler, Daniel. 1980. "Mexican Indian Policy in New Mexico." NMHR 55:2 (April):101–120.

Tyler, S. Lyman. 1973. "Some Economic Aspects of Indian Contacts in the Spanish Southwest." Pp. 35–45 in Schroeder (1973).

Ulibarri, Richard O. 1963. "American Interest in the Spanish Southwest, 1803–1848." Ph.D. diss., Dept. of History, University of Utah, Salt Lake City. Reprint, 1974, San Francisco: R & E Associates.

Undreiner, George J. 1947. "Fray Marcos De Niza and His Journey to Cibola." *The Americas* 3:4(April):415–486.

United States Bureau of the Census. 1975. *Historical Statistics of the United States, Colonial Times to 1970, Bicentennial Edition.* Washington, DC: U.S. Government Printing Office.

Upham, Steadman. 1982. *Polities and Power: An Economic and Political History of the Western Pueblo.* New York: Academic Press.

Utley, Robert M. 1984. *The Indian Frontier of the American West 1846–1890.* Albuquerque: UNMP.

Van Alstyne, R. W. 1960. *The Rising American Empire.* New York: OXUP.

———. 1972. "Empire in Midpassage, 1845–1867." Pp. 83–133 in *From Colony to Empire: Essays in the History of American Foreign Relations,* edited by W. A. Williams. New York: Wiley.

van den Berghe, Pierre L. 1981. *The Ethnic Phenomenon.* New York: Elsevier.

Van Ness, John R. 1976. "Spanish American vs. Anglo American Land Tenure and the Study of Economic Change in New Mexico." *Social Science Journal* 13:3(Oct.):45–52.

———. 1979. "Hispanic Village Organization in Northern New Mexico: Corporate Community Structure in Historical and Comparative Perspective." Pp. 21–44 in *The Survival of Spanish American Villages,* edited by Paul Kutsche. Colorado College Studies, No. 15. Colorado Springs: The Colorado College.

Vicens Vives, Jaime. 1969. *An Economic History of Spain* (with the collaboration of Jorge Nadal Oller). Frances M. López-Morillas (trans.) (from 1964, 3rd ed. in Spanish). Princeton, NJ: Princeton University Press.

———. 1970a. "The Decline of Spain in the Seventeenth Century." Pp. 121–167 in Cipolla (1970).

———. 1970b. *Approaches to the History of Spain,* 2d rev. ed. Berkeley: UCALP.

Vigness, David. 1954. "Relations of the Republic of Texas and the Republic of the Rio Grande." SWHQ 57:3(Jan.):312–321.

Vishanoff, John. 1975. "Review of Gene Brack, *Mexico Views Manifest Destiny,*

1821–1846: An essay on the origins of the Mexican War." Journal of Mexican American History 5:122–124.

Vivian, R. Gordon. 1964. *Gran Quivira: Excavations in a 17th-Century Jumano Pueblo.* U.S. National Park Service Archaeological Research Series 8. Washington, DC: U.S. Government Printing Office.

Voss, Stuart F. 1982. *On the Periphery of Nineteenth-Century Mexico: Sonora and Sinaloa, 1810–1817.* Tucson: UAZP.

Wallace, Ernest, and E. A. Hoebel. 1952. *Lords of the South Plains.* Norman: UOKP.

Wallerstein, Immanuel. 1974a. "The Rise and Future Demise of the World Capitalist System: Concepts for Comparative Analysis." CSSH 16:4(Sept.): 387–415, reprinted in Wallerstein (1979, Ch. 1).

_____. 1974b. *The Modern World-System: Capitalist Agriculture and the Origins of European World-Economy in the Sixteenth Century.* New York: Academic Press.

_____. 1979. *The Capitalist World-Economy.* Cambridge: CUP.

_____. 1980. *The Modern World-System: Mercantilism and the Consolidation of the European World-Economy, 1600–1750.* New York: Academic Press.

_____. 1984. *The Politics of the World-Economy: The States, the Movements, and the Civilizations.* New York: CUP.

Wallerstein, Immanuel, and William G. Martin. 1979. "Peripheralization of Southern Africa, II: Changes in Household Structure and Labor-Force Formation." *Review* III:2(Fall):193–207.

Warner, Ted J. 1966. "Frontier Defense." NMHR 41:1(Jan.):5–19.

Weber, David J. 1972. *Taos Trappers: The Fur Trade in the Far Southwest, 1540–1846.* Norman: UOKP.

_____. 1981. "American Westward Expansion and the Breakdown of Relations Between Pobladores and 'Indios Bárbaros' on Mexico's Far Northern Frontier, 1821–1846." NMHR 56:3(July):221–238.

_____. 1982. *The Mexican Frontier, 1821–1846.* Albuquerque: UNMP.

Weber, David J., ed. 1973. *Foreigners in Their Native Land: Historical Roots of the Mexican American.* Albuquerque: UNMP.

_____. 1979. *New Spain's Far Northern Frontier: Essays on Spain in the American West, 1540–1821.* Albuquerque: UNMP.

Weigand, Phil C. 1982a. "Introduction." *Anthropology* 6:1&2:1–6.

_____. 1982b. "Mining and Mineral Trade in Prehistoric Zapatecas." *Anthropology* 6:1&2:87–134.

_____. 1982c. "Sherds Associated with Turquoise Mines in the Southwestern U.S.A." *Pottery Southwest* 9:2(April):4–6.

Weigand, Phil C., Garman Harbottle, and Edward V. Sayre. 1977. "Turquoise Sources and Source Analysis: Mesoamerica and the Southwest U.S.A." Pp. 15–34 in Earle and Ericson (1977).

Weigand, Phil C., and Michael W. Spence. 1982. "The Obsidian Mining Complex at La Joya, Jalisco." *Anthropology* 6:1&2:175–188.

West, Robert C. 1949. *The Mining Community in Northern New Spain: The Parral Mining District.* Ibero–Americana 30. Berkeley: UCALP.

White, Leslie. 1943. "Punche: Tobacco in New Mexico History." NMHR 18:4(Oct.):386–393.

Whitecotton, Joseph W., and Richard A. Pailes. 1979. "Mesoamerica as an Historical Unit: A World-System Model." Paper presented to XLIII International Congress of Americanists, Vancouver, Canada, August.

———. 1983. "New World Precolumbian World Systems." Paper presented at Society for American Archaeology, Pittsburgh, April.

———. 1986. "New World Precolumbian World Systems." Pp. 183–204 in Mathien and McGuire (1986).

Wilcox, David R. 1981a. "The Entry of Athapaskans into the American Southwest: The Problem Today." Pp. 213–256 in Wilcox and Masse (1981).

———. 1981b. "Changing Perspectives on the Protohistoric Pueblos, A.D. 1450–1700." Pp. 378–409 in Wilcox and Masse (1981).

———. 1984. "Multi-Ethnic Division of Labor in the Protohistoric Southwest." During the Protohistoric Period." *Papers of the Archaeological Society of New Mexico* 9:141–154. Albuquerque: Archaeological Society Press.

———. 1986. "The Tepiman Connection: A Model of Mesoamerican-Southwestern Interaction." Pp. 135–154 in Mathien and McGuire (1986).

Wilcox, David R., and W. Bruce Masse (eds.). 1981. *The Protohistoric Period in the North American Southwest, AD 1450–1700*. Anthropology Research Papers, No. 24. Tempe, AZ: Arizona State University Press.

Willey, Gordon R. 1966. *An Introduction to American Archaeology. Vol. 1: North and Middle America*. Englewood Cliffs, NJ: Prentice-Hall.

Williams, William A. 1972. *From Colony to Empire: Essays in the History of American Foreign Relations*. New York: Wiley.

Wolf, Eric R. 1955. "The Mexican Bajio in the Eighteenth Century." Middle American Research Institute, publication 17:177–200.

———. 1959. *Sons of the Shaking Earth*. Chicago: UCP.

———. 1982. *Europe and the People Without History*. Berkeley: UCALP.

———. 1984. "Culture: Panacea or Problem?" *American Antiquity* 49:2(April): 393–400.

Wolf, Eric R., and Edward C. Hansen. 1967. "*Caudillo* Politics: A Structural Analysis." CSSH 9:2(Jan.):168–179.

———. 1972. *The Human Condition in Latin America*. New York: OXUP.

Wolpe, Harold (ed.). 1980. *The Articulation of Modes Production*. London: Routledge, Kegan Paul.

Woodbury, Richard B. 1979. "Prehistory: Introduction." Pp. 22–30 in Ortiz (1979), [1978].

Woodbury, Richard B., and E. B. Zubrow. 1979. "Agricultural Beginnings, 2000 B.C.–A.D. 500." Pp. 43–60 in Ortiz (1979), [1978].

Woodruff, William. 1973. "The Emergence of an International Economy, 1700–1914." Pp. 656–737 in Cipolla (1973).

Worcester, Donald E. 1944. "The Spread of Spanish Horses in the Southwest." NMHR 19:3(July):225–232.

———. 1979. *The Apaches: Eagles of the Southwest*. Norman: UOKP.

Worcester, Donald E. (ed. and trans.). 1951. *Instructions for Governing the Interiour Provinces of New Spain, 1786*. Berkeley: UCALP.

Wright, Henry T. 1977. "Recent Research on the Origin of the State." *Annual Review of Anthropology* 6:379–397.

Yancey, William, E. P. Ericksen, and R. N. Juliani. 1976. "Emergent Ethnicity: A Review and Reformulation." ASR 41:3(June):391–402.

Young, Robert W. 1983. "Apachean Languages." Pp. 393–400 in Ortiz (1983), [1981].

Zeleny, Carolyn. 1944. "Relations Between the Spanish-Americans and Anglo-Americans in New Mexico: A Study of Conflict and Accommodation in a Dual-Ethnic Situation." Ph.D. diss., Dept. of History, Yale University, New Haven, CT. Reprint, 1974, New York: Arno Press.

Zevin, Robert B. 1971. "The Growth of Cotton Textile Production after 1815." Pp. 122–147 in *The Reinterpretation of American Economic History,* edited by R. W. Fogel and S. L. Engerman. New York: Harper and Row.

Zubrow, Ezra B. W. 1974. *Population, Contact, and Climate in the New Mexican Pueblos.* Anthropological Papers of University of Arizona No. 24. Tucson: UAZP.

Index